Co
OF

CW00321674

COLLINS GUIDE TO BIRDS

A photographic guide to the birds of Britain and Europe

John Gooders

Photographs assembled by FLPA

HarperCollins*Publishers*

HarperCollins*Publishers*
London . Glasgow . New York . Sydney
Auckland . Toronto . Johannesburg

First published 1998

ISBN 0 00 220011 2

Edit and page make-up by D & N Publishing, UK

Colour origination by United Graphics, Singapore
Printed and bound in Italy by Rotolito Lombarda, Italy

CONTENTS

AUTHOR'S PREFACE

The first *Collins Bird Guide* was published in 1980 and achieved a place in *The Sunday Times* bestselling book listings for several consecutive weeks – something seldom, if ever, achieved by any other bird book and certainly not by any other book written by me. It was subsequently translated into several European languages, and went on to become one of the best-selling bird books of all time. The present *Collins Guide to the Birds of Britain and Europe* is, however, far from being a second edition. All the photographs are new, the maps have been updated and the text has been completely rewritten in the light of better knowledge. The first *Collins Bird Guide* was co-authored by Stuart Keith, but Stuart's other commitments – mainly to the monumental *Birds of Africa*, Academic Press (1982) – prevented him from participating in the writing of the present edition.

Nevertheless, I have felt free to draw upon his original contributions, while taking full responsibility for expressing them in my own way. I have been fortunate in having Myles Archibald at Collins as a publisher, David Price-Goodfellow and his team at D & N Publishing as editors and designers and in being able to call once again upon the services of Marion Waran to produce a clean typescript on the magic word processor. To Stuart, Myles, David, and Marion my sincerest thanks. But above all my thanks must go to the huge number of photographers whose skill and dedication have made possible one of the greatest collections of bird photographs ever assembled.

John Gooders, 199
East Sussex, England

INTRODUCTION

Almost every new bird book comments on the boom that birding, formerly bird-watching, is enjoying at the present time. That was true when the first edition of this book was published in 1980, and it is equally true today. In fact, over the past sixteen years the birdwatching boom has continued to gather momentum so that now the number of birding devotees is greater than ever. The increased number of clubs and societies, journals and magazines, field guides and even holiday companies, has reflected this growth, but now there are also bird telephone hotlines, bird pagers, bird videos, bird computer programmes and bird fairs. And the word is spreading: there are birders in Spain, France, Italy, Portugal, Greece; and in other countries where, only a few years ago, there were only a few ornithologists. Even manufacturers have cottoned-on to the idea that in birders they have a large, ever expanding market for their products. Specifically designed binoculars and telescopes are now widely available and birders are now far and away the largest market for them.

The birding boom has also changed the way we identify birds. More and more expertise is applied to 'problem' species, and the very criteria by which we put a name to a bird have been revolutionized. As a result the species accounts in this book have been completely rewritten. The old photographs have been discarded and replaced by newer and better ones showing more plumages, of more species, in more typical poses.

But while the primary aim of this book is to aid the identification of every regular European bird, it also seeks to satisfy the demand to know more about the birds we see. And, incidentally, it forms a treasure trove of the best bird photographs ever published.

Geographical Scope   This guide covers all of Europe including that part of Russia west of the 30th meridian (*see* map). Iceland is included as

well as the larger Mediterranean islands and
that part of Turkey lying west of the
Bosphorus. I have 'bent' the 30th meridian
to include those areas of Norway and
Finland that lie to the east of the line.

Choice
of Species
Over 450 species are fully described and
illustrated in this guide. As a rule, I have
included a species if it occurs in Europe
virtually every year. A few birds, such as
American Bittern and Pallas's Sandgrouse,
which occurred more frequently in the past
but very rarely in recent years have been
omitted.

Organization
of the Guide
The illustrations in conventional bird
guides are organized by families and
scattered throughout the text, which
means that the reader must leaf through
the entire book to find the picture of a
particular bird. Instead, we have placed all
the colour plates in one section and then
grouped the family and species descriptions
in a separate section. The unified visual key
arranges birds by characteristics that they
have in common. Simple silhouette
symbols direct the reader to the group of
birds most resembling the one sighted. The
reader can then narrow the search to a few
birds or find exactly the one he has seen.
Reading the species descriptions will
confirm the identification.

Photographs as
a Visual Guide
For our illustrations we have used colour
photographs of birds in their natural
habitats. The last 25 years have seen a
revolution in bird photography with the
introduction of lightweight cameras,
interchangeable lenses, and fast colour film.
The results have been spectacular.
Photographers are no longer restricted to
taking pictures of birds at the nest or in
other predictable settings, but can capture
birds flying, in display, or feeding – images
of behaviour that simply were not possible
previously.

Besides being a pleasure to look at, these
photographs show birds as they really are in
nature, rather than an artist's

interpretation. This was the first book to bring together colour photographs of almost every European bird in a single volume. By starting from scratch, this new edition sets new standards and is as much a breakthrough as the first. It brings together the work of dozens of outstanding bird photographers in a total of over 980 photographs. The result is a book that is a delight to look at as well as to use.

How the Visual Guide Works
Birds are arranged in the established systematic order that has the advantage of grouping similar birds together. Thus all the ducks appear consecutively as do all the birds of prey. Occasionally, however, birds have been grouped out of order to facilitate comparison. So, swifts have been grouped with swallows and martins because all are small, fast fliers that are usually seen in the air.

The Gannet, Fulmar, albatross, shearwaters, and petrels are found in the section on oceanic birds because they all share that distinctive habitat. The perching birds are by far the largest category. I have placed most of them in seven groups based on such generally recognized types as Chats and Thrushes, and Warblers and Flycatchers. Within each group the photographs have been arranged by colour and plumage pattern. Thus the sparrows, finches and buntings group begins with birds with primarily red plumage like the crossbills and then progresses to those with rusty-orange, yellow, yellowish-brown, brown, and brown streaked with black plumage, ending with grey and black buntings.

Groups The colour plates are arranged in the following groups:

Divers and Grebes
Pelagic Birds
Cormorants and Pelicans
Herons, Storks and Ibises
Wildfowl
Birds of Prey

Gamebirds
Crakes and Allies
Waders
Gulls, Terns and Auks
Sandgrouse, Parakeets, Cuckoos and
    Pigeons
Owls, Nightjars and Colourful Exotics
Woodpeckers
Swifts and Swallows
Larks, Pipits and Wagtails
Waxwing, Dipper, Wren and Accentors
Chats and Thrushes
Warblers and Flycatchers
Tits, Nuthatches and Shrikes
Crows, Jays and Starlings
Sparrows, Finches and Buntings

What the   Where the sexes are similar the
Photographs   photographs show adult males in breeding
Show   plumage, since males are usually the most
                brightly coloured and easiest to identify.
                Females and birds in winter plumage that
                differ appreciably from breeding males are
                also illustrated, as are distinctive juveniles.
                As often as space has allowed, I have also
                included flight shots of birds such as swifts
                and raptors that are usually seen in the air.
                Beneath each colour plate is a caption
                giving the bird's English name, scientific
                name, and the page number of the text
                description. The age, sex, or plumage is
                given whenever the photograph is of other
                than a breeding male.

Key to the   The organization of the colour plates is
Colour Plates   summarized in a chart preceding the
                photographic section (*see* page 22). A
                silhouette of the most typical bird within
                each group has been selected to represent
                the entire group. It appears on the left of
                the chart and is repeated as a thumb-tab
                on the left side of each double page of
                colour plates that illustrate that group.
                Thus, a silhouette of a shearwater
                represents the group Pelagic Birds, and a
                silhouette of a hawk represents the group
                Birds of Prey, which also includes eagles,
                vultures, harriers, kites, falcons, buzzards,
                and Osprey. This chart will lead you to the

double-page introductions to each group. Each introduction depicts the typical birds within the group and will lead you to the page on which the bird you are trying to identify appears.

Text Organization In the text the bird descriptions are arranged in systematic or scientific order. The families are arranged on an evolutionary time scale: birds believed to be the oldest (divers and grebes) are placed first, while the much younger passerine families, which are still rapidly evolving, appear at the end. Families are grouped in a larger category, the order; and within each family birds are arranged in a 'family tree', according to their evolutionary relationships. Thus, the species *Anthus campestris*, Tawny Pipit, is placed in the genus *Anthus* along with other pipits. *Anthus* is one of several genera included in the pipit and wagtail family, Motacillidae, which in turn belongs, with other families, in the order Passeriformes (the perching birds).

Family Descriptions Each group of species descriptions is preceded by a general paragraph on the family. Characteristics common to all species within that family are given in addition to the number of species worldwide and the number that occur in Europe.

Common and Scientific Names I have adopted many of the common names used in *List of Birds of the Western Palearctic* published by *British Birds* (1997), except where the name in common use seems preferable. Most readers will, I trust, find this less confusing than the wholesale and often cumbersome changes used by that journal. At present there is considerable overlap and confusion in names, and many ornithologists believe that a standard list of English names for all birds of the world is desirable. *Charadrius alexandrinus*, for example, is known as Snowy Plover in North America, Kentish Plover in Europe, and Red-capped Dotterel in Australia.

To avoid confusion in cases where a species is known by different common names, every bird has a scientific name that is recognized throughout the world. It consists of two Latinized words: the first is the genus, the second the species. Thus the Latin name of the Grey Wagtail, *Motacilla cinerea*, identifies it first as a member of the genus *Motacilla* and then specifically as *cinerea* meaning 'grey'. With a few exceptions, I have used the scientific names and systematic order of the *List of Recent Holarctic Bird Species* by K. H. Voous, published by The British Ornithologists' Union and reprinted from *Ibis*, 1977.

The widespread use of DNA as a key to ornithological, and other, relationships over the past few years has thrown systematics into disorder. One of the most significant results has been a multiplicity of 'new' species resulting from 'splitting' previous species into two, or more. Thus, as this book was in production, Taiga Bean Goose and Tundra Bean Goose were split, Western and Eastern Bonelli's Warblers were recognized and Great Grey Shrike and Southern Grey Shrike were divided. With this DNA-derived process progressing so furiously, it is inevitable that further new species will be recognized before this book is published.

Species Descriptions I have avoided technical terms wherever possible. Occasionally, such terms have been necessary, and these are defined in the glossary. However, the reader should study the labelled drawings on page 19 in order to become familiar with the various parts of a bird's body.

Measurements The size of a bird as given in the text and captions is the average overall length from the tip of its bill to the tip of its tail. When significant, the wingspan, length of bill, or length of tail also appears.

Shape and Colour In the description of each species, the key, identifying features are italicized. In the waders, the key characteristics are the rump, tail, and wing patterns; in gulls, the wingtip pattern, and bill and leg colours; in leaf warblers, wing and head patterns; and so on. In each case, descriptions of these characteristics will be given in italics. When plumage within a species varies, the text first describes the appearance of the breeding male, followed by seasonal changes and the female and juvenile plumages. In some birds, such as Sky Lark and Carrion Crow, the sexes are similar and change little during the year. In others, such as ducks and finches, the sexes have a very different plumage. Still others, like the divers and grebes, have a change of plumage from summer to winter. In many species the young are very different from the adults. For example, the adult Robin has a red breast, whereas the juvenile is mottled-brown and is in fact driven from the adult's territory as soon as its red breast develops. While most young birds moult into adult plumage during their first year, some, such as the larger gulls and birds of prey, take several years to acquire full adult plumage, and in each year the plumage becomes progressively nearer to that of the adult. When distinctive subspecies occur in Europe, these are also described. The colour plates likewise show as many plumage variations for each species as space has allowed. In the case of easily confused species, the text helps distinguish one from the other.

Voice Birds use their voices for a variety of purposes: to defend a territory, to attract a mate, to maintain contact with other birds, or as an alarm. Some have a wide vocabulary. The Great Tit, for example, has been credited with 57 different calls. To identify most species, however, it is sufficient to learn the common contact notes and song. In fact some birds are so similar in appearance that they are best distinguished by their voices. However, while phonetic descriptions of voices are certainly helpful, they are no substitute for hearing the actual songs and calls. Very good recordings of bird songs are available, but by far the best way to learn songs is to go into the field with someone who knows them.

Habitat Birds are mobile and adaptable and some may occupy a wide range of habitats. Nevertheless, most species have a preferred breeding habitat, and this is described in the text. When the winter habitat is different, this is also described. For example, geese nest in the Arctic tundra but feed in fields and arable land in winter. Petrels, shearwaters, and other seabirds spend most of their lives at sea, coming to land only to nest.

Breeding A description of the eggs, nest, nest site, duration of incubation and role of the sexes is given for each species. The number of eggs cited is that normally found in a nest, although the number can vary considerably according to geographical location, whether the eggs are of a first or second brood, and other factors. Some birds construct elaborate nests: the Egyptian Vulture, which breeds in caves or holes in cliffs, builds a nest of sticks, bones, fur, paper, and dung, and lines it with hair, wool and rags. Others, including many waders, lay their eggs in a bare scrape. Some birds, like the Gannet, nest in vast colonies; others, such as the Nightingale, nest as a solitary pair.

Range The geographic range given for each bird focuses on its world and European distribution and supplements the information in the individual range maps. The range description generally moves from west to east and north to south. Breeding range appears first; winter range is given if different. For species that appear in Europe only as migrants, information on their general route is given. In some cases, range can help confirm identification of a species. For example, a nightjar seen in Britain has to be the European Nightjar because the Red-necked Nightjar – the only other species – is confined to Iberia. The ranges of species are constantly changing: the White-rumped Swift, for instance, is a relative newcomer to Europe, having extended its range northward from Africa into southern Spain in the last couple of decades. A number of Asian species, such as the Paddyfield Warbler and the Citrine Wagtail, are expanding their ranges west into Europe.

Range Maps   Maps accompany each range description except for those species whose range is so restricted that a written description suffices or for those that appear in Europe only as migrants. The maps show both breeding and winter ranges, using the following key:

 Breeding range

 Winter range

 Permanent range – areas in which a species occurs in both winter and summer.

Comments   At the end of each species description, additional notes discuss behaviour, feeding habits, population status, migration, conservation, origin of names, and other points of general interest. There, for example, is described the dramatic tracking of a Russian eagle by satellite, the fantastic transcontinental flight of the Richard's Pipit, and the fact that swifts often sleep in flight.

How to Find   Some advance planning will enable you to
Birds   increase the number of birds seen on a field trip. Since many species remain more or less in one habitat, you should plan to visit as many habitats as possible. A good system is to begin a field trip very early in the morning and go first to freshwater marshes, since many of the species to be found there are most active shortly after dawn. As the day progresses, move to woodland and then to open fields and coastal and open water habitats, where most species are conspicuous all day. While many species are rather tame, others are shy or secretive. Learn to move

slowly and quietly. Avoid sudden movements and bright-coloured clothing, which serve to make an observer more visible to shy or wary species. Some of these elusive birds can be lured into view by 'squeaking', or 'pishing', an imitation of the sound of a bird in distress. Rails and elusive forest species can be attracted by tape recordings of their songs and calls, though the overuse of tapes, especially at sites visited regularly by birders, can lead to dangerous interference in the birds' breeding routine. Information on particularly good birdwatching areas in Britain and Ireland and on the Continent is available in books and magazines. There are also several well-established bird 'hotlines' that can be telephoned for the very latest news. In an unfamiliar area, it is wise to contact members of the local bird club, since they can provide specific, up-to-date information on the birds of their area and the best places to see them. Many birders also belong to their own local bird club or natural history society, where they make contact with fellow *aficionados* and join group excursions to the best birdwatching areas.

Appendices Information on birdwatching equipment, a list of accidentals, and notes on conservation are included in the appendices.

PARTS OF A BIRD

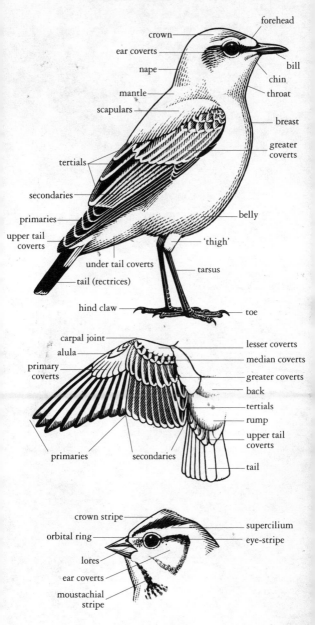

HOW TO USE THIS GUIDE

Example It is early winter and you see a medium-
small bird hopping around your garden. Its
back and wings are brown, and it has dark
speckles on its chest and belly. Its shape and
upright stance remind you of the familiar
thrush that nests behind the ivy, but it is
slightly smaller and has a white
supercilium (eyebrow) and rusty colour
along the flanks.
1. Turn to the spread of silhouettes that
precedes the colour plate section and find
the silhouette that fits a thrush-like bird.
2. Look for the thumb tab with the thrush
silhouette in the colour plate section.
3. Among the colour photographs of
thrush-like birds, you will find there are
only three birds with the combination of
plain brown above and dark spots below:
Song Thrush, Mistle Thrush, and Redwing.
Only the Redwing has a white supercilium
and rusty flanks.
4. Under the photograph you will find the
page number that refers you to the text
description of the Redwing. Reading the
description confirms your identification of
the Redwing, an autumn migrant from
Scandinavia.

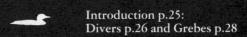
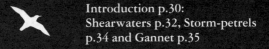

Introduction p.204:
Larks p.206, Pipits p.208
and Wagtails p.210

Introduction p.214:
Waxwing p.216, Dipper p.216,
Wren p.217 and Accentors p.217

Introduction p.218:
Chats p.220, Wheatears p.224
and Thrushes p.226

Introduction p.228:
Warblers p.230 and
Flycatchers p.244

Introduction p.246:
Tits p.248, Nuthatches p.252,
Treecreepers p.253 and
Shrikes p.254

Introduction p.256:
Orioles p.258, Crows p.258
and Starlings p.261

Introduction p.262:
Sparrows p.264, Waxbills p.265,
Finches p.266 and Buntings p.274

Divers and Grebes

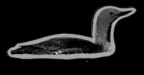

These are medium to large, aquatic birds that dive with consummate ease, often for lengthy periods. The feet, set well back on the body, are unsuited to walking and divers and grebes are extremely ungainly on land. Most species have distinctive seasonal plumages and many spend the winter on or near the sea. All divers are larger than all grebes and fly with a distinctive 'humped' back shape.

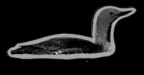

Divers pp.26–7

Grebes pp.28–9

Red-throated Diver *Gavia stellata* p.283
1. summer; 2. winter

Great Northern Diver *Gavia immer* p.285
1. summer; 2. winter

Little Grebe or Dabchick *Tachybaptus ruficollis* p.287
1. summer; 2. winter

Red-necked Grebe ***Podiceps grisegena*** p.289
1. summer; 2. winter

Slavonian Grebe ***Podiceps auritus*** p.290
1. summer; 2. winter

Black-necked Grebe ***Podiceps nigricollis*** p.291
1. summer; 2. winter

Albatross p.32

Fulmar p.32

Shearwaters pp.32–3

Storm-petrels p.34

Gannet p.35

Pelagic Birds

This is a diverse group of birds brought together by a common oceanic lifestyle. They vary in size from the huge albatrosses, with 3 m (10 ft) wingspans, to the tiny, almost sparrow-sized storm-petrels. Many have a stiff-winged, shearwater-type flight that utilizes lift, created by the movement of waves and swell, for propulsion. All species come to land only to breed, or under duress during heavy weather. Many species are essentially nocturnal during the breeding season, but both Gannet and Fulmar are diurnal and are easily seen at their bustling breeding colonies.

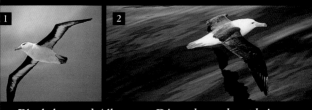

Black-browed Albatross *Diomedea melanophris*
p.292 1. & 2. adult

Fulmar *Fulmarus glacialis* p.293
1. & 2. adult

Levantine Shearwater
Puffinus yelkouan
p.295

Balearic Shearwater
Puffinus mauretanicus
p.296

Sooty Shearwater *Puffinus griseus* p.296
adult

Great Shearwater *Puffinus gravis* p.297
adult

Cory's Shearwater *Calonectris diomedea* p.298
adult

Manx Shearwater *Puffinus puffinus* p.294
1. & 2. adult

Leach's Storm-petrel *Oceanodroma leucorhoa*
p.300 adult

European Storm-petrel *Hydrobates pelagicus*
p.301 adult

Cormorants pp.38–9

Pelicans pp.40–1

Cormorants and Pelicans

These large fish-eating, aquatic birds
haunt both coasts and inland waters, and
frequently spend much time ashore
perched on sand bars, shoals, buoys, and
other structures. Pelicans are largely white,
cormorants predominantly black. Though
both groups are gregarious, pelicans
indulge in communal fishing expeditions.
Cormorants are unusual among aquatic
birds in lacking a fully waterproofed
plumage. As a result they can often be
seen hanging out their wings to dry.

Shag *Phalacrocorax aristotelis* p.305
1. adult summer;
2. adult winter;
3. juvenile

Pygmy Cormorant *Phalacrocorax pygmeus* p.306 adult summer

Dalmatian Pelican *Pelecanus crispus* p.307
1 adult summer; 2 adults and juveniles; 3 adult summer

Herons, Storks and Ibises

 This is a group of long-legged wading birds that mostly find their food in an aquatic environment. Most have long pointed bills suited to a sudden pounce on prey, such as fish or frogs, but ibises have decurved, probing bills and spoonbills and flamingoes have sifting bills. In flight, herons and egrets tuck their neck back into their shoulders, whereas ibises, spoonbills and flamingoes fly with neck and bill extended.

Bittern *Botaurus stellaris* p.316
adult

Little Bittern *Ixobrychus minutus* p.316
1. male; 2. female; 3. juvenile; 4. male

Squacco Heron *Ardeola ralloides* p.314
1. adult summer; 2. juvenile; 3. adult winter.

Cattle Egret *Bubulcus ibis* p.313
1. adult summer; 2. adult winter; 3. mixed-plumage flock

Great White Egret *Egretta alba* p.311
1. & 2. adult

Purple Heron *Ardea purpurea* p.309
1. adult; 2. sub-adult; 3. juvenile

Glossy Ibis
*Plegadis
falcinellus* p.318
1. adult winter;
2. adult summer

Black Stork *Ciconia nigra* p.320
1. & 2. adults

White Stork *Ciconia ciconia* p.321
1. & 2. adults

Swans pp.54–5

Grey geese pp.56–7 and 60–1

Black-and-white geese pp.58–9 and 61

Shelduck pp.62–3

Dabbling ducks pp.64–70

Diving ducks pp.71–5

Seaducks pp.76–81 and 84–5

Stifftails p.81

Wildfowl

Swans, geese and ducks are essentially
aquatic birds that feed on or adjacent to
water. They vary in size from the huge
Mute Swan to the dainty Common Teal.
Many species, such as the swans, geese
and most duck, are vegetarian, but some
of the duck dive in pursuit of fish and other
aquatic life. Many frequent marshes and
other fresh waters, but some, especially
duck, are essentially marine outside the
breeding season. Many are winter visitors
to much of Europe.

Sawbills pp.82–3 and 85

Whooper Swan *Cygnus cygnus* p.324
1. juveniles and adults; 2. adult

Bean Goose *Anser fabalis* p.327
adults. *See also p.60*

Greylag Goose *Anser anser* p.326
adults. *See also p.60*

White-fronted Goose *Anser albifrons* p.329
1. adults ssp. *albifrons*; 2. juvenile ssp. *flavirostris*. See also p.60

Canada Goose *Branta canadensis* p.331
adult. *See also p.61*

Barnacle Goose *Branta leucopsis* p.331
adults. *See also p.61*

Brent Goose *Branta bernicla* p.332
1. ssp. *nigricans* adult; 2. ssp. *bernicla* 1st winter;

Bean Goose
Anser fabalis
p.327.
See also p.56

Greylag Goose
Anser anser
p.326. *See also p.56*

Pink-footed Goose *Anser brachyrhynchus* p.328. *See also p.56*

White-fronted Goose *Anser albifrons* p.329. *See also p.57*

Lesser White-fronted Goose *Anser erythropus* p.330. *See also p.57*

Canada Goose *Branta canadensis* p.331. *See also p.58*

Barnacle Goose *Branta leucopsis* p.331. *See also p.58*

Ruddy Shelduck **Tadorna ferruginea** p.335
1. pair (male right); 2. pair (female right)

Eurasian Wigeon *Anas penelope* p.337
1. male; 2. female. *See also p.68*

Common Teal *Anas crecca* p.338 1. pair (female left);
2. male ssp. *carolinensis* (Green-winged Teal). *See also p.68*

Pintail *Anas acuta* p.341
1. male; 2. female. *See also p.69*

Eurasian Wigeon *Anas penelope* p.337
males and females. *See also p.64*

Gadwall *Anas strepera*
p.338 male (left) and female.
See also p.64

Mallard *Anas*
platyrhynchos p.340 male
(below) and female. *See also p.6*

Garganey *Anas querquedula* p.339
male. *See also p.66*

Pintail *Anas acuta* p.341
males and female (top left). *See also p.67*

Mandarin Duck *Aix galericulata* p.336
1. male; 2. female

Marbled Duck *Marmaronetta angustirostris*
p.342 adult. *See also p.74*

Pochard *Aythya ferina* p.344
1. male; 2. female. *See also p.74*

Tufted Duck *Aythya fuligula* p.346
1. male; 2. female; 3. female 'Scaup-faced'. *See also p.75*

Barrow's Goldeneye *Bucephala islandica* p.354
1. males; 2. female. *See also p.75*

Marbled Duck *Marmaronetta angustirostris* p.342
adults. *See also p.70*

Red-crested Pochard *Netta rufina* p.343
males and female (left). *See also p.70*

Pochard *Aythya ferina* p.344
males and females. *See also p.71*

Tufted Duck *Aythya fuligula* p.346
males and females (top). *See also p.72*

Scaup *Aythya marila* p.346
males and females. *See also p.72*

Barrow's Goldeneye *Bucephala islandica* p.354
male (below) and female. *See also p.73*

King Eider *Somateria spectabilis* p.348
1. female; 2. male.

Common Scoter *Melanitta nigra* p.351
1. male; 2. female

Surf Scoter *Melanitta perspicillata* p.353
1. males and females. *See also p.85*

Ruddy Duck *Oxyura jamaicensis* p.358
1. male summer; 2. female

Smew *Mergus albellus* p.355
1. male summer; 2. female. *See also p.85*

Common Eider *Somateria mollissima* p.347 males and female (below). *See also p.76*

Steller's Eider *Polysticta stelleri* p.349 male. *See also p.77*

Harlequin Duck *Histrionicus histrionicus* p.350 males (centre) and females. *See also p.78*

Velvet Scoter
Melanitta fusca p.352
male. *See also p.80*

Surf Scoter *Melanitta*
perspicillata p.353
males and females. *See also p.81*

Smew *Mergus albellus*
p.355 males. *See also*
p.82

Red-breasted Merganser
Mergus serrator p.356
male. *See also p.82*

2

Birds of Prey

This is a relatively homogeneous group of birds, most of which hunt their prey in flight. They vary in size from the huge vultures to relatively small falcons, and several are colonial breeders and gregarious throughout the year. Many of the larger species depend to a varying extent on carrion, while the smaller hawks and falcons are among the most efficient hunters. Over Europe as a whole, these birds have suffered a significant decline due to persecution and changing land use during the twentieth century. In contrast, Britain's populations are showing a healthy growth as the century draws to a close.

Lammergeier *Gypaetus barbatus* p.364
1. adult; 2. immature; 3. adult

Griffon Vulture *Gyps fulvus* p.366
1. & 2. adults

Lesser Spotted Eagle *Aquila pomarina* p.376
1. adult; 2. immature. *See also p.94*

Spotted Eagle *Aquila clanga* p.377
1st winter. *See also p.94*

Spanish Imperial Eagle *Aquila adalberti* p.379
adult. *See also p.94*

Imperial Eagle *Aquila heliaca* p.379
adult. *See also p.94*

White-tailed Eagle
Haliaeetus albicilla
p.363 adult. *See also p.95*

Booted Eagle *Hieraaetus*
pennatus p.382
adult pale phase. *See also p.95*

Short-toed Eagle
Circaetus gallicus p.381
adult. *See also p.95*

Lesser Spotted Eagle *(left)* p.376
adult. *See also p.90*

Spotted Eagle *(right)* p.377
adult. *See also p.90*

1 **2** **3**

1 **2**

Steppe Eagle *(above)* p.378
1. adult; 2. 1st winter; 3. 2nd summer. *See also p.*

Spanish Imperial Eagle *(left)* p.379
1. adult;
2. immature.
See also p.91

1 **2**

Golden Eagle p.380
1. juvenile; 2. adult. *See also p.91*

White-tailed Eagle *(right)*
p.363
1. adult;
2. immature.
See also p.92

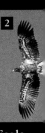

Booted Eagle *(left)*
p.382
1. pale form;
2. dark form.
See also p.92

Bonelli's Eagle *(left)* p.383
1. adult;
2. immature.
See also p.92

Honey Buzzard *Pernis apivorus* p.360
1. dark form; 2. pale form

Rough-legged Buzzard *Buteo lagopus* p.374
1. & 2. adult

Black-shouldered Kite
Elanus caeruleus p.361
adult. *See also p.100*

Black Kite
Milvus migrans p.362
adult. *See also p.100*

Red Kite *Milvus milvus* p.362
adult. *See also p.100*

Hen Harrier *Circus cyaneus* p.368
1. male with young; 2. female. *See also p.101*

Pallid Harrier *Circus macrourus* p.369
1. male; 2. female. *See also p.101*

Black-shouldered Kite
Elanus caeruleus p.361.
See also p.98

Black Kite
Milvus migrans (above)
p.362. *See also p.98*

Red Kite *Milvus milvus*
p.362. *See also p.98*

1

2

3

4

Hen Harrier *Circus cyaneus* p.368
1. male; 2. female. *See also p.99*

Pallid Harrier *Circus macrourus* p.369
1. male; 2. juvenile. *See also p.99*

European Sparrowhawk *Accipiter nisus* p.372
1. male; 2. female; 3. juvenile female

Lesser Kestrel *Falco naumanni* p.385
1. male; 2. female. *See also p.108*

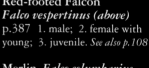

Red-footed Falcon
Falco vespertinus (above)
p.387 1. male; 2. female with
young; 3. juvenile. *See also p.108*

Merlin *Falco columbarius*
(left) p.388 1. male; 2. female.
See also p.108

Eleonora's Falcon *Falco eleonorae* p.389
1. pale form; 2. dark form. *See also p.109*

Lanner Falcon *Falco biarmicus* p.390
adult. *See also p.109*

Gyr Falcon *Falco rusticolus* p.392
1. pale form; 2. dark form. *See also p.109*

Lesser Kestrel
Falco naumanni
p.385
1. male;
2. female.
See also p.104

Common Kestrel
Falco tinnunculus
(right) p.386
female. See also p.104

Red-footed Falcon *Falco vespertinus* p.387
1. male; 2. female. *See also p.105*

Eleonora's Falcon *Falco eleonorae* p.389
1. pale form; 2. dark form. *See also p.106*

Lanner Falcon
Falco biarmicus
p.390 adult. *See also p.106*

Saker Falcon
Falco cherrug
p.391 adult. *See also p.106*

Gyr Falcon *Falco rusticolus* p.392
1. pale form; 2. dark form. *See also p.107*

Gamebirds

Grouse, partridge and pheasants have been the sportsman's traditional quarry ever since man developed the shotgun. As a result, a considerable industry has invested vast resources in protection, bird management and artificial propagation to the birds' benefit. In many areas, the prime gamebirds, pheasants, grouse and partridge, enjoy a healthy overpopulation, while in contrast Capercaillie, Black Grouse and Common Quail have exhibited serious declines. All gamebirds are essentially terrestrial and most fly only to escape danger.

Hazel Grouse *Bonasa bonasia* p.394
1. male; 2. female

Ptarmigan *Lagopus mutus* p.396
1. female (left) and male summer; 2. winter

Capercaillie *Tetrao urogallus* p.397
1. male; 2. female

Chukar *Alectoris chukar* p.399
female with chicks

Rock Partridge *Alectoris graeca* p.400
adult

Grey Partridge *Perdix perdix* p.402
1. male; 2. female

Common Quail *Coturnix coturnix* p.405

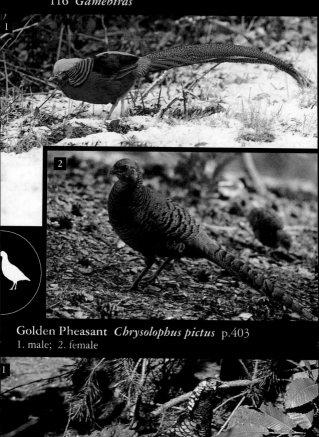

Golden Pheasant *Chrysolophus pictus* p.403
1. male; 2. female

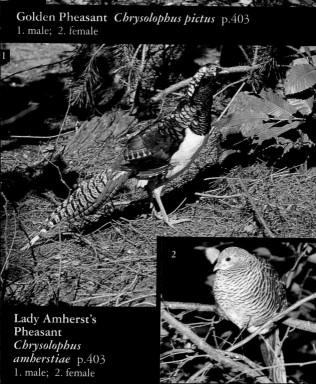

Lady Amherst's Pheasant *Chrysolophus amherstiae* p.403
1. male; 2. female

Common Pheasant *Phasianus colchicus* p.404
1. ring-necked male; 2. male; 3. female

Crakes and Allies

This is a group of predominantly aquatic birds which spend much of their time exploring dense emergent vegetation. Some, like the gallinules and coots, have become more aquatic and spend their time swimming, while others, such as the Corn Crake, are essentially dry-land birds. Most have long legs and toes, and are marked in camouflaged shades of brown and cream. Despite their apparent poor flying abilities, many perform lengthy migrations. Associated with the crakes are two groups of larger species, the cranes and bustards, which are among Europe's most spectacular birds.

Water Rail *Rallus aquaticus* p.408
adult

Spotted Crake
***Porzana porzana* p.408**
1. adult; 2. juvenile

Little Crake *Porzana parva* p.409
1. male; 2. female

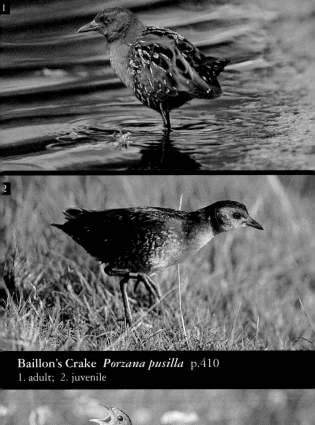

Baillon's Crake *Porzana pusilla* p.410
1. adult; 2. juvenile

Moorhen *Gallinula chloropus* p.412
1. adult; 2. juvenile

Common Coot *Fulica atra* p.414
1. adult; 2. juvenile

Common Crane *Grus grus* p.416
1. adult pair; 2. adults and a juvenile

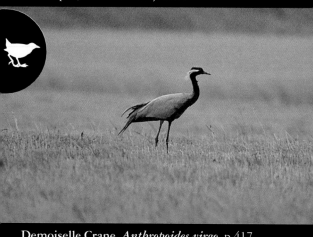

Demoiselle Crane *Anthropoides virgo* p.417
adult

Great Bustard *Otis tarda* p.419
1. male; 2. male displaying; 3. females

Stone-curlew *Burhinus oedicnemus* p.423

Stone-curlew p.125

Black-and-white waders
pp.128–9

Coursers and pratincoles
pp.130–1

Plovers pp.132–7

Calidris sandpipers
pp.138–41

Snipe p.143

Godwits and curlews
pp.144–5

Tringa sandpipers
pp.146–51

Waders

These are long-legged, long-billed birds, many of which share an aquatic habitat. Many are 'shorebirds' that feed on shoals and mud banks exposed by the receding tide and which then form enormous flocks at favoured high-tide roosts. Many such birds are winter visitors to Europe that breed in the high Arctic wastes of Siberia, while others merely pass through Europe in spring and autumn while travelling between their breeding and wintering grounds. The typical *Calidris* and *Tringa* sandpipers are often regarded as difficult to identify by beginners.

Phalaropes pp.152–3

Black-winged Stilt *Himantopus himantopus* p.421
1. male summer; 2. winter; 3. adult

Cream-coloured
Courser
Cursorius curso[r]
p.424 adult

Ringed Plover *Charadrius hiaticula* p.428
1. adult; 2. juvenile

Kentish Plover *Charadrius alexandrinus*
p.429 1. male summer; 2. juvenile

American
Golden Plover
*Pluvialis
dominica*
p.432
juvenile

Pacific Golden Plover
Pluvialis fulva p.431
1. & 2. juveniles

European Golden Plover *Pluvialis apricaria*
p.431 1. summer, northern race; 2. winter; 3. flock in flight

Dotterel *Charadrius morinellus* p.430
1. summer; 2. juvenile

Spur-winged Plover *Hoplopterus spinosus* p.434
1. & 2. adults

Knot *Calidris canutus* p.437
1. summer; 2. winter

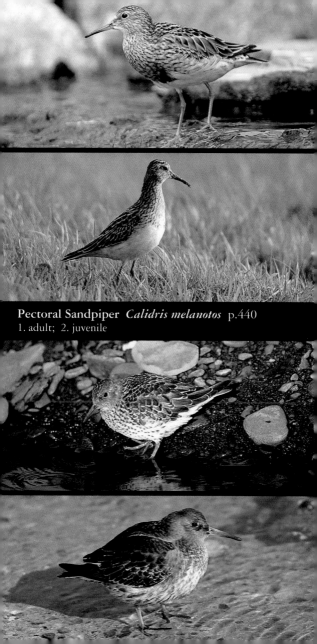

Pectoral Sandpiper *Calidris melanotos* p.440
1. adult; 2. juvenile

Little Stint *Calidris minuta* p.439
1. summer; 2. winter; 3. juvenile

Curlew Sandpiper
Calidris ferruginea p.441
1. summer; 2. winter; 3. juvenile

Dunlin *Calidris alpina*
p.443
1. summer; 2. winter;
3. juvenile

Common Snipe *Gallinago gallinago* p.446
adult

Jack Snipe
Lymnocryptes
minimus p.446
adult

Great Snipe
Gallinago media p.447
adult

2

Black-tailed Godwit *Limosa limosa* p.449
1. summer; 2. winter

Whimbrel *Numenius phaeopus* p.451
adult

Slender-billed Curlew *Numenius tenuirostris* p.451
adult

Spotted Redshank *Tringa erythropus* p.452
1. summer; 2. winter. *See also p.150*

Marsh Sandpiper *Tringa stagnatilis* p.454
winter. *See also p.150*

Green Sandpiper *Tringa ochropus* p.456
adult. *See also p.151*

Common Sandpiper *Actitis hypoleucos* p.457
1. adult; 2. juvenile. *See also p.151*

Spotted Redshank *Tringa erythropus* p.452
winter. *See also p.146*

Common Redshank *Tringa totanus* p.453
winter. *See also p.146*

Greenshank *Tringa nebularia* p.455 winter. *See also p.147*

Common Sandpiper *Actitis hypoleucos* p.457 winter. *See also p.149*

Turnstone *Arenaria interpres* p.459
1. summer; 2. & 3. winter

Red-necked Phalarope *Phalaropus lobatus*
p.460   1. female summer;   2. juvenile;   3. winter

 Skuas pp.156–7

 Gulls pp.158–69

 Sea terns pp.170–3

 Marsh terns pp.174–5

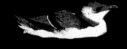 Auks pp.176–7

Gulls, Terns and Auks

This is a group of large to medium-sized seabirds, some of which have adopted a freshwater marshland habitat, while others, more recently, have spread inland to exploit man-made environments. Gulls and terns are largely white in adult plumage, while exhibiting variable degrees of brown while immature. Auks, in contrast, are black and white at all times. Most species are gregarious and colonial, and auks form the core of all the great cliff seabird colonies.

Pomarine Skua *Stercorarius pomarinus* p.463
1. adult dark form; 2. adult light form; 3. juvenile

Long-tailed Skua *Stercorarius longicaudus* p.464
1. adult; 2. juvenile; 3. adult

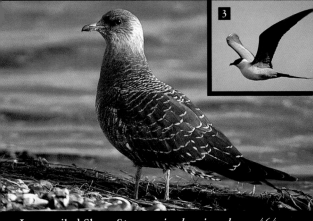

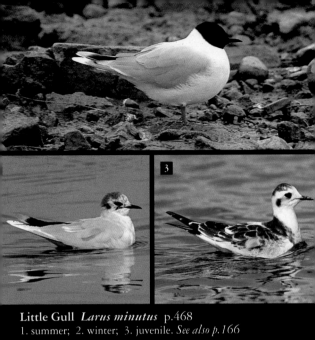

Little Gull *Larus minutus* p.468
1. summer; 2. winter; 3. juvenile. *See also p.166*

Slender-billed Gull *Larus genei* p.470
1. adult; 2. 1st winter. *See also p.166*

Ring-billed Gull
Larus delawarensis p.472
1. adult summer;
2. adult winter;
3. 1st winter.
See also p.166

Lesser Black-backed Gull *Larus fuscus* p.474
1. summer; 2. winter; 3. 2nd winter; 4. 1st winter. *See also p.167*

Herring Gull *Larus argentatus* p.477
1. summer; 2. winter; 3. juvenile. *See also p.167*

Iceland Gull *Larus glaucoides* p.475
1. winter; 2. 1st winter. *See also p.168*

Glaucous Gull
Larus hyperboreus p.476
1. summer;
2. winter;
3. 1st winter.
See also p.168

Ivory Gull *Pagophila eburnea* p.480
1. adult; 2. 1st winter. *See also p.169*

Kittiwake *Rissa tridactyla* p.481
1. adult; 2. 1st winter. *See also p.169*

Mediterranean Gull *(left)* p.467
adult winter. *See also p.158*

Little Gull
(above) p.468
1. summer;
2. 1st winter.
See also p.159

Black-headed
Gull *(left)*
p.470 summer.
See also p.159

Slender-billed
Gull p.470
adult. *See also p.1C*

Common Gull
p.473 adult winter.
See also p.161

Lesser Black-backed Gull
p.474 adult summer.
See also p.162

Great Black-backed Gull
p.478 adult. *See also p.162*

Herring Gull *(right)* p.477
adult. *See also p.163*

2

Iceland Gull p.475
1. adult; 2. 1st winter.
See also p.164

Glaucous Gull p.476
winter. *See also p.164*

Ivory Gull p.480
1st winter. *See also p.165*

Kittiwake p.481
1. adult; 2. 1st winter. *See also p.165*

Caspian Tern *Sterna caspia* p.484
1. winter; 2. summer; 3. winter

Common Tern *Sterna hirundo* p.483
1. summer; 2. 1st winter; 3. juvenile; 4. summer

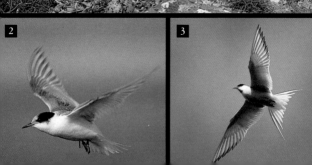

Roseate Tern *Sterna dougallii* p.486
1. & 2. summer

Gull-billed Tern *Gelochelidon nilotica* p.488
1. summer; 2. moulting to winter; 3. summer; 4. winter

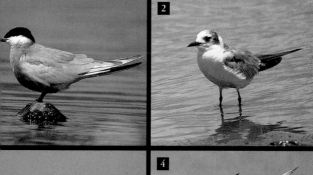

White-winged Black Tern *Chlidonias leucopterus*
p.490 1. summer; 2. juvenile; 3. summer

Common Guillemot *Uria aalge* p.492
1. summer; 2. winter; 3. summer

Brünnich's Guillemot *Uria lomvia* p.493
1. summer; 2. winter

Black Guillemot *Cepphus grylle* p.495
1. summer; 2. winter

Little Auk *Alle alle* p.496
1. summer; 2. winter; 3. summer

Sandgrouse p.180

Parakeets p.181

Cuckoos pp.182–3

Pigeons and doves pp.184–

Sandgrouse, Parakeets, Cuckoos, and Pigeons

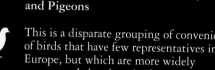

This is a disparate grouping of convenience of birds that have few representatives in Europe, but which are more widely represented elsewhere in the world. Thus we have two sandgrouse, a single parakeet, two cuckoos and six pigeons (or doves) all of which are strong, fast fliers. They inhabit a wide variety of landforms, though sandgrouse are confined to semi-desert and arid grasslands.

Black-bellied Sandgrouse *Pterocles orientalis* p.498
1. male; 2. female; 3. males and females

Pin-tailed Sandgrouse *Pterocles alchata* p.499
1. male; 2. female; 3. pair

Common Cuckoo *Cuculus canorus* p.502
1. adult; 2. female hepatic form; 3. juvenile; 4. adult

Rock Dove
Columba livia
p.504 adult

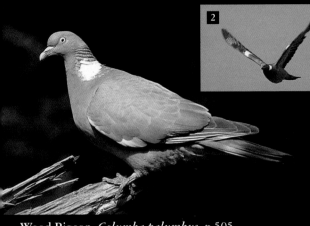

Wood Pigeon *Columba palumbus* p.505
1. & 2. adults

Collared Dove *Streptopelia decaocto* p.506
adult

Turtle Dove
Streptopelia turtur
p.507 adult

Laughing Dove
Streptopelia senegalensis
p.508 adult

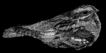

Owls, Nightjars and Colourful Exotics

This is a diverse group of birds of which only the owls are well represented in Europe in terms of the number of species. There are thus only two nightjars, plus a single hoopoe, bee-eater, roller and kingfisher representing families that are far more numerous and diverse elsewhere in the world. Owls are largely nocturnal hunters, though the Short-eared Owl is essentially a daytime predator and several northern species enjoy the long days of summer in the Arctic. Nightjars too are nocturnal, but hunt on the wing taking large flying insects. The other species are brightly coloured and, like the nightjars, largely summer visitors.

Barn Owl *Tyto alba* p.509
1. ssp. *alba*; 2. ssp. *guttata*; 3. pale form

Snowy Owl *Nyctea scandiaca* p.510
1. male; 2. female

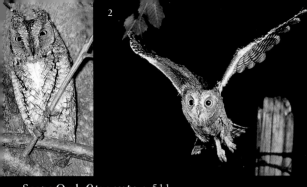

Scops Owl *Otus scops* p.511
1. & 2. adult grey form

Pygmy Owl *Glaucidium passerinum* p.512
1. & 2. adults

Tawny Owl *Strix aluco* p.513 adult

Ural Owl *Strix uralensis* p.514 adult

Great Grey Owl *Strix nebulosa* p.515 adult

Eagle Owl *Bubo bubo* p.515 adult

Long-eared Owl *Asio otus* p.516
adult

Short-eared Owl *Asio flammeus* p.517
1. & 2. adults

Tengmalm's Owl *Aegolius funereus* p.518
1. & 2. adults

European Nightjar
Caprimulgus europaeus
p.520
1. female; 2. male

Red-necked Nightjar
Caprimulgus ruficollis
(below) p.520
male

**Common
Kingfisher**
Alcedo atthis
(below) p.525
adult

European Roller *Coracias garrulus* p.527
adult

European Bee-eater *Merops apiaster* p.526
adult

2

Woodpeckers

These are predominantly arboreal birds and expert tree climbers which are mostly resident in Europe. The 'green' woodpeckers, while remaining tree-hole nesters, frequently forage on the ground, while the Wryneck is a long-distance migrant and summer visitor. Other woodpeckers are predominantly pied and are best identified by their back and face patterns. Most excavate a new tree-hole nest chamber each year and are the primary suppliers of such holes for other species. They vary in size from the huge Black Woodpecker to the sparrow-sized Lesser Spotted Woodpecker.

Grey-headed Woodpecker *Picus canus* p.531
1. male; 2. female

Wryneck
Jynx torquilla p.530
adult

Three-toed Woodpecker
Picoides tridactylus
(right) p.536 adult

Black Woodpecker *Dryocopus martius* p.536
1. male; 2. female

Great Spotted Woodpecker *Dendrocopos major*
p.532 1. male; 2. female

Swifts and Swallows

Though not related, swifts and swallows share an aerial lifestyle and are dependent on flying insects for food. All species are long-winged and spend much of their time in flight. They have short bills but large gapes and, with a single exception, are all summer visitors to Europe. Swifts are the most aerial of all birds, collecting nesting material, mating and even sleeping on the wing. The swallows (including the martins) construct their characteristic mud nests mainly on human structures.

Common Swift *Apus apus*
p.522 1. & 2. adults

Pallid Swift
Apus pallidus
p.523

Alpine Swift
Apus melba
p.523

White-rumped Swift *Apus caffer*
p.524

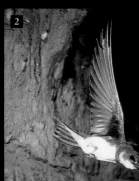

2

Crag Martin
Ptyonoprogne rupestris
p.546
1. & 2. adults

2

Swallow *Hirundo rustica* p.547
1. adult; 2. 1st year

2

Red-rumped Swallow
Hirundo daurica
p.547
1. & 2. adults

2

Larks, Pipits and Wagtails

 These are mostly small terrestrial birds of
open ground that spend much of their time
walking. While the larks are robust in
build and clothed in shades of brown and
buff, the pipits and wagtails are slim and
elegant and, in the case of the wagtails,
delicately marked in black, white and
yellow. Though wagtails and many pipits
have a distinct preference for aquatic
environments, larks are essentially birds of
dry and even arid landforms.

Calandra Lark
Melanocorypha calandra
p.537

Short-toed Lark
Calandrella brachydactyla
p.538

Lesser Short-toed Lark
Calandrella rufescens p.539

Crested Lark
Galerida cristata p.540

Thekla Lark *Galerida theklae*
p.541

Wood Lark *Lullula arborea*
p.541

Sky Lark *Alauda arvensis*
p.542

Richard's Pipit *Anthus novaeseelandiae*
p.550

Tawny Pipit *Anthus campestris* p.550
1. adult; 2. juvenile

Red-throated Pipit *Anthus cervinus* p.551

Water Pipit *Anthus spinoletta* p.552
1. summer; 2. winter

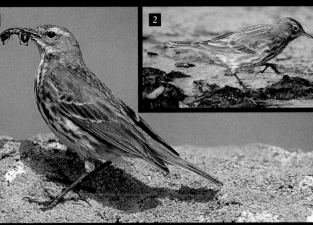

Rock Pipit *Anthus petrosus* p.553
1. summer ssp. *petrosus*; 2. winter ssp. *littoralis*

Tree Pipit
Anthus trivialis p.553

Meadow Pipit
Anthus pratensis p.554

Grey Wagtail *Motacilla cinerea* p.555
1. male; 2. female; 3. juvenile

Citrine Wagtail *Motacilla citreola* p.557
1. male; 2. female; 3. juvenile

Pied Wagtail *Motacilla alba yarrellii* p.555
1. male summer; 2. female summer; 3. juvenile

White Wagtail *Motacilla alba alba* p.556
1. male; 2. female; 3. juvenile

Yellow Wagtail *Motacilla flava* p.556
1. ssp. *flavissima* male; 2. ssp. *feldegg* male;

Waxwing p.216

Dipper p.216

Wren p.217

Accentors p.217

Waxwing, Dipper, Wren, and Accentors

Although there are fifty or more wrens in the world, only one of which occurs in Europe, there are relatively few other species of waxwing, dipper and accentor. Over most of Europe waxwings are sporadic winter visitors in highly variable numbers. Outside these irruptions, which occur about every seven or so years, they are virtually unknown. Dippers, in contrast, are resident and totally confined to fast-running permanent streams. Accentors are mountain birds, one of which, the Hedge Accentor, has adapted to a wide variety of lowland habitats. The single non-American wren has occupied virtually every landform in Europe.

Waxwing *Bombycilla garrulus*
p.559

1

2

Wren *Troglodytes troglodytes*
p.561

Hedge Accentor *Prunella modularis*
p.562

Alpine Accentor *Prunella collaris*
p.563

Chats and Thrushes

Although easily divisible into two or more groups, this is a family of closely related mainly terrestrial birds many of which are summer visitors, or at least partial migrants. Chats are generally smaller than thrushes, with medium-length to long tails that are frequently cocked or distinctively coloured like in the redstarts, wheatears or Bluethroat. Thrushes are more soberly coloured, often with streaked or spotted breasts. All species are strong fliers.

Rufous Bush-robin *Cercotrichas galactotes*
p.564

1

2

Robin *Erithacus rubecula* p.565
1. adult; 2. juvenile

Red-flanked Bluetail *Tarsiger cyanurus* p.568
1. fresh autumn male; 2. female; 3. 1st winter

Black Redstart *Phoenicurus ochruros* p.569
1. male; 2. female

Common Redstart
Phoenicurus phoenicurus
p.570
1. male; 2. female;
3. fresh autumn male

Whinchat *Saxicola rubetra* p.570
1. male; 2. female

Pied Wheatear *Oenanthe pleschanka* p.572
1. fresh autumn/spring male; 2. female

Black-eared Wheatear *Oenanthe hispanica* p.573
1. ssp. *melanoleuca* male; 2. ssp. *hispanica* male;
3. ssp. *melanoleuca* female; 4. ssp. *hispanica* female

Black Wheatear
Oenanthe leucura
573 male

Isabelline Wheatear
Oenanthe isabellina
p.574 adult

Rock Thrush *Monticola saxatilis* p.575
1. male; 2. female

Blue Rock Thrush *Monticola solitarius* p.576
1. male; 2. female

Ring Ouzel *Turdus torquatus* p.577
1. male; 2. female

Blackbird
Turdus merula
p.578
1. adult male;
2. female

Song Thrush
Turdus philomelos p.578

Redwing *Turdus iliacus*
p.579

Warblers and Flycatchers

 These are mainly small insectivorous birds
many of which are only summer visitors to
Europe. Flycatchers frequently perch quite
openly and catch their prey in the air.
Warblers may also practice 'flycatching', but
more usually scour vegetation in search of
adult insects and their larvae in an ever-
active manner. Warblers are divisible into
four main groups which largely follow their
generic names: the marsh warblers (*Locustella*
and *Acrocephalus*), the tree warblers
(*Hippolais*), the scrub warblers (*Sylvia*) and
the leaf warblers (*Phylloscopus*). Placing an
individual in the correct grouping is the first
step in accurately identifying what can be a
difficult group of birds.

Fan-tailed Warbler *Cisticola juncidis*
p.581

Cetti's Warbler *Cettia cetti*
p.582

Grasshopper Warbler *Locustella naevia*
p.583

Aquatic Warbler *Acrocephalus paludicola*
p.586

River Warbler
Locustella fluviatilis p.584

Savi's Warbler
Locustella luscinioides p.58

Blyth's Reed Warbler
Acrocephalus dumetorum
p.588

Marsh Warbler
Acrocephalus palustris
(right) p.589

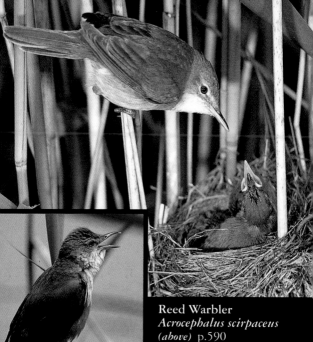

Reed Warbler
Acrocephalus scirpaceus
(above) p.590

Great Reed Warbler
Acrocephalus arundinaceus
p.590

Olivaceous Warbler *Hippolais pallida*
p.591

Olive-tree Warbler *Hippolais olivetorum*
p.592

Icterine Warbler
Hippolais icterina p.593

Melodious Warbler
Hippolais polyglotta p.5

Marmora's Warbler *Sylvia sarda* p.594
1. male; 2. juvenile

Spectacled Warbler *Sylvia conspicillata* p.595
1. male; 2. female

Sardinian Warbler *Sylvia melanocephala* p.597
1. male; 2. female

Rüppell's Warbler *Sylvia rueppelli* p.598
1. male; 2. female

Orphean Warbler *Sylvia hortensis* p.598
1. male;
2. juvenile

Barred Warbler *Sylvia nisoria* p.599
1. adult; 2. 1st winter

Lesser Whitethroat *Sylvia curruca* p.600
1. male; 2. female

Common Whitethroat *Sylvia communis* p.600
1. male; 2. female

Garden Warbler *Sylvia borin*
p.601

Blackcap *Sylvia atricapilla* p.602
1. male; 2. female

Greenish
Warbler
*Phylloscopus
trochiloides*
p.603

Arctic Warbler
*Phylloscopus
borealis (below*
p.603

Bonelli's Warbler *Phylloscopus bonelli*
p.606

Chiffchaff *Phylloscopus collybita* p.607
1. summer; 2. 1st winter

Willow Warbler *Phylloscopus trochilus* p.608
1. summer; 2. 1st winter

Pallas's Warbler *Phylloscopus proregulus*
p.604

Yellow-browed Warbler *Phylloscopus inornatus*
p.605

Wood Warbler *Phylloscopus sibilatrix*
p.607

Goldcrest *Regulus regulus* p.609
1. male; 2. female

Spotted Flycatcher *Muscicapa striata*
p.611

Red-breasted Flycatcher *Ficedula parva* p.612
1. male; 2. female

Collared Flycatcher *Ficedula albicollis* p.613
1. male; 2. female; 3. juvenile

Pied Flycatcher *Ficedula hypoleuca* p.614
1. male; 2. female; 3. 1st winter

Tits, Nuthatches and Shrikes

Tits and nuthatches are predominantly arboreal birds that are mostly resident. Shrikes, in contrast, are birds of heath and open countryside that are mostly summer visitors, or at least partial migrants. While tits and nuthatches are ever active scouring woodland for small items of food, shrikes perch openly waiting to pounce in the manner of a bird of prey. Most members of the group are well marked and relatively easy to identify.

Bearded Tit *Panurus biarmicus* p.616
1. male; 2. female

Marsh Tit *Parus palustris*
p.619

Willow Tit
Parus montanus p.620

Sombre Tit
Parus lugubris p.620

Coal Tit *Parus ater*
p.622

2

Blue Tit *Parus caeruleus* p.623
1. adult; 2. juvenile

2

European Nuthatch *Sitta europaea* p.625
1. ssp. *europaea*; 2. ssp. *caesia*

Krüper's Nuthatch *Sitta krueperi*
p.625

Wallcreeper *Tichodroma muraria* p.628
1. & 2. adults

Red-backed Shrike *Lanius collurio* p.632
1. male; 2. female

Lesser Grey Shrike *Lanius minor* p.633
1. adult; 2. 1st winter

Woodchat Shrike *Lanius senator* p.634
1. male; 2. female; 3. juvenile

Masked Shrike *Lanius nubicus* p.635
1. adult male; 2. juvenile

Crows, Jays and Starlings

This is a group of closely related species that includes some of the best-known and most obvious of European birds. While the typical crows, such as the Carrion Crow, Jackdaw and Raven are predominantly black, the jays and orioles are more colourful. Similarly, while some such as Nutcracker, Rook and starling are gregarious, others are essentially solitary. Most are resident, but the Golden Oriole is a summer visitor.

Golden Oriole *Oriolus oriolus* p.631
1. male; 2. female

Eurasian Jay
Garrulus glandarius
p.636

Siberian Jay
Perisoreus infaustus
p.637

Alpine Chough *Pyrrhocorax graculus* p.639
1. & 2. adults

Red-billed Chough *Pyrrhocorax pyrrhocorax* p.640
1. & 2. adults

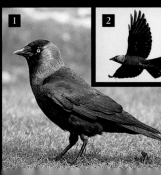

Rook *Corvus frugilegus* p.642
1. & 2. adults; 3. juvenile

Carrion Crow *Corvus corone* p.642
1. & 2. ssp. *corone*; 3. Hooded Crow, ssp. *cornix*

Common Starling *Sturnus vulgaris* p.644
1. summer; 2. winter

Spotless Starling *Sturnus unicolor* p.645
1. summer; 2. winter

Rose-coloured Starling *Sturnus roseus* p.646
1. adult; 2. juvenile

Sparrows, Finches and Buntings

This is a large group of thick-billed, seed-eating, small birds that includes some of Europe's most familiar species. Despite their similarity, they exhibit considerable diversity in food and habitat preferences and, particularly, in bill structure. The massive nut-cracking bill of the Hawfinch contrasts with the delicate tweaking bill of the Goldfinch, while the crossed prizing bills of the crossbills vary in size from species to species depending on the cone size of the conifers they inhabit. Buntings are longer-tailed than finches and sparrows, spend more time on the ground and in female and immature plumages pose serious identification problems.

House Sparrow
Passer domesticus
p.647
1. male;
2. female;
3. ssp. *italiae*

Spanish Sparrow *Passer hispaniolensis* p.648

Tree Sparrow
Passer montanus
p.649

Rock Sparrow
Petronia petronia
p.650

Common Waxbill *Estrilda astrild*
p.651 adult

Chaffinch *Fringilla coelebs* p.653
1. male; 2. female

Serin *Serinus serinus* p.654
1. male; 2. female

Greenfinch *Carduelis chloris* p.655
1. male; 2. female

Goldfinch *Carduelis carduelis* p.656
1. adult; 2. juvenile

Citril Finch *Serinus citrinella*
p.656

Siskin *Carduelis spinus* p.657
1. male; 2. female

Linnet *Carduelis cannabina* p.658
1. male summer; 2. female

Twite *Carduelis flavirostris* p.659
1. summer; 2. winter

Common Redpoll *Carduelis flammea* p.659
1. male; 2. female

Arctic Redpoll *Carduelis hornemanni* p.660
1 & 2. adults

Common Crossbill *Loxia curvirostra* p.662
1. & 2. males; 3. female

Two-barred Crossbill *Loxia leucoptera* p.661
1. male; 2. juvenile

Scottish Crossbill *Loxia scotica* p.662
male (left) and female

Trumpeter Finch *Bucanetes githagineus* p.664
1. male; 2. female

Common Rosefinch *Carpodacus erythrinus* p.664
1. male; 2. female

Pine Grosbeak *Pinicola enucleator* p.666
1. male; 2. female

Bullfinch *Pyrrhula pyrrhula* p.666
1. male; 2. female

2

Snow Bunting
Plectrophenax nivalis p.669
1. male summer;
2. adult male winter (right) and females winter/1st winter males (left);
3. female winter

2

Rustic Bunting
Emberiza rustica (*above*) p.674
1. male summer;
2. female summer

Little Bunting
Emberiza pusilla p.675
male summer

Yellowhammer *Emberiza citrinella* p.670
1. male; 2. female

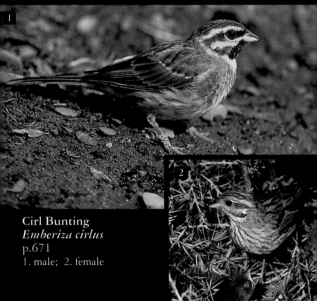

Cirl Bunting
Emberiza cirlus
p.671
1. male; 2. female

Ortolan Bunting *Emberiza hortulana* p.672
1. male summer; 2. female

Cretzschmar's Bunting *Emberiza caesia* p.673
1. male; 2. female

Cinereous Bunting
Emberiza cineracea

Corn Bunting
Miliaria calandra

Rock Bunting *Emberiza cia* p.672
1. male; 2. female

Reed Bunting
Emberiza schoeniclus
p.676
1. male;
2. female;
3. juvenile

Yellow-breasted Bunting *Emberiza aureola* p.677
1. male summer; 2. female

The number preceding each species
description in the following pages
corresponds to the page number in the
colour section on which that species can be
found.

DIVERS (GAVIIDAE)

Five species; northern Eurasia and North America. Three breed in Europe, and another is a regular but scarce winter visitor. These are large waterbirds with long, pointed bills and large webbed feet set well back on the body. While they are accomplished swimmers and expert divers, they are very clumsy on land and never venture far from water margins, even to nest. In flight their long, pointed wings and hump-backed, neck-down appearance is characteristic. They breed on fresh waters, mostly lakes of variable size depending on species, and winter along coasts where they form loose flocks. In summer, their loud, wailing calls are far-carrying; in winter they are silent. The sexes are similar.

p.26 **Red-throated Diver** *Gavia stellata*

Description: 53–59 cm (21–23 in). The only diver with *thin, uptilted bill* and, when breeding, a *plain unmarked back*. In summer, head and neck pale grey, marked by narrow black and white stripes on hind neck and rusty-red throat patch that at any distance is difficult to see and appears black. Back plain rather than chequerboard, at all times. In winter, pale head with prominent dark eye and uptilted bill are diagnostic.

Voice: Loud wailing cries, various cackles and growls, and repeated duck-like quacking uttered on breeding grounds. Silent in winter.

Habitat: Small lakes and ponds among tundra and moorland, usually within a short distance of the sea. Winters on coasts, coming inland only when storm-driven, oiled or sick.

Breeding: Two dark-olive eggs, spotted and blotched with black, laid in simple scrape among waterside vegetation. Incubation 24–29 days, mainly by female.

Range: Circumpolar. Breeds in Iceland and Scotland, and through most of Fennoscandia; winters on adjacent coasts as well as along all British and Irish coasts south to Biscay and Iberia. Also locally in Mediterranean.

The Red-throated Diver breeds on smaller
pools than other divers and commutes to the
sea, as well as to larger fresh waters, to feed.
Such behaviour enables it to exploit
breeding grounds that are not available to
the other divers which prefer to nest and feed
on the same water. It sometimes forms large
flocks at favoured feeding grounds in winter.

p.26 **Black-throated Diver** *Gavia arctica*

Description: 56–59 cm (22–27 in). Similar in size to
Red-throated Diver, but more like Great
Northern in plumage. In summer, head and
neck grey, marked by black patch on throat
and bold black and white neck-stripes. Back
shows clear chequerboard pattern. In winter
back is darker, without scaly pattern, than any
other diver. Dark crown extends below dark
eye. At all times *white flank-patch* at
waterline is invaluable, though not totally
dependable, distinguishing feature. Bill
straight and regular in shape, not thin and
uptilted as in Red-throated, nor as heavy
and strong as in Great Northern. Crown
lacks 'bumps' of both Great Northern and
White-billed Divers.

Voice: A mournful wail and deep *kow-hoo* during
breeding season; silent in winter.

Habitat: Breeds on large lakes in open country and
among extensive conifer forests. Does not
commute to other waters to feed.
Essentially marine in winter, frequenting
inshore coastlines; inland mostly when
storm-driven or sick.

Breeding: Two olive-green eggs, boldly spotted black,
laid in scrape among vegetation near
water's edge, often on small island.
Incubation 28–29 days, by both sexes.

Range: Breeds from Scotland and Scandinavia across
northern Eurasia to northern Pacific and
across North America. The similar, but
smaller, Pacific Loon (diver) *G. pacifica*
replaces it in Bering Straits, but is often
regarded as no more than a subspecies. In
winter, Black-throated Diver ranges from
ice-free coasts of Scandinavia through North
Sea, Biscay and eastern Mediterranean.

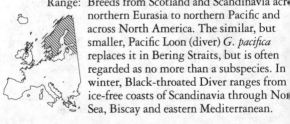

Along with other divers that winter in the Mediterranean and Black Seas, it performs a long overland migration from its breeding grounds in northern Russia and can then often be found on large inland fresh waters. Small numbers regularly winter inland in Switzerland and Hungary.

---

p.27 **Great Northern Diver** *Gavia immer*

Description: 69–81 cm (27–32 in). Largest of the regular European divers, distinguished by *large straight grey-black bill* in all plumages. In summer, head and neck black, broken only by narrow black and white striped patches on throat and sides of neck. Black upperparts show chequerboard pattern similar to, but more extensive than, Black-throated Diver. In winter, upperparts dark grey lightened by *pale scaly barring*. Dark crown separated from eye by bold pale ring-like Red-throated Diver, but unlike Black-throated. Steep forehead and flat crown create more angular head than in other common divers, but not as pronounced as 'bumpy' head of the rarer White-billed Diver.

Voice: Loud, wailing calls with mournful quality that evokes the wilderness wherever this bird commonly breeds. Also a hollow laughing and abrupt *gek* in flight.

Habitat: In summer frequents large tundra and boreal lakes. In winter mainly at sea, but in shallow offshore waters. Decidedly rare inland.

Breeding: Two olive-green to dark-brown eggs, liberally spotted with black, laid on small mound of waterside vegetation with slipway to the lake. Incubation 29–30 days, by both sexes.

Range: Breeds from Iceland (the only regular European site), westwards through Greenland, and right across Canada to Alaska and western USA. Iceland birds winter around Norway, Britain and Atlantic coast southwards to Portugal.

Divers, as their name implies, are excellent underwater swimmers that can remain submerged for up to two minutes at a time, cover a distance of up to 100 m (110 yd), and reach depths of 60 m (200 ft). When disturbed at their breeding grounds they frequently submerge and disappear by diving to marginal vegetation some distance away.

p.27 **White-billed Diver** *Gavia adamsii*

Description: 75–90 cm (29–35 in). Largest and rarest of the divers. Similar to Great Northern, which it replaces in the high Arctic. In all plumages the *heavy ivory-coloured bill has upswept lower mandible* and is held uptilted like that of Red-throated Diver. The 'bumpy' head has steep forehead and flat, even indented, crown. In summer, plumage very similar to Great Northern, but with larger and fewer white squares on its chequerboard back. In winter, 'face' distinctly patchy, with dark extending below white-ringed eye. Barred upperpart more prominent than in Great Northern.

Voice: Loud wails and laughs similar to those of Great Northern, but louder and even more discordant.

Habitat: Treeless tundra marshes with lakes and pools. Shows no particular preference for large lakes and will nest on quite small ponds. In winter frequents coastlines most distant from Arctic breeding grounds.

Breeding: Two olive or brown eggs, with widely scattered dark spotting, laid in nest that may be quite obvious along relatively bare shoreline and may consist of no more than mound of mud. Incubation shared by both sexes, but exact duration remains unrecorded.

Range: Breeds from northern Russia across Siberia and into Alaska and northern Canada. Winters in small numbers along coasts of Norway, wandering southwards as vagrant to shores of North Sea. Elsewhere found along both coasts of northern Pacific.

This is a rare European bird and one that sets the telephone lines humming, the pagers paging, and twitchers twitching.

GREBES (PODICIPEDIDAE)

20 species; worldwide. Five species regularly occur in Europe; all breed. A group of small to medium-sized waterbirds that spend virtually their entire lives afloat. They are expert divers. Like the divers, their feet are set well back on the body making them entirely unsuited to a terrestrial life. Even their nests are floating structures anchored to emerging aquatic vegetation. The feet are lobed, rather than fully webbed like divers and duck. Take-off is somewhat laboured with a long pattering over the water surface. Once airborne, however, they fly quite strongly and several species make lengthy migrations. All breed on freshwater lakes and pools, but several spend the winter at sea, though mostly close inshore. During the summer several develop elaborate and colourful plumes that are used in ritualized displays.

---

p.28 **Little Grebe** *Tachybaptus ruficollis*

Description: 25–29 cm (10–11 in). Smallest of the grebes, marked by short, *stubby bill and vertically 'sawn-off' rear end* which, combined with short neck, create a chunky, rather than elegant, appearance. In summer both sexes show rich-chestnut foreneck and sides to head. A pale-yellow area of bare skin marks base of lower mandible. In winter becomes buff-brown with dark cap. At all times overall shape is quite different to all other small grebes.

Voice: Far-carrying, whinnying trill; *whit, whit* of alarm.

Habitat: Predominantly fresh water; lakes, ponds, marshes, slow-moving rivers and canals with good growth of emergent vegetation. In winter occasionally on sea and estuarine waters, but mostly on lakes and reservoirs.

Breeding: Four to six white eggs laid in floating nest anchored to and hidden among aquatic vegetation. Like those of other grebes the eggs soon become stained. Incubation 25–29 days, by both sexes.

Range: Through most of Europe across Eurasia an
Southeast Asia; also throughout sub-
Saharan Africa. East European birds are
only summer visitors.

Like other members of its family, the Littl
Grebe often dives and reappears some
distance away. In late summer it may dive
in deep water, swim close to the bottom,
and attack the shoals of fry that frequent
the shallow margins where it surfaces. Thi
technique may be used over and over agai
to attack the same shoal.

p.28 **Great Crested Grebe** *Podiceps cristatus*

Description: 45–51 cm (18–20 in). Largest of the grebe
and marked in summer by elaborate and
colourful head-plumes that are erected in
display. Plumes are tipped chestnut on hir
crown and upper neck and contrast with
white of face and foreneck. Upperparts da
grey, flanks mottled and streaked chestnu
In winter, plumes are lost, the long slende
neck is white, and a *dark cap does not extend t
eye* which stands out as a result. At all
times, bill pink, slender and pointed. Red
necked Grebe has dusky foreneck and
yellow base to bill.

Voice: A variety of growls, cackles and barks.

Habitat: Breeds on good-sized fresh waters; lakes,
reservoirs and large marshland pools with
emergent or overhanging vegetation. In
winter frequents similar areas, but also
occurs on the sea, though seldom at any
great distance from land.

Breeding: Three to six white eggs laid on floating
platform anchored to vegetation. On
leaving nest, eggs are covered with
decaying aquatic plants that soon stain
them. Incubation 25–29 days, by both
sexes.

Range: Breeds right across Europe and southern
Asia as far as China, but also locally in
Africa and Australia. East European birds
move south and west in winter when their
breeding grounds become frozen over,
many to the Mediterranean.

The elaborate displays of the Great Crested Grebe, studied first by Julian Huxley, played a significant part in the development of ethology – the study of animal behaviour. The courting pair perform extraordinary movements that involve raising their crests, facing up virtually standing on the water to present each other with nest-building weeds, and much head dipping and false preening.

---

p.29 **Red-necked Grebe** *Podiceps grisegena*

Description: 40–46 cm (16–18 in). The only European grebe that could be confused with the slightly larger Great Crested. Shorter neck, heavier head, and shorter and thicker bill are the major structural differences. In summer the combination of chestnut-red foreneck, silvery-white cheeks and black cap makes identification straightforward; but in winter, when these features are lost or masked, the *dusky foreneck, cap extending below eye, and the yellow-based bill* are the features that most reliably separate it from Great Crested, though the silvery-grey cheeks remain prominent.

Voice: A variety of wailing and whinnying calls, plus a few harsh quacks during the breeding season; silent at other times.

Habitat: Freshwater lakes and pools, often quite small and invariably shallow, with strong growth of emergent vegetation. In winter haunts shallow bays and estuaries along protected coasts; also frequents large inland fresh waters such as lowland reservoirs, but generally frequents more marine environments than Great Crested.

Breeding: Four to five white eggs laid in floating nest well hidden among dense stands of reeds or other emergent vegetation. Often nests in association with colonies of Black-headed Gulls. Incubation 22–25 days, shared by both sexes.

Range: Breeds in northern and eastern Europe as far as Urals, in Pacific Russia and Japan, and across Alaska and Canada. Winter visitor westward across remaining Europe.

Red-necked Grebes show remarkable dietary adaptation. By feeding almost exclusively on aquatic invertebrates in summer they are able to exploit waters that fish-eating grebes cannot utilize. In winter they switch their diet to small fish found at sea, but are less efficient hunters than other grebes that occupy similar areas.

---

p.29 **Slavonian Grebe** *Podiceps auritus*

Description: 31–36 cm (12–14 in). Small-sized grebe, a little larger than Little Grebe and no more than slightly larger than Black-necked Grebe. Generally more streamlined than either of those species, with rear end sloping to water rather than being 'cut off' and square-ended. In summer, shows combination of dark upperparts, rufous-chestnut foreneck and golden horns. (The Black-necked Grebe has black foreneck and golden fan.) In winter, Slavonian has clear *white foreneck and head marked by clear-cut black cap.* Black-necked is always dusky and smudgy rather than pure white.

Voice: A rippling trill while breeding; otherwise generally silent.

Habitat: Frequents variety of shallow waters generally to the north of other species. Most overlap is with Red-necked Grebe, with which it shares need for emergent vegetation, although it can breed successfully where this is lacking. Winters at sea in bays and estuaries.

Breeding: Three to five white eggs laid on floating nest, usually hidden among dense growth of vegetation. Also in the open, anchored to the bottom in shallow water. Incubation 22–25 days, by both sexes.

Range: Circumpolar, from Iceland to Scotland and Scandinavia, across Siberia to Pacific and northern North America. Birds from easter Europe move south and west in winter.

Though the breeding ranges of the Slavonian and Black-necked grebes are virtually complementary and overlap only in southern Sweden, both species migrate to share common wintering grounds. At this time, however, they are largely separated by habitat preference: Black-necked is essentially a freshwater bird, while Slavonian prefers the sea.

p.29 **Black-necked Grebe** *Podiceps nigricollis*

Description: 28–33 cm (11–13 in). A small grebe, only a bit larger than Little Grebe. At all times, thin, uptilted bill is invaluable field mark. In summer, chestnut flanks contrast with black neck and head, the latter marked by golden fan behind the eye. When wet, this fan can resemble golden horn of Slavonian Grebe. In winter, dark cap extends to eye, but rises above eye level on ear coverts. *Foreneck smudgy grey. Lack of clear-cut black cap* contrasting with white face and foreneck in winter is major distinction from Slavonian Grebe.

Voice: Generally less vocal than other grebes. In summer a soft trill and various peeping notes.

Habitat: Shallow fresh waters with emergent vegetation. Highly erratic in establishing and abandoning colonies. In winter frequents large fresh waters rich in molluscs; only occasionally resorts to estuaries or the sea.

Breeding: Three to four white eggs laid on floating nest well concealed among reeds or sedges. Incubation 20–21 days, by both sexes. Usually colonial, with nests only 100 cm (3 ft) apart.

Range: Patchily distributed right across Europe from Spain to Scotland, and eastwards across temperate Europe to central Siberia. Also in Pacific Asia and through much of North America. Most birds move south and west in winter.

Frequent changes in the location of breeding colonies by this species is largely due to variations in water levels, particularly in the warmer parts of its range. Shifting rainfall patterns can quickly create or destroy suitable nesting conditions and the species is quick to take advantage of changes, such as the creation of new reservoirs.

ALBATROSSES (Diomedeidae)

13 species; mostly confined to southern oceans, though several range northwards and breed in the North Pacific. Only one species has genuinely occurred in the wild in Europe. Albatrosses are huge seabirds, with extremely long and narrow, stiffly he. wings. They have large heads and bills, bu short tails. Their aerial mastery allows the to wander the oceans, returning to land on to breed on a longer than annual cycle. Th feed mainly on squid that rise to the surfac at night, though many follow fishing vesse to obtain offal. They breed colonially on remote islands.

p.32 **Black-browed Albatross**
Diomedea melanophris

Description: 80–95 cm (31–37 in). With a wingspan o over 210 cm (7–8 ft), this huge seabird cannot be mistaken for any other Europea species, though the inexperienced should beware distant views of Great Black-back Gull. *Stiff-winged, shearwater-like flight,* combined with white head marked by prominent eyebrow, and entirely black ba and upperwings separate it from all other European birds. *Underwing broadly edged white.*

Voice: Various harsh croaks when fighting for fo around fishing vessels.

Habitat: Remote, mostly uninhabited islands; nest on or near cliffs to ease take-off problems. Otherwise ranges across cold, open oceans travelling huge distances in search of food

Breeding: One white egg laid on large, neatly constructed mound of earth. Incubated by both sexes in shifts that last for a week or more without food.

Range: Oceans of the southern hemisphere, particularly around the Antarctic continent, but ranging northwards to rich feeding grounds off New Zealand and South Africa. Single long-stay individuals summered on Faeroes 1860–1894, and Ba Rock and Shetland from 1967 to at least

1994. Otherwise very rare vagrant to North Atlantic, mainly British, coasts.

This is the only albatross to have occurred in Europe under its own power. Though there are records of other albatross species, most are usually regarded as having been assisted by being captured by seamen and subsequently released. The occurrences of Yellow-nosed Albatross off the Atlantic coasts of North America show that this species is potentially a European bird.

SHEARWATERS AND PETRELS
(PROCELLARIIDAE)

66 species; worldwide, though with a distinct southern hemisphere bias. Six species breed in Europe and two more are visitors in variable numbers. These are medium-sized seabirds that fly low over the open oceans and come to land only to breed on remote, uninhabited islands or headlands. They are characterized by long, stiff wings that are held straight as they obtain lift from air rising over the waves. They have webbed feet, hooked bills and tube noses. They feed on fish, squid and will follow fishing boats in search of offal. Their conservation depends on suitable rat-free and cat-free islands on which to breed.

NOTE: the systematics of this group have been and continue to be the subject of argument and heated debate among ornithologists.

p.32 **Fulmar** *Fulmarus glacialis*

Description: 44–50 cm (17–20 in). A grey, gull-like petrel, distinctly *thick set, strongly built and bull-necked*. Upperparts and upperwings pale grey and thus more like a gull than any other petrel; underparts white. Grey rump and tail, together with stiff-winged flight, easily distinguish it from any gull. Northern birds are darker above and below and often called 'Blue Fulmar'.

Voice: Growls and chuckles uttered on breeding grounds; at sea a variety of grunts and cackles, especially when disputing food around fishing boats.

Habitat: Breeds on sea cliffs, usually among crumbling tops, but also in stone walls and derelict buildings, sometimes some distance inland. Rest of year spent at sea roaming the oceans.

Breeding: One white egg laid on bare ledge or depression in turf. Incubation 55–57 days, by both sexes.

Range: Breeds throughout North Atlantic and North Pacific. In Europe, distributed around Iceland and Britain and Ireland with localized colonies in Norway and France. Winters at sea, but scarce southwards of breeding areas.

A population explosion over the past 200 years has made the Fulmar a far more familiar bird in northern Europe. Once confined to two major breeding sites, in Scotland and Iceland, it has doubtless benefited from deep-sea trawling and its associated waste.

p.33 Manx Shearwater *Puffinus puffinus*

Description: 30–38 cm (12–15 in). Medium-sized, typical shearwater, black above and white below. Black on crown extends to below eye (*see* Little Shearwater). Careers over water in long glides broken by bouts of *flapping of stiffly held wings showing alternately black and white*.

Voice: Loud wailing, cackling and groaning at breeding sites creates a wild and eerie atmosphere. Generally silent at sea.

Habitat: Breeds on islands and remote headlands and on rocky mountain tops. Otherwise found totally at sea ranging well out of sight of land.

Breeding: One white egg laid in specially excavated burrow, old rabbit hole, or crevice among rocks. Incubation 47–55 days, by both sexes.

Range: By far the most common shearwater around northern and western coasts of Europe.

Replaced in Mediterranean by recently separated Balearic and Levantine Shearwaters. European birds breed mainly around coasts of Britain and Ireland, with isolated colonies in France and Iceland. Outside the breeding season ranges westwards across North Atlantic and northwards to Norway.

Manx Shearwaters can often be seen resting in rafts on the sea near their breeding colonies, awaiting cover of darkness before coming ashore. This tactic avoids the threat of predation posed by Great Black-backed Gulls, though it is far from successful as witness the number of shearwater skins turned inside out wherever the two species share a breeding ground.

p.32 Levantine Shearwater *Puffinus yelkouan*

Description: 30–38 cm (12–15 in). Very similar to Manx Shearwater, with dark upperparts and pale underparts clearly separated by a sharp line obvious on head and rear flanks. *Upperparts always dark brown,* rather than solid black of same-sized Manx. Dirty-grey undertail coverts, flanks and underwing are other features to watch for. Distinguished from closely related Balearic Shearwater by *clear-cut dark and light pattern.*

Voice: Silent at sea. Series of wailing and cackling calls at breeding sites.

Habitat: Nests in burrows and rock crevices on isolated islands; otherwise found only at sea.

Breeding: One white egg. Incubation 47–55 days by both sexes. The chick is similarly tended by both parents.

Range: Confined to Greek Aegean islands and Crete, though it ranges as far as Black Sea, Cyprus, and coasts of Israel in winter.

The extraordinary, large-scale and easily visible, daily movements of these birds through the narrow straits of the Bosphorus, between the Aegean and Black Seas, have led to speculation on the existence of as yet undiscovered colonies in the latter. Alternatively, they may be no

more than Aegean birds flying in and out of
the Black Sea to feed.

---

p.32   **Balearic Shearwater** *Puffinus mauretanicus*

Description: 33–40 cm (13–16 in). Recently separated
from Manx and Levantine Shearwaters and
the most distinctive of the three. Similar in
structure to those species, though slightly
larger and longer winged. Upperparts
distinctly brown, merging with buffy-brown
underparts fading to cream on the belly. The
*lack of a sharp demarcation between dark
upperparts and pale underparts* distinguishes it
from both Manx and Levantine Shearwaters.
Flight attitude similar, careering over waves
on stiffly flapped wings interspersed with
shearwatering glides.

Voice: Silent at sea, but series of wailing and
cackling calls at breeding colonies.

Habitat: Nests in burrows on islands, but at all other
times found only at sea. Large numbers pass
through the narrows at the Strait of
Gibraltar.

Breeding: One white egg laid in burrow or crevice
among rocks from mid-March onwards.
Incubation, 47–55 days, and care of young
shared by both sexes.

Range: Breeds in western half of Mediterranean from
Balearics to Corsica, Sardinia and Sicily; also
off coasts of North Africa and in the
Adriatic. Outside breeding season roams
western Mediterranean and eastern Atlantic.

Balearic Shearwaters are relatively common
offshore in the eastern North Atlantic and
regularly reach as far north as the English
Channel having passed through the Strait
of Gibraltar. Some individuals are as large
as a small Sooty Shearwater and they should
therefore be identified with care.

---

p.32   **Sooty Shearwater** *Puffinus griseus*

Description: 39–44 cm (15–17 in). An all-dark, brown-
black shearwater, marked only by *pale centres
to underwing*. Slimmer and more narrow-

winged than any other shearwater, with
wings generally held more angled (swept
back) and set well back on body to create a
'weight-forward' impression. Flaps more
frequently than other shearwaters.

Voice: Silent at sea; on breeding grounds makes
various choking and guttural calls.

Habitat: Breeds on islands where burrows can be
excavated in earth. At other times
essentially pelagic, mainly concentrated at
cold waters with good feeding.

Breeding: One white egg laid at end of long burrow
excavated by the birds themselves.
Incubation period and role of sexes unknown.

Range: Breeds only in southern hemisphere on
remote islands off coasts of South America,
New Zealand and Australia, but is a
widespread winter visitor to both North
Atlantic and North Pacific. In Europe it is
an autumn, mainly August to September,
visitor to Atlantic and North Sea coasts.

The huge loop migrations of Sooty
Shearwaters bring them northwards to the
Atlantic coasts of North America in the
summer. Many, but not all, then move
eastwards to European coasts in early
autumn before heading southwards once
more along the western coasts of Africa.

p.33 **Great Shearwater** *Puffinus gravis*

Description: 42–49 cm (16½–19 in). A large shearwater
that alternates long glides with brief spells
of wing flapping on long, stiffly held
wings. Similar in size to Cory's Shearwater,
but distinguished by being darker above
and whiter below. Shows distinctive *dark
cap separated from back by white collar;* a clear-
cut white 'horseshoe' at base of tail, and
dark smudge at centre of belly.

Voice: Utters various croaking calls in colonies at
night. Silent at sea.

Habitat: Breeds colonially on remote islands where
earth can be excavated for burrows. Spends
other times at sea roaming oceans.

Breeding: One white egg laid in burrow usually
excavated on a grassy slope. Incubation

period and roles of sexes is unknown. Highly colonial.

Range: Breeds only on Gough Island and Tristan da Cunha group in central South Atlantic. In the southern winter moves northwards through western Atlantic to coasts of North America, thence eastwards to coasts of Europe in late summer and autumn. Mostly seen off coasts of Ireland and southwest England, in Biscay and coasts of Portugal.

Breeding birds return to their colonies in the South Atlantic by September, so those that frequent European waters in August and September must be presumed to be immature or non-breeding birds, though these too move southwards soon after.

p.33 **Cory's Shearwater** *Calonectris diomedea*

Description: 43–48 cm (17–19 in). Large, chunky shearwater similar to Great Shearwater, but with bulkier body, broader wings and heavier flight involving slower, but more frequent, wingbeats. Upperparts brown; underparts dull whitish with distinctly pale, greyish head. *Pale crown and prominent eye* distinguish it from Great Shearwater, even at considerable distances. Closer approach shows uniformly pale underwing with black margins, unlike complex dark margins to underwing coverts of Great Shearwater.

Voice: Wide variety of harsh, rasping, screaming and wailing calls that produce a cacophony of sound at breeding colonies. Silent at sea.

Habitat: Breeds on remote islands and coasts among rocks or bushes, as well as in specially excavated burrows which may be shared. Otherwise pelagic. Will gather around fishing boats. Highly colonial.

Breeding: One white egg. Incubation about 60 days, by both sexes.

Range: Confined to Mediterranean and islands of eastern Atlantic from Portugal to Azores, though not Cape Verde Islands which are home to the similar, recently separated Cape Verde Shearwater *Calonectris edwardsii*. In

winter wanders westwards across Atlantic to
North America, and southwards to Cape of
Good Hope.

Cory's Shearwater colonies have been
systematically plundered by local people for
centuries and some doubtless still suffer in
this way. Young birds are taken for their
oil, down and as food, and more recently
fishermen have plundered adults and eggs.

---

p.33 **Little Shearwater** *Puffinus assimilis*

Description: 25–30 cm (10–12 in). Small version of
Manx Shearwater showing similar pattern
of black upperparts and white underparts.
Main plumage difference is that *black of
crown does not extend to eye* which, as a
result, is left as black spot on white 'face'.
More significant differences result from
different structure: wings are
proportionately shorter, with rounded tips,
and are flapped more frequently creating a
Common Sandpiper-like impression –
much *more fluttering* than Manx. Subspecies
P. a. baroli of Azores, Madeira and Canaries
has white undertail coverts; *P. a. boydi* of
Cape Verde Islands has dark undertail
coverts.

Voice: Laughing, with emphasis on second syllable
and ending in a *hoo*. Silent at sea.

Habitat: Breeds on uninhabited islands in turf-
covered areas near coast. Winters at sea,
usually not moving far from breeding
colonies.

Breeding: One white egg laid in hole in the ground or
rock crevice. Incubation 52–58 days, by
both sexes.

Range: In Europe breeds only on Atlantic islands;
seldom seen further north than the waters
of Portugal. Otherwise found in southern
hemisphere, with colonies in South
Atlantic and South Pacific as far away as
New Zealand.

Less than 100 records of Little Shearwater
have been accepted for Britain and Ireland,
the majority in late summer in August and

September. Most have been seen in the
southwestern approaches, often in company
with Manx Shearwaters, by dedicated sea-
watchers peering for many hours from
prominent, favoured headlands.

STORM-PETRELS (HYDROBATIDAE)

20 species; worldwide. Two species breed in
Europe and another is a scarce autumn
visitor to the extreme southwest. Storm-
petrels are mostly small black-and-white
swallow-like birds that flutter and glide
over the sea, picking small food items from
the surface, often with their legs dangling
or pattering over the surface. They come to
land only to breed on some of the most
remote islands of the world. Though locally
abundant, they usually give only the
briefest of views and are notoriously
difficult to identify.

p.34   **Leach's Storm-petrel** *Oceanodroma leucorhoa*

Description: 19–22 cm (7½–9 in). Typical black storm-
petrel marked by white rump. Differs from
other species in having white rump divided
by black line, a distinctly *forked tail, and
obvious pale upperwing coverts*. Most obviously
differs in having long wings held more
shearwater-like than in other storm-petrels,
with more prolonged gliding and bounding
and less fluttering flight.

Voice: On breeding grounds produces a deep,
prolonged purring and a distinct
chuckling. Silent at sea.

Habitat: Breeds on the most remote, generally
uninhabited, islands among rocky slopes.
Otherwise totally pelagic, keeping well out
of sight of land.

Breeding: One white egg, speckled reddish at the
more rounded end, laid in rock crevice or
hollow. Incubation 41–42 days, by both
sexes.

Range: In Europe confined to a few colonies off
north and west coasts of Scotland, to single

islands off Iceland and Norway, and probably to several islands off southwestern Ireland. Elsewhere found off eastern and western Canada and islands of Aleutian chain. In winter ranges across Atlantic southwards to Brazil and South Africa.

Leach's Storm-petrel never follows ships in the manner of the European Storm-petrel and, to all intents and purposes, ignores their passage. It is seen from the shoreline only after severe autumn storms, but may occasionally be 'wrecked' inland, sometimes in numbers.

---

p.34 **European Storm-petrel**
Hydrobates pelagicus

Description: 14–16 cm (5–6 in). Most common of the storm-petrels of Europe and the one that most regularly follows ships. Small black seabird marked by *square white rump and square-tipped tail*. Upperwing uniformly black; underwing marked by bold white bar across coverts. Feet do not extend beyond tail, but are often dangled as the bird picks food from water's surface. Flight generally more fluttering than Leach's Storm-petrel.

Voice: On breeding grounds utters a purring sound terminating in distinct hiccup. Silent at sea.

Habitat: Breeds on isolated, rat-free, uninhabited islands with turf and rocks. Spends rest of life at sea, usually out of sight of land.

Breeding: One rounded white egg, frequently spotted brown at larger end, laid in burrow or rock crevice. Incubation 38–40 days, by both sexes.

Range: Endemic European breeding bird with largest colonies around coasts of Britain and Ireland, but also in western Mediterranean, where it is the only storm-petrel. In winter ranges southwards off coasts of North and South Atlantic oceans as far as Cape of Good Hope.

This bird feeds mainly on crustaceans and squid picked from the surface of the sea without alighting, and it is therefore in the habit of following ships to find such food disturbed or killed by revolving propellers. In the breeding season it feeds mainly on small sprats that are often abundant in late summer off rocky western shores.

p.34 **Wilson's Storm-petrel** *Oceanites oceanicus*

Description: 17–18 cm (6½–7in). Very similar to European Storm-petrel in being black with *white rump and square-cut tail*. But feet extend beyond tail, and *pale upperwing coverts* have distinct pattern, the latter similar to, but not as marked, as Leach's Storm-petrel. Lacks pale underwing line of European Storm-petrel. Frequently patters over water with feet dangling to surface. Close examination reveals yellow webs to feet. Generally less fluttering and more gliding flight than other species.

Voice: Chattering calls at breeding sites and at sea. Usually silent in winter.

Habitat: Remote, rocky islands during breeding season. Winters at sea; ranging the oceans where flocks may gather in enormous numbers at favoured feeding grounds.

Breeding: One white egg laid in burrow or rock crevice. Incubation for 39–48 days, by both sexes.

Range: Breeds on Antarctic and sub-Antarctic islands around South Pole. Ranges northwards across South Pacific and Indian Oceans and Antarctic seas. Performs loop migration through Atlantic that extends northwards as far as Newfoundland in the west and western approaches to English Channel in the east.

Though less than twenty records of Wilson's Storm-petrel are accepted for Britain and Ireland, there are many that are never seen from land. Pelagic trips to the area between Wexford, Lands End and to the south-west regularly record this species, albeit in small numbers. As a result this area has become known as The Wilson's Triangle.

GANNETS AND BOOBIES (SULIDAE)

Nine species; virtually worldwide. One species breeds in Europe, and there are claims that another may have occurred as an exceptional vagrant. These are large seabirds with long necks, long pointed bills, long pointed tails and long pointed wings, giving them a quite distinctive shape. They feed by diving from the air, and fly on stiff wings in a flap-glide manner similar to that of shearwaters. Though they are exclusively seabirds, they seldom venture far beyond the continental shelf.

p.35 **Gannet** *Morus bassanus*

Description: 86–96 cm (34–38 in). A large, white seabird marked by extensive black wingtips and unique *cigar-like shape,* tapering fore and aft. Long neck and long, sharply pointed tail. Long wings also distinctly pointed. *Flies on stiff wings,* low over waves, rising on series of flaps before gliding once more. Passes through series of plumages: brown juvenile becomes progressively whiter with each moult. Shape, flight and behaviour distinguishes it from all other European seabirds.

Voice: Variety of grunts and cackles at breeding grounds; a hoarse *urrah* when disputing food.

Habitat: Breeds on cliffs, stacks and remote offshore islands. At other times at sea, though usually over shallower waters of continental shelf rather than truly pelagic.

Breeding: One white egg laid in shallow cup of seaweed. Incubation for 43–45 days, by both sexes. Gannets are highly colonial and construct their nests evenly spread, just out of pecking distance of their neighbours. Some colonies are huge, containing tens of thousands of pairs.

Range: Breeds on both eastern and western coasts of North Atlantic. In Europe most colonies are around Iceland, Britain and Ireland, with a few in northern France and along

Norwegian coast. In winter young birds move south along coasts of West Africa.

Gannets frequently gather in enormous numbers to feed around trawlers and over large shoals of surface-swimming fish. Their diving – headfirst from considerable heights – creates an outstanding wildlife spectacle.

CORMORANTS (PHALACROCORACIDAE)

32 species; worldwide. Three species breed in Europe. Cormorants are medium to large waterbirds that are mainly black in colour. They have long necks, long tails and large, fully webbed feet. In flight the long neck is extended, giving a somewhat goose-like impression. They swim and dive, from the surface with great expertise, often showing only head and neck above the water's surface. Characteristically they spend long periods perched with wings spread to dry in the sun or wind. Though they are found on both salt and fresh waters, most species specialize on one or the other. They breed colonially on cliffs or among trees. The sexes are similar.

p.38 **Cormorant** *Phalacrocorax carbo*

Description: 84–89 cm (33–38 in). Large, black waterbird marked by *long thick neck and long heavy bill*. In breeding season adult has golden glossy sheen on mantle and bold white patches on face and thigh. In winter only a smudgy face-patch remains. Juveniles browner with pale, even white, belly. Southern European birds have variable amount of white streaking on crown and nape. Often flies in 'V' formation like geese. In all plumages, larger, thicker necked and heavier billed than Shag.

Voice: Growls, croaks and grunts during breeding season; usually silent at other times.

Habitat: At sea, but never far from shoreline; also haunts estuaries, large inland lakes, and marshes with large areas of open water.

Breeding: Three to four pale-blue eggs laid in substantial nest. Inland breeders site nest in a tree, constructing it with sticks and lining it with grass and leaves. Coastal nesters use any flotsam and seaweed to form rotting, smelly nest at the foot of cliffs. Incubation 28–29 days, by both sexes.

Range: Widespread throughout Old World from Europe to Japan, southwards through Asia to Australasia, and in Africa. In New World breeds only in northeastern Canada. Widely scattered breeder throughout Europe, though only a winter visitor to southwest.

A great fisherman that can often be seen swimming through the water's surface, with head submerged like a snorkeller. They dive from the surface and use their huge webbed feet to propel themselves with speed and agility in pursuit of fish. These are invariably brought to the surface and swallowed whole. Most prey consists of bottom-dwelling fish, only 10 per cent of which is marketable. Daily intake varies from 400–700 g (14–25 oz).

---

p.39 **Shag** *Phalacrocorax aristotelis*

Description: 72–80 cm (28–31½ in). Smaller and slimmer than closely related Cormorant, though size notoriously difficult to judge, especially at sea. Shag's *thin neck, smaller head and distinctively thinner bill* are main differences, though Shag never shows white in any plumage. Adult black with greenish gloss and small crest in summer. Juvenile brown, darker above and paler below, but never white below like juvenile Cormorant. Swims, dives, snorkels and hangs out wings to dry like Cormorant.

Voice: Various grunts and hisses at breeding grounds; silent at sea.

Habitat: Essentially marine, so an inland 'shagorant' is most likely a Cormorant. Frequents rocky coasts and breeds among tumbled boulders and screes among cliffs.

Breeding: One to six, mostly three, pale-blue eggs laid in a substantial nest of seaweed situated in rock crevice. Incubation 30–31 days, by both sexes. Mostly colonial.

Range: More or less confined to Europe from Iceland to Scandinavia, and from Morocco to Crimea. Winters near breeding sites.

This is an excellent diver that can stay submerged for up to three or four minutes at a time. It preys mainly on mid-water fish and especially sand-eels, but also takes small cod, whiting and saithe. Its reputation as a competitor of commercial fisheries seems unjustified as in most areas sand-eels form over half its food by volume.

---

p.39 **Pygmy Cormorant** *Phalacrocorax pygmeus*

Description: 45–55 cm (18–21½ in). Smallest of cormorants, and marked by very *long tail, thin neck, large head and tiny bill*. The combination of these features creates highly distinctive and unmistakable silhouette. Highly gregarious and marsh dwelling. Summer adult has black body, wings and tail, with head and neck washed dark warm brown. In winter, throat and foreneck dull white and, in juvenile, white extends to underparts. Swims and dives easily and perches openly in trees.

Voice: Croaking and barking calls while breeding; otherwise silent.

Habitat: Extensive reed-marshes with trees and scrub Frequently nests colonially alongside herons

Breeding: Four to six white, washed green, eggs laid in well-constructed cup-shaped nest among reeds or a low tree. Incubation 27–30 days, by both sexes, starting with the first egg. Care of young is shared.

Range: Breeds in major marshes of southeastern Europe in Romania, Greece and former Yugoslavia. Also eastwards to Iraq and southern Siberia. Winters near breeding grounds.

Though it is locally abundant there has been a serious decline in the Pygmy Cormorant's numbers, mainly due to the drainage of large marshes for agricultural use. The growing demand for water for irrigation and tourist developments may create more lowland wetlands where this dainty cormorant can re-establish itself.

PELICANS (Pelecanidae)

Eight species; virtually worldwide. Two species breed in Europe. Pelicans are large waterbirds that fly on huge, square-shaped wings. They soar like vultures, but also glide over water like gannets. All are marked by a large bill with an equally large and capacious pouch. They swim buoyantly and have huge, fully webbed feet that are well used when lifting off. European species feed by upending themselves, like duck, but do so in small groups. A group of opened underwater pouches creates an avian trawl that panics shoals of fish into their bills. One foreign pelican plunge-dives for food like gannets. Nesting is colonial either among marshy vegetation, on islands, or in trees.

p.40 **Dalmatian Pelican** *Pelecanus crispus*

Description: 160–180 cm (63–71 in). Very similar to, but slightly larger than, White Pelican, with similar structure including large orange bill-pouch. Differs in having black legs and, in flight, *dark-greyish, not black, primaries,* lacking contrast with greyish, not white, wing coverts. Underwing of Dalmatian can appear virtually uniform; that of White Pelican always shows contrast. Adult shows ragged crest. Juvenile grey, not brown.

Voice: A variety of grunting, hissing and spitting calls during breeding season.

Habitat: Though frequently found alongside White Pelican on extensive lowland marshes, also

uses smaller waters at high altitudes not
frequented by its close relative.

Breeding: Two to five white eggs laid in bulky
structure of sticks and other vegetation on
the ground. Incubation 30–32 days, mainl
by female.

Range: More widespread in smaller colonies than
White Pelican, from Albania and Greece t
Romania, eastwards through Persian Gulf
to south-central Siberia. Winters in Greec
and Turkey.

A rapid decline in numbers, particularly i
Romania where it was formerly abundant,
can be ascribed to disturbance, direct
persecution and marshland drainage. A
similar story can be told for the great Volg
Delta on the Black Sea where a population
crash has just been halted in time by rigid
protection measures.

p.41 **White Pelican** *Pelecanus onocrotalus*

Description: 140–180 cm (55–70 in). Huge, white
waterbird that can be confused only with
closely related Dalmatian Pelican. At rest
whole plumage appears white, marked by
yellow patch on breast in summer and by
deep orange-yellow pouch. Legs reddish
pink. In the air, *flight feathers black
contrasting clearly with white coverts.* Juvenil
brown above with pale-yellowish legs.
Dalmatian Pelican differs in having less
clear-cut contrast between greyish flight
feathers that fade to whitish coverts, and i
having black legs.

Voice: Grunts, growls and mooing calls when
breeding; a low croak is uttered in flight.

Habitat: Large marshes with large areas of open
water, large lakes and deltas; coastal lagoo
and sandbanks.

Breeding: Two to three white eggs laid in scrape on
the ground, with little or no lining, often
on low-lying island screened by substanti
reed beds. Incubation 29–30 days, by bot
sexes. Breeds in very large colonies.

Range: Breeds in southeastern Europe only in
Greece and Romania. Also eastwards

through Turkey to south-central Siberia; elsewhere in Africa, India and Vietnam. European birds are mainly summer visitors.

The decline of the White Pelican throughout its European range can be blamed on persecution and disturbance, but perhaps equally on the lack of large secluded breeding grounds rich enough in fish to support 2,000-plus birds and their young. Throughout the nesting and rearing cycle, each individual consumes about 1 kg (2 lb) of fish per day.

HERONS AND EGRETS (Ardeidae)

61 species; worldwide. Nine species breed in Europe, some of which are resident, some summer visitors. These are medium to large waterbirds, marked by slim bodies and long necks and legs. Their bills are relatively long and mostly pointed, and the toes are long and unwebbed. In flight the neck is tucked back between the shoulders – unlike storks and ibises – which creates a characteristic shape as their long legs trail behind. Even at rest, or while hunting, the neck is folded back, suddenly to snap out to its full length as the bird grabs its prey. Most species are expert fishermen, but some specialize on other aquatic life forms. Nesting is often colonial, either in trees or in extensive reed beds, depending on species preference.

p.49 **Purple Heron** *Ardea purpurea*

Description: 75–85 cm (29–33 in). Only slightly smaller than Grey Heron, but in the field appears distinctly smaller. Grey wings with black flight feathers are common to both species, but Purple Heron has brown plumes on back and *brown neck marked by black lines* front and rear. Bill yellow; legs olive-green. In flight, underwing distinctly dark with maroon coverts. In all plumages, 'warmth' of colour quite distinct from 'cold' greys of its larger cousin. Juveniles virtually brown and black.

Voice: A harsh *snark*, like Grey Heron, but a little higher pitched and less far carrying. Guttural croaks at breeding colonies.

Habitat: Marshes with extensive reed-beds; riverside swamps and backwaters; deltas.

Breeding: Four to five greenish-blue eggs laid in nest of reeds hidden deep inside a reed bed. Incubation 24–28 days, by both sexes. Usually solitary breeders, but other herons and cormorants may nest nearby.

Range: Found widely throughout Eurasia and sub-Saharan Africa as far as Java, Celebes and Cape Town. European birds are summer visitors as far north as Holland.

Everywhere the Purple Heron is less numerous than the Grey and more confined to extensive wetlands. The propensity to drain reed beds over the past two centuries has doubtless destroyed much suitable habitat and reduced the Purple Heron's numbers as a result. On migration it often flies along coasts in sizeable flocks.

---

p.48 **Grey Heron** *Ardea cinerea*

Description: 90–100 cm (35–39 in). Largest European heron, marked by *large grey wings* with black flight feathers. At rest mainly grey above, with distinctive white crown bordered by extended black plumes. *White foreneck* with narrow black stripes extends t breast. Long neck; long grey-green legs that trail in flight; yellow bill. Deeply bowed wings and slow, even ponderous wingbeats emphasize size. Stalks in water to catch fish.

Voice: Distinctive, loud *snark*; at breeding colonie produces a variety of croaking and gruntin, calls.

Habitat: Virtually all types of wetland, from muddy estuaries and rocky coasts to tiny streams, river backwaters and marshes, floods and damp meadows.

Breeding: Three to five pale greenish-blue eggs laid in solidly constructed, tree-top nest of sticks and twigs. Also nests among reeds or on cliff ledge. Incubation 23–28 days, by both sexes. Highly colonial birds. Many heronries are a century or more old.

Range: Throughout Old World from Britain to Japan southwards to Java; also throughout sub-Saharan Africa. In Europe breeds beyond Arctic Circle in coastal Norway. Eastern European birds are summer visitors; western birds resident.

The Grey Heron was one of the first bird populations to be accurately censused. Since 1928 the number of nests in England and Wales has fluctuated between 2,000 and 5,000, largely depending on the severity of the previous winter. The relatively quick recovery in numbers to a norm after a hard winter shows that there is a limit to the number of herons that can be sustained.

p.47 **Great White Egret** *Egretta alba*

Description: 85–100 cm (33½–39 in). Large, white heron, similar to Little Egret, but much larger, with heavier, longer and more robust bill. In summer, all-white plumage decorated with elaborate plumes that cascade from lower back. In all plumages, long *neck is held in remarkable kinked fashion*, with sharp, distinct angles. Legs and feet black, often yellowish on tibia; *bill yellow*, with darkened tip in summer. Almost the size of a Grey Heron, the wingbeats are similarly ponderous, quite unlike Little Egret.

Voice: Croaks and crow-like *caws* when breeding; otherwise silent.

Habitat: Extensive marshes with mixture of reed-beds and open water; lakes, lagoons, riverside margins and backwaters.

Breeding: Three to four pale blue eggs laid in nest of dead reeds raised as a platform on debris of extensive reed-bed. Incubation 25–26 days, by both sexes. Nests solitarily, or in loose colonies with nests some distance apart.

Range: Cosmopolitan, breeding on all large
landmasses on every continent. In Europe
confined to Balkans and to Hungarian
plain. Winters in Greece and Turkey.

Once persecuted for its nuptial plumes,
the Great White Egret made a significant
recovery during the more enlightened
latter part of the twentieth century. Its
numbers increased and it has recently
spread northwards to Holland, where it
retains a precarious toe-hold. Continued
drainage of its reed-bed homes – rather
than direct persecution – is a new danger.

p.46   **Little Egret** *Egretta garzetta*

Description: 53–58 cm (21–23 in). A medium-sized,
tall, thin, elegant egret with all-white
plumage marked by beautiful, long, nuptial
plumes in summer. In all plumages, long,
dagger-like *bill black, a*nd *legs black marked
by contrasting yellow feet.* In flight, feet are
held claw-like upwards and trail well
beyond tail. Can be confused only with
Great White Egret, but Great White is
almost as large as Grey Heron and has
yellow bill and black feet.

Voice: A variety of growls and croaks at breeding
colonies.

Habitat: Occupies wide range of wetland habitats,
often more open, less well vegetated than
that of other herons. From estuaries and
salt-pans to lagoons, marshes, rivers and
pools. Quickly occupies flooded
agricultural land and rice-fields.

Breeding: Four pale, greenish-blue eggs laid in twig-
based nest, usually in a tree but sometimes
in low bush or even reeds. Incubation
21–25 days, by both sexes. Essentially
colonial, usually in association with other
tree-nesting herons.

Range: Breeds widely throughout Old World from
Iberia to Japan and from South Africa to
Australia. Widespread through Europe
extending northwards to western France.
Mostly summer visitor, though winters in

southern Iberia, with vast majority crossing Sahara to western Africa.

The increasing occurrence of this bird in southern England, where flocks up to 30 or 40 strong have been observed throughout the year, culminated in the first breeding in Poole Harbour, Dorset in 1996.

p.46 **Cattle Egret** *Bubulcus ibis*

Description: 48–53 cm (19–21 in). Small, white heron marked by stubby yellow bill and medium-length back legs. In summer plumage it is decorated with orange plumes on crown, back and breast, and legs are green. In all plumages, throat reaches forward on lower mandible to create *distinctly 'jowled' look*. Hunts on dry land, as well as marshes, frequented by domestic stock; invariably gregarious. Often stands upright with neck extended. Flights to favoured tree roosts in sizable groups at dusk.

Voice: Various croaking calls, but only at breeding sites.

Habitat: Marshes and floods, fields and meadows, and even dry open plains where domestic or wild mammals gather.

Breeding: Four to five blue-washed white eggs laid in neatly constructed nest of twigs situated in a tree, usually alongside water or on an island. Will also nest among low, marshland vegetation. Colonial, forming dense single-species colonies with tens of nests in a single tree. Incubation 21–25 days, by both sexes.

Range: A temperate and tropical Old World species from Spain to China and from South Africa to Australasia. Colonized Americas during twentieth century where it has since expanded range and prospered. In Europe restricted to Iberia and southern France. Immatures may migrate to Africa; adults disperse locally.

Though named for their association with domestic cattle, these successful little

herons are equally at home among the herd
of big game animals of Africa. They also
associate with pigs, sheep and even tractors
where they follow the plough.

---

p.45   **Squacco Heron** *Ardeola ralloides*

Description: 43–48 cm (17–19 in). A small, mainly
buff-brown heron; easily overlooked
among marshside vegetation but bursts
into visibility with flash of *brilliant-white
wings* when it takes to the air. Adult a
warm orange-buff above and below, with
fuzz of black and white plumes on crown
and nape in summer. Bill long, pointed,
blue with black tip; legs dull pink. In
winter and juvenile plumages, upperparts
dull brown; crown, neck and breast heavily
streaked; legs yellow-green. In all
plumages, white wings form obvious
contrast with body in flight.

Voice: Occasional harsh *karr*, but generally silent.

Habitat: Well-vegetated marshes, lake and marsh
edges, backwaters, rice-fields, and other
wetlands. Generally among low, emergent
vegetation rather than tall stands of reeds o
thickets. Occasionally on open marshes
where it is easily seen.

Breeding: Three to five greenish-blue eggs laid in
twiggy, cup-shaped nest in tree, bush, or
among marshland vegetation. Often nests
colonially with species such as Glossy Ibis,
Pygmy Cormorant, or other herons. Where
these species begin to nest earlier, Squaccos
will use a nearby tree rather than face direc
competition.

Range: Summer visitor to southern Europe from
Spain to Turkey and Caspian region. More
common and widespread in east than west.
Also breeds across sub-Saharan Africa,
where European birds winter.

Squacco Herons are mainly insectivorous,
though they will take amphibians and fish
where available. In several parts of their
European range they make much use of
rice-fields; their nearest relatives are the
pond herons, or paddybirds, of Asia, where

insects and their larvae are virtually the only food available.

p.45 Black-crowned Night Heron
Nycticorax nycticorax

Description: 58–65 cm (23–25½ in). Generally a rather secretive bird, roosting unobtrusively in well-vegetated trees by day, feeding along waterside margins at night. Adult chunky, rather thickset, with black cap and back that contrast with grey wings and white underparts, particularly in flight. Neck is always hunched between shoulders, and in the air it has a *distinctive cartoon-cigar-like shape*. Juveniles heavily streaked cream on dark brown, and could be mistaken for Bittern. Generally gregarious when roosting, flighting and feeding.

Voice: A harsh *kwok*, generally uttered in flight.

Habitat: Waterside thickets, trees, reeds and tangles, with suitable perches over open water to feed. Favours more extensive wetlands than some other herons.

Breeding: Three to four pale-blue eggs laid in neatly constructed cup in waterside tree or bush, usually in association with others, often alongside other heron species. Incubation 21 days, by both sexes.

Range: Breeds throughout the world, except Australasia. Summer visitor to most of southern Europe extending northwards to Holland in west. Winters in Africa across the sub-Saharan Sahel zone, extending southwards through East Africa to Cape Province of South Africa.

Night Herons feeds mostly at night (or among darkened backwaters during the day). They regularly flight between their roosting or nesting sites and favoured feeding grounds each dawn and dusk. Only during such fly-overs can their numbers be estimated. At other times they can prove remarkably elusive even where they are relatively common. When hunting, the long neck is snapped forward to expose its extraordinary length.

p.44 **Little Bittern** *Ixobrychus minutus*

Description: 33–38 cm (13–15 in). Smallest of the
European herons. Both sexes marked by dar
wings showing bold, pale-pink or pinkish-
buff patch on inner wing. Male has black ca
and back, and wings broken by *pale-pink
upperwing coverts*. Underparts buffy and
lightly streaked. Females and immatures
dark rather than black above, with less
prominent, pale wing-patch and heavily
streaked breast. Bill long, pointed and pale
based; legs medium length, strong and pale
green. Frequently flies short distances over
reed tops and alights perched near the top o
a reed or bush. Generally rather shy.

Voice: A low croaking *hoof* repeated at two-second
intervals both by day and night; a *gak* of
alarm, often in flight.

Habitat: Dense aquatic vegetation, with reeds and
bushes mingled to form impenetrable
thickets, on pond, lake and riverside
margins.

Breeding: Five to six white eggs laid in neatly
constructed cup of aquatic and other
vegetation placed among reed debris or in
thick bush. Incubation 16–19 days, by
both sexes.

Range: Widespread throughout Old World from
Spain to India, Africa and Australia.
European birds are summer visitors to mos
of the continent, wintering in sub-Saharan
Africa.

In suitable areas Little Bitterns can be quit
numerous and easily seen, especially durin
early spring when territories are being
established. After years of suspected
breeding in Britain, a pair finally nested at
Potteric Carr, Yorkshire, in June 1984,
rearing three young.

p.44 **Bittern** *Botaurus stellaris*

Description: 70–80 cm (27–31½ in). Large, brown and
buff heron, heavily streaked and barred in
black to create remarkably well-*camouflage
plumage* that merges perfectly with the

creamy-brown reed-beds it inhabits. Most obvious field mark is bold, black moustachial streak. In flight, wings are rounded and neck tucked back in typical heron fashion. The resemblance to an old sack has struck many observers. Generally shy and secretive.

Voice: A deep booming sound, audible at considerable range, more like a distant foghorn than a bird. At close range it can be heard to consist of two notes, the first sounding like a deep intake of breath – *urr-hump*.

Habitat: Confined to extensive reed-beds; in winter may stray to thickets and other well-vegetated aquatic margins.

Breeding: Three to four pale greenish-blue eggs laid on platform of reeds and other vegetation, well hidden among dense stands of reeds. Incubation 21 days, by both sexes.

Range: Breeds right across northern Eurasia from Britain to Japan. West European birds are largely resident; eastern and Asiatic birds migrate south to Africa (where it breeds locally), India and China.

Its crepuscular nature means that seeing a Bittern is a lot harder than hearing one. Best times are very early morning and late evening, though in severe winters birds may be forced from their reed beds in search of open waters on which to feed. Caught in the open, they adopt a sky-pointing posture that exposes the reed-like stripes on the neck and breast, and they sway from side to side like wind-caught reeds – a particularly inept form of camouflage behaviour against a background of a grass-covered flood.

IBISES AND SPOONBILLS
(THRESKIORNITHIDAE)

33 species; most confined to tropics. Only two species breed in Europe. These are mainly medium-sized waterbirds, with long legs and long, decurved or spatulate

bills. In flight the neck is extended, unlike
a heron's which is folded back on the
shoulders. They feed on a variety of
aquatic foods, which are picked and
probed out by ibises, and sieved by
spoonbills. Highly gregarious birds, they
form large feeding flocks and nest in
colonies, sometimes in association with
herons and cormorants. The sexes are all
but identical.

p.49 **Glossy Ibis** *Plegadis falcinellus*

Description: 50–65 cm (20–25½ in). Medium-sized
waterbird that, at a distance, appears all
black; marked by a *long decurved bill* and
long legs. At closer range, purple and green
sheen is apparent, with yellow-green legs.
At distance in poor light could be confused
with Curlew, but shorter legs, deliberate
feeding movements and overall shape
different. Flies with *neck extended* and legs
trailing behind.

Voice: Mostly silent, but a harsh *graa* when
breeding.

Habitat: Most types of fresh water, but especially
well-vegetated marshes with open water
and dense reed beds. Frequents lagoons and
even open salt-pans on passage.

Breeding: Three to four blue eggs laid in neat nest
constructed in tree, bush or reeds.
Incubation 21 days, mainly by female.
Highly gregarious, forming dense colonies
at favoured sites.

Range: Widespread in Old World from Balkans to
Australia and tropical Africa. Also in West
Indies and eastern North America.
Confined to south-east in Europe, where it
is only a summer visitor. Largest numbers
breed in Danube Delta; winters in sub-
Saharan Africa.

The Glossy Ibis is a comparatively recent
colonizer of the Americas, where the closely
related White-faced Ibis differs only in the
extent of white around the base of the
latter's bill. The White-faced Ibis is
probably the result of an earlier

colonization by Glossy Ibises that have since diverged into a full species.

---

p.47 Spoonbill *Platalea leucorodia*

Description: 78–90 cm (31–35½ in). Large, white waterbird with long black legs and remarkable, *long, spoon-shaped bill.* Somewhat egret-like and can be confused with Little Egret when bill cannot be seen. Spoonbill is always a warmer, *almost creamy, white,* never the detergent-white of egrets. In flight, head and bill held straight ahead, not tucked back like egret. In breeding season adult has yellow patches on face, breast and at tip of black bill. Juvenile has pink bill and black tips to wing.

Voice: Clatters bill and makes odd grunts during breeding season; otherwise silent.

Habitat: Variable, from estuaries and even shorelines to salt-pans, lagoons and well-vegetated marshes. Breeds among marshes that have growths of reeds or adjacent trees.

Breeding: Four white eggs, speckled with reddish, laid in well-constructed cup in a tree or among dense reeds. Incubation 21 days, by both sexes. Highly colonial, often nesting in association with herons and storks.

Range: Breeds across Eurasia from Atlantic to Sea of Japan; also southwards through India with a few isolated pockets in Africa. European birds based mainly in southeast, with colonies in Spain and Holland; these are summer migrants that winter in West and East Africa.

Even at considerable distances Spoonbills can be recognized by three major characteristics: their warm-white coloration; their gregariousness – even when asleep a tightly grouped flock of white birds are Spoonbills not egrets; and their characteristic side-to-side, scything feeding technique. The latter enables a feeding Spoonbill to be identified at ranges of a kilometre, or more. Only Avocet shares this feature.

STORKS (CICONIIDAE)

17 species; mainly in the tropics. Only two
species breed in Europe. Storks are large
birds with long legs and long necks. Their
bills are large, often colourful, and usually
well pointed, though some (the open-bills)
have a gap between the mandibles like a pair
of pincers. Many species, including the two
European birds, are predominantly black and
white. Neck and legs are held extended in
flight; and their flight technique makes
much use of thermals to enable them to soar
like birds of prey. Though often associated
with water, they also frequent dry arid areas.
They are colonial nesters, mainly in trees but
also on cliffs and buildings. Feeding is often
opportunistic, though some species are
highly specific. Fish, amphibians, insects,
crustaceans and molluscs feature highly in
their diet.

---

p.50 **Black Stork** *Ciconia nigra*

Description: 90–100 cm (35–39 in). Large, black and
white bird marked by long neck, long red
bill, and long red legs. Whole plumage
black except lower breast and belly; thus a
black bird with some white. White Stork,
the only confusable species, is white with
some black. In flight *black head and neck
terminate abruptly on breast,* forming distinct
band. Juvenile similar, but with green bill
and legs. Somewhat solitary and shy – a
contrast with the confiding behaviour of
White Stork.

Voice: Various hisses and whistles; more vocal
than White Stork, but less inclined to bill
clattering.

Habitat: Various wetlands, mostly secluded or well
vegetated. In summer frequents damp
forests, riverine woodland, and other forested
areas near water; also mountain regions.

Breeding: Three to five white eggs laid in bulky
structure of twigs constructed in major fork
of a large forest tree; sometimes also on cliff
ledge or in narrow cave. Incubation 30–35
days, by both sexes.

Range: Eurasia, from Portugal to Japan with a
secondary population in southern Africa.
Iberian population (largely resident) quite
separate from central and eastern European
birds, which are summer visitors.

The Black Stork is generally less confined
to narrow sea-crossings than the White,
which has broader wings, though Gibraltar
and the Bosphorus are the major migration
routes. It is often solitary, except on
migration, and always more secretive and
difficult to locate than its tame cousin.

p.50 **White Stork** *Ciconia ciconia*

Description: 95–105 cm (37–41 in). Large, *white bird
marked by black flight feathers* that create a
pied effect both on the ground and in the
air. Long legs and neck extend fore and aft
in flight; large, sharply pointed bill and
long legs, both deep red. Only confusable
species, Black Stork, has black plumage
broken only by white belly. Confiding;
frequently found alongside man, nesting
mostly on human-built structures. Highly
gregarious during all phases of its life.

Voice: Weak hissing and frequent loud bill-
clattering displays at nest.

Habitat: Highly variable, from marshes and pools to
dry open plains, farmland, estuaries and
salt-pans.

Breeding: Three to five white eggs laid in massive
structure that is often added to year after
year. Basic nest consists of twigs, but is
adorned with all manner of other material
including rags and polythene. Incubation
29–30 days, by both sexes.

Range: Confined to Palearctic as a breeding species,
with separate populations in Europe, south-
central Siberia and far-eastern Siberia near
Sea of Japan. European birds show
migrational divide: western birds
concentrate at Gibraltar, eastern birds at
the Bosphorus. 'Spring' arrivals start in
November; 'autumn' departures under way
by July. Regularly winters in southern
Portugal and Andalucian region of Spain.

Nest sites include houses, telegraph poles, pylons, specially erected platforms and, more naturally, trees. Colonies of Spanish and House Sparrows often construct their nests in the base of the White Stork's massive home.

FLAMINGOES (PHOENICOPTERIDAE)

Five species; confined mainly to the tropics. A single species breeds in Europe. Flamingoes are large waterbirds marked by long legs and, equally exceptionally long necks. Their bills, held upside-down while feeding, are strangely curved and marked by an elaborate series of lamellae that filter minute food particles mainly from salty or brackish waters. The plumage is white, with pink flushes and patches, or distinctly pink all over. They fly with neck and legs extended and are highly gregarious at all times, forming flocks that provide some of the most outstanding bird spectacles in the world.

p.51 **Greater Flamingo** *Phoenicopterus ruber*

Description: 125–145 cm (49–57in). A very large, quite unmistakable bird, marked by pinkish-white plumage, pink and black wings, *exceptionally long pink legs, and long neck with chunky black and pink bill*. Only confusable with other flamingoes that have escaped from captivity; or, exceptionally, with the smaller and pinker Lesser Flamingo that has, on occasion, wandered northwards from tropical Africa. Highly gregarious, forming breeding colonies thousands or tens of thousands strong.

Voice: Goose-like gobbling and honking at all times, both on the ground at colonies and in flight.

Habitat: Saline lagoons and lakes, estuaries, freshwater marshes, and open tidal mud flats.

Breeding: One to two green-washed white eggs laid on cone of mud raised from the ground and constructed by the birds themselves.

Usually an island forms base of colony and nests are crowded closely together. Incubation 28–32 days, by both sexes.

Range: Breeds from Europe to central Siberia and in Middle East and India; also in West Indies and Central America. In Europe, breeds at a few sites including traditionally the Camargue in France and Laguna de Fuenta Piedra in Spain. More recently colonized Doñana, Valencia and the Ebro Delta, all in Spain.

Synchronized laying is essential: isolated pairs or small groups seem incapable of breeding. Sometimes breeding is abandoned in mid-season, and occasionally no attempt at breeding is made at all. Yet the Flamingo seems capable of maintaining its numbers, despite these apparent disasters.

SWANS, GEESE AND DUCK
(ANATIDAE)

144 species; worldwide. Some 46 species occur in Europe, of which 31 breed, seven are regular visitors, and four have been deliberately or accidentally introduced. These are small to very large aquatic birds that swim well and spend most of their lives on or near water. They are robust in build, have flattened bills (except the sawbills), and large, fully webbed feet. Some are expert divers, finding most of their food underwater; others skim the water's surface, or upend in shallow water. Some, including the geese and swans, find much of their food on dry land, but resort to water for safety when breeding or roosting. Many are highly gregarious. At the end of the breeding season, a post-nuptial moult sees all of the flight feathers shed at once and, for a short period, every bird becomes flightless. Sexual dimorphism is common among the ducks, but not among swans and geese. Europe is particularly important as a wintering ground for many species, and concentrations in that season are often spectacular.

p.54 **Bewick's Swan** *Cygnus columbianus*

Description: 116–128 cm (45½–60½ in). Large, white
waterbird confusable only with two other
swans, both of which are considerably
larger. Like Whooper Swan, holds neck
straight rather than curved like Mute Swan;
neck is, however, shorter than either species
creating a more goose-like impression.
Yellow at the base of the bill is *truncated,
rather than forming a point* like a Whooper's.
Bill profile concave rather than straight like
Whooper, a particularly useful feature in
juvenile birds which are greyer.

Voice: Loud, goose-like honking in flight and
musical babbling while feeding.

Habitat: Breeds on Arctic tundra swamps and pools.
In winter frequents seasonal floods, large
lowland lakes and reservoirs, arable and
grassy fields with nearby wetland for
roosting.

Breeding: Three to five creamy-white eggs laid in
well-constructed nest of lichens and mosses
lined with down, usually on a secure island.
Incubation 29–30 days, mostly by female.

Range: Circumpolar in north, but excluding Arctic
Scandinavia. In Europe, a winter visitor
mainly to North Sea coasts westwards
through Britain and Ireland; largest
numbers in Britain and Holland.

The lumping together of Bewick's Swan of
Eurasia and the Whistling Swan of North
America as a single species created one of
those silly mid-Atlantic wrangles about the
English name for the species. Instead of
letting things be, and letting Americans
and Brits call their own birds what they
will, the new name Tundra Swan was
invented. Like other such artificialities it
seems doomed to oblivion – thank heaven.

p.55 **Whooper Swan** *Cygnus cygnus*

Description: 145–160 cm (57–63 in). An all-white
swan, much the same size as Mute Swan,
but with straight neck and yellow bill-
patch as Bewick's. Larger and longer necked

than Bewick's, with *straight, not concave, bill profile, and pointed, not truncated, yellow patch on bill*. Long, straight neck creates a much more swan-like impression than shorter-necked, goose-like Bewick's. In several areas the two winter-visiting swans form mixed flocks in which Whoopers stand out by being both larger and taller.

Voice: A double, trumpeting *whoop-whoop* repeated among members of a flock; highly vocal.

Habitat: In summer frequents islands and margins of lakes, marshy tundra pools, Arctic deltas and estuaries. In winter occurs on agricultural land with adjacent lakes, estuaries, and floods.

Breeding: Five to six creamy-white eggs laid on large nesting mound of vegetation near water's edge, often on a small island. Incubation 35–42 days by female.

Range: Breeds right across northern Eurasia from Iceland to Bering Straits. In Europe breeds in Iceland and Scandinavia and, rarely, in Scotland. Winters through much of temperate Europe from Britain to Greece, around North Sea and Baltic, to Black Sea.

The Icelandic population winters in northern Britain and Ireland, but it is outnumbered by Continental birds that mainly winter around the mouth of the Baltic. These in turn are outnumbered by more eastern birds that winter in the Black Sea. Some 45,000 to 50,000 birds winter in total.

p.55 **Mute Swan** *Cygnus olor*

Description: 145–160 cm (57–63 in). Large, all-white waterbird – the familiar long-necked swan of parks and ponds in many parts of Europe – with long, curved neck and *deep-orange bill marked by large, black knob* at base. Sexes similar but black knob larger in male. Bill colour and serpentine neck distinguish Mute from the two other swans, both of which are predominantly winter visitors.

Voice: Various hisses when threatened; in flight wings produce beating noise.

Habitat: Variety of fresh waters in summer, from park ponds to wild marshes, with mixture of dense emergent vegetation and open waters; also rivers and estuaries. In winter also at sea in sheltered bays and on intertidal shores.

Breeding: Five to seven white eggs laid in huge mound of aquatic vegetation on waterside margin or among shallow waters. Incubation 34–38 days, mainly by female.

Range: Breeds from Faeroes eastwards across Siberia. Also in North America, South Africa and Australasia where introduced. West European birds largely resident; eastern birds move south and west in winter.

Mute Swans have been introduced and/or domesticated in so many parts of Europe that their natural range is somewhat mysterious. In England they were domesticated for food (served at medieval banquets) and, with some exceptions, are still officially the property of the monarch. Such regal protection no doubt accounts for their highly successful survival in this country. A decline in numbers resulting from the swans' ingestion of lead fishing weights has been recognized and, where steps have been taken to ban lead weights, the population has shown a remarkable recovery.

---

pp.56 & 60 **Greylag Goose** *Anser anser*

Description: 71–89 cm (28–35 in). Largest of the 'grey' geese, with buff-brown barred plumage, large orange bill, and strong, pink legs and feet. The large, buff-brown (not dark) head and neck combined with *large orange bill* are the best field marks when birds are at rest. In flight, pale *grey forewing* is a feature shared only with much smaller and dark-headed Pink-footed Goose and, to a much lesser extent, with similarly small White-fronted. Only the dark-headed Bean Goose approaches it in size.

Voice: Deep *aahng-ung-ung*; highly vocal producing all the sounds associated with farmyard geese, which are descended from wild Greylags.

Habitat: Variety of fresh waters, with extensive growth of emergent vegetation and adjacent grasslands. In the north breeds among tundra marshes and pools. In winter frequents pastures, estuaries, marshlands and lakes with grazing nearby. Less inclined than other wild geese to commute long distances to feed.

Breeding: Four to six white eggs laid in scrape lined with down, or atop pile of vegetation in marshy reed-bed. Incubation 27–28 days, by female alone.

Range: Breeds right across Palearctic from Iceland to Sea of Japan. Winters in western Europe, India and Far East. Icelandic birds winter in Scotland while Scandinavian and east European birds are found mainly in Spain.

Though its natural range was severely reduced by over hunting and capture for domestication, the later part of the twentieth century saw successful attempts at reintroduction in many areas. None more so than in Britain, where the native population is confined to a small part of the Outer Hebrides.

pp.56 & 60 **Bean Goose** *Anser fabalis*

Description: 71–89 cm (28–35 in). Virtually the same size as Greylag Goose, though not so robust in build and with smaller head and bill. Easily distinguished by black and orange bill, and orange legs and feet; and even more readily by *dark head and neck* that contrasts with paler, buff-brown body. In flight, upperwing is uniform brown, lacking grey forewing of Greylag and smaller Pink-footed.

Voice: A low-pitched *ung-unk*, but generally less noisy than other geese.

Habitat: In summer frequents lakes and marshes among conifer forests of the Scandinavian Arctic, extending northwards into open tundra swamps in Siberia. In winter found on grasslands and arable land within reach of suitable waters for roosting.

Breeding: Four to six white eggs laid in scrape lined
with grasses and down, adjacent to water
and often sheltered by vegetation.
Incubation 27–29 days, by female alone.
Though not strictly colonial, several
nests may be found relatively close
together.

Range: Breeds right across northern Europe from
Scandinavia to Bering Straits. In winter, a
regular visitor to temperate western Europe
from Britain to Bulgaria.

Bean Geese have recently been split into
two species: Taiga Bean Goose *A. fabalis*
and Tundra Bean Goose *A. semirostris*. Taiga
is long-necked with a long orange bill.
Tundra is short-necked with a short dark
bill marked by an orange patch. Small
numbers of Taiga Bean Geese winter in the
fenlands of England. All other British Bean
Geese are Tundra.

pp.56 & 60 **Pink-footed Goose** *Anser brachyrhynchus*

Description: 61–76 cm (24–30 in). A small 'grey' goose
that is highly gregarious and forms some
of the most spectacular winter flocks in the
whole of Europe. Small size coupled with
short neck produce duck-like impression.
*Small head and small black and pink bill,
together with dark neck,* clinch
identification. Legs pink. In flight shows
pale-grey forewing like much larger
Greylag.

Voice: Highly vocal, with high-pitched *unk-unk*
and *wink-wink* calls.

Habitat: Breeds among Arctic tundra with marshes
and pools, favouring a variety of nest sites
from flat dry ground to vertical cliff-faces.
In winter frequents pastures, stubbles,
waste potatoes and winter cereals, and
roosts on large lakes or sheltered estuaries.
Makes lengthy flights between roosts and
feeding grounds.

Breeding: Four to five white eggs laid in scrape lined
with moss, lichens and down, in variety of
tundra sites. Incubation 25–28 days, by
female alone.

Range: Confined as breeding bird to eastern Greenland and Iceland, wintering in Britain and Ireland (70,000 to 90,000 birds); and to Spitzbergen, wintering southern North Sea (12,000 to 15,000 birds). Has prospered under protective regime in winter quarters.

Once considered a 'dwarf' subspecies of Bean Goose, the Pink-footed Goose has learned to live happily alongside man during the winter. Though apparently causing some damage to the crops on which they feed, there is considerable evidence that the cropping of winter cereals grazed by the geese may be actually improved. Their autumn predilection for potatoes is confined only to waste roots left in the fields.

pp.57 & 60 **White-fronted Goose** *Anser albifrons*

Description: 65–76 cm (26–30 in). Small 'grey' goose of brown and buff plumage marked by *white base* to pink or orange bill, orange legs, and characteristic and variable *smudged barring on belly*. Only Lesser White-fronted shows similar belly-bars and white 'front'. In flight shows greyish base to primaries, but never as marked as grey forewing of Greylag and Pink-footed. Russian birds *A. a. albifrons* have pink bills; Greenland birds *A. a. flavirostris* have orange.

Voice: Highly pitched, almost ringing *kow-yow* and *ryo-ryok*; noisy in large flocks.

Habitat: Bare, open tundra wastes; winters mainly on grassland, marshes and bogs. Less frequently found on arable land than some other 'grey' geese.

Breeding: Five to six white eggs laid in scrape on the ground lined with down. Incubation 27–28 days, by female alone.

Range: Circumpolar in Arctic, though absent from Iceland and Scandinavia. Winter visitor from Ireland across Britain, Holland and central Europe to Balkans. Some 160,000-plus birds winter in Europe, mostly from Russia. Greenland White-fronted Geese

confined to Ireland and Wales (12,000 birds).

In winter quarters White-fronted Geese are regular commuters between their safe roost on an estuarine sandbar or mud flat, and favoured feeding grounds. They are highly gregarious, and the sight and sound of the flocks across the dying sunset is always evocative of the wild.

pp.57 & 61 **Lesser White-fronted Goose**
Anser erythropus

Description: 53–66 cm (21–26 in). Similar to White-fronted, but slightly smaller, with more extensive white at base of bill and conspicuous *yellow eye-ring* in adult. Black barring on belly much less extensive; legs orange, bill pink. Shorter neck and more rounded head distinguish this species among flocks of its more abundant relative. In flight shows uniformly brown upperwing, lacking grey-based primaries of White-fronted.

Voice: A *kow-yow*, faster and higher pitched than White-fronted, perhaps even squeaky.

Habitat: Marshes and bogs at northern margin of conifer forests, forest clearings, and taiga valleys among forested hills. In winter frequents pastures, steppes and crops.

Breeding: Four to five white eggs laid in down and feather-lined scrape atop marshland hummock. Incubation 25–28 days, by female alone. Nest sites are often among boulder-strewn hillsides and raised bogs, rather than lowland marshes or precipitous cliffs.

Range: Breeds in a narrow band from Scandinavia to Bering Straits, mostly beyond Arctic Circle. In winter bulk of population in China, with secondary centre in Balkans and Middle East. In Europe winter concentrations in Romania declining.

For most European birders the Lesser White-fronted Goose is to be picked out among the large flocks of wintering White-fronted Geese of Continental (rather than Greenland) origin. The increasing frequency of this species in western Europe is doubtless a reflection of greater skill and effort in finding it, rather than a genuine increase in numbers of birds.

---

pp. 58 & 61 **Canada Goose** *Branta canadensis*

Description: 90–100 cm (35½–39½ in). The largest of European geese, with particularly long neck that makes it 'taller' than similar-sized Greylag. Body brown above, buffy below. Neck and head black, broken only by *prominent white chin-strap* that extends to behind eye. Only the diminutive Barnacle Goose is even vaguely similar, but that is a grey, rather than brown, bird. Introduced and prospering, mainly in Britain; generally tame.

Voice: A loud *wagh-onk*, with the second syllable higher pitched.

Habitat: In native North America, breeds on tundra and winters among southern swamps and marshes. Largely resident in Europe, frequenting ponds, lakes and ornamental waters.

Breeding: Five to six white eggs laid in substantial nest of grasses lined with down and placed at water margin. Incubation 28–30 days, by female alone.

Range: Resident in Britain. Scandinavian breeders are summer visitors, but make only short migrations to the shores of the ice-free Baltic.

Most European Canada Geese are large, though there is some variation in size due to the introduction and interbreeding of different subspecies. Occasional tiny individuals, the size of a Shelduck, may be genuine transatlantic vagrants, or escapees from wildfowl collections.

---

pp. 58 & 61 **Barnacle Goose** *Branta leucopsis*

Description: 58–69 cm (23–27 in). Attractive 'black' goose that is actually grey. Upperparts grey with bold black barring; underparts white, barred grey on flanks. Breast, neck and crown black broken by *bold white 'face'*. In flight, wings show steel-grey across flight feathers. Larger Canada Goose is brown rather than grey; similar-sized Brent lacks white face.

Voice: Dog-like growls and puppy-like yaps.

Habitat: Breeds on cliffs and crags of Arctic islands; winters on grassland and coastal marshes, with safe wetland roost nearby.

Breeding: Three to five white eggs laid in neat nest of vegetation, lined with down and placed on safe cliff ledge or small island. Incubation 24–25 days, by female alone.

Range: Breeds on east coast of Greenland, on Spitzbergen and in Arctic Russia on Novaya Zemlya. The three distinct populations all migrate to winter in the same region, but remain separate.

Greenland birds winter in Ireland and northwest Scotland; Spitzbergen birds winter on Scotland's Solway Firth; and Russian birds in Holland. All have increased in numbers, bringing the world and European population to over 70,000 birds. In both Britain and Holland farmers are compensated for crop damage caused by dense flocks of Barnacles, and some are contracted to produce special 'sweet-grass' crops for the birds. Despite such measures there are still demands to control their numbers by shooting.

---

pp.59 & 61   **Brent Goose** *Branta bernicla*

Description: 56–61 cm (22–24 in). Small 'black' goose that occurs in two distinct subspecies. Upperparts grey or greyish brown, neatly barred with black and white. Underparts whitish, with barring on the flanks in *B. b. hrota*; or virtually black with a little pale flank-barring in *B. b. bernicla*. Head, short neck and breast black, with *white neck-slash* visible in good light. In flight the contrast between pale underparts and black breast forms notable breast-band in *hrota*, absent in all-dark *bernicla*. American birds *B. b. nigricans* are occasional vagrants, recognized by very dark underparts separated from dark upperparts by bold pale flanks, and bolder white neck-slash.

Voice: Grumbling and growling *grrack*, especially in disturbed flocks.

Habitat: Summers on open tundra with marshes and islands; in winter essentially marine, feeding on estuaries and open shorelines. Has recently begun exploiting adjacent grasslands, but still virtually unknown away from coasts.

Breeding: Three to five white eggs laid in down-lined scrape adjacent to water on mound or islet. Incubation 24-26 days, by female alone.

Range: Circumpolar in high Arctic. Winter visitor in large numbers to Britain and Ireland, North Sea and French Atlantic coasts. Greenland birds winter in Ireland; all others are from Spitzbergen and Russia.

A serious decline in numbers during the 1930s was put down to overshooting and a disease that affected zostera, the main food plant. The species' recovery and increase are due largely to a ban on shooting and the birds' adapting to other marine and terrestrial food plants.

---

p.58 **Red-breasted Goose** *Branta ruficollis*

Description: 51–58 cm (20–23 in). Neat little 'black' goose marked by *harlequin face pattern* and bright-rufous breast. Upperparts black, separated from black underparts by bold, but narrow, white flank-slash. Undertail and lower belly white. Throat, neck and breast rufous, separated from black belly by narrow white breast-band. Head and upper neck a distinctive pattern of rufous, white and black. Small black bill. In flight wings uniformly black above and below. Despite such distinctive plumage, can be hard to locate among flocks of other geese.

Voice: A shrill *kee-waa*.

Habitat: Breeds beside rivers in high Arctic tundra. In winter frequents grassy steppes and shallow margins of large lakes. In Europe mainly on winter cereals.

Breeding: Three to eight creamy-white eggs laid in scrape lined with down, adjacent to a riverbank or among dwarf tundra vegetation. Incubation 24–30 days, by female alone.

Range: Breeds only in north-central Siberia. In winter, found in region of Caspian Sea, Iraqi marshlands and Romania. Numbers present in Europe in Romania have declined, but even fewer now found in Greece and Bulgaria.

The serious decline in numbers to a present world population of less than 8,000 pairs makes this attractive goose a seriously endangered species. Though hunting and loss of breeding habitat are probably the main causes, its propensity to nest close to that of avian predators, such as Peregrine, may be linked to its decline.

---

p.62 **Common Shelduck** *Tadorna tadorna*

Description: 58–64 cm (23–25 in). Large, rather goose-like duck. Both sexes white, marked by black 'braces', black head and neck, and broad, *chestnut breast-band*. Legs pink; bill red, surmounted in the male by swan-like red knob. In the air, the flight feathers are black contrasting with white coverts.

Voice: Male whistles; female quacks.

Habitat: Mostly shorelines, estuaries and other marine habitats and adjacent marshes, though will breed some distance inland.

Breeding: 8–15 creamy eggs laid in rabbit's or similar burrow, or in hollow tree or some other ground cavity, lined with down. Incubation 28–30 days, by the female. On hatching, the young are led to water which may involve a walk of several kilometres.

Range: Breeds in northwestern Europe and sporadically through Mediterranean, and eastwards through southern Siberia almost to Pacific. Scandinavian birds migrate south and west in winter.

Virtually the whole European population of Common Shelduck, over 100,000 birds, migrates to moult in the German Bight in late summer. Young birds are left in the care of 'aunties', which guard crèches of youngsters.

p.63 Ruddy Shelduck *Tadorna ferruginea*

Description: 61–67cm (24–26½ in). Like Common Shelduck in shape, but virtually *whole plumage is chestnut-orange*. Male has narrow black neck-ring; female a white head. In flight both show bold pattern of black wing feathers with white coverts.

Voice: A loud goose-like, honking *aang*.

Habitat: Shores of inland lakes and marshes, often salt-lakes, as well as river margins and even small pools, often at considerable altitude.

Breeding: 8–12 white eggs laid in nest of down in a hole in riverbank or tree, or in other crevice. Incubation 27–29 days, by female.

Range: Breeds in a huge belt from Morocco to central Siberia and northern China. Decidedly scarce in Mediterranean and Balkans; though large numbers winter in Turkey, there are few in Romania, Bulgaria and Greece.

Ruddy Shelduck occur on a variety of waters that, lacking strong growths of emergent vegetation, are seldom used by other wildfowl. Their highly variable diet, which includes both vegetable and animate matter, depends largely on local availability. They are thus able to exploit waters that cannot support other ducks. In Europe large bare salty marshlands are used, but in Siberia they frequent large rivers with extensive shoals.

---

p.63 Egyptian Goose *Alopochen aegyptiacus*

Description: 66–72 cm (26–28½ in). Structure unlike typical goose: legs long and neck short. Brown above and creamy buff below, with white undertail and small dark-brown belly-patch. Best field marks are large, *maroon-brown patch surrounding yellow eye*, and dark hind neck with neat neck-ring. Small bill and long legs both pink. In flight shows bold white forewing contrasting with black flight feathers and black tail. Sexes similar.

Voice: Mostly silent, but with some hissing and loud strident calls.

Habitat: Lakes, grassy margins and adjacent marsh in Africa frequents riverside woodlands (frequently perches), ponds and lakesides.

Breeding: Eight to nine creamy eggs laid on mound vegetation protected by waterside bush or scrub; also in tree hole or rock cleft. Incubation 28–30 days, by both sexes.

Range: Resident in Africa south of Sahara as far south as Cape of Good Hope; also northwards as far as Upper Egypt. In Europe confined to East Anglia.

Despite suffering no persecution by man and generally being aggressive in defence of its territories – even against larger species – the Egyptian Goose has never really prospered like other introduced wildfowl and its numbers and feral range remain small.

p.70 **Mandarin Duck** *Aix galericulata*

Description: 41–47 cm (16–18½ in). A dainty, ornamental duck that now finds its major world stronghold in England, where it was introduced during the nineteenth century. Male a remarkable combination of features and colours confusable only with related North American Wood Duck: a long black crest extends from crown, over white face marked by dark eye; foreneck is a cascade of rich ginger; brown breast is marked by two parallel white rings; brown *upperparts boast two ginger 'sails';* tiny bill is red. In contrast female is brownish grey marked by neatly spotted flanks and white eye-ring and bridle. Both sexes have white undertail and in flight show green speculum on dark wing.

Voice: Male utters a shrill whistle; female a brief *ke*

Habitat: Largely confined to extensive old woodland with small, well-hidden and undisturbed ponds, lakes and slow-flowing rivers.

Breeding: 9–12 creamy eggs laid in tree hole or cavity lined with down. Incubation 28–30 days, solely by female.

Range: Breeds naturally only in northern China, far eastern Russia and Japan; migrates south and east in winter, though only within those countries. In Europe confined to

southeast and central England and central Scotland where it is resident.

These attractive duck find Britain's parks and ornamental gardens perfectly suited to their needs, especially where these are surrounded by extensive wooded grounds and are undisturbed by public access. They are at home among the woods and hammer ponds of Surrey and Sussex, as anywhere. The British population is a stable 260 pairs.

---

p.68 **Eurasian Wigeon** *Anas penelope*

Description: 43–45 cm (17–17½ in). Northern breeding duck that forms large winter flocks in many areas of western and southern Europe; often coastal, mainly wet marshes or flooded grazing. Male grey, marked by rufous head with golden-yellow crown; rear end shows *black and white with white flank-slash*. Female brown with less pronounced flank-slash. Both sexes have neat rounded head with small silver-grey bill. In flight male shows *white on inner wing, lacking in female*. Therefore large flocks of duck in flight with some birds with white in wing, some without, are potentially this species.

Voice: Highly distinctive whistle in male; female growls.

Habitat: Breeds among tundra pools with or without trees; also among marshes in southern parts of range. Winters on flooded grasslands and estuary margins, often in association with geese.

Breeding: Seven to eight creamy eggs laid on the ground in down-lined hollow. Incubation 22–25 days, by female alone.

Range: Breeds right across northern Palearctic from Iceland to Bering Straits. Highly migratory, wintering in Europe and from India and Southeast Asia to China and Japan.

Winter flocks of Eurasian Wigeon whistling overhead as they flight to and from their roosting grounds at dusk and dawn bring an evocative sense of the wild to many parts of temperate northern and western Europe.

Their association with Brent Geese on coastal saltings, and Pink-footed Geese at inland floods, is more a matter of shared habitat preferences than of mutual benefi

---

pp.64 & 68 **Gadwall** *Anas strepera*

Description: 48–54 cm (19–21 in). Slightly smaller th Mallard and, unusually among male surfa feeding duck, discreetly coloured in shade of grey and brown. Only close examinatio reveals finely vermiculated plumage to advantage. At any distance, male resembl female Mallard, but marked by a *black rea end and distinct white speculum*. White speculum is also best feature of female an particularly obvious in flight.

Voice: Male whistles; female quacks like Mallar

Habitat: Marshes, lakes, pools with extensive grow of vegetation; frequents larger waters including reservoirs and estuaries in wint

Breeding: 8–12 creamy eggs laid in down-lined depression well hidden among scrub near water. Incubation 25–27 days, by female alone.

Range: Disrupted circumpolar from Europe to central and eastern Siberia in conifer and steppe zones, as well as in similar areas of North America. Migrant, wintering in India and Southeast Asia as well as in southern and western Europe.

Originally introduced to several parts of west European range, including England 1850, the Gadwall has since spread and prospered. There are also indications of natural spread from the east. It is general a shy species that prefers wild marshes to smaller ornamental waters.

---

pp.66 & 68 **Common Teal** *Anas crecca*

Description: 34–38 cm (13½–15 in). Tiny duck that flie on fast-beating wings and often forms tightly knit flocks like waders. Male grey, with distinctive chestnut head broken by yellow-bordered, bold green patch around eye. At any distance dark head contrasts with pale body. Bold, *pale-yellow patch at rear end bordered black*. Female similar to other female surface-feeding ducks, though small size distinguishes it from all save female Garganey. *Green speculum* and plain, unstriped face are main distinctive features.

Voice: Male whistles; female quacks.

Habitat: Ponds, lakes and especially marshes with good growth of emergent vegetation. Breeds at high latitudes and often among moorland and tundra wastes.

Breeding: 8–12 creamy-buff eggs laid in down-lined hollow sheltered by vegetation, usually near water. Incubation 21–28 days, by female alone.

Range: Circumpolar in northern hemisphere, though absent in Greenland and Canadian archipelago. In Europe breeds in north; winters south and west.

Though considered to be a member of the same species, the American Green-winged Teal *A. c. carolinensis* is easily identifiable in the field: the male has a white vertical breast-slash as well as a broken, ill-defined yellow border to the green eye-patch. It is a vagrant to Europe, mostly to Britain and Ireland.

pp.66 & 69 **Garganey** *Anas querquedula*

Description: 37–41 cm (14½–16 in). Teal-sized duck. Male has maroon-brown head marked by *bold, white supercilium*, obvious at great distance; flanks grey with extended blue scapulars that cascade from back. In flight, pale-blue inner forewing obvious. Female very similar to female Common Teal, but with distinct *striped face* pattern and blue-grey inner wing.

Voice: Male utters crackling rattle, female a high-pitched quack.

Habitat: More marsh orientated than Common Teal, with preference for swampy ground with secluded areas of open water and extensively vegetated margins. Also reservoir and gravel-pit margins.

Breeding: 8–11 buffy eggs laid in depression lined with down. Incubation 21–23 days, by female alone.

Range: Summers right across Palearctic, from Britain to Pacific, mainly in steppe zone, though also among conifer forests; but nowhere common. In winter whole of breeding area is vacated as European birds move to Sahelian region south of Sahara.

One of the earliest returning summer visitors with first arrivals in early March; th is often the most abundant duck among the floods of Senegal, Niger and Chad. Number present at the Niger Inundation Zone can b spectacular, indicating strong breeding populations probably east of our region.

pp.65 & 68 **Mallard** *Anas platyrhynchos*

Description: 55–62 cm (22½–24½ in). Widespread, common and familiar as the 'pond duck' throughout Europe. Male is beautifully marked duck with metallic-green head bordered by neat white neck-ring. Body grey, with black flank-line and black rear end with curled-up tail feathers. Female mottled in shades of brown with orange bi and often a well-marked eye-stripe and supercilium. In flight both sexes show prominent *blue speculum bordered white,* and pale, silvery underwing.

Voice: Loud, distinctive quacking, but also a conversational gabbling.

Habitat: From semi-tundra marshes to city parks vi ponds, lakes, rivers and reservoirs. Virtuall any wetland area may support these highly adaptive birds.

Breeding: 10–12 creamy eggs laid in down-lined hollow near water, well hidden among vegetation, though often quite openly where cover is unavailable. Incubation 28–29 days, solely by female, that is remarkably well camouflaged. Replacemen broods are common.

Range: Circumpolar in northern hemisphere. Breeds throughout Europe, but northern and eastern birds are only summer visitors.

Mallard are the ancestors of the vast majority of domestic duck types. Yet even in the all-white 'call ducks' the male retains the curled-up feathers of the upper tail. Wild birds frequently interbreed with domestic forms and are as at home alongside man as the House Sparrow.

pp.67 & 69   **Pintail** *Anas acuta*

Description: ♂ 63–70 cm (25–27½ in); ♀ 53–59 cm (21–23 in). Although both sexes have characteristically pointed tails, the male's extended tail feathers make it significantly longer overall. An exceptionally elegant duck marked by long neck, well-proportioned head and bill, and foreparts that *sit low in the water*. Spends more time upending than other ducks. Male grey, with black and creamy-yellow rear end; head chocolate-brown with white of the neck extending upwards to form stripe on the side. Female similar to other female surface-feeding duck, but with pale, featureless 'face'. In flight, *long pointed tail* is prominent feature.

Voice: Male utters nasal wheezes and growls; female quacks.

Habitat: Shallow waters from tundra pools to temperate marshes, though generally avoids large open waters. In winter will gather in large flocks on flooded grassland and at favoured estuaries.

Breeding: Seven to nine creamy or greenish eggs laid in scrape lined with down and well hidden among vegetation near water. Incubation 21–23 days, by female alone.

Range: Circumpolar. In Europe confined to north and east and only a winter visitor to south and extreme west. Some European birds cross Sahara to winter in Sahelian region.

Among mixed flocks of duck gathered at a favoured sanctuary, Pintail are easily picked out at distance by their more or less continuous upending feeding action. They often gather in discrete sub-flocks where their pointed tail feathers instantly confirm their identity.

pp.67 & 69 **Shoveler** *Anas clypeata*

Description: 47–53 cm (18½–21 in). Medium-sized
duck marked in all plumages *by huge
spatulate bill*. Male has silver bill, metallic
green head, white breast, and rich-chestnu
underparts; at rest, white breast often mo
prominent feature. Female mottled in
shades of dark brown and cream with
orange bill margins. In flight both sexes
show prominent *pale-blue inner wing* with
bottle-green speculum, but shape and siz
of bill still best feature.

Voice: Male utters harsh *tuk-tuk*; female quacks.

Habitat: Shallow waters at all times: tundra pools,
marshes, pond and lake margins, floods a
estuaries.

Breeding: 8–12 buffy eggs laid in hollow, lined wit
vegetation and down, near water.
Incubation 22–23 days, by female alone.

Range: Circumpolar in tundra and boreal zones.
Scattered distribution through temperate
Europe and decidedly scarce breeder in sou
Winter visitor from north and east to most
parts of Europe. Some birds cross Sahara.

The unique bill of the Shoveler is perfectl
adapted to sieve small aquatic animals fro
soft mud by pumping water through in a
more or less continuous flow. An individu
may spend an hour or more feeding in th
way without moving more than a metre,
which demonstrates either the richness o
the mud or the efficiency of the Shoveler'
bill as a feeding tool; probably both.

pp.70 & 74 **Marbled Duck** *Marmaronetta angustirostr*

Description: 39–42 cm (15½–16½ in). Small, buff-bro
duck that has become very scarce and
elusive during the past century. Head lar
with a ragged hind crest and marked by
dark eye-patch that is the most obvious fiel
mark. The rest of the plumage is buff-
brown liberally spotted with bold blobs o
white. Sexes alike. In flight, wings are
uniform, broken only by darker tips and
carpal patches on upper surface.

Voice: Generally silent, but male utters a soft squeak, female a two-note whistle.

Habitat: Shallow, freshwater pools with extensive emergent vegetation, marshes and lakes with shallow margins. Generally secretive, spending much of its time hidden.

Breeding: 9–13 creamy eggs laid in down-lined depression among dense vegetation near water. Incubation 25–27 days; despite the sexes being so similar, the female, like other ducks, incubates alone.

Range: Virtually confined to western Palearctic, but highly sporadic in Europe. Confined to Spain and Turkey, extending eastwards to southern Russia. Some local movements, with largest winter numbers in Turkey.

The Marbled Duck was locally abundant in the Doñana area of southern Spain during the last part of nineteenth century, and the subsequent decline to no more than 100 pairs today is something of a mystery. This is always a shy, retiring species that simply melts into vegetation whenever it becomes aware of being observed.

pp.70 & 74 **Red-crested Pochard** *Netta rufina*

Description: 53–59 cm (21–23 in). Male marked by over-large head, rich *orange-rufous crest* and red bill; upperparts, buffy brown, underparts white; breast, rear end and belly-stripe black. Unmistakable. Female brownish with *darker cap above paler face*, resembling female Common Scoter, but with small, delicate bill. In flight, both ~~se~~s show very bold white wingbar. ~~~~lly gregarious and often the ~~~~uck at favoured waters. ~~~~hough female utters

~~~~ng growth of ~~~~ially semi- ~~~~ter more ~~~~f fresh ~~~~re.

tunnel through dense vegetation, mostly reeds. Incubation 26–28 days, by female.

Range: Predominantly south European. From Spain northwards through France to Holland and Germany, thence eastwards to central-southern Asia. European birds winter in Spain, Greece and Balkans.

Though properly regarded as a diving duck, Red-crested Pochard frequently upend like surface feeders and graze like geese. They tend to be highly localized and have very particular habitat requirements. Thus the strongest population is centred on a few lakes in central Spain where well over half the European population can be found throughout the year.

pp.71 & 74   **Pochard** *Aythya ferina*

Description: 44–48 cm (17½–19 in). Well-marked diving duck with tail held at water level and distinctly sloping bill shape. Male grey with black breast and rear end, and dark rusty head; bill silver. At any distance it appears *pale-centred with solid black fore and aft*. Female similar shape but dark-greyish brown with prominent pale bars. A pale eye-ring extends in a bridle. In flight, both sexes show broad, pale-grey wingbar. Often found in large rafts; dives easily from the surface.

Voice: Generally quiet. Male has soft wheezing call; female growls.

Habitat: Lakes and ponds of some depth, among forests and steppes, and with abundant aquatic vegetation. In winter also on large bare waters including reservoirs devoid of even marginal vegetation.

Breeding: 6–11 pale-greenish eggs, laid in hollow, or on heap of aquatic vegetation, often away from dry land. Incubation 24–26 days, by female alone.

Range: Breeds from western Europe to eastern Siberia. Vast majority move south or west in winter with over 250,000 birds in northwest Europe and 500,000 in southern Europe, the Mediterranean and Black Sea.

A westward spread during the twentieth century has resulted in a somewhat patchy distribution throughout most of Europe. Pochard now breed as far south as Andalucia in Spain and as far west as Myvatn in Iceland. It is also a familiar visitor to city ponds, gravel pits and recreational waters.

p.71 **Ferruginous Duck** *Aythya nyroca*

Description: 39–43 cm (15½–17 in). An all-dark diving duck marked by *white rear end*, the boldest of all white wingbars in flight and, in the male, by clear-cut white eye. Resembles Pochard in general shape, though with larger silver bill. Close approach reveals plumage to be rich, dark chestnut. Female differs by buffy, barred flanks. Replaces Pochard southwards in steppe region.

Voice: Male produces a chattering, female a definite croaking.

Habitat: Shallow freshwater lakes with dense growth of emergent and marginal vegetation, particularly reeds. Confined as breeder to shallow steppe lakes and brackish pools. More widespread in winter.

Breeding: 7–11 creamy eggs laid in down-lined hollow well protected by dense growth of waterside vegetation. Incubation 25–27 days, by female alone.

Range: Scarce and highly localized breeder in Spain, France, and central and eastern Europe eastwards across steppes of southern Russia. Winters in Greece, Turkey, Middle East, and northern India.

Though it is scarce or unknown outside eastern Europe, the Ferruginous Duck is relatively common on Russian steppes. Unlike most other ducks, it does not undertake regular migrations to special moulting grounds, but heads directly for winter quarters, pausing in large numbers at favoured localities along the way. It is therefore regular in Hungary in autumn, but virtually absent in winter. It is decidedly scarce in northwest Europe.

pp.72 & 75   **Tufted Duck** *Aythya fuligula*

Description: 41–45 cm (16–17½ in). Neatly proportioned, black and white diving duck with small crest on rounded head. Male black marked by *bold white flanks*. Close approach reveals metallic-blue wash over head, a droopy crest and yellow eye. Female brown with similar rounded head shape and vestigial crest. In flight both sexes show broad white wingbar. Dives easily and forms rafts, often with Pochard in winter quarters.

Voice: Male whistles, but only during breeding season; female growls.

Habitat: Lakes and pools, as well as natural-banked reservoirs, and open water among extensive marshes, all with good growth of emergent vegetation. In winter also at bare open waters and estuaries.

Breeding: 5–12 greenish eggs laid in down-lined depression under cover and adjacent to water. Incubation 23–25 days, solely by female.

Range: Breeds right across Palearctic from Iceland to Kamchatka. In Europe, breeds in temperate north and locally in the former Yugoslavia. Absent in Mediterranean. Winters widely in western Europe where over half a million birds can be found.

Although the Tufted Duck is frequently found alongside and feeding with Pochard, especially in winter, the two species avoid competition by taking predominantly different foods. Tufted Duck feed on molluscs, crustaceans and insect larvae, while the Pochard is predominantly a vegetarian, though both are bottom feeders.

pp.72 & 75   **Scaup** *Aythya marila*

Description: 46–51 cm (18–20 in). Similar to, and easily confused with, more widespread Tufted Duck, of which Scaup is actually the maritime equivalent. Male similarly dark headed, dark breasted and dark tailed with white flanks. Major difference is *barred-grey (rather than black) back.* A larger bill, differently shaped, sloping hind crown and metallic-green-washed head are further features. Female even closer in appearance to female Tufted Duck, though sloping hind crown is different. Female Scaup has clear-cut *white area at base of bill*. Some female Tufted show this feature, but white never as extensive or as clear cut. Both sexes show bold white wingbar in flight. Highly gregarious in tightly knit flocks in winter.

Voice: Mainly silent, though female growls.

Habitat: Breeds on ponds and lakes among open tundra and among adjacent wooded taiga zone. Winters mainly on the sea in estuaries and sheltered bays where it may gather in enormous flocks over good feeding grounds.

Breeding: 8–11 grey eggs laid in down-lined depression. Incubation 26–28 days, by female.

Range: Circumpolar in far north of Palearctic and Nearctic, though absent in Greenland. Widespread winter visitor to coasts of northwestern Europe.

Although it is said to be omnivorous, the largest rafts of Scaup are invariably concentrated over rich beds of molluscs, mostly mussels, in winter. Other concentrations occur at distilleries and breweries where waste grain is released into estuaries or bays.

pp.76 & 84 **Common Eider** *Somateria mollissima*

Description: 55–61 cm (21–24 in). Robust, *chunky sea-duck* that rides out the roughest of seas with apparent ease. At any distance, male is black and white and only close approach reveals pale-green hind neck. Confusable only with other eider from which it is distinguished by its *white back*. Characteristic sloping crown and bill profile shared with all-brown female. In flight, both sexes show white wing-linings; male with white upperwing coverts. Generally gregarious and found close inshore among rocky bays and headlands.

Voice: Male has cooing courtship calls; female growls.

Habitat: Breeds along rocky coastlines and, especially, low offshore islands. Highly colonial.

Breeding: Four to six greenish eggs laid in depression lined with down. Incubation 27–28 days b female alone; sitting females are highly approachable and tame at this time. Colonies number from a few to several thousand pairs and are utilized year after year.

Range: Circumpolar in high Arctic. In Europe breeds along coasts of Iceland, northern Britain and Ireland, and Scandinavia. Most winter near breeding colonies, though Baltic birds move southwestwards to ice-free waters.

The eiderdown with which these birds line their nests has been 'farmed' for centuries for its highly insulative qualities. Despite the advent of modern synthetics, it is still regarded as the highest-quality filler for duvets and is collected annually by Icelandic farmers who protect the colonies from predators. The best-quality down is taken before the eggs are laid.

p.77 **King Eider** *Somateria spectabilis*

Description: 47–63 cm (18½–25 in). Male has all-black body broken only by white flank-patch. Foreparts a harlequin pattern of grey crown green face and peachy breast marked by large *red comb at base of red bill*. The latter creates remarkably rectangular head shape. Female similar to female Common Scoter, but sloping bill profile has pronounced bump.

Voice: Silent away from breeding grounds.

Habitat: Breeds alongside pools, lakes and rivers on Arctic tundra. Winters along coasts in sheltered, often rocky bays.

Breeding: Four to seven pale-green eggs laid in depression lined with down, usually amon; dwarf vegetation near water. Incubation 22–24 days; by female alone.

Range: Circumpolar in high Arctic; localized
winter visitor to Scandinavian coasts and in
tiny numbers to northern Scotland.

Although regarded as no more than a
vagrant away from Norwegian coasts,
King Eider occur regularly in Northern
Scotland in small numbers. Most occur in
Shetland and Fair Isle and are usually
adult males that make extended stays and
then return for several consecutive
winters. Females may be scarcer or simply
overlooked among the vast flocks of
Common Eider, with which these birds
regularly associate.

pp.77 & 84 **Steller's Eider** *Polysticta stelleri*

Description: 43–48 cm (17–19 in). Male largely black
above and peachy white below. White head
shows patches of black and pale green;
unlike other eider, *bill profile does not slope*
and is thus more duck-like. In flight, a
white inner wing contrasts with black
flight feathers and back. Female similar
shades of brown to Common and King
Eider, but given good views, concave bill
profile easily distinguishes it.

Voice: Male utters low growls, female a guttural
chattering.

Habitat: Breeds among tundra on pools and marshes;
winters along rocky coasts and sheltered
fjords.

Breeding: Six to eight pale-green eggs laid in
depression well lined with lichens, moss,
feathers and down. Incubation, by the
female alone, for unknown period.

Range:  A high-Arctic breeder, regular only along
Norwegian coast. Breeds either side of Bering
Straits along north-facing tundra coastlines
extending only relatively short distances
inland. Regularly winters, summers and
occasionally breeds in Varanger Fjord in
northern Norway. In winter extends
southward along adjacent coasts.

Despite wintering in the same area as
King Eider in northern Norway, this

attractive duck is an extremely rare vagrant elsewhere in Europe. Even northern Britain has seen only 14 records since the first in 1830, and Denmark fare little better. Long-staying drakes inevitably attract much attention.

pp.78 & 84 **Harlequin Duck** *Histrionicus histrionicus*

Description: 41–45 cm (16–17½ in). Highly localized torrent specialist with exceptional swimming ability. Male dark blue-grey with rich-chestnut flanks and various whit spots and streaks creating *harlequin face* pattern. Female brown with pattern of *thre diffuse spots on face* and, therefore, easily confusable with female Long-tailed Duck and particularly Velvet Scoter. Both sexes show uniform dark wings in flight.

Voice: Male utters long whistle that terminates i a trill and a high squeaking call; female croaks.

Habitat: Breeds alongside raging torrents, rapids and waterfalls among Arctic tundra where it navigates and hunts with consummate ease. Winters along rocky coasts, often clo inshore where its swimming abilities enab it to avoid being crushed by violent breakers, and seldom wandering further afield.

Breeding: Six to eight creamy eggs laid in depressior lined with down. Incubation 27–29 days, by female alone.

Range: Circumpolar in high Arctic, but with a ga that extends eastwards from Scandinavia t eastern Siberia and another in north-centra Canada. Also extends surprisingly southward in Rocky Mountain system of USA. In Europe confined to Iceland.

The swimming and diving abilities of this little sea-duck are remarkable. In summer it catches insects and larvae from among the rapids; in winter it tears molluscs from sea-girded rock faces. It is one of the rarest of vagrants south of Iceland and had occurred a mere 14 times in Britain up to the end of 1996.

pp.79 & 84 **Long-tailed Duck** *Clangula hyemalis*

Description: ♂ 54–58 cm (21–23 in); ♀ 41–45 cm (16–17½ in). This stocky sea-duck has distinctive male and female as well as summer and winter plumages. Male's long tail characteristic. In all plumages, *chunky head* marked with variable face patterns in dark brown and white. Summer male, and summer and winter females have brown backs and white underparts; winter male has white upperparts with broad brown 'braces' terminating in narrow breast-band. In flight, *all-dark wings contrast with white underparts* at all seasons, and head is held above body level on longish neck.

Voice: Male utters wide range of yodelling calls; female quacks.

Habitat: Breeds among bare, high-Arctic tundra on pools and lakes, often at some altitude. Winters along coasts in sheltered bays and estuaries.

Breeding: Five to nine pale-yellowish eggs laid in depression lined with down and usually concealed by low vegetation. Incubation 23–25 days, by female alone.

Range: Circumpolar. In Europe breeds in Iceland and northern Scandinavia. Winters along adjacent coasts as well as British coasts of North Sea.

On its breeding grounds, the Long-tailed Duck is perhaps the most vocal of all ducks. Males arrive early, often before the iced-over rivers and lakes have fully melted. Like seals, they often hunt beneath the ice, using only a small hole through which to surface for breath.

p.80 **Common Scoter** *Melanitta nigra*

Description: 46–51 cm (18–20 in). An *all-black sea-duck* that gathers in offshore flocks and flies low over the sea. Male black, with typical duck-like, concave bill profile; close approach reveals yellow bill surmounted by small black knob. Female dark brown with pale sides to head and dark cap; thus, at rest, it is confusable with female Red-crested Pochard. Both sexes uniformly dark in flight.

Voice: Various plaintive whistles and growls.

Habitat: Tundra lakes, pools and marshes among dwarf vegetation; sometimes at altitude among moorland. Essentially marine in winter, frequenting shallow bays and wide estuaries, usually in flocks.

Breeding: Six to nine creamy eggs laid in waterside depression lined with down. Incubation 27–31 days, by female alone.

Range: Breeds right across northern Palearctic, crossing Bering Straits into western Alaska. Also in Newfoundland and irregularly elsewhere in Canadian Arctic. In Europe, breeds in Iceland, northern Britain and Scandinavia, wintering around North Sea and Atlantic coasts.

Common Scoter are highly gregarious and often form quite substantial flocks at particularly favoured feeding grounds. They fly in wavering lines, low over the sea with one group leaving and joining another for no apparent reason. Flocks often contain other scoters including Velvet and the rare Surf Scoter.

pp.80 & 85 **Velvet Scoter** *Melanitta fusca*

Description: 53–59 cm (21–23 in). Very similar to Common Scoter, though slightly larger and marked by *bold white speculum in both sexes*. Despite illustrations, this white mark in the wing can be difficult to see and is often obscured. Male black with white speculum and small white patch behind eye. Bill yellow with extended black centre creating sloping profile that is shared with the brown female. At rest female is often easier to pick out from flocks of Common Scoter by having two diffuse, pale face-patches.

Voice: Piping whistles on breeding grounds; generally silent at sea though a harsh *karr* uttered in flight.

Habitat: Ponds and lakes among conifer forests and taiga zone, so generally breeds to south of Common Scoter. Also at or above tree line in mountain areas and along bare coastlines.

Breeding: Seven to ten cream-coloured eggs laid in nest of twigs and grasses lined with feathers and down. Incubation 27–28 days by female alone.

Range: Circumpolar in boreal and taiga zones, though absent in eastern Canada, Greenland and Iceland. In Europe essentially Scandinavian in distribution. Migrants move south and west to North Sea and mouth of Baltic.

In winter the Velvet Scoter is usually found in small parties rather than in the large flocks favoured by Common Scoter. It often prefers rocky, rougher shorelines, but also mixes with its more abundant cousin. When watching mixed scoter flocks, patience is often required to pick out the white wing-flash of Velvet, though the face pattern of females is sometimes easier to see, even at a distance.

---

pp.81 & 85 **Surf Scoter** *Melanitta perspicillata*

Description: 45–56 cm (17½–22 in). Like other scoter, male is black, though nape and crown marked with *bold patches of white* visible at considerable range. Close approach reveals straight, eider-like profile and orange-yellow-white coloration of bill. Female shares profile, but is dark-capped like Common Scoter and patchy faced like Velvet. Uniformly dark in flight.

Voice: Both sexes utter croaks and gurgling calls during courtship; otherwise silent.

Habitat: Lakes and pools among open tundra and wooded taiga. Thus replaces Common Scoter over much of North America. In winter frequents inshore waters, mostly sheltered bays.

Breeding: Five to seven creamy-buff eggs laid in hollow lined with down and hidden beneath shrubs near water. Incubation by the female alone; period unknown.

Range: Western North America from Alaska through northern Canada. In Europe, a regular vagrant to west coasts of Britain and Ireland, mainly Scotland. There are about ten reports a year, mostly in winter and mostly long-staying.

The nest of the Surf Scoter was first found only in 1920, and even today knowledge of its breeding routines are far from complete. Even in winter it favours deeper water than other scoter and is therefore more difficult to observe. Vagrants to Europe are more likely to occur with Velvet than with Common Scoter.

---

pp.73 & 75 **Barrow's Goldeneye** *Bucephala islandica*

Description: 42–53 cm (16½–21 in). Male black above and white below, with black head marked by *white oval spot*. Main differences from Goldeneye are remarkable raised crown, steep forehead and sloping nape, blue rather than green metallic wash to head, oval rather than round face patch, and black back with white spots rather than white back with black lines. Female much closer to female Goldeneye, but with steep forehead and sloping nape. Bill smaller than Goldeneye.

Voice: Rolling, grunting *kaa* by male in courtship; female utters a few croaks. Silent outside breeding season.

Habitat: Lakes, ponds and rivers, mainly among conifer forests, though in open country in Iceland and elsewhere. Winters on similar waters, but also along coasts.

Breeding: 8–14 grey-green eggs laid in down-lined hole among rocks or in a cliff. Incubation 30 days, solely by female.

Range: Mainly from Alaska southwards through Rocky Mountain system, but also in Labrador, Greenland and Iceland. Vagrant elsewhere in Europe.

The Icelandic population numbers some 800 pairs and is decidedly resident, moving no further than the nearest coastline. Vagrants elsewhere in Europe

are exceptionally rare, only a singleton for
Britain, and may well have their origins in
North America rather than Iceland.

pp.73 & 75 **Goldeneye** *Bucephala clangula*

Description: 40–48 cm (16–19 in). Compact, diving
duck. Male largely white with black central
back, black lines over wings, black rear end,
and black head washed bottle green. A
white circle marks face between bill and eye.
Sloping hind crown gives head peculiar
triangular shape. Female grey-bodied, with
brown triangular-shaped head. In flight
both sexes show white inner wing, larger in
male than female.

Voice: Variety of nasal and rasping calls during
elaborate courtship; otherwise silent.

Habitat: Equally at home on fresh and salt water.
Lakes and ponds among extensive conifer
forests. In winter frequents lakes, reservoirs,
gravel pits, estuaries, and sheltered sea
bays.

Breeding: 6–11 blue-green eggs laid in tree hole or
nest box lined with down. Incubation
27–32 days, by female.

Range: Circumpolar in northern boreal forests. In
Europe, from Scotland eastwards through
Scandinavia and from eastern Germany
through Russia. Common in northwestern
Europe in winter with over 200,000 birds
in Europe as a whole.

Colonization of Scotland during the second
half of the twentieth century was
significantly aided by the provision of nest
boxes in suitable habitats. In Finland
similar nest-box provision has built up the
population to no less than 50,000 pairs in
recent years.

p.82 **Smew** *Mergus albellus*

Description: 36–43 cm (14–17 in). Adult male is quite
simply stunning. White, with large head;
flanks vermiculated grey with narrow black
lines extending over back and flanks. Black

mask encloses eye, and hind crown has black mark. Bill silver, its small size accentuated by vertical forehead. Female and all immatures grey, marked by *maroon cap (black at any distance)* and white cheeks. In this plumage Smew could be confused with winter Slavonian Grebe. Generally gregarious, forming large flocks in several winter zones.

Voice: Various grunts in courtship; otherwise silent.

Habitat: Breeds on lakes and ponds among conifer and taiga forests. In winter frequents sheltered waters including estuaries, reservoirs and gravel pits.

Breeding: Six to nine creamy eggs laid in tree hole lined with down and feathers. Incubation 30 days, by female alone.

Range: Breeds from northern Scandinavia right across northern Palearctic in boreal zone. Large numbers winter in Pacific region around Japan. In Europe most winter at mouth of Baltic and in Holland. Hard weather moves birds westward as far as southern England.

Female and immature birds of both sexes are jointly referred to as 'redheads', which is somewhat confusing as there is a diving duck bearing this name in America, and other sawbills are also red-headed in female and immature plumages. Flocks in Holland may number up to 10,000 individuals, a remarkable sight as they bob over the waves of the Ijsselmeer.

pp.82 & 85 **Red-breasted Merganser** *Mergus serrator*

Description: 51–61 cm (20–24 in). Large, streamlined duck, with long, thin, serrated bill ideally suited to grasping slippery fish. Male has grey flanks and black back separated by *bold white slash* visible at great distances. Head black, washed metallic green; neck white, with *breast-band of buff speckled black*. Most obvious feature at close range is *ragged crest* that extends horizontally from hind crown. Female grey with rust-

red head extending to ragged crest. In
flight both sexes show white on inner
wing

Voice: Wheezing and rattling calls during
courtship; otherwise silent.

Habitat: Large rivers, lakes and pools among tundra
and conifer forests. Also on sheltered sea
inlets such as fjords. In winter, mainly
marine in sheltered bays and estuaries, but
also upstream on larger rivers.

Breeding: 7–12 buffy eggs laid in down-lined hollow
well hidden among rocks or dense
vegetation near water. Incubation 29–35
days, by female alone.

Range: Circumpolar in tundra and boreal zones. In
Europe, breeds from Iceland and Britain
eastwards through Scandinavia. In winter,
locally distributed as far south as Portugal
and Greece.

Mainly a fish eater, the Merganser uses both
wings and feet when swimming underwater
and is extremely adept at catching even
fast-swimming species such as trout and
salmon parr. It is seldom regarded as
anything but an enemy by fishermen and is
persecuted as a result.

pp.83 & 85 **Goosander** *Mergus merganser*

Description: 57–69 cm (22½–27 in). Largest of the
'sawbill' ducks. Male white with *pinkish
wash,* particularly on breast. Dark head
washed metallic green and boasts *smooth
crest* at rear of crown. Female grey, with
rufous-chestnut head that is same shape as
male's. Smooth crest of both sexes contrasts
with ragged crest of similar Red-breasted
Merganser. In flight both sexes show white
on inner wing .

Voice: Both male and female produce a variety of
croaking calls during courtship, but are
silent for the rest of the year.

Habitat: Found mostly on fresh water at all seasons.
Lakes and large rivers mostly among
forested country, particularly conifer, but
also in more open tundra locations. In
winter, maintains preference for fresh

waters, frequenting lakes, reservoirs, barrages and gravel pits.

Breeding: 8–11 creamy eggs laid in down-lined hole in tree, among rocks or in dense vegetation. Incubation 32–35 days, by female alone.

Range: Circumpolar in northern boreal and tundra zones; also southwards on Himalayan plateau. Winters south of breeding range and, in Europe, from Iceland in a line southeastwards to former Yugoslavia.

The shortage of suitable nest holes in trees often leads to two females laying in a single nest and even to laying in the nests of other species. In Finland, the provision of nest boxes has been rewarded with a 63 per cent take-up rate by these birds, a fact that does not endear the local conservationists to fishermen.

p.81 **Ruddy Duck** *Oxyura jamaicensis*

Description: 36–43 cm (14–17 in). An American duck that has been introduced to Europe over the past 30 years and prospered. Male typical 'stifftail' with long tail held vertically, or invisible at water level, giving the bird a curious weight-forward appearance. In summer, body is rich chestnut and head is white, with *black cap that extends to eye*; bill bright blue. In winter, buff-bodied with dark bill. Female brownish at all seasons, with dark cap and prominent facial bar that closely resembles female White-headed Duck. Shows silvery underwing in flight.

Voice: Various hisses and grunts produced by both sexes during courtship.

Habitat: Lakes, ponds and marshes in breeding season, but larger waters in winter.

Breeding: Six to ten white eggs laid in substantial nest of vegetation placed among reeds. Incubation 20–21 days, by female alone.

Range: Breeds naturally in western North and South America. Introduced to Britain in Gloucestershire in 1960s; has since spread, reaching the Continent in the 1980s.

The introduction of alien species regularly causes problems, particularly in isolated and fragile landscapes. Only in the late 1980s was it realized that the expanding population of Ruddy Ducks posed a threat to the highly endangered White-headed Duck of southern Europe. Through hybridization this native European bird could be wiped out and, at present, ornithologists and conservationists are debating the appropriate course of action. So Nero fiddles while Rome burns.

---

p.81 **White-headed Duck** *Oxyura leucocephala*

Description: 43–48 cm (17–19 in). Native 'stifftail' duck. Both sexes buffy brown. Male has white head with small *black cap that does not extend to eye,* and bulging, pale-blue bill. Female has dark cap extending to eye, bold dark stripe across face, similar to female Ruddy Duck. Bill shape and bolder facial stripe are major distinctions.

Voice: Male makes winding and piping calls, female a quiet *gek*.

Habitat: Shallow lakes and pools with extensive growth of emergent vegetation including marginal reeds and reed-beds. Such lakes easily dry out during Mediterranean summer. Largely resident.

Breeding: 5–12 white eggs laid in substantial, reed-lined nest of aquatic vegetation, usually over water. Incubation 25–27 days by female.

Range: Highly fragmented, precarious populations from Spain and Black Sea to Russian steppes. Largely resident and highly localized in Iberia, but large numbers of presumed Russian birds winter on lakes of southwestern Turkey. World population *c.*15,000.

Active conservation measures in Spain only just saved this duck in its major European stronghold during the 1980s. Having now built up numbers from the danger level, the species once again faces extinction through interbreeding with the fast-colonizing, alien Ruddy Duck.

EAGLES, BUZZARDS, HAWKS AND VULTURES (Accipitridae)

217 species; worldwide. Twenty-seven species breed in Europe. Species vary enormously in size from the small sparrowhawks to the enormous vultures, which are among the largest of all living birds. These are large-winged birds that soar easily. They have strong legs with large powerful talons for grabbing prey, and strongly hooked bills for tearing it apart. Most are coloured in subdued shades of brown; some share very similar plumage and are among the most difficult of all birds to identify. Shape, particularly, in the air, is usually more important than coloration. While many species are highly opportunistic in their feeding habits, others are highly specialized or seasonally specialized. Most are solitary breeders, though some gather in large, wheeling flocks on migration. Overall Europe's rapacious birds have experienced a serious decline during the twentieth century, a decline that mostly continues and may see the extinction of some species within the young birder's lifetime.

p.96 **Honey Buzzard** *Pernis apivorus*

Description: 50–58 cm (19½–23 in). Medium-sized, broad-winged hawk, like Common Buzzard but longer, slimmer and more angular, with distinctive *small head on long neck* creating pigeon-like appearance. Long tail has three well-defined bars. Wings rounded and definitely 'waisted' where they join the body, held drooping while soaring. Underwing always heavily and *regularly barred*. Occurs in pale and dark phases. Unique butterfly-like display flight over territory in early part of breeding season.

Voice: Shrill *kee-aa* or *kee-uu*.

Habitat: Frequents extensive mature woodland, mostly deciduous, but also mixed, and sometimes stands of pure conifers.

Breeding: One to three white eggs generously speckled reddish, laid in nest of sticks in tall

tree, sometimes in old nest of Carrion Crow.
Incubation 30–35 days, mainly by female.

Range: Almost confined to western Palearctic,
breeding throughout Europe save for most of
Britain and northwestern Scandinavia.
Summer visitor to Europe, wintering in
Africa south of Sahara.

This is generally a stronger flier than most
other migrant soaring birds of prey. As a
result, it is less confined to the two major
sea-crossings and regularly occurs on
Mediterranean islands where other migrant
raptors are unknown. Its passage through
Tunisia and Sicily to Italy makes it prime
game for Sicilian hunters, in total
contravention of EC and Italian laws.

pp.98 & 100 **Black-shouldered Kite** *Elanus caeruleus*

Description: 31–35 cm (12–14 in). Small, delicately
patterned, grey and black hawk. Basically
grey above and white below, with large
black patches at carpal joint and bold-black
wingtips. Large, almost *owl-like head* and
short, notched tail are characteristic.
Hovers like a kestrel on *sharply pointed
wings,* but spends most of its time sitting
atop a telegraph pole, pylon or dead tree.
Voice: Various weak whistles.
Habitat: Open, park-like groves, particularly of olives
but also cork oaks, broken by dry open areas.
Breeding: Three to four cream-coloured eggs blotched
with brown and grey, laid in nest of twigs
in outer branches of low tree. Such nests are
used for several years in succession.
Incubation 25–28 days, by female alone.
Range: Widespread through Africa, India and
Southeast Asia; in Europe confined to
Iberia. Mainly resident, though African
breeders move northward to edge of Sahara
to winter.

Thirty years ago it was said that the Black-
shouldered Kite perhaps bred in Portugal.
Today some 50 pairs breed in Portugal and
Spain, mainly in Extremadura and
Alentejo. Whether this is an increase, or

merely the result of more intensive observation, it is impossible to say. These are easily overlooked birds that are best sought at dawn and dusk.

---

pp.98 & 100 **Black Kite** *Milvus migrans*

Description: 53–59 cm (21–23 in). Large, dark raptor with *long angular wings and long, slightly forked tail.* Dark-brown coloration that is paler on upperwing coverts, and angular build, eliminate all other European birds o prey except female and immature Marsh Harrier. Black Kite flies on bowed, not upswept, wings and uses tail in circling an twisting flight. Small head and bill obviou when perched.

Voice: High-pitched squeals and chattering during breeding season.

Habitat: Variable from open country with woodland clumps and belts to towns and villages. Often found at rubbish tips and along rivers, where it scavenges for food.

Breeding: Two to three cream-coloured eggs, blotche with brown, laid in twiggy nest in high tree, often near the trunk. Incubation 25–28 days, by female alone.

Range: Found throughout Old World. From Europe to Pacific it is a common summer visitor; resident from Japan to Asia, Australia and Africa. Most authorities regard African Black Kite, which has a yellow bill, as a separate species.

At Gibraltar and the Bosphorus, this is often the dominant migrant bird of prey, passing in hundreds per day during peak periods. In India the bird is so common that it is often run over by traffic and will scavenge around people while they eat.

---

pp.98 & 100 **Red Kite** *Milvus milvus*

Description: 58–64 cm (23–25 in). Large, slim bird of prey, with long angular wings and long tai similar to Black Kite, but coloration and *deeply forked tail* quite distinct. Rich rufo body and inner wings contrast with black flight feathers and almost white head. Underwing shows *white patches at base of primaries*. Forked tail rufous and virtually translucent against the light.

Voice: Repeated *he-ha-heea* similar to, but higher pitched than, Common Buzzard.

Habitat: Deciduous woodland and forests with open ground. Also parkland and open country with woodland clumps or breaks.

Breeding: Two to three white eggs, spotted with red, laid in nest of twigs usually constructed on the base of an old nest of a Carrion Crow or hawk. Incubation 28–30 days, by female alone.

Range: Almost the entire world population is found in Europe. Breeds from Wales to Southern Scandinavia and from Portugal to Black Sea. Northern and eastern birds are summer visitors, but only a few cross either the Bosphorus or Gibraltar.

A catastrophic decline due to direct persecution by shooting and poisoning was halted during the twentieth century, though not before the Red Kite was eliminated from the whole of England and Scotland. Reintroduction schemes have seen Red Kites breeding in both countries for the first time in almost 100 years, though it will take a long time for these birds to reach the abundance they enjoyed during the sixteenth and seventeenth centuries.

pp.92 & 95 **White-tailed Eagle** *Haliaeetus albicilla*

Description: 69–71 cm (27–28 in). Huge eagle marked by large wings, head and bill, and *short, wedge-shaped tail*. In flight, long, broad wings are dominant feature. Full adult plumage brown with pale, almost white, head and *white tail*. Immature uniformly dark brown with no more than pale centres to tail feathers. Associated with water at all seasons. Regularly perches on ground; thus, from a distance, it resembles an old tree stump.

Voice: Loud, far-carrying *kok-kok-kok* during courtship.

Habitat: Rocky coasts and islands, extensive marshes, large rivers and lakes. In winter occupies similar terrain, plus large reservoirs and barrages.

Breeding: Two white eggs laid on huge grass-lined platform of sticks in tree or cliff. Incubation 34–45 days, by both sexes.

Range: Breeds right across Palearctic from Scandinavia and Baltic to Bering Straits. In Europe, highly fragmented range due to persecution and habitat destruction. Strongest population along coasts of Norway. Eastern birds migrate, some reaching France.

The reintroduction of this magnificent fish-eating eagle to Scotland after an absence of 80 years has yet to prove a total success, though several pairs now breed annually. The conflict in Serbia and Croatia during the 1990s doubtless took its toll on what was previously a major European stronghold.

p.88 **Lammergeier** *Gypaetus barbatus*

Description: 100–115 cm (39½–45½ in). Huge vulture marked by long, pointed wings and *long, wedge-shaped tail*. Adult has golden head and body with slate-grey wings and tail. Face has black extending from eye to bill, where extended feathers cascade to form a 'beard' (hence its former name, Bearded Vulture). Immatures are brown, speckled white, rather than golden.

Voice: High-pitched scream in display, otherwise silent.

Habitat: Confined to high mountain fastnesses where disturbance is minimal: high cliff-faces, gorges and screes with wild mammals and domestic stock.

Breeding: One to two white eggs laid on platform of sticks sheltered well inside a cave in a precipitous cliff-face. Incubation 53 days, by female alone.

Range: Breeds in South Africa and Ethiopia, and from Turkey eastwards through mountains of Middle East to Himalayas. In Europe now

confined to Pyrenees (30 pairs), Corsica (5 pairs), Greece (3 pairs) and Crete (5 pairs).

Over the past 30 years the Greek population has been all but wiped out. How long can it survive elsewhere? Lammergeiers are unique in feeding mostly on the bones that remain after other vultures have picked them clean. Their habit of dropping bones to break them on rocks has been documented in Greece since 4,000 BC.

p.88 **Egyptian Vulture** *Neophron percnopterus*

Description: 60–70 cm (23½–27½ in). A boldly *black and white bird* and the smallest of the European vultures. Adult white, with bare, yellow face surmounted by tuft of feathers forming ragged crest. In the air all flight feathers are black, contrasting with white linings. Only Booted Eagle in its pale phase shares this pattern, but Egyptian Vulture differs in *wedge-shaped tail and tiny, pointed head.* Immatures similar in shape, but coloured in variable shades of brown.

Voice: A quiet mewing during the breeding season.

Habitat: Open countryside, though progressively confined to more mountainous areas with cliffs and gorges. A scavenger that is running out of scavengable material in an ever-tidier Europe.

Breeding: Two white eggs, blotched with brown, laid on cliff ledge lined with variable mass of debris that now includes rags, wool and polythene. Incubation 42 days, by both sexes.

Range: Breeds in Iberia and Greece, and in isolated pockets in between. A summer visitor that crosses into Europe at Gibraltar and Bosphorus, it numbers not much more than 2,000 pairs. Also breeds across Sahelian region of Africa and through Middle East to India.

This is the snapper-up of unconsidered trifles, having waited around the fringes of a vulture feast until the larger species have finished. It picks at bones, swallows strips of skin and will consume all manner of unmentionables from around villages and towns. It is an adaptable bird that has learned to break Ostrich eggs with stones, but it is unlikely to adapt to a tidy Europe without help.

---

p.89 **Griffon Vulture** *Gyps fulvus*

Description: 95–105 cm (37½–41½ in). Huge vulture with long, broad wings, and *small head and tail*. Basic plumage pattern buff-brown, with black wings and tail. Head white and woolly forming obvious ruff around base of neck. Contrast between *buffy coverts and bla flight feathers* precludes confusion with any other vulture, but see juvenile Imperial and Spanish Imperial Eagles. Long neck often extended when disputing food on the ground. Immature darker and less buffy.

Voice: Usually silent, but various hisses and growls when disputing food.

Habitat: Formerly more widespread, but progressively confined to mountain region with cliffs and gorges that offer feeding opportunities over adjacent lowlands.

Breeding: Single white egg laid on cliff ledge or inside cave with no more than a little debr to act as a nest. Incubation 48–54 days, by both sexes. Colonial.

Range: Breeds across southern Palearctic from Portugal to Turkey, Middle East and northern India. Mostly resident, though Turkish birds migrate. In Europe some 5,000 pairs concentrated mainly in Spain, but with good populations still in Crete.

Changes in traditional agricultural practices in the Mediterranean region over the past 50 years, especially the decline in the number of mules and donkeys, has seriously reduced the scavenging opportunities for vultures. The widespread use of the pick-up, as a substitute offers nothing for vultures. As a result these bird are becoming increasingly dependent on artificial food dumps provided by conservationists.

p.89 **Black Vulture** *Aegypius monachus*

Description: 100–110 cm (39½–43½ in). Largest of all
Old World vultures and *uniformly dark* in
coloration. Close approach reveals brownish
wash on all-black bird. Wings are long,
broad and almost square tipped. Bald head
small, pale and surrounded by neck ruff;
tail short and distinctly wedge-shaped. Though
immature Griffon Vulture is darker than
adult, there should be no confusion
between the species given reasonable views.
Soars effortlessly.

Voice: Aggressive croaks and hisses when
disputing food; otherwise silent.

Habitat: Open countryside with large trees for
nesting. As with other vultures,
progressively confined to wild upland areas,
though not dependent on cliffs and gorges
like other species.

Breeding: Single white egg laid in substantial nest of
sticks used year after year and added to
every season. Incubation 48–54 days, by
both sexes. As fledging takes over 100 days,
Black Vultures spend half their year rearing
their single youngster.

Range: Resident through huge range extending
across southern Palearctic from Spain and
Greece to northern China. In Europe
confined to central Spain, Majorca and
Greece, with a total of probably less than
300 pairs.

Although it is the largest and most
powerful of the vultures, this species is
nowhere common. Nests may be grouped
quite close together, but it is never truly
colonial like the Griffon. Feeding stations
are an essential conservation tool as Europe
becomes progressively more tidy.

pp.98 & 100 **Marsh Harrier** *Circus aeruginosus*

Description: 48–56 cm (19–22 in). Largest of the
harriers, with typical flap-and-glide flight
low over the ground on upswept wings.
Long narrow wings and long tail shared
with other harriers. Male brown, paler on

head, with contrasting *grey flight feathers* and
tail. Younger males show less grey than
older birds. Female and immatures dark
brown marked by *creamy-white crown* and, in
adult female, by creamy-white forewing.
Larger and bulkier than other harriers and
more confined to wetlands.

Voice: A high-pitched *kee-aa* in courtship.

Habitat: Extensive marshes, with large reed-beds,
are used in summer. In winter more
widespread, especially on estuaries, coastal
grazing marshes and floods.

Breeding: Four to five bluish-white eggs laid on
platform of reeds or other available
vegetation, usually hidden among dense
reeds over water. Incubation 33–38 days,
by female alone. The 'food-pass' in flight,
from male to female, is common to all
harriers.

Range: Summer visitor to most of Palearctic,
though western European birds are largely
resident. Winters in sub-Saharan Africa and
Asia. Resident in Australasia. Highly
fragmented European distribution due
partly to specific habitat requirements, but
also to direct persecution.

The expansion of a Marsh Harrier
population, following successful
conservation measures, may lead to an
enforced change of habitat. In England,
such measures have seen the population
boom from an all-time low of three birds.
As a result these harriers have now adapted
to nesting in cereal fields as well as the
much scarcer reed-beds.

pp.99 & 101   **Hen Harrier** *Circus cyaneus*

Description: 43–51 cm (17–20 in). The largest of the
grey-male, brown-female harriers, and
considerably more bulky than either
Montagu's or Pallid Harriers. Male *grey
above, white below, marked by black wingtips
and white rump*. Female brown with barred
underwing and broad white rump,
distinguished from other female harriers by
broader white rump and darker, more uniform

face with neat, pale, facial 'collar'. With experience, it is easy to pick out the heavier build of Hen Harrier, but always check plumage features.

Voice: Chattering *chick-ik-ik-ik*; also high-pitched plaintive *wee-aa*.

Habitat: Moorland, especially with young plantations of conifers, coastal marshes and steppes. More widespread in winter over heaths, scrub and adjacent land.

Breeding: Four to six pale-blue eggs laid in hollow lined with grasses. Incubation 29–39 days, by female alone.

Range: The world's most widespread harrier, absent only from Africa and Australasia. Called Northern Harrier in North America. In Europe a summer visitor to north and east, and widespread winter visitor to south and west where it breeds as far south as northern Spain.

Like other harriers, this bird quarters the ground, flying low in a flap-flap-glide, to surprise its prey. Mostly it takes small mammals, but it also attacks small birds and the chicks of larger species. As these include the young of several gamebirds, it is regarded as the enemy of gamekeepers, whose role it is to maintain an artificially high population of birds for their masters to shoot.

pp.99 & 101 **Pallid Harrier** *Circus macrourus*

Description: 41–48 cm (16–19 in). About the same size and bulk as Montagu's, but substantially lighter in build than Hen Harrier. Male grey above, with *diamond-shaped black wingtips,* and white below. Female brown above and below, broken by narrow white rump. *Facial pattern* is best means of distinguishing it from other female harriers. Pallid has pale facial 'collar' extending from supercilium, with dark ear coverts enclosing white beneath eye. This is more complex (and obvious) than 'faces' of either Montagu's or Hen Harriers and can be clearly seen even in flight.

Voice: A chattering *kee-kee-kee* and wailing *preeee*.

Habitat: Essentially a steppe bird of grassy plains that has, inevitably, turned to crops of cereals to a limited extent. Also frequents floods and marshes.

Breeding: Four to five pale-blue eggs laid in tussock lined with grass among grassy fields or light scrub. Incubation 28–30 days, by female alone.

Range: Summer visitor to eastern Europe. Breeds from northeastern Bulgaria eastwards across Russian steppes to south-central Siberia. Migrates to winter in savannah Africa south of Sahara and in India. A few winter locally in Greece. Decidedly scarce west of breeding range.

The migrations of Pallid Harriers follow two distinct routes southeast and southwest. The actual migrational divide between these two populations remains unknown. Western birds mostly follow the rift valley through Israel and Jordan to the Nile in Egypt, thence southwards before spreading westwards as far as Senegal: a journey of 8,000 km (5,000 miles).

pp.99 & 101 **Montagu's Harrier** *Circus pygargus*

Description: 39–46 cm (15½–18 in). Lightly built harrier. Male grey above, with black wing-tips and *black bar across wing*. White underparts boldly *streaked chestnut*. Female brown with narrow, white rump. Face pattern differs from other harriers in having white below eye and contrasting dark ear coverts, but *lacking facial 'collar'*.

Voice: High-pitched chattering *kek-kek-kek* in courtship.

Habitat: Open grassy plains, heaths, crops of cereals, and freshwater marshes.

Breeding: Four to five bluish eggs laid on platform of available vegetation – typically reeds, grasses or stems – on the ground, often on hummock or ridge. Incubation 27–40 days by female alone.

Range: Summer visitor to south and temperate Europe. Breeds right across temperate

Europe to Russia and central Siberia.
Winters in savannah Africa and India. In
Europe has patchy distribution except in
Spain where it is locally abundant.

The English name of this bird stems from
the work of George Montagu, a disgraced
former lieutenant-colonel in the Wiltshire
militia, who discovered in 1803 that the
grey harriers were not, as previously
thought, a single species, but rather the
males of two species, Montagu's and Hen.
It was named in his honour by
MacGillivray in 1836, though Montagu
died in 1815.

---

p.102 **Goshawk** *Accipiter gentilis*

Description: 48–58 cm (19–23 in). Large, powerful,
round-winged hawk. Female considerably
larger than male. Both sexes have rounded
wings and long tails and fly in typical
accipiter fashion, with fast dashes through
cover to secure prey and, while soaring, a
series of wingbeats followed by circling
glide on still wings. Male grey above, the
larger female brown. Both closely barred
dark grey below. Main feature is large size,
with consequent slower wingbeats than
Sparrowhawk, *deep chest and bulging
secondaries*. Often shows powder-puff of
white at base of undertail. A small male
Goshawk is little bigger than a large female
Sparrowhawk.
Voice: Loud, chattering *gek-gek-gek* in early part of
breeding season only.
Habitat: Extensive forests, both deciduous and
coniferous, with clearings and open
margins. Also copses in more open areas.
Breeding: Two to three pale-blue eggs laid in large
cup constructed of twigs and placed high
up next to trunk of substantial tree.
Incubation 36–41 days, by female.
Range: Circumpolar in northern forest zones.
Breeds throughout Europe with recent
colonization and spread in Britain by
escaped falconers' birds. Largely resident.
Nowhere common.

A female Goshawk is as large as a Common Buzzard, and a fearsome predator quite capable of downing birds as large as a pheasant or grouse. It often adopts a falcon-like diving approach when attacking pigeons, but will also jink among trees in pursuit of woodland birds. In some areas both chicken and rabbits feature largely in the diet.

p.103 **European Sparrowhawk** *Accipiter nisus*

Description: 28–38 cm (11–15 in). Agile, *round-winged* hawk with *long tail;* adept hunter both among dense woodland and through ground cover. Male grey above, barred rufous below; female brown above, barred grey below. Both show clearly barred tail and soar with series of fast flaps between glides. The lighter build, particularly depth of chest, and faster wingbeats while soaring, are best means of distinguishing it from the similar Goshawk. The smaller Levant Sparrowhawk is a very different bird.

Voice: Loud *kek-kek-kek.*

Habitat: Woodland of both deciduous and coniferous trees as well as open farmland broken by belts and copses. Often uses farm buildings to hide its approach to prey, flying low over the ground, even along ditches.

Breeding: Four to five white eggs, liberally blotched with rust, laid in stick nest situated high in a tree. Incubation 42 days, by female alone.

Range: Breeds right across Palearctic, from Atlantic to Bering Straits and southwards to Himalayas. European birds resident, except those breeding in northern Scandinavia. Siberian birds migrate south to Asia.

Since it feeds mostly on small birds, the Sparrowhawk was severely affected by pesticide poisoning during the 1960s; in many areas it was wiped out. A slow recovery saw a return to former territories and numbers during the 1980s. Today it is probably as common as at any time during the twentieth century.

p.103 **Levant Sparrowhawk** *Accipiter brevipes*

Description: 32–38 cm (12½–15 in). The same size and
shape as European Sparrowhawk, but quite
different in plumage. Male grey above,
with finely barred pinkish breast. Female
grey-brown, with more coarsely barred
dirty-pink breast that extends across
underwing coverts. Both sexes have
distinctive white underwing and *black tips
to more pointed wings,* precluding confusion
with the more widespread European
Sparrowhawk. Could be confused with
similarly pale Lesser Kestrel, though latter
has narrow wings and broad terminal tail-
band.

Voice: Shrill *kee-wick*.

Habitat: Extensive deciduous woodland and wooded
river valleys.

Breeding: Four to five lightly spotted, blue-white
eggs laid in neat twig nest high in a tree.
Incubation 30–35 days, by female alone.

Range: Summer visitor to Balkans and Greece,
eastwards through Ukraine; thus confined to
relatively small area of western Palearctic.
Nowhere common and probably declining.
Migrates over Bosphorus and may be
numerous, but winter quarters in eastern
Africa remain unknown.

The total European population is certainly
less than the near 6,000 that have been
counted crossing the Bosphorus in autumn.
No doubt some Ukraine birds take this
westerly route around the Black Sea. Birds
also tend to move through in a rush in mid-
September, when over 2,000 have been
counted in a single day.

p.96 **Common Buzzard** *Buteo buteo*

Description: 50–56 cm (19½–22 in). Highly variable in
plumage and best identified by structure
and flight attitude. Typical birds brown
above, with dark breast forming band with
paler belly. Dark underwing coverts
contrast with pale flight feathers.
However, underwing may be wholly dark

showing only a pale area at base of
primaries; or completely pale, save a dark
patch at carpal joint. In flight, *wings held
in shallow 'V' with small head and well-
spread, shortish tail*. Russian birds – called
Steppe Buzzard *B. b. vulpinus*, are more
rufous with pale-rufous tail and resemble
Long-legged Buzzard.

Voice: High-pitched, far-carrying, mewing *pee-o*

Habitat: Forests and woodlands, agricultural land
with wooded copses and shelter belts,
moorland and cliff-girt coasts. In winter,
also in more open country, including
marshes.

Breeding: Three to four white eggs blotched reddish
laid in neat cup of twigs usually in tree or
on cliff. Incubation 42 days, by female
alone.

Range: Breeds right across Palearctic from Atlantic
to Pacific. Northern and eastern birds are
migratory. In Europe, Scandinavian birds
cross the narrow straits from Falsterbo to
Denmark in late autumn. Many Russian
birds pass over the Bosphorus considerably
earlier to winter through eastern Africa.
Others winter in Asia.

The most common and widespread,
medium to large European raptor. The best
approach is to assume an unknown bird is
Common Buzzard until it can be proved
that it is something more exciting. Thus it
is the 'bench-mark' from which other
soaring raptors must be differentiated.

p.97 **Rough-legged Buzzard** *Buteo lagopus*

Description: 50–61 cm (19½–24 in). Similar in shape
and structure to Common Buzzard, but
hovers more frequently and soars on flat,
not upswept, wings. Brown above, with
pale whitish head. Whitish, streaked
breast and dark belly-patch. Similarly
coloured Common Buzzards show the
reverse pattern: dark breast and pale belly.
In flight, *tail whitish with broad terminal
band*; underwing white with bold, dark,
carpal patches.

Voice: Mews like Common Buzzard.
Habitat: Predominantly tundra-breeding buzzard: open tundra with cliffs and rocky outcrops, occasionally in open forested country at higher altitudes.
Breeding: Two to three white eggs brown-blotched laid in substantial, grass-lined nest of twigs and placed on cliff ledge or outcrop, or in a tree. Incubation 28 days, by female alone.
Range: Winter visitor to most of northeast Europe. Circumpolar in northern latitudes, though absent from Greenland and Iceland. European range confined to Scandinavian mountain chain and far north. Winters from eastern Britain across temperate Europe to Black Sea, as well as eastwards across southern Siberia to northern Japan.

The appearance of this Arctic raptor in temperate Europe depends entirely on the population of lemmings, which is cyclical and reaches peaks every five or six years. When these small mammals erupt, Rough-legged Buzzards have no choice but to follow. In more normal years they may be scarce in their winter quarters.

p.97 **Long-legged Buzzard** *Buteo rufinus*

Description: 50–65 cm (19½–25½ in). Very similar to Common Buzzard, especially the eastern subspecies known as Steppe Buzzard *B. b. vulpinus*. At rest it is brown above and below with paler creamy head. In flight, white flight feathers contrast with *rufous wing linings* and dark carpal patches. Head and breast creamy, belly dark brown, and *tail unbarred pinkish*. Dark belly and rufous wing linings are best field marks; larger and longer winged than Steppe Buzzard.
Voice: A brief mewing, similar to Common Buzzard.
Habitat: Steppes, plains, open hillsides, mainly drier and with fewer trees than preferred by Common Buzzard.
Breeding: Two to three, brown-blotched white eggs laid in substantial nest of sticks placed on

rock outcrop or on the ground. Incubation minimum of 28 days; the role of the sexes unknown.

Range: Southern replacement of Common Buzzard, resident in southeastern Europe. Breeds from Morocco to Greece, Cyprus, Bulgaria, Romania, and Turkey, eastwards across steppes of southern Siberia. European and Siberian birds are summer visitors.

Although the European population of this species is probably under 100 pairs, its virtual absence from the classic migration watchpoints is confusing. No doubt it is often overlooked among the more abundant Steppe Buzzards and there is some doubt about reports of birds in Tunisia and along the eastern shores of the Black Sea. Nevertheless, these birds must move through either the Bosphorus or Tunisia and, in the latter, are more likely than Steppe Buzzard.

pp.90 & 94 **Lesser Spotted Eagle** *Aquila pomarina*

Description: 60–65 cm (23½–25½ in). Medium-sized eagle, easily confused with Steppe, Spotted and Imperial Eagles. Lesser Spotted is all-dark, marked by prominent head and substantial tail to give neatly proportioned appearance. In flight adult shows small white patches at base of primaries on upperwing and narrow white horseshoe on rump. Juvenile has wider rump-patch and additional white line along secondary coverts joining bold white wing-patch. In all plumages, *coverts paler than flight feathers*. Length of *tail over half the width of wing*. Spotted Eagle has coverts same dark colour as flight feathers, or even darker, and tail is only a third of wing width.

Voice: High-pitched, dog-like yapping.
Habitat: Extensive woodlands, often among hills. In winter haunts savannahs.
Breeding: Two white eggs, spotted reddish brown, laid in twig nest in a tree near woodland

edge. Incubation 40–45 days, by female alone.

Range: Virtually confined to eastern Europe, extending into westernmost Russia. Winters in eastern Africa. A separate population is resident in northern India.

Most of the European population of Lesser Spotted Eagles crosses the Bosphorus twice each year. In September, the spectacle of over 1,000 a day circling as they pass from Europe is one of the highlights of 'Eurobirding'. The total of just under 20,000 birds gives the best estimate of the European breeding population, i.e. about 7,000 pairs. Eastern breeders pass around the eastern shores of the Black Sea.

---

pp.90 & 94 **Spotted Eagle** *Aquila clanga*

Description: 67–72 cm (26½–28½ in). Much broader winged than similarly dark Lesser Spotted Eagle and shows reverse pattern of *dark coverts and pale flight feathers* in all plumages. Adult has narrow, white horseshoe on rump and small white patch at base of primaries on upperwing. Juvenile has more prominent rump and wing patches, plus three rows of white spots across wing coverts. The *short, rounded tail is only a third of wing width*, and secondaries show prominent obvious bulge.

Voice: Dog-like barking, slightly lower pitched than Lesser Spotted.

Habitat: Woodlands associated with wetlands, especially along seasonally flooded rivers and among extensive marshes. More widespread in winter, but still usually near water.

Breeding: Two grey, sometimes spotted, eggs laid in substantial twig nest in forest tree. Incubation 42–44 days, by female alone.

Range: Summer visitor to extreme east of Europe. Breeds from Poland eastwards right across Palearctic to Sea of Japan. Winters from China to India and in Middle East and Turkey. European birds, perhaps 30 pairs in

Poland, Finland and Baltic states, winter in northern Greece and European Turkey, and in Po Valley of northern Italy.

Surprisingly few Spotted Eagles have been identified crossing the Bosphorus or, come to that, around the eastern shores of the Black Sea. However, in 1994, a radio-tagged individual was tracked from Yemen via Tehran and the Aral sea to its presumed breeding grounds near Omsk.

pp.90 & 94 **Steppe Eagle** *Aquila nipalensis*

Description: 67–87 cm (26½–34 in). Large, well-proportioned, all-dark eagle. Uniformly dark adult shows no distinguishing plumage features. In flight, *short inner primaries create distinct dent on trailing edge of wing*. Juvenile has tawny-rufous underwing coverts contrasting with black flight feathers and separated by bold, white, mid wing line. Black tail, tipped white. In this plumage Steppe resembles immature Imperial Eagle, but latter much more buff on coverts. Sheer size should prevent confusion with similarly dark, Spotted and Lesser Spotted Eagles.

Voice: Harsh *caw-caw*.

Habitat: Dry, open, lowland steppes and semi-desert; avoids mountains.

Breeding: One to three white eggs, sometimes lightly spotted, laid in nest of twigs and other available materials on the ground, or on haystack or deserted building. Incubation takes about 45 days, by female.

Range: Breeds from near Black Sea eastwards across the steppes to central and eastern Siberia. Winters in Middle East and India. Rare vagrant westwards across continental Europe.

The Steppe Eagle has only recently split from the Tawny Eagle to be classified as a separate species, even though the two are quite different in appearance. Steppe Eagles regularly migrate around, through and over the Himalayas, the world's highest mountains. Some have even been observed flying over Everest at 8,840 m (29,000 ft).

pp.91 & 94	**Spanish Imperial Eagle** *Aquila adalberti*
Description:	75–83 cm (30–33 in). Large, dark eagle of impressive proportions, that flies on stiff, straight and level wings with consummate ease. Adult all dark, marked by white crown and nape, *white 'braces' and white leading edge to wing,* visible at considerable distance. Juvenile tawny below and above with contrasting dark flight feathers. Upper surface shows bold white rump and white line along wing coverts, pale inner primary patch visible above and below.
Voice:	Dog-like *yowk-yowk-yowk.*
Habitat:	Woodlands among dunes and marshes, but more typically among hills and mountains.
Breeding:	Two white eggs, spotted brown, laid in tree nest that is used year after year and reaches staggering proportions. Incubation some 43 days, by both sexes.
Range:	Confined to Spain, though formerly also in Portugal and Morocco; largely resident with some juvenile wandering.

The species has recently split from Imperial Eagle, from which it differs mainly in showing white along the leading edge of the adult wing. Though their usual ranges are separated by virtually 1,600 km (1,000 miles), recent occurrences of Imperial Eagle in Italy indicate that a meeting between the two species is far from impossible.

pp.91 & 94	**Imperial Eagle** *Aquila heliaca*
Description:	72–80 cm (28½–31½ in). Large, dark eagle, very similar to Spanish Imperial Eagle though averages a little smaller. Adult shows same pale golden crown and *white braces,* but *lacks white leading edge to wing.* Juvenile has tawny coverts contrasting with

black flight feathers and pale inner
primaries; above shows broad, white rump
and narrow, white, mid-wing bar.
Confusable only with rare juvenile Steppe
Eagle and distinguishable from similar-
aged Spanish Imperial Eagle by heavily
streaked underparts.

Voice: Crow-like *yowk-yowk-yowk*.

Habitat: Wooded parkland and marshes; steppes and
plains with trees.

Breeding: Two or three white eggs, spotted brown,
laid in substantial nest in either deciduous
or conifer tree. Incubation 43 days, mostly
by female.

Range: From central Europe eastwards through
steppes of Siberia. Resident in Balkans, but
most migrate southwards to winter in
Middle East, India and China. Decidedly
rare and in need of conservation in Europe.

Though it is a strongly built and
formidable eagle, the Imperial regularly
avoids competition with both Golden and
Steppe Eagles where their ranges overlap.
It thus avoids both mountains and bare
steppes, confining itself to lightly wooded
lowlands and hill districts. It is a confiding
eagle that regularly allows a close
approach, particularly in winter, and is
easily shot as a result.

pp.91 & 95 **Golden Eagle** *Aquila chrysaetos*

Description: 76–90 cm (30–35½ in). Huge, powerful,
dark eagle of distinctive structure and
flight. Adult dark brown marked by *golden
crown, nape and upperwing coverts*. Juvenile
lacks gold colour, but has white tail with
broad terminal band, and broad white bar
across underwing, boldest at base of
primaries. In flight, prominent, aquiline
head, *wings 'waisted'* where they join body
and held in *noticeable 'V' when soaring*, and
large tail are sure means of identification in
all plumages. Quarters hillsides like a
harrier.

Voice: Yelping *kaa* and *yo-yo-yo*, but generally less
vocal than other eagles.

Habitat: Mainly mountains with cliffs and gorges, but also wild lowlands and forests where not persecuted.

Breeding: Two white eggs, boldly blotched rufous-brown, laid in substantial structure of sticks that is added to each year. Each territory has two or more traditional nests that may be used in different years. Incubation 43–45 days, usually by female; only a single eaglet is reared.

Range: Circumpolar in northern forest zones. In Europe resident mainly in mountain and hill regions and thus somewhat fragmented. Northern birds move southwards in winter.

This is a magnificent eagle that sails majestically over high mountains and along fearsome cliffs in its search mainly for mammals such as rabbits and hares. It is, however, also a scavenger, and its taking of sheep afterbirths and stillborn lambs has brought it into conflict with farmers. Despite persecution it is still probably the world's most numerous *Aquila* eagle species.

pp.93 & 95 **Short-toed Eagle** *Circaetus gallicus*

Description: 62–67 cm (24½–26½ in). Medium-sized, snake-eating eagle, grey-brown above and barred white below; one of the easiest of all eagles to identify. In flight *pale body, with darker head and pale underwing* cannot, given good views, be confused with any other European raptor. Its propensity to hover or hang on the wind, coupled with a flat-faced, thick-necked appearance, facilitates identification at considerable distance.

Voice: Various mewing and barking calls.

Habitat: Mainly open country with scrub and scattered trees, hillsides, and more extensive forests with adjacent open areas for hunting.

Breeding: Single white egg laid in nest of twigs placed at top of small tree. Incubation 47 days, by female alone.

Range: Breeds right across Europe to western
Siberia and through Middle East, though
absent from much of central Europe.
Winters in Sahelian zone of Africa, and in
India where it also breeds.

This migrant crosses the Mediterranean ov
the two major narrow routes at Gibraltar
and the Bosphorus. This is a snake-eating
eagle marked by a flat, owl-like face, a thic
short neck and strong, heavily scaled legs
and feet. It is closely related to the harrier
eagles of Africa and is sometimes regarded
as conspecific with one or two of them.

---

pp.92 & 95 **Booted Eagle** *Hieraaetus pennatus*

Description: 45–53 cm (17½–21 in). A small, buzzard-
sized eagle that occurs in two distinct
colour phases. Pale phase is white below
and pale grey-brown above. In flight, tail,
body and underwing coverts white,
contrasting with black flight feathers – a
pattern shared only with adult Egyptian
Vulture. Dark phase has pale tail
contrasting with uniform dark-brown boc
and wings. The latter can be confused wit
Common Buzzard, but *prominent head and
tail* of eagle create quite different shape.
Soars on flat wings.

Voice: High-pitched *ki-kii* and a *pi-pi-pi-peu*.
More vocal than most other eagles.

Habitat: Deciduous, coniferous and mixed
woodlands, usually on slopes in hilly
districts, but also in lowlands, with
adjacent open country.

Breeding: One to two white eggs, lightly spotted
brown, laid in substantial stick-and-twig
nest, usually placed high in a forest tree,
occasionally on cliff-face. Incubation 42–
days, by both sexes.

Range: Summer visitor from Atlantic coasts acros
Europe to eastern Siberia. In Europe abser
from centre of continent. Winters in
savannah Africa and India.

The absence of this eagle from central
Europe, from Italy northwards through

Germany to Scandinavia, may be attributed to a migrational divide, which sees western birds migrate through Gibraltar and eastern birds over the Bosphorus. Doubtless, this divide reflects the direction of colonization northwards after the last ice age, rather than the species' elimination from this part of the Continent.

---

pp.92 & 95 **Bonelli's Eagle** *Hieraaetus fasciatus*

Description: 65–72 cm (25½–28½ in). A well-proportioned, medium to large eagle that flies effortlessly on straight, flat wings. Upperparts grey-brown, underparts white with clear streaking on breast. *White patch on upper back,* visible at rest and in flight, is certain means of identification. In flight, *white body contrasts with dark underwing.* Prominent head, good-length tail, and straight, flat wings produce typical eagle silhouette. Juvenile has tawny body and wing coverts, with pale primaries and dark wingtips.

Voice: Plaintive *kee-aoo*; also a *klu-klu-klu* and a shrill whistle.

Habitat: Wooded hillsides and shallow gorges with rocky outcrops, usually among dry scrubby country.

Breeding: Two white eggs, spotted with brown and lilac, laid in substantial nest of sticks used year after year on cliff or large tree. Incubation 42–44 days, by both sexes.

Range: Highly fragmented, with separate populations in Mediterranean basin, India, China and southern Africa, all of which are resident.

These are powerful birds capable of taking substantial prey. Food is captured mostly on the ground, but they can also catch large birds in the air and there are many examples of co-operative hunting techniques where one member of a pair flushes prey that the second then captures. Food is then shared, or taken to the nest for the young.

OSPREYS (PANDIONIDAE)

One species; worldwide. The species breed
in Europe, where it is a summer visitor. Th
is a large bird of prey, with long wings,
small head and bill, and long powerful
talons. The feet have spines that are well
suited to grasping slippery fish – the bird'
staple diet – which it catches by diving, fe
first, into the water. It is a highly specializ
predator that is as at home on an Arctic
river as it is along some tropical shoreline.

pp.93 & 95 **Osprey** *Pandion haliaetus*

Description: 51–59 cm (20–23 in). A large, long-
winged, angular bird of prey that flies,
gull-like, on *bowed wings*. Grey-brown
above, white below, marked by narrow
breast-band of black streaks. Small white
head, ragged crest on hind crown and
prominent dark eye-stripe are obvious wh
perched. In flight, white body and white
underwing marked by *prominent black carp
patches*. Long, narrow, bowed wings are be
distinguishing feature.

Voice: A whistled *chew-chew-chew*.

Habitat: Lakes, ponds, rivers and sheltered sea
coasts; usually, but not invariably, with
adjacent forests or woodland clumps.
Plentiful supply of suitably sized fish is
main essential.

Breeding: Three cream eggs, blotched red-brown, la
in substantial stick nest placed in tree, or
sometimes on cliff or island cliff top. Nes
used year after year. Different populations
show propensity for either tree or cliff.
Incubation 35–38 days, mainly by female

Range: Virtually cosmopolitan. Summer visitor t
north, wintering from tropics southwards
In Europe breeds from Scandinavia and
Germany eastwards, but also on islands ir
western Mediterranean.

The recolonization of Scotland during the
second half of the twentieth century followe
and coincided with, a similar recolonizatior
of Norway from Sweden. These newcomers

are tree nesters, whereas the former British breeders were cliff and castle specialists. It is therefore highly unlikely that Ospreys will return to famous Loch an Eilean, where the last of the former population made their final stand against Booth and other nineteenth-century collectors.

FALCONS (FALCONIDAE)

60 species; worldwide. Ten species breed in Europe. These are among the most attractive and charismatic birds in the world. Long-winged and fast flying, many catch their prey in the air in spectacular stoops. Some are highly gregarious, and some have a remarkable migrant-orientated lifestyle. Most have long, pointed wings, long tails, rounded heads, and powerful legs and talons. Principal prey is birds and insects caught in the air, but some (outside Europe) are bat specialists. Some species are in high demand by falconers whose depredations threaten several populations.

pp.104 & 108 **Lesser Kestrel** *Falcon naumanni*

Description: 29–32 cm (11½–12½ in). Highly gregarious, insect-eating falcon. Male *unspotted brown above*, with long, black-banded grey tail and grey secondaries that, together, create unique upperwing pattern in flight. Female spotted brown above. Male has grey head lacking moustache; female shows only a vestigial one. From below, both sexes much paler, with less barring, than Common Kestrel, and both have *extended, central tail feathers* that protrude to form a distinctive wedge shape. Flight more flickering, with shallow wingbeats, than Common Kestrel; they hover less frequently and feed in the air.
Voice: Screeching *kee-kee-kee*; noisy at colonies.
Habitat: Towns, cliffs and ruins, with plentiful nest holes and surrounding open grasslands.

Breeding: Four to five lightly spotted, white eggs lai
in unlined hole in building or cliff, even i
modern multi-storey blocks. Incubation 2
days, by female.

Range: Summer visitor through Mediterranean to
central Siberia and northern China. Whole
population winters in savannah Africa
involving huge migration by far-eastern
breeders.

These are town-dwelling falcons that hunt
over surrounding open countryside. They
are declining in most areas due (probably)
to pesticides that are successfully reducing
the quantity of prey available. Many
colonies have been abandoned completely,
though the provision of nest boxes may
help to build up colonies where insects
remain abundant.

pp.104 & 108 **Common Kestrel** *Falco tinnunculus*

Description: 33–36 cm (13–14 in). Small, hovering
falcon, and Europe's most common raptor
Male has grey head and tail with heavily
speckled brown back and wings. Head
shows narrow moustache and tail has broa
terminal band. Female heavily speckled
brown above; lacks grey, but shows narrow
moustache. Long *pointed wings and long tai*
Spends much time hovering in search of
terrestrial prey, mainly small mammals.

Voice: Shrill *kee-kee-kee.*

Habitat: Farmland, moorland, coasts, marshes,
woodland, towns, and even city centres.

Breeding: Four to five white eggs, heavily speckled
red-brown, laid in hole or on ledge.
Incubation 27–39 days, mainly by female

Range: Breeds throughout most of Old World fro
Europe to Pacific, through China and
Southeast Asia to Middle East and sub-
Saharan Africa. Northern and eastern
populations are migrants, many winterin
in India.

This highly successful falcon feeds mainly
on mice and voles upon which it drops
vertically after prolonged hovering. It has

however, spread into towns and even the hearts of large cities where, in the absence of small mammals, it has switched to a diet of House Sparrows. Its propensity to hunt motorway margins may be attributed either to the lack of human disturbance (cars are not people) or to the numbers of frightened or injured small mammals.

---

pp.105 & 108 **Red-footed Falcon** *Falco vespertinus*

Description: 28–31 cm (11–12 in). Adult male dark *slate-grey above and below,* marked by red feet and rust-red undertail coverts. Base of bill and eye-ring also red. Female *gingery buff on head and breast,* with dark mark through eye and a faint moustache. Wings and back slate-grey heavily barred black. Juvenile has gingery crown and is streaked below and barred above. Long, pointed wings reach tail tip at rest. Frequently hovers and perches on telegraph wires. Highly gregarious.

Voice: High *kee-kee-kee* uttered by both male and female. Being gregarious at all seasons, these are among the most vocal of all birds of prey.

Habitat: Steppes and open farmland broken by copses and shelter belts.

Breeding: Three to four creamy-buff, speckled red-brown eggs laid in old nest of another species high in tree. Incubation 28 days, by female alone. Colonial.

Range: Summer visitor to eastern Europe. Breeds from Hungary through eastern Europe and Russia to eastern Siberia in the steppe zone. Winters in small area of southwestern Africa.

Being highly colonial, and reusing old nests of other species, these falcons are largely dependent on rookeries. They usually arrive late – after the Rooks have reared their young – but, after a hard and extended winter, they may arrive to find that their would-be nests are still occupied by unfledged Rooks. In these circumstances disputes are inevitable, noisy and spectacular.

pp.105 & 108 **Merlin** *Falco columbarius*

Description: 27–32 cm (10½–12½ in). Small, northern
falcon. Male blue-grey above, warm buff
streaked black below, with *faint moustache*
and prominent terminal tail-band. Female
brown above, white below, with extensive
black streaking and only a hint of a
moustache. In flight, the combination of
small size and thickset, even chunky build is
good feature. It is neither as long-winged,
nor as slim as, Hobby, and it is much mor
Peregrine-like in its hunting than Red-
footed Falcon.

Voice: Chattering *kee-kee-kee.*

Habitat: Rough, open, rolling country with low
vegetation and general lack of trees.
Moorlands, often among hills, rather than
bare mountain slopes. In winter, often
coastal on marshes and estuaries.

Breeding: Five to six buffy eggs, heavily spotted wit
rusty red, laid in hollow on the ground,
though sometimes on a cliff or disused nes
of other species in a tree. Incubation 25–3
days, mainly by female.

Range: Circumpolar in the north, including tund
and open areas of taiga. In Europe breeds i
Iceland, on northwestern hills of Britain
and Ireland, and through Scandinavia. Mc
migrate to winter over lowland Europe.

These are highly aggressive little falcons
that take small birds, usually captured in
flight. They are often somewhat crepuscul
and, at favoured winter marshes, will spen
much of the day atop a small bush awaitin
the arrival of small birds, often Starlings,
coming to roost. Their level-flight speed i
impressive and they fly with great agility
pursuit of their chosen victim.

pp.105 & 108 **Hobby** *Falco subbuteo*

Description: 30–36 cm (12–14 in). Long-winged, fast-
flying falcon. Adult slate-grey above, heavi
streaked black on white below. Undertail
coverts are rusty, and black moustache is
prominent on *white cheeks that extend, almos*

unbroken, to form an incomplete neck-ring – one of the best identification features. The *wings not only reach beyond the tail tip when folded, but are so narrow* as to occasionally cause confusion with a large swift. Juvenile brown above and heavily streaked brown below; but with same prominent 'collar' as adult. Eleonora's Falcon is similar size, but has dark underwing and buffy, not white, streaked breast.

Voice: A *keu-keu-keu* that is both high pitched and whining.

Habitat: Open country, including marshes, broken by copses, clumps, and wind breaks of deciduous or coniferous trees. In winter frequents park-like savannah with trees and open grasslands.

Breeding: Two or three yellowish eggs, speckled with reddish, laid in old nest of another bird, usually a Carrion Crow. Incubation 28 days, mainly by female.

Range: Summer visitor to Europe. Breeds right across Palearctic, including most of temperate Europe, from Portugal to Kamchatka. Winters in northern India and southern Africa.

For most of the year these fast-flying falcons depend on a diet of large, flying insects, caught and consumed in flight. On arrival in Europe they frequently concentrate over marshes where dragonflies are hatching, and they may then appear to be gregarious. However, they switch to a diet of small birds to rear their young and, remarkably, then concentrate their hunting on swallows, martins and even swifts, among the fastest flying of all small birds.

---

pp.106 & 109 **Eleonora's Falcon** *Falco eleonorae*

Description: 36–40 cm (14–16 in). Similar to, though a little larger than, Hobby, and marked by similar long, slim wings. In all plumages, tail broader than Hobby's. Occurs in dark and pale phases. Dark birds are uniformly sooty black, though underwing shows paler flight feathers than coverts. Pale birds have similarly *dark underwing* that distinguishes it from all other falcons, but pale-buffy (no white like Hobby) body lightly streaked. Cheeks white with clear dark moustache. Pale phase outnumbers dark. Gregarious throughout the year and colonial during breeding season.

Voice: High-pitched scream of complaint.

Habitat: Breeds only on sea cliffs of mostly uninhabited rocky islands, but regularly hunts over nearby marshes and other wetlands, even commuting to nearby mainlands to bathe.

Breeding: Two to eight white, brown-blotched eggs laid on bare cliff ledge, sometimes in old nest of another species, overlooking the sea and within a short distance of other pairs. Incubation 28–33 days, by both sexes.

Range: Breeds from Atlantic coasts of North Africa, through Mediterranean to Cyprus, with largest numbers among Greek islands. Winters in Madagascar.

These falcons are largely insectivorous, but change to a diet of small birds in autumn. They arrive and breed late in the summer so that the abundance of small, nocturnal, migrant birds that flood over the Mediterranean provide ample autumn food rear their young. They often hunt after dark and they have 'larders' where prey is stored t see them through poor hunting conditions.

pp.106 & 109 **Lanner Falcon** *Falco biarmicus*

Description: 34–50 cm (13½–19½ in). Similar to Peregrine, but *lighter in both build and coloration*. Pale and dark grey above, with multiple dark-barred tail, sandy crown, ar white cheeks with narrow dark moustache In flight, underparts white, with sparse, narrow, black streaks on breast and underwing. Much *paler than other similar-sized falcons*, with significantly narrower wings, thinner, less bulky body, and longer tail. Juvenile brown, with dark body and underwing coverts contrasting with pale flight feathers.

Voice: Repeated, high-pitched *ki-ki-ki*.
Habitat: Bare hillsides, park-like savannahs, broken country and mountainsides.
Breeding: Three to four buff-spotted white eggs laid on cliff ledge or, sometimes, in disused tree nest of another species. Incubation 31–38 days, by both sexes.
Range: Resident from Mediterranean and Middle East southwards through Africa, including mountains of central Sahara.

Highly favoured by falconers and severely persecuted as a result, with young birds fetching high prices in the Middle East. This is a fast-flying falcon that catches much of its prey in flight, but which is quite capable of adapting its technique to small terrestrial mammals and reptiles. In mid-Sahara, small passerine migrants, especially Yellow Wagtails, are taken in quantity, while sandgrouse form the most important food during non-migration periods.

pp.106 & 109 **Saker Falcon** *Falco cherrug*

Description: 45–55 cm (17½–21½ in). Like a brown Peregrine, but even more *heavily built* and thickset and thus not easily confused with the lightly built Lanner. Adult brown above, with whitish head, marked by dark eye-stripe and *faint moustache*. Underparts and underwing coverts white, heavily streaked black. Flight feathers contrastingly white, with only palest of barring. Tail faintly barred above and below. From below could be confused with dark Gyr Falcon, though the two species seldom overlap in range.
Voice: Screaming *kee-kee-kee*.
Habitat: Open steppes and plains, flat agricultural land, and bare plateaux.
Breeding: Four creamy eggs, spotted with reddish, laid on bare cliff ledge or in old nest of another species. Incubation 28 days, by both sexes.
Range: Summer visitor to eastern Europe eastwards across Russian steppes to eastern

Siberia. Winters in eastern China, Pakista
and East Africa.

Birds breeding in eastern Europe occupy
typical steppe-type habitats, but they are
increasingly resorting to the disused nests
of other birds built in power pylons. Prey
often taken in the air, but small mammals,
mostly susliks, predominate and may be
hunted from a perch or even on the ground
Aerial prey consists mostly of medium-
sized birds, though species as large as
herons and bustards have been recorded.

pp.107 & 109 **Gyr Falcon** *Falco rusticolus*

Description: 50–62 cm (19½–24½ in). Very large,
powerfully built falcon that occurs in two
phases with various intermediate coloration
Pale phase, (more northerly birds), is *white
above and below,* marked only by a few flecks
black on back, wings and tail. Dark phase
(more southerly birds), is *dark grey speckled
white* with white cheeks and prominent
moustache. In all plumages, from below the
flight feathers are either white or paler than
underwing coverts. The sheer *body bulk and
broad-based wings* of this falcon are usually
sufficient to distinguish it from other falcon

Voice: Harsh *kee-kee-kee.*

Habitat: Open tundra, bare cliffs and ravines,
mountains, coasts, and islands at high
altitudes. In winter, other open, usually
coastal, areas.

Breeding: Three to four buffy eggs, spotted with
reddish, laid on bare cliff ledge or old nest
of Raven or Rough-legged Buzzard.
Incubation 28–29 days, by female.

Range: Circumpolar in Arctic, where it breeds; in
winter regularly moves southwards to taiga
zone and beyond. In Europe breeds only in
Iceland and through Scandinavian mounta
chain and on northern tundra and coasts.

From time to time the odd Gyr Falcon
wanders further south than normal and
delights those fortunate enough to find it.
Sadly such vagrants are becoming rarer, an

only a few stay long enough for the word to spread and the bird to be enjoyed by the mass of birders. Most of those that have occurred in Britain have been of the pale phase, but escapees and especially hybrids pose serious identification problems.

pp.107 & 109 **Peregrine Falcon** *Falco peregrinus*

Description: 38–48 cm (15–19 in). Large, powerful falcon. Adult dark slate-grey above marked by white cheeks and *clear-cut, bold moustache*. Underparts white, heavily barred black. In flight, viewed from below, lightly barred flight feathers significantly paler than more heavily barred wing linings. Barred *tail considerably shorter* than in other falcons. Juvenile brown above and heavily streaked brown below. Broadly based pointed wings, deep chest, and sense of speed and power are always impressive.

Voice: Shrill, repeated *kee-kee-kee*.

Habitat: Mountains, with gorges and cliffs, among open moorland and tundra. Also sea cliffs. In winter, often coastal among marshes and particularly estuaries.

Breeding: Three to four buffy eggs, liberally speckled reddish, laid on bare cliff ledge or old cliff nest of another species. Incubation 35–42 days, mainly by female.

Range: Widespread but not numerous. Breeds on all the world's large landmasses, though somewhat sporadically through Europe where Britain holds largest population. More widespread in winter.

Following years of direct persecution, the Peregrine population, especially in Europe and North America, was dealt what could have been a final blow by the pesticide fiasco of the 1960s. The voluntary and compulsory ban in the use of these persistent substances has enabled Peregrine populations to increase once more, in some countries via deliberate reintroduction schemes. Sadly, the popularity of these birds with falconers, particularly in the newly rich oil states of the Middle East, has renewed pressure on these superb raptors.

GROUSE (TETRAONIDAE)

16 species; Holarctic region. Five distinct species breed in Europe. These are medium- to large-sized gamebirds with broad, rounded wings that produce very fast acceleration, but are completely unsuited to extended flight. They are predominantly terrestrial, though several species spend significant periods in trees, mostly conifers, and find much of their food among the shoots and berries of small shrubs. The sexes are mostly dissimilar, males being both larger and more boldly marked. Males often resort to communal 'leks', or display grounds, and are polygamous as a result. They are regarded as prime targets by sportsmen and several are very good to eat. Though generally declining, several species are maintained at artificially high numbers for sport.

p.112	**Hazel Grouse** *Bonasa bonasia*
Description:	35–37 cm (14–14½ in). A medium-sized gamebird, about the same size as a partridge, notoriously difficult to locate and see. Male grey and brown above, heavily barred and streaked, marked by large *tail with diagnostic, broad, black terminal band* on most of outer feathers. Head has short crest, a little red above eye, and black, white-bordered chin. Underpart richly spotted with large chestnut arrows. Female similar, but lacks crest and black chin. When flushed, wings produce rolled beating sound.
Voice:	Repeated whistling, plus loud wingbeating in display.
Habitat:	Conifer and mixed forests, with generous growth of shrubby understorey of alder and birch, often near water.
Breeding:	Six to ten buffy speckled eggs laid in well-lined hollow under cover of shrubs. Incubation 23–27 days, by female alone.
Range:	Resident right across Palearctic from eastern France to Bering Straits. Confined to hill forests in western parts of range, but

widespread throughout boreal zone further north and east.

This elusive, arboreal gamebird is closely related to the American Ruffed Grouse, which produces a remarkable wingbeating display by beating its wings on a hollow log that acts as an amplifier. The Hazel Grouse, still sometimes called Hazel Hen, also produces loud wingbeats. It is best located in late autumn or early spring when setting out its territory.

---

p.112 **Willow Grouse and Red Grouse**
Lagopus lagopus

Description: 33–39cm (13½–15½ in). Two well-marked subspecies, formerly regarded as separate species, that are prime hunting targets wherever they occur. Male Willow Grouse *L. l. lagopus* rich chestnut on head, neck and breast, marked by red wattle above eye. Back is chestnut-brown heavily barred black. *Wings and underparts white* with a few chestnut bars on flanks. Similar to Ptarmigan but chestnut where Ptarmigan is grey. In winter, whole plumage white with black outertail, like male Ptarmigan, though latter shows black lores. Female barred chestnut and black throughout in summer, but with white wings like male; similar to male in winter. Red Grouse *L. l. scoticus* is *chestnut-brown* throughout, with no seasonal change; female less rufous than male. Lack of white wings in Red Grouse at any time easily distinguishes it from Ptarmigan.

Voice: A crowing *go-bak, go-bak, go-bak, bak, bak*.

Habitat: Willow Grouse occupies moorland and tundra with dwarf scrub; Red Grouse mostly heather moors. Both subspecies found at lower levels in winter.

Breeding: 6–11 yellowish eggs blotched dark brown, and laid in hollow lined with moss and grasses. Incubation 20–26 days, by female.

Range: Circumpolar in tundra, taiga and boreal zone, with local movements southward to avoid harshest winter conditions. In

Europe, Red Grouse confined to Britain and
Ireland; Willow Grouse circumpolar,
through most of Scandinavia except
Swedish lowlands.

Though these species are hunted
throughout their range, only in Britain
and Ireland has the sport of grouse
shooting become the preserve of the rich
and aristocratic. The 12th August, 'the
Glorious Twelfth', which opens the British
grouse-shooting season, is as much a part
of the social calendar as horse racing, tennis
and rowing among the upper classes.

---

p.113 **Ptarmigan** *Lagopus mutus*

Description: 33–36 cm (13–14 in). High altitude and
high latitude equivalent of Willow and
Red Grouse, but marked in shades of *grey
rather than brown*. Like Willow Grouse has
distinct summer and winter plumages. In
summer, male grey, heavily streaked and
barred black, with white belly and wings,
and bold red comb over eye. In winter,
whole plumage, except *black lores* and black
tail, is white. Female similar, if more
subdued, but lacks red comb.

Voice: A rattling *kuh-kuh-kurrrrrr*. Male produces
crowing 'song' during breeding season.

Habitat: Bare mountain plateaux and high tundra
well beyond tree line.

Breeding: Five to ten white eggs, blotched brown,
laid in scrape lined with grasses. Incubation
24–28 days, by female alone.

Range: Circumpolar in tundra zone, but also
southwards into high mountains. In
Europe, breeds in Iceland, the Scandinavian
and Scottish mountains, as well as in high
Pyrenees and Alps.

The seasonally variable camouflage of
Ptarmigan is remarkable, and it is quite
easy to walk through a flock without being
aware of their presence until the last
second. In summer, their mottled greys
blend perfectly with the sparsely vegetated
rocky areas they prefer, while in winter

their white feathering hides them in snow. Even in transitional patchy grey and white state they are easily overlooked as this plumage pattern effectively breaks up their outline.

---

p.113 **Capercaillie** *Tetrao urogallus*

Description: ♂ 82–90 cm (32½–35½ in); ♀ 58–64cm (22–25 in). A huge black grouse that is difficult to find, but bold or even ferocious when confronted. Male is turkey-like bird with *huge, wedge-shaped black tail* that is fanned in display. Head has ragged beard, white bill, and red comb around eye. Female largely brown, broken by bars of buff and white, with orange throat and breast; heavily barred *tail square,* rather than notched like otherwise similar female Black Grouse.

Voice: Male produces series of clicks that accelerate to a terminal *pop.* Also a raucous, crowing *ko-ko-kok.*

Habitat: Extensive conifer forests, mostly among hills.

Breeding: Five to eight buffy eggs, blotched reddish, laid in hollow lined with a few grasses and hidden among low vegetation. Incubation 26–29 days, by female.

Range: Breeds from mountains of Spain and Scotland, eastwards through conifer forests of European mountain chains, to Scandinavia, Russia and eastern Siberia. Resident. It was exterminated in Scotland by 1770, but was reintroduced from 1837.

Like so many other grouse, male Capercaillies gather at special display grounds, called 'leks', where they strut around, tails spread, clicking furiously to attract visiting females. Their stylized jousting is, however, far from continuous and generally triggered off by the arrival at the lek of an interested female. Having mated, females depart to take full and sole charge of the rearing process. Usually only one or two dominant males are responsible for mating with all visiting females.

p.113 **Black Grouse** *Tetrao tetrix*

Description: ♂ 51–56 cm (20–22 in); ♀ 40–44 cm
(15–17 in). Large grouse like much larger
Capercaillie and similarly best seen at
communal display grounds. Male black,
marked by large red comb over eye, two
white bars on the folded wing, and extensive
white undertail coverts that are shown off in
display. Female brown, heavily barred black
and buff, to form highly effective camouflage
while incubating. *Tail lyre-shaped in male and
deeply notched in female.*

Voice: A sneezed *chew-oosh* and repeated *koo-roo* at lek

Habitat: Margins of conifer forests and open
meadows and moorland; moors with
clumps of conifers.

Breeding: Six to ten buffy eggs, spotted with brown,
laid in scrape lined with grasses. Incubation
23–26 days, by female.

Range: Breeds right across Palearctic from Scotland
to Pacific, as well as among European
mountains as far south as Macedonia.
Resident throughout.

Leks of Black Grouse are traditionally sited
near conifer woods at particular areas of
moorland grass that have been used for
many generations. Their tenacity in using
such areas may even outlast the building of
new homes, and there are several examples
of houses with leks in front gardens. As
with other lekking species, actual fights are
rare since dominance is established and
accepted by the majority of lekking males.

PARTRIDGES, PHEASANTS AND QUAIL (PHASIANIDAE)

189 species; worldwide. Seven species are
native to Europe and another three are
introduced and present in self-supporting
feral populations. These are small to large,
ground-dwelling gamebirds that, like grouse
have large, rounded wings that are capable of
great speed off the mark but unable to
support extended flight. Common Quail is a

exception in having long, pointed wings and in being a long-distance migrant. They are ground feeders, often scratching for their food among leaves and earth, chicken-like, with strong and powerful legs and feet. Tails are mostly short, though among the pheasants they are long and attenuated. Pheasants are also atypical in being sexually dimorphic. Most are vegetarians feeding on grain and shoots, though worms, insects and snails feature in the diets of some species. Several species are highly regarded as gamebirds and are strenuously protected as a result.

p.114 **Chukar Partridge** *Alectoris chukar*

Description: 33–36 cm (13–14 in). Very similar to Rock Partridge: greyish-brown above, creamy below. Face pattern of white chin enclosed by *black line extending through eye, but not to bill* as in Rock Partridge. Also has wider and fewer flank-stripes, though difficult to count and compare in the field. Flies low in brief flight on bowed wings, like other partridges.

Voice: Far-carrying *chuck-chuck-chuckar*.

Habitat: Stony hillsides and dry plains, usually at lower altitude than similar Rock Partridge.

Breeding: 8–14 buffy, reddish-spotted eggs, laid in hollow lined with grasses and sheltered by bush or rock. Incubation 24–26 days, by female alone.

Range: Replaces other 'red-legged' partridges in north-eastern Greece. Extends across Palearctic from northern Greece, through Turkey and Middle East, to Siberia and Northern China. Resident; introduced elsewhere and frequently interbreeds with other 'red-legged' partridges.

Although the Chukar is so very similar in appearance to Rock Partridge, and considered conspecific until comparatively recently, these two gamebirds do not overlap in range and make contact only in northeastern Greece. Even here, there is no evidence of interbreeding. The difference in their calls is a significant factor in regarding them as two distinct species.

p.114 **Rock Partridge** *Alectoris graeca*

Description: 32–35 cm (12½–14 in). Like Red-legged Partridge and almost identical in plumage to Chukar: grey-brown above, creamy below with flanks heavily barred black. Chin white, enclosed by *black border that extends to eye and bill*. Chukar has fewer, wider flank-bars, and black facial border does not extend to bill. These are fine differences, difficult to see in the field. Range and calls are more reliable methods of distinguishing these two very closely related species.

Voice: A clicking *whit-whitit*, repeated rhythmically and quite distinct from both Chukar's and Red-legged Partridge's call.

Habitat: Dry, stony, hillsides up to bare mountainsides and rocky screes; often at some altitude.

Breeding: 8–14 creamy-buff, brown-blotched eggs, laid in depression lined with thin layer of grasses and hidden by rock or small shrub. Incubation 24–26 days, by female alone.

Range: Confined to mountains of southern Europe from Italy and Alps to Greece and southern Bulgaria. Resident, even at altitude.

Living mainly at altitude there is little or no meeting with the other partridges that just overlap in range in both west and east. In southeast France, the Red-legged overlaps the range of the Rock Partridge, but it is a bird of dry plains and fields. In northern Greece, the Chukar similarly overlaps, but is also confined to lowland habitats. The difference in calls between the Rock and the other two is significant as well as the best means of identification.

p.114 **Red-legged Partridge** *Alectoris rufa*

Description: 33–36 cm (13–14 in). Medium-sized, chunky gamebird, very similar to the three other 'red-legged' partridges of Europe, with brown upperparts and grey flanks heavily barred with black and chestnut. Chin white, bordered by *black margin that breaks up into series of spots and streaks on neck and breast.* Latter marking is best means of distinguishing it from both Rock and Chukar Partridges.

Voice: Loud, far-carrying *chuk-chuk-chukar.*

Habitat: Bare grassy plains and arable fields, as well as low, stony hillsides and chalk downs.

Breeding: 10–16 yellowish, reddish-spotted eggs, laid in hollow lined with a few grasses. Incubation 23–25 days, by female alone.

Range: Confined to, and resident in, Iberia and France, and in England where it was introduced about 1770 and is more common in the dry east than the wetter west.

One of the few species of birds endemic to Europe, the Red-legged Partridge is regarded as the primary sporting quarry in its native Iberia. Driven by beaters, quite phenomenal 'bags' are shot by highly efficient commercial sporting organizations. Spanish partridge shooting is highly regarded and extremely expensive as a result. Most shot birds are sent to the restaurant market in Madrid where they again fetch high prices.

p.114 **Barbary Partridge** *Alectoris barbara*

Description: 32–34 cm (12½–13½ in). Buffy brown above; creamy below, with series of narrow buff and black flank-bars. Differs from European species in having *grey face bordered rust,* rather than white face bordered black. Rusty crest and white-spotted rust neck-band are sure means of identification.

Voice: A repeated *kutch-uk* and a harsh *crrick-crrick-crrick-jacar.*

Habitat: Maquis covered, rocky hillsides and gullies with bare rocky areas and screes, as well as open woodlands and groves.

Breeding: 8–16 yellow-buff, brown-blotched eggs laid in hollow sheltered by low scrub. Neither the incubation period, nor the roles of the sexes is known, though there is little reason to think them much different from that of other related partridges.

Range: Confined to and resident in North Africa, from Mauritania to Libya, where it replaces European Red-legged Partridge.

This bird was introduced to Gibraltar to provide sport for British officers garrisoned on the Rock. It is also resident in Sardinia, where the Red-legged Partridge is absent. Since there is no evidence of introduction, the origins of these Sardinian birds remains unknown, though it hardly seems likely that they could have arrived there under their own steam.

---

p.115 **Grey Partridge** *Perdix perdix*

Description: 29–32 cm (11½–12½ in). Typical, medium-sized, chunky, ground-dwelling bird, but quite differently marked to other European partridges. Upperparts heavily streaked and barred in shades of black, buff and brown. *Face orange,* breast grey with *dark chestnut horseshoe on belly,* larger in male than female. In flight, shows reddish outertail like other partridges. Flies low over ground with rapid wingbeats broken by glides on bowed wings.

Voice: Harsh *kirr-ik* and decelerating *krikrikri-kri-krikri.*

Habitat: Heaths, arable field, moorland and grassy plains.

Breeding: 9–20 buffy-brown eggs laid in hollow lined with grass and well hidden among low vegetation and scrub. Incubation 23–25 days, by female alone.

Range: Resident from Spanish mountains eastwards throughout temperate and upland Europe to the steppes of southern-central Siberia.

The most widespread and abundant of the European partridges. Several hundreds of thousands are 'put down' (released) each year, particularly in England and France, for sporting purposes. Its range overlaps that of most of the 'red-legged' partridges; but interbreeding is exceptional, the species seemingly able to co-exist.

p.116 **Golden Pheasant** *Chrysolophus pictus*

Description: ♂ 89–109 cm (35–43 in); ♀ 61–71 cm (24–28 in). Male is staggeringly colourful bird with bold patches of gold and red predominating, but with extraordinary *neck-fan* of gold and black that is expanded in display. Long tail heavily barred. Female like small Common Pheasant, heavily barred in brown and black, but marked by a *pale-buffy eye-patch*. Legs brown.

Voice: A harsh, crowing *chak-chak*.

Habitat: Occurs naturally among densely vegetated hillsides with scrub. In England frequents dense stands of rhododendron scrub among woodland.

Breeding: 5–12 buff-coloured eggs laid in depression lined with vegetation and hidden among dense scrub. Incubation 22–23 days, by female alone.

Range: An introduced pheasant that has established feral population in Britain; otherwise confined to hills of north-central China. In Britain feral populations are found only in southwestern Scotland (Galloway) and eastern England (Norfolk), though new releases occur quite frequently.

This fine little pheasant has been kept in captivity for years and frequently interbreeds with the closely related Lady Amherst's Pheasant. As a result pure birds are somewhat rare and may show confusing characters drawn from both species. With such a limited world distribution, most birders are happy to see these feral populations.

p.116 **Lady Amherst's Pheasant**
Chrysolophus amherstiae

Description: ♂ 105–120 cm (41½–47½ in); ♀ 58–68 cm (23–27 in). Male is splendidly marked bird, with bold patches of black and white, green and blue, red and yellow plumage, with *huge tail of black, silver and gold*. Female heavily barred brown and black, with *pale-blue eye-patch* and grey legs. Female may be confused with similar female Golden Pheasant, and the two species freely interbreed in captivity.

Voice: Harsh crow-like call of male, similar to that of Golden Pheasant.

Habitat: Naturally occurs on high rocky slopes covered with dense vegetation, including bamboo, among tall forests. In England occurs in scrub among woodland.

Breeding: 6–12 buff-coloured eggs laid in scrape lined with vegetation, and hidden among dense ground cover. Incubation 23 days, by female alone.

Range: Found only in mountains of western China and adjacent Burma, where it is resident. In England a feral population is established at borders of Bedfordshire, Buckinghamshire and Hertfordshire northwest of London.

Sarah, Lady Amherst, was the wife of the governor-general of India and resident in Calcutta from 1823 to 1828. In 1825 she was presented with two pheasants that had originally belonged to the King of Burma. She returned with them to Britain in 1828, but they died within weeks of reaching Europe. Lady Amherst showed them to an expert who published their first description and named them in her honour.

---

p.117 **Common Pheasant** *Phasianus colchicus*

Description: ♂ 75–90 cm (29½–35½ in); ♀ 52–64 cm (20½–25 in). Bulky, long-tailed gamebird. Male rich chestnut above, marked with streaks and pale arrowheads, and chestnut streaked and barred black below. Head *bright iridescent green,* with bold red eye-wattle and, often, a white neck-ring. Female mottled and barred in shades of buff, brown and black. Both sexes have long tails, the male's longer and barred chestnut and black. Pheasants fly strongly at medium height and glide on slightly bowed wings. They are therefore the perfect sporting bird.

Voice: Loud, far-carrying *kok—kok-kok.*

Habitat: Woods, heaths with copses and shelter
belts, arable farmland and marshes.

Breeding: 7–15 olive-brown eggs laid in hollow lined
with grasses and well hidden among low
scrub. Incubation 23–27 days, by female
alone.

Range: Natural range extends from Middle East,
through central-southern Siberia to
Southeast Asia and China. Introduced
birds, now ferally established, breed right
across temperate Europe.

The world's most popular gamebird has
been introduced to many far-flung regions
of the world, from Europe to North
America and Australasia. It was probably
the Romans who first introduced it to
Europe, but it has been the subject of so
many introductions from so many different
parts of the species range, that various,
often well-marked, subspecies have
interbred to create a huge mixture of
different male plumages.

---

p.115 **Common Quail** *Coturnix coturnix*

Description: 17–18.5 cm (6½–7 in). Small, dumpy, but
fast-flying, brown gamebird, heavily
streaked above, buffy with streaked breast
and flanks below. Both sexes show pattern
of black stripes on crown and face, but
more marked in male than female. In flight,
cigar-shaped body, with short pointed tail
and *long pointed wings,* are obvious features.
Usually heard, but seldom seen except
when flushed, which requires almost
stepping on the bird.

Voice: Liquid *whit-ti-whit*, rendered 'wet-me-lips'.
Also a harsh *creek*.

Habitat: Open grasslands, steppes; also hay fields
and cereals.

Breeding: 7–12 creamy, spotted-brown eggs laid in
scrape lined with grass and hidden among
low vegetation. Incubation 16–21 days, by
female alone.

Range: Summer visitor right across Mediterranean
and temperate Europe as far as east-central
Siberia and southwards across northern

India; also in southern and eastern Africa.
Some European birds winter along coasts of
Iberia and North Africa, but most cross
Sahara to Sahelian zone.

Changing agricultural techniques and
genetically engineered shorter growing
periods have made it difficult for the
Common Quail successfully to rear its
brood during the short northern summer.
Its decline has been hastened by the
ridiculous sport of spring shooting in the
Mediterranean, where it is still regarded as
prime quarry, along with Turtle Dove.

BUTTON-QUAIL (Turnicidae)

14 species; exclusively in Old World in
warm tropical regions. A single species
maintains a precarious foothold in Europe.
These are tiny, gregarious birds that run to
avoid danger and disappear among deep
cover when disturbed. They are chunky,
with short tails and short, rounded wings,
and are mostly clothed in cryptic shades of
brown and buff. They exhibit role reversal
when breeding: a single female mates with
several males and produces separate clutches
in separate nests for her mates to care for.
They feed chicken-like on seeds and insects.

Little Button-quail *Turnix sylvatica*

Description: 15–16 cm (6–6½ in). Smaller and much
rarer than Common Quail, which is only
potential confusion species. Dark brown
above, buffy orange below. *Tiny, ground-
dwelling bird* that runs fast for cover and
seldom, if ever, flies. Its orange-chestnut
patch on rounded wings is thus seldom
shown to advantage. When feeding, head is
held down, but when running for cover
head is held up like a miniature chicken.
Gregarious at all times.

Voice: A quavering *whooo* repeated; sounds like a
distant fog horn.

Habitat: Dry, bare land with scanty grass and growth of separated bushes or clumps.

Breeding: Four creamy-buff eggs, speckled black and brown, laid in scrape lined with grasses, often with surrounding grasses forming a canopy. Incubation 12–14 days, solely by male. Females may mate with and lay different clutches for two or more males to incubate in separate nests.

Range: An extremely rare and elusive resident of southwestern Iberia, North Africa, savannah Africa, and from India into Southeast Asia. Highly localized Iberian breeding sites, but not seen every year.

Formerly called Andalusian Hemipode, a wonderful and unique name that seems inappropriate for a species that is virtually extinct in Andalucia, but widespread in Asia and Africa where the names Little, Common and Kurrichane Button-quail are widely used. The lack of reports of this bird in southern Iberia partially reflects its status, but it is a very difficult bird to locate and might be a little less rare than it seems.

RAILS, CRAKES, GALLINULES AND COOTS (RALLIDAE)

130 species; worldwide. Nine species breed in Europe. These are small to medium-sized aquatic birds with short, often cocked, tails, broad, rounded wings, and long legs. The particularly long toes, which spread the bird's weight over floating vegetation, are lobed for swimming among the coots. Rails and crakes are clothed in shades of brown and cream, and merge well with their background. In contrast, gallinules and coots are boldly coloured. In flight, their rounded wings and dangling legs give an impression of weakness, but several species are powerful fliers and perform long-distance migrations. Rails, in particular, have colonized many oceanic islands where they have evolved into endemic species and become flightless or virtually so.

p.120   **Water Rail** *Rallus aquaticus*

Description: 27–29 cm (10½–11½ in). Secretive,
wetland species that is more often heard
than seen. Brown with dark feather centre
above; grey on face, breast and belly, with
white barring on black flanks and white
undertail, particularly apparent as the bird
walks away with jerks of its cocked tail.
Best feature is *long, red bill,* unlike any
similar European species. In flight long,
pink legs trail behind.

Voice: Loud, squealing, pig-like shrieks.

Habitat: Reed beds and other dense aquatic
vegetation among marshes, swamps and
ditches. Often resorts to more open waters
in winter.

Breeding: Six to ten cream-coloured, reddish-spotted
eggs laid in well-constructed cup of
vegetation, over or adjacent to water.
Incubation 19–20 days, mainly by female.

Range: Breeds right across Palearctic from
Iceland to Japan and southwards to
central Asia. West European birds are
resident, but are joined by winter visitors
from further east.

Like other rails – and there are many
species outside Europe – the Water Rail is
highly adapted to a life among aquatic
vegetation. The long bill is an effective
probe, though it is also sometimes used as a
dagger, and the strong legs and long toes
ease its passage over floating vegetation. It
is also laterally compressed, which enables
it to pass between dense reeds without
getting tangled up.

---

p.120   **Spotted Crake** *Porzana porzana*

Description: 22–24 cm (8½–9½ in). Significantly larger
than either Baillon's or Little Crake. Adult
blotched and barred brown and black
above; underparts greyish, with mass of
small *white spots on head, neck and breast*
merging into white bars on flanks and belly.
Undertail buff. Bill yellow, with red base.
Legs greenish yellow. Juvenile has yellow-

green (not red and yellow) bill and warm buff breast, though equally as spotted as adult. A highly secretive bird, mostly located by call.

Voice: A distinctive *quip–quip–quip*, which is repeated for long periods and has been likened to a tap dripping into a half-filled barrel of water.

Habitat: Densely vegetated swamps, marshes and bogs with sedges and long coarse grasses. Also similar margins of lakes and large, slow-moving rivers.

Breeding: 8–12 buffy, reddish-blotched eggs laid in cup of vegetation hidden in tussock or on the ground. Incubation 18–21 days, by both sexes.

Range: Highly secretive summer visitor to temperate Europe, eastwards to central Siberia. Very patchily distributed in Europe, with birds present one year and absent the next. Winters in northern India and South and East Africa.

Viewing Spotted and other crakes requires a quite different approach to general birding. These are mostly crepuscular birds – more active at dawn and dusk than during the day. A walk through suitable habitat is unlikely to be rewarded with success. Instead, choose the right time, the right habitat, and sit and watch patiently over an area between patches of cover where moving birds must walk openly. If not alarmed they will continue feeding as they walk.

p.120 **Little Crake** *Porzana parva*

Description: 18–20 cm (7–8 in). Small, elusive summer visitor that closely resembles both Spotted and Baillon's Crakes. Upperparts brown and black in all plumages. Adult male grey below, with *flank barring confined to rear* and generally insignificant. Female buffy below, but with similar rear flank bars. Both have yellow bills with *small area of red at base and yellow-green legs*. Juvenile resembles female, but with more extensive and obvious flank bars, and distinctive, pale tips to tertials forming a pale patch on the folded upperwing. In all plumages Little Crake shows *prominent primary projection,* whereas in Baillon's Crake the primaries are mostly hidden beneath tertials on the folded wing.

Voice: Repeated *kook-kook-kook*, accelerating and gradually fading away; also a loud trilling.

Habitat: Swamps and marshes with extensive growth of water-lilies and other emergent vegetation, as well as similar margins of lakes and rivers.

Breeding: Seven to eight yellowish eggs, spotted brown, laid in nest of aquatic vegetation well hidden among similar material. Incubation 20–21 days, by both sexes.

Range: Breeds patchily across Europe into Russia and Ukraine and as far as south-central Siberia. Some winter in the Rann of Kutch, but most fly to Ethiopia and Kenya.

All these species of European crake are significantly affected by changes in water level at their chosen breeding sites and, particularly, by drying out during hot summers. Large-scale agricultural drainage has therefore caused their decline. However the Little Crake is less affected than the other two species since it is more tolerant of both rises and falls in water level.

p.121 **Baillon's Crake** *Porzana pusilla*

Description: 17–18 cm (6½–7 in). Smallest of the crakes, but must be distinguished from Little Crake with care. Adult male brown and black above, grey below with black and white *barring extending prominently along the flanks. Bill green;* legs brownish. Primaries *tightly bunched* and project only slightly beyond covering tertials. Female similar to female Little Crake, being buffy below, but with obvious flank-barring. Juvenile even more heavily barred, with bars extending to breast. Bolder and more extensive barring, compared with Little Crake, is usually most obvious field mark, but should be checked against bill and leg colour and extent of primary projection.

Voice: A rattled trill *trrrr-trrrr*, repeated at close intervals and sounding like a ruler passed over the teeth of a comb.

Habitat: Marshes and swamps with scattered growth of sedge clumps; also similar margins of ponds and rivers.

Breeding: Six to eight buff, brown-spotted eggs laid in neat cup-shaped nest of leaves hidden among vegetation. Incubation 20–21 days, by both sexes.

Range: Highly localized summer visitor to Europe, extending eastwards across southern Siberia to Japan and northern China. Also resident in southern Africa, Madagascar and Australasia. Palearctic birds migrate to India and Southeast Asia, though European birds probably mix with local birds in East Africa having crossed Sahara.

Baillon's Crake generally occupies smaller marshes and swamps than other crakes and is, if possible, even more secretive and difficult to see. This is, however, more a matter of habit and habitat, rather than a distinct shyness, for these birds can be quite confiding in human presence.

p.121 Corn Crake *Crex crex*

Description: 25–28 cm (10–11 in). A stocky bird that is significantly larger than other crakes but, owing to its severe decline, increasingly difficult to see. Buff and black above. Grey on head and foreneck, the latter fading into unique pattern of chestnut and white bars on flanks. Short, *stubby bill* is pale horn; legs pale pink. Wings *rich chestnut* both when folded and, especially, when in flight. Combination of size and habitat makes this one of the simplest of all crakes to identify, while calls make it easy to locate. The problem is to see it.

Voice: Harsh, grating, long repeated *crek-crek-crek*, mostly at dawn and dusk.

Habitat: Grasslands, hay fields and rough pastures mainly growing to height of bird; therefore tends to avoid cereals.

Breeding: 8–12 green, brown-blotched eggs laid on flat nest of grasses hidden among vegetation. Incubation 15–18 days, by female alone.

Range: Breeds right across temperate Europe and Russian steppes to eastern Siberia. Whole population, including birds breeding almost as far away as Japan, winters in southeast Africa.

The decline of the Corn Crake from being a familiar sound of summer to an endangered rarity can be fairly ascribed to agricultural mechanization. Cutting hay by hand enabled nests to be seen (and avoided) and young birds to escape; modern hay-making machinery cuts without care. Even more destructive is the practice of cutting fields earlier in the season for successive crops of silage.

---

p.122 Moorhen *Gallinula chloropus*

Description: 31–35 cm (12–14 in). Both confiding and obvious. Adult brown-black above and blue-black below, separated by narrow, white flank-line. Undertail white; tail cocked; *bill and narrow frontal shield red*; legs and long toes yellow-green. Juvenile slate-brown, with white undertail and flank-line, and pale, buffy-grey breast. Swims buoyantly and walks easily over waterside vegetation, on adjacent grassland, and even among low trees and waterside shrubs.

Voice: Explosive *quark* or *currick*; high-pitched *kik-kik-kik-kik*.

Habitat: Marshes, swamps, bogs, ponds, lakes, reservoirs, rivers; indeed virtually any manner of wetland with sloping margins and emergent vegetation.

Breeding: 5–11 buffy eggs, liberally spotted black, laid in substantial nest constructed of any available material hidden on the ground, occasionally in a shrub, near water. Incubation 19–22 days, by both sexes.

Range: Widespread and common. Virtually cosmopolitan breeding on all the world's landmasses except Australasia. Mainly resident, though birds from eastern Europe and northern Palearctic are summer visitors.

The Moorhen is by far the most successful member of its family, being highly adaptable and at home alongside man. Despite its huge range and limited migrations only 12 subspecies are recognized, even on isolated islands such as the Galapagos and Seychelles. The tendency not to speciate is in sharp contrast to its close relatives the rails, which have evolved into many quite distinct island species.

p.122 **Purple Gallinule** *Porphyrio porphyrio*

Description: 45–50 cm (17½–19½ in). Unmistakable, large, blue waterbird marked by *large red bill* and enormous red legs and feet. Adult dark blue with white undertail beneath permanently cocked, short tail. Large, *conical bill, large feet and long toes red*. Though it can swim and fly, it is usually seen walking over aquatic vegetation. Juvenile blue above and grey below, with dark legs and feet.

Voice: Variety of snoring and trumpeting calls.

Habitat: Marshes and swamps with dense stands of sedges, as well as reeds and other emergent vegetation.

Breeding: Two to five buffy, brown-spotted eggs laid in substantial nest of aquatic vegetation in tussock or hidden among waterside vegetation. Incubation 22–25 days, mainly by female.

Range: Widespread resident through much of Old World, though in Europe confined to a few locations in Mediterranean and absent from eastern Palearctic.

This is not so much a shy species as a bird that moves slowly, devouring vegetation as it goes. Thus it may spend long periods hidden, but equally may spend long periods on static view. It feeds, remarkably, on the pith of sedges, which it holds in its feet and strips with its large bill. It also takes shoots and seeds, invertebrates, and the eggs and young of other species, which is just as well because the pith of sedges seems unlikely to provide much in the way of nourishment.

---

p.123 **Common Coot** *Fulica atra*

Description: 38–42 cm (15–16½ in). Medium-sized, all-black waterbird that can be confused with Moorhen in juvenile plumage and with extremely rare Red-knobbed Coot. Adult sooty black marked by *white bill and large white frontal shield*. Legs strong, with lobed feet, yellow-green in colour. A dumpy, rotund bird that swims buoyantly and walks easily over the ground. When disturbed it patters fast over water surface, rather than flies. Red-knobbed Coot has two dark red knobs at top of frontal shield in summer and lacks small wedge of black at base of bill.

Voice: Explosive *kook* or *kick-kick*.

Habitat: Lakes, ponds, marshes and slow-flowing rivers with open water and areas of emergent vegetation. In winter, also on more open waters, including reservoirs, usually in large numbers.

Breeding: Six to nine buffy, black-spotted eggs laid in substantial nest of vegetation, usually among emergent growth above the water. Incubation 21–24 days, by both sexes.

Range: Breeds right across the Palearctic, southwards into Oriental and Australasian regions. In Europe largely resident, but Scandinavian and east European birds migrate south and west in winter. There may be as many as two million birds wintering in Europe.

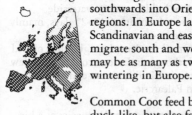

Common Coot feed by diving, upending duck-like, but also feed at the surface of water and on dry land. Most food is vegetable matter, but insects and molluscs are also taken. Substantial areas of open water are required for take-off, though the habit of pattering over the surface when disturbed may confuse predators, particularly when members of large flocks all patter at once. In the air they fly strongly with legs trailing behind.

p.123 Red-knobbed Coot *Fulica cristata*

Description: 38–42 cm (15–16½ in). Very similar to Common Coot in shape and coloration. All sooty black with green legs, and white bill and frontal shield. Main differences are presence of two red knobs at top of frontal shield in summer that give head a *peaked shape* at any distance; these are lost in winter. There is no *small black wedge at base of bill*, and no narrow white trailing edge to secondaries in flight. All are fine points and should be thoroughly checked, preferably at close range.

Voice: Explosive *cronnk* differs from Common Coot, but should be carefully checked against a recording. It is, however, of great help in locating this rare and elusive species when both coots occur together.

Habitat: Much the same as Common Coot: lakes and marshes with open water and areas of emergent vegetation. In Europe tends to keep closer to cover.

Breeding: Four to six pale-buffy, black-spotted eggs laid in substantial nest of vegetation among emergent growth. Incubation 21–24 days, by both sexes.

Range: In Europe breeds only in southern Spain, but is extremely rare. Elsewhere breeds in Morocco, in southern and eastern Africa, and in Madagascar.

This is actually the ecological replacement of the Common Coot in Africa, whose range it overlaps only in southern Spain. Its rarity in Andalucia is quite genuine, as every year many birders make a special attempt to add it to their Eurolists. In Morocco, where Common Coot has a toehold in the far north, it is more obvious and common among the lakes of the Middle Atlas.

CRANES (Gruidae)

14 species; Old World and North America.
A single species breeds in Europe and another
is a scarce visitor. These are tall, long-necked
and long-legged terrestrial birds that fly with
neck and legs extended. They are gregarious,
forming large flocks outside the breeding
season that fly noisily, goose-like, across the
sky. Their trumpeting far-carrying calls are
evocative of the wild. Most are migratory,
some performing prodigious, length-of-the-
continent flights, adults leading the young.
All species are in decline and some are rare
and highly endangered. Their size and
charisma, however, has led to intensive and
expensive programmes to bring them back
from the brink of extinction.

p.124 **Common Crane** *Grus grus*

Description: 106–118 cm (42–46½ in). Very large, noisy,
gregarious, grey and black bird that flies
with neck extended forward and legs
trailing aft. Basically grey above and below
with long neck and head, and substantial,
dagger-like bill. Adult has black crown and
black chin and foreneck *separated by bold
white slash*. Crown has tiny red patch. Legs
long and black. Conspicuous rear end has
cascade of drooping grey feathers. Juvenile
buffer, especially on plain head and neck.
Gregarious, flying in goose-like skeins and
with similar, but more trumpeting, calls.
Voice: Loud, trumpeting and rolling *krrrr*.
Habitat: Marshes and swamps among conifer forests
and forested tundra. In winter frequents
open agricultural land with large water as
nearby roost.
Breeding: Two grey, brown-blotched eggs laid on
platform of vegetation or hummock, in
swamp or adjacent to water. Incubation
28–30 days, by both sexes.
Range: Breeds right across northern Palearctic from
Scandinavia virtually to Pacific, as well as
locally in Turkey and Middle East. Winters
in western Europe, Turkey, Sudan, and in
northern India and China.

Cranes in Europe exhibit a clear migrational divide. After breeding, Scandinavian birds gather in northeast Germany before heading southwest through Holland and France to Spain. Main winter concentrations are in Extremadura and Gallicia, with traditional stop-overs in Vendee and Marne. The creation of large reservoirs in northeastern France has tempted large numbers to winter, or partially winter, much further north than previously.

<p.124> **Demoiselle Crane** *Anthropoides virgo*

Description: 90–100 cm (35½–39½ in). Similar in shape, structure and coloration to Common Crane, but significantly smaller. Adult grey above and below with *black face extending onto foreneck to form drooping crest* on breast. A white tuft extends from ear coverts. The drooping rear end is grey, tipped black. Flies with neck and legs extended. Smaller size and marked black breast distinguishes it from larger Common Crane.

Voice: Rolling, trumpeted calls like Common Crane, but higher pitched.

Habitat: Marshes, rivers, steppes, plains, and more arid areas. Winters on dry agricultural land and marshes with nearby waters.

Breeding: Two pale buffy-grey eggs, spotted and blotched brown, laid in scrape near water. Incubation 27–29 days, by both sexes, though mainly by female.

Range: Breeds across central Palearctic from Black Sea to northern China, with small isolated populations in Turkey and probably still in Morocco. Although small numbers winter elsewhere, bulk of population is found in north-central India.

Though concentrated in India during winter, it is possible to travel extensively through likely habitats without seeing a single bird. Even world-famous Bharatpur seldom holds more than a handful. Travel west to the Rann of Kutch, however, and the numbers are simply spectacular with thousands often concentrated on a single roadside pool.

BUSTARDS (OTIDIDAE)

23 species; confined to Old World. Two breed in Europe and another is an exceptionally rare vagrant. Bustards are large turkey-like, ground-dwelling birds of open grassland, steppe and savannah. They have long necks and legs, and a horizontal carriage as they walk sedately over their range. In flight they appear heavy, with slow, noisy beats of huge wings. Males of most species have ornate plumes on head and neck, which are erected in display and then make the bird visible at great range, which is, of course, the object. The majority of species is found among the savannahs of Africa, but the two Indian species are endangered and another, the Houbara, is the prime quarry of falcon-toting sheiks wherever it is found.

p.124 **Little Bustard** *Tetrax tetrax*

Description: 41–45 cm (16–17½ in). Large, heavily-built, ground-dwelling bird, much smaller than related Great Bustard. In summer male is delicately mottled brown above, white below with prominent *black and white neck pattern* that is puffed up in display. Female similar, but darker above and lacking neck pattern. Long and strong, walking legs. In flight, resembles similar-sized duck, but *wingbeats are fast and fluttering*. Shows large area of white on flight feathers. Gregarious, especially outside breeding season.

Voice: Both sexes utter grunted *ogh*. Male has snorting, territorial, raspberry-like *prrit*.

Habitat: Open grasslands, steppes, cereals, grassy parkland, and groves.

Breeding: Three to four greenish, brown-streaked eggs laid in bare scrape. Incubation 20–21 days, by female alone.

Range: Breeds across Europe to Russian steppes beyond Caspian, but absent from most of central and south-central Europe. French population are summer visitors.

The absence of these birds from middle Europe is probably due to changing land

use and deliberate persecution by hunters, although this absence extends well back into the nineteenth century. In their Iberian strongholds, where some 50,000 to 70,000 birds are found, this process can be seen in action as known haunts are gradually abandoned as they are progressively ploughed.

p.125 **Great Bustard** *Otis tarda*

Description: ♂ 95–105 cm (37½–41½ in); ♀ 75–85 cm (29½–33½ in). Huge, ground-dwelling bird that vies with Mute Swan for the title of world's heaviest flying bird. Both sexes mottled and barred black on buff-brown above, white below, and with long thick necks and legs. Larger male has *grey head and neck* marked by extensive white whiskers and large, heavily barred tail. In display, neck is held back on the body, the breast pumped up, the tail raised, and the wings semi-spread and turned inside out to show large areas of white. The bird is then visible at great range. Female similarly marked, but does not perform displays. Gregarious.

Voice: A low bark, but mostly silent.

Habitat: Grassy plains and steppes, and large fields of cereals; also locally among open grassy groves.

Breeding: Two to three grey-green, brown-blotched eggs laid in hollow among grass. Incubation 25–28 days, by female alone.

Range: Patchily distributed across Palearctic from Portugal to far-eastern Siberia. Siberian birds are migrants to Turkey, Middle East and northern China.

European birds are concentrated in several main areas, with over half in Portugal and particularly Spain. Elsewhere it breeds in northeastern Germany and adjacent Poland, in Austria and Hungary, and in Romania. Everywhere there has been a recorded decline in numbers owing to changing agriculture and hunting. Just how long a bird of this size can survive in an increasingly mechanized Europe is a matter of conjecture.

OYSTERCATCHERS
(HAEMATOPODIDAE)

Seven species; worldwide. A single species
breeds in Europe. These are medium-sized,
chunky, black or black and white birds foun
mostly along seashores, but also inland alon
rivers and lakes. They are structurally simila
with strong pink legs and a long, thick red
bill. They feed predominantly on molluscs,
which are opened or smashed to obtain the
contents. Generally gregarious, they form
immense high-tide flocks at particularly
favoured intertidal resorts.

---

p.128 **Oystercatcher** *Haematopus ostralegus*

Description: 41–45 cm (16–17½ in). Large, tubby, blac
and white wader marked by *long and heavy,
red bill, and long, thick, pink legs*. In summe
black above, extending to form clear-cut
breast-band; white below. In flight, black
wings show prominent white wingbar. In
winter, a white neck-strap develops on
foreneck. Gregarious and noisy.

Voice: A loud, shrill *kleep* and a piping *kleep-a-kle*
that is repeated.

Habitat: Rocky shorelines, estuaries, mud flats, and
sandy intertidal areas, rich in shellfish,
particularly mussels. Also inland along river

Breeding: Three buff, black-blotched eggs laid in bar
scrape in shingle or sand. Incubation 24–2
days, by both sexes.

Range: Breeds along coastal Europe from Iceland,
Britain and Scandinavia, and thence inland
across Russia. Also along coasts of Sea of
Japan and Kamchatka, and locally through
Mediterranean. Northern birds migrate
westwards to winter around North Sea.

Though named for their presumed
predilection for oysters, European
oystercatchers are mussel specialists.
Some birds specialize in prising these
molluscs open and neatly severing the
tendon that holds them to their shell.
Others are less refined and smash mussels
open with a vigorous hammering

technique. Such specialized opening techniques are not geographically orientated, though smash-and-grab birds do have shorter bills as a result.

AVOCETS AND STILTS (RECURVIROSTRIDAE)

13 species; worldwide. Two species breed in Europe. These are medium-sized, black and white birds, with long, or exceptionally long, legs and fine bills that are pointed in the stilts and upturned in the avocets. Both are highly specialized feeders that show a distinctive preference for more saline habitats. They are therefore more coast orientated than many other waders, though inland salt-lakes also hold them in good numbers. Stilts feed by picking insects mainly from the surface in water that is too deep for other waders. Avocets feed with a side-to-side, scything motion that sifts crustaceans from soft mud in shallow water.

p.129 **Black-winged Stilt** *Himantopus himantopus*

Description: 36–40 cm (14–16 in). A neatly proportioned, black and white wader with extremely long legs. Adult black above, white below, with fine, *needle-like bill* and *long pink legs* that trail behind in flight. Male has smudgy black crown and nape lacking in female. In flight, pointed wings are uniform black above and below. Generally gregarious.

Voice: Clear *kick*; also a double *kee-uk*, often repeated.

Habitat: Saline lagoons, marshes and salt-pans, mostly near the sea, but also inland. Also frequents fresh marshes, where it breeds as the wetland dries out.

Breeding: Four black-spotted, buffy eggs laid in scrape with a token array of stems as nesting material, usually in a drying-out marsh only slightly above the prevalent water level. Incubation 25–26 days, by both sexes.

Range: Widespread through Europe, eastwards across Siberia to China and India, and southwards to central Africa. A summer visitor to Europe that winters mostly in African Sahelian region.

The long legs of this bird are an adaptation feeding in deeper waters than other waders, where it picks most of its food from the water's surface. On dry land it has to bend almost vertically forward to feed in mud while, when settling on its nest, a controlled 'crash' is the best it can manage. When sitting, the folded legs project beyond tail.

---

p.129 **Avocet** *Recurvirostra avosetta*

Description: 41–45 cm (16–17½ in). Large, pied wader, basically white with bold black areas on crown, nape, back and wings. Legs long, blue, and trail in flight. *Bill long, fine and upturned* (recurved), and swept from side to side when feeding. Distant black and white birds may be gulls, but sideways sweeping identifies this species.

Voice: Shrill *kleet*.

Habitat: Bare or scantily vegetated, saline lagoons and marshes, preferably coastal. Winters on estuaries and salt-pans.

Breeding: Four buffy eggs, spotted and blotched with black, laid in bare scrape, often alongside tuft of vegetation. Incubation 22–24 days, by both sexes. Colonial.

Range: Summer visitor across Palearctic from Atlantic to northern China. Also breeds across southern and eastern Africa. European range fragmented. Most of Atlantic and North Sea population winter in Portugal.

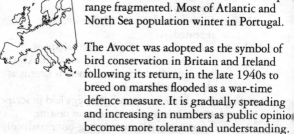

The Avocet was adopted as the symbol of bird conservation in Britain and Ireland following its return, in the late 1940s to breed on marshes flooded as a war-time defence measure. It is gradually spreading and increasing in numbers as public opinion becomes more tolerant and understanding. Such understanding is gradually spreading through the adjacent Continent.

THICK-KNEES (BURHINIDAE)

Nine species; Old World and Central America, with majority in Africa. Only one species in Europe. Thick-knees are well-camouflaged birds in shades of brown and buff. They frequent bare, stony ground and are generally both secretive and crepuscular. For such a large bird their camouflage is highly effective, and it is enhanced by their habit of standing stock still to avoid detection. They have long, walking legs and in flight show large white wing-patches. In many parts of their range, stony ground is most common along river-banks, and so many species are associated with water. The prominent tarsal joint is responsible for the vernacular name 'thick-knee'.

p.125 **Stone-curlew** *Burhinus oedicnemus*

Description: 38–43 cm (15–17 in). Large, brown, buff-and-cream streaked bird, marked by large head and eye, and long, thick yellow legs. Easily overlooked among dry stony wastes, but long, round-tipped wings show *prominent black and white pattern in flight*. Generally adopts slow-moving, hunched-up attitude and is most active at dawn and dusk.

Voice: Thin, whistled *coor-lee*, likened to a tin whistle.

Habitat: Scant grasslands on poor soils; bare heaths, downland and poor arable fields. Local on shingle beaches and dry river beds.

Breeding: Two creamy eggs, spotted and blotched brown, laid in bare scrape. Incubation 25–27 days, by both sexes.

Range: Resident or summer visitor through Mediterranean and temperate Europe eastwards through Siberia to India and Southeast Asia. Most European birds (except Iberia) move out for the winter, though few move further than Mediterranean basin.

The decline in numbers and distribution of this secretive bird is largely due to changing agricultural techniques and practice. In particular, the ploughing up of old heathland and downland for food productio[n] and the widespread use of fertilizers have destroyed much Stone-curlew habitat. Mor[e] recent 'set-aside' schemes designed to redu[ce] food production have not yet been utilized [to] produce suitable habitat.

PRATINCOLES AND COURSERS (GLAREOLIDAE)

16 species; Old World. In Europe one species breeds, another is a regular passage migrant, and another is a vagrant. These a[re] small to medium-sized birds that fly on long, pointed wings. Coursers are long-legged, running birds of dry, semi-desert areas. Pratincoles are short-legged, predominantly aerial birds of dried-out marshes. While coursers look and behave like plovers, pratincoles look and behave like terns. Both groups are predominantly brown and merge exceptionally well with the different landscapes they inhabit. Coursers feed on insects and reptiles foun[d] by making running pounces on the groun[d;] pratincoles feed on insects taken high in t[he] air and have a swallow-like bill and gape.

p.130 **Cream-coloured Courser** *Cursorius cursor*

Description: 19–21cm (7½–8 in). A semi-desert, ground dwelling, fast-running bird. Whole of plumage sandy cream, marked by bold crow[n] pattern of pale blue, black and white that meets to form characteristic 'V' shape on nape[.] Black bill distinctly decurved; legs long and grey. In flight, whole outer wing is black, contrasting with creamy inner wing and body. Behaves like a plover, interspersing short, fast runs with stock-still pauses. Well camouflaged and easily overlooked.

Voice: Piping whistle and hard *praak*.

Habitat: Dry semi-desert with scant vegetation is natural habitat. Vagrants frequent similar areas where they exist, but also occur on beaches and dry fields.

Breeding: Two buffy eggs, streaked and spotted brown, laid in bare hollow. Incubation and role of sexes unknown, though both sexes present during hatching period.

Range: Breeds through North Africa and Middle East. Many of these are migrants, wintering in the northern Sahelian zone, where there is also a resident population. Overshoots to southern Europe, where it is an irregular vagrant probably overlooked in Spain.

The movements of these birds are a matter of some conjecture and based on relatively little evidence by virtue of the inhospitable nature of their breeding grounds. Many birds leave the Sahelian region in early spring to breed in North Africa, while others remain to breed locally. Northward movements do continue, however, to mid-summer, and it seems likely that some individuals rear broods in the Sahelian region before flying to North Africa to rear a second.

---

p.130 **Collared Pratincole** *Glareola pratincola*

Description: 24–27 cm (9½–10½ in). A stockily built, short-legged bird marked by very long wings and long forked tail. Upperparts brown; underparts white with creamy wash over breast. Black line running from eye to breast encloses creamy patch. Bill short, decurved like a swallow's, and dark with red base. In flight, outer wing darker than inner, and secondaries show *narrow, white, trailing edge* – the best means of distinguishing the species from very similar Black-winged Pratincole. Chestnut underwing coverts, if visible, are diagnostic, but mostly appear dark like Black-winged. Tern-like appearance, with long, angular wings, forked tail and buoyant flight identify a pratincole.

Voice: Screeching *kirrick*, like a tern.

Habitat: Marshes, drying floods, damp agricultural land; wetlands that dry out in summer.

Breeding: Three black-blotched, creamy eggs laid in bare scrape. Incubation 17–18 days, by both sexes.

Range: Summer visitor to Mediterranean and
          eastwards through Middle East. Winters i
          savannah Africa where it also breeds.

          These are highly gregarious birds that oft
          fly high, with only their noisy calls
          betraying their presence. On arrival they
          will hawk tern-like over marshes, creating
          colonies on islands that become no more
          than raised areas as the sun dries out the
          surroundings. Though highly localized,
          they are often abundant where found.

p.131   **Black-winged Pratincole**
         Glareola nordmanni

Description: 24–27 cm (9½–10½ in). Very similar to
               Collared Pratincole and distinguished onl
               with the greatest of care. Generally darke
               above than Collared, with less contrast
               between inner and outer wing. Underwin
               coverts black, but in most lights and mos
               conditions, so are those of Collared
               Pratincole. Black-winged *lacking white
               trailing edge to secondaries* is best field mark
               but still requires care.
Voice: Tern-like *kirrick*.
Habitat: Drying-out marshes and floods.
Breeding: Three olive-green eggs, blotched and streak
               black. There is no information available ab
               incubation period and role of sexes.
Range: Summer visitor to northwestern shores of
               Black Sea eastwards to central Siberia, th
               effectively north and east of Collared
               Pratincole. Winters in south and west
               Africa, overlapping with cogenor in some
               areas. Wanders westwards to eastern
               Europe, though scarce breeder in Romani

               Distinguishing the two closely related
               European pratincoles is never easy and oft
               impossible. A glimpse of a chestnut
               underwing is a sure indication of Collared
               Pratincole, but a similar glimpse of a dark
               underwing may be a Black-winged, or
               equally a Collared in poor lighting
               conditions such as bright sunlight. There
               therefore a built-in bias towards the posit

identification of Collared. The narrow white trailing inner wing of the Collared is similarly a positive feature while its absence may again be just a matter of poor views.

PLOVERS (CHARADRIIDAE)

60 species; worldwide. Seven species breed in Europe, one is a winter visitor and three are vagrants. Plovers are small to medium-sized shorebirds, marked by a rotund even tubby body, a neatly rounded head on a short neck, and a short, stubby bill. The legs are long and the characteristic hunting method consists of short, fast runs followed by stock-still freezes similar to the popular children's party game. Darker, mainly brown, upperparts contrast with pale, mainly white, underparts. Smaller species are often marked by dark rings and other head and neck markings. Larger species often show dark underparts, or prominent breast-bands, particularly in breeding plumage, while the lapwings are marked with crests and facial wattles. Many species are typical shorebirds, but some favour inland marshes and even damp grasslands and dry fields.

p.132 Little Ringed Plover *Charadrius dubius*

Description: 14–16 cm (5½–6½ in). Smaller, but otherwise similar to Ringed Plover. Adult upperparts grey-brown; underparts white. Head shows pattern of clear, though narrow, black breast-band and black facial mask extending over crown, with narrow white anterior margin lacking in Ringed Plover. Bold *yellow eye-ring,* black bill and yellow legs are best field marks separating it from larger species. Juvenile has pale margins to all feathers of upperparts, creating a scaly appearance similar to juvenile Ringed. In all plumages, small size, together with *long wings* that create a slimmer, more attenuated appearance are good features. In flight, *lacks white wingbar* of Ringed.

Voice: Brief *piu*, quite different from Ringed Plov

Habitat: Rivers, lakes and gravel pits with extensi
shingle margins. More catholic at marshe
and floods on passage and in winter
quarters.

Breeding: Four buffy eggs, streaked and spotted
brown, laid in bare scrape. Incubation
24–26 days, by both sexes.

Range: Summer visitor to inland fresh waters rig
across temperate zone of Palearctic from
Europe to Japan. Also in India and
Southeast Asia, where resident. European
birds winter in Sahelian zone of Africa
south of the Sahara.

This is a river-based species that finds its
ideal conditions along the shingle banks
large rivers after the spring snow-melt an
floods have passed. The widespread use of
concrete during the second half of the
twentieth century, and the consequent
demand for ballast, created huge number
of gravel pits that have proved a perfect
alternative. The species' numbers and ran
have exploded as a result.

p.133   **Ringed Plover** *Charadrius hiaticula*

Description: 18–20 cm (7–8 in). Adult brown above a
white below, marked by broad, black
breast-band, and black face and crown
pattern. A narrow, white supercilium
behind eye does not extend over crown li
Little Ringed Plover. Legs and bill orang
the latter with black tip. Juvenile scaly
brown above with breast-band that may
incomplete. Bill black; legs dark and dul
pinkish. In flight shows *prominent white
wingbar* in all plumages.

Voice: A musical *toor-lee*.

Habitat: Shorelines of shingle and sand, together
with similar inland areas. Also coastal
lagoons, mountains and Arctic tundra.
Outside breeding season, on shorelines,
estuaries and marshes.

Breeding: Four buffy, brown-spotted eggs laid in ba
scrape, usually among shingle. Incubatio
23–26 days, by both sexes.

Range: Virtually circumpolar in tundra zone, though absent from central Canada and Alaska. Widespread and common summer visitor or resident in northern Europe: breeds in Iceland, Britain and Ireland, northwestern France (its lowest latitude), Baltic and Scandinavia. Winters in savannah Africa and western Europe.

West European birds can be found along coasts virtually throughout the year. British birds, for example, are absent only in mid-winter in December and January and probably move no further than the estuaries of Portugal. Siberian birds, in contrast, migrate thousands of miles from the Bering Straits to South Africa.

p.133 **Kentish Plover** *Charadrius alexandrinus*

Description: 15–17 cm (6–6½ in). Small version of Ringed Plover, with broken breast-band. *Paler and more sandy* upperparts; in summer male has warm-rufous crown. Breast-band consists of *black patches at sides* and face pattern of no more than broad extended eye-stripe and narrow crown-bar. Female similar, but lacks rufous crown. Juvenile has scaly feather margins to upperparts and no more than pale, vestigial smudges at sides of breast. Bill and legs black at all times. In flight shows white wingbar between black flight feathers and sandy coverts.

Voice: Musical *choo-it* and softer *wit-wit-wit*.

Habitat: Mainly coastal on saline lagoons and estuaries, salt-pans, and open sandy and muddy shorelines.

Breeding: Three to four buffy eggs, streaked and spotted black, laid in bare scrape in sandy or shingly flats. Incubation 24 days, by both sexes.

Range: Widespread through Old World. Breeds right across Palearctic from Europe and Middle East to Japan. Winters in tropics. European birds are summer visitors, with northern birds wintering in Mediterranean and coastal West Africa.

Named after the English county of Kent,
where it bred on the shingle peninsular o
Dungeness until a light railway was
constructed through the middle of the
breeding grounds. Specimen and egg
collectors made short work of the rest and
the bird has not bred in England since.

p.136 **Dotterel** *Charadrius morinellus*

Description: 20–23 cm (8–9 in). Attractive, but well-
camouflaged plover. More boldly marked
female is grey-brown above with bold
white supercilia that meet on nape. Brea
grey separated by narrow black and whit
bands from *rich-chestnut lower breast and
belly*. Male is dull version of female.
Juvenile mottled brown and buff above,
with brown streaking on buffy backgrou
on sides of breast, broken by faint white
breast-band. Legs and feet yellow in all
plumages. Compare with dark-legged
Sociable Plover.

Voice: A trilled *titti-ri-titti-ri* repeated.

Habitat: Stony and lightly vegetated plateaux of
high mountains and extensive Arctic
tundra; occasionally on large, bare fields
sea level. On passage, on extensive open
pastures and plough, often downland.
Winters in similar open, semi-desert area

Breeding: Three buffy eggs, spotted brown-black, l
in depression lightly lined with mosses a
lichens. Incubation 21–26 days, by male

Range: Breeds among mountains and tundra of
Scotland and from Scandinavia right acr
northernmost Siberia to Bering Straits.
Also among high mountains of central
Asia and locally among mountains of
southern Europe. Winters North Africa
and Middle East.

Several Arctic breeding species of waders
like the Dotterel, have adopted a role-
reversal strategy to deal with the short,
Arctic breeding season. Having produced
eggs weighing about a third of her own
body weight or, if she takes another mate
two-thirds of her body weight, the femal

recovers while the male takes full charge of incubation and tending the young. This division of duties makes sense in the mad dash to rear a brood before the onset of autumn. It also accounts for the male's duller plumage.

p.134 **Pacific Golden Plover** *Pluvialis fulva*

Description: 23–26 cm (9–10 in). Smallest and rarest of the three golden plovers, but very similar to American Golden Plover and distinguished from it only with the greatest care. Pacific has more gold on upperparts and a yellow wash on sides of breast and flanks. *Bill longer and heavier; supercilium buffy rather than white;* and long legs project beyond tail tip in flight. Underwing similarly grey, rather than white like European Golden Plover.

Voice: A loud *cher-it* bearing a resemblance to the *chu-it* of Spotted Redshank.

Habitat: Breeds on Arctic tundra; in winter and on passage haunts grasslands and ploughed fields.

Breeding: Three to four brown-spotted buff eggs laid in hollow. Incubation probably 26 days, by both sexes.

Range: Breeds on both sides of Bering Straits, in western Alaska and in eastern Siberia. Winters India and Southeast Asia through to Australasia.

Much rarer in Europe than American Golden Plover, this is the species that makes an extraordinary landfall in Hawaii each autumn. It also regularly overshoots Asia to reach the Seychelles, only a 1,000 miles from Africa.

p.134 **European Golden Plover**
Pluvialis apricaria

Description: 27–29 cm (10½–11½ in). Typical, medium-sized plover with tubby body, *rounded head, short neck, small bill,* and long legs. In summer, upperparts spangled

black and gold; underparts, from face to
belly, black with broad white margin.
Black underparts more extensive and clea
cut in northern subspecies *N. a. apricaria*
than in southern *N. a. oreophilos* of Britai
Denmark and Germany. In winter, gold
upperparts less apparent, and breast
streaked black and dull gold. In flight
shows only faint wingbar and *white
underwing.*

Voice: A whistled *tlui* in flight.

Habitat: Breeds on Arctic tundra and at altitude
further south among moorlands and even
lowland heaths. In winter frequents
estuarine margins, damp pastures, and
open, ploughed hillsides.

Breeding: Four brown-blotched, buffy eggs laid on
tussock in lightly lined nest. Incubation
27–28 days, mainly by female.

Range: Summer visitor from Iceland to central
Siberia north of the tree line and
southwards to hills of England and Dani
heaths. Strangely, the whole population
heads west, or southwest, to winter in
Mediterranean and around North Sea.

While most British and Irish birds make
only local movements, huge numbers fro
Iceland and Scandinavia arrive in Britain
Ireland and northwestern France to wint
They are, however, highly susceptible to
frost and, like Lapwings, make quite
extensive movements during the course
a winter.

---

p.134   **American Golden Plover**
Pluvialis dominica

Description: 24–28 cm (9½–11 in). Very similar to
European Golden Plover, and classified a
separate species only recently. Easily
overlooked among flocks of that relativel
common and widespread bird. Upperpar
darker, less golden than European;
underparts more buffy with flank-bars in
first winter. Differs structurally in being
smaller, *slimmer* and less pot-bellied, wit
longer legs, longer wings, shorter neck and

more *prominent whitish supercilium*. In flight underwing is grey rather than white.

Voice: A *klee-ee*, with the emphasis on the *klee*.

Habitat: Breeds on Arctic tundra among pools and marshes with dwarf vegetation. On passage, frequents grasslands and plough.

Breeding: Three to four brown-spotted buff eggs laid in hollow lined with lichens. Incubation 26 days, by both the sexes.

Range: Vagrant westward from native North America. Breeds in Canadian Arctic, but replaced by Pacific Golden Plover in western Alaska. Winters in South America.

This diminutive version of the European Golden Plover is regular in Europe in small numbers each autumn. Most are found in Britain and Ireland, where annual totals average about eight a year. From their northwestern breeding grounds in Canada, birds fly eastwards on a great circle route to Labrador and over the western Atlantic to make a landfall in South America. This is the classic route of transatlantic vagrants.

p.135 **Grey Plover** *Pluvialis squatarola*

Description: 28–31 cm (11–12 in). Medium-sized and chunky. In summer, black and white spangled upperparts are separated from black face and underparts by broad white line. In winter, upperparts dull grey and black; underparts greyish, with fine streaking on breast and flanks. In flight shows white wingbar, white rump, and diagnostic *black axillaries (armpits)*. Despite obvious differences, can still be confused with coastal Golden Plovers outside breeding season.

Voice: Whistled *tlee-oo-ee*.

Habitat: Almost exclusively along shorelines. Breeds on Arctic tundra. In winter and on passage frequents rocky and muddy shorelines, estuaries and coastal lagoons. Scarce inland.

Breeding: Four buff-coloured eggs, with dark spots and blotches, laid in scrape lined with a few

bents or stones. Incubation 26–27 days, l
both sexes.

Range: Circumpolar in northernmost tundra zon
called Black-bellied Plover in North
America. Breeding range does not reach
Europe where it is a regular passage
migrant and winter visitor.

This bird is a real globe-spanner, wintering
along the coasts of all the world's great
landmasses as far south as Chile, Cape of
Good Hope and Perth. It finds its way to t
world's most isolated islands, but also wint
as far north as Scotland, no more than 10
degrees latitude south of its breeding range

p.136   **Spur-winged Plover** *Hoplopterus spinosus*

Description: 25–27 cm (10–10½ in). Medium-sized
plover, pale buffy above with distinctive
black cap that reaches eye level, and black
chin and foreneck widening out over brea
and belly. In flight, *black underparts and
flight feathers contrast with white wing linin*
Above, body and wing coverts are buffy a
contrast with black flight feathers. Long
black legs trail in flight. Wings distinctl
rounded and Lapwing-like.

Voice: A harsh *kik*, and plaintive *did-e-do-it*.

Habitat: Open marshes and lagoons, estuaries and
salt-pans, rivers with mud banks.

Breeding: Four black-blotched, buffy eggs laid in b
scrape adjacent to water. Incubation 22–2
days, by both sexes.

Range: Widespread through tropical Africa; also
scarce summer visitor northwards throug
Turkey and Greece.

The expansion of range into Greece was
first noted in 1959. It now breeds along
the coasts of Thrace and Macedonia, whe
there may be over 100 pairs. It has also
spread inland to larger lakes, though ther
is no evidence of a population boom and
remains one of Europe's scarcer breeding
birds. A vagrant to Britain (and Holland)
stayed for several months in Kent and
Sussex, but may have been an escape.

p.136 **Sociable Plover** *Chettusia gregaria*

Description: 27–30 cm (10½–12 in). In summer, basically warm buff above and below, marked by bold head pattern of black cap, white supercilium and black eye-stripe. Underparts have *black and chestnut belly*, with white undertail coverts. In winter has buffy crown with broad, *creamy supercilium* and warmly streaked breast fading to white belly. In flight, warm underparts contrast with white wing linings and secondaries, and with black primaries. From above, black outer wing and buff coverts contrast with white secondaries. Generally gregarious forming small flocks, but vagrants usually alone.

Voice: A shrill whistle away from breeding grounds.

Habitat: Open steppes, dry grassy plains; winters in open savannah country, often near water.

Breeding: Four buff-brown eggs, streaked and spotted blackish. Incubation about 25 days, probably by both sexes.

Range: Vagrant westwards from Russia mainly to southeast Europe. Breeds across Russian steppes; winters in Pakistan and northwest India, and in East Africa. Regular on passage in Turkey.

This is an extremely rare vagrant westwards as far as Britain, where only 32 were identified prior to 1990. It now occurs about once a year, mostly in autumn and mostly associated with flocks of Lapwings. In winter plumage it could perhaps be overlooked as a European Golden Plover.

p.137 **Lapwing** *Vanellus vanellus*

Description: 29–32 cm (11½–12½ in). Medium-sized, *round-winged* plover that appears black and white at any distance. Closer approach shows upperparts to be washed metallic green, with undertail coverts warm chestnut. Head marked black and white, with *wispy crest* rising from hind crown. Chin and breast black contrasting with white face and white lower breast to form

distinct band. In flight, rounded wings a
dark above, but with contrasting white
linings below. Generally gregarious.

Voice: Plaintive *pee-wit*.

Habitat: Damp meadows, marshes, moorland and
open, ploughed fields. In winter, also on
grasslands and estuaries.

Breeding: Four buff-brown, black-blotched eggs lai
in hollow lined with grasses hidden amor
grass. Incubation 24–29 days mainly by
female.

Range: Breeds in broad swathe across Palearctic
from Britain and Portugal to Sea of Japan
Mostly a summer visitor that winters in
China, Pakistan, Middle East, around
Mediterranean and in western Europe.

This is a remarkably adaptable plover tha
occupies a vast range of different habitats
from muddy estuaries to dry upland
plough. It is Europe's most common wad
and its aerial displays and plaintive calls ;
familiar signs of spring. Until quite
recently, its eggs were served as a delicacy
in restaurants in many countries.

SANDPIPERS, SNIPE AND PHALAROPES (Scolopacidae)

93 species; worldwide. Twenty-five breed i
Europe, four are regular passage migrants,
and many others are scarce migrants or
vagrants. Many are long-distance migrant:
that, from time to time, wander and may
then occur thousands of miles off course.
This is a highly diverse family, varying in
size from large to really tiny birds. Most a:
brown above and white below, with variab
amounts of streaking, but are more bright
coloured when breeding. They have long
legs and most have long bills that are used
probes in soft mud. The sexes are mostly
similar. They occupy a wide variety of
wetland habitats, though mud flats and
estuaries hold the largest concentrations ir
terms of the number of individuals. Most :
gregarious, and flocks of tens of thousands

a single species may occur at favoured winter feeding grounds. In contrast, other species are solitary and never frequent estuaries at all. Many species perform huge migrations, from one end of the earth to the other, and breed among the high Arctic tundra as far north as ice-free land exists. Several have adopted interesting breeding routines to cope with the very short summer at these latitudes. Many species are highly specialized feeders and have the longest bills, for their size, of all the world's birds. Others are remarkably adaptable and will feed on almost anything edible.

---

p.138 **Knot** *Calidris canutus*

Description: 24–27 cm (9½–10½ in). In breeding season, entire underparts rich chestnut with chestnut spangling on otherwise greyish upperparts. In winter, grey above and white below, with streaks of arrowheads on breast and flanks. *Bill short,* about the same length as head, and yellowish-green legs also relatively short. In flight, shows white wingbar and grey, not white, rump. Stocky, even *tubby, build, short bill and size* distinguish it from Dunlin.

Voice: A muttered *knot.*

Habitat: Breeds on high Arctic tundra with marshy pools among scant vegetation. In winter, frequents intertidal flats and estuaries in huge flocks, but also in small numbers along rocky shorelines.

Breeding: Four brown-spotted, pale-greenish eggs laid in a scrape lined with lichens. Incubation 20–25 days by both sexes, though male takes larger share.

Range: Breeds central and eastern Siberia, among Canadian archipelago and in north and eastern Greenland. Winters mainly in western Europe and West Africa, where about 430,000 birds are concentrated at a few major sites.

There are good grounds for believing that these birds fly from their remote breeding grounds to their winter haunts around the

North Sea in a single non-stop flight. Its name may commemorate King Canute, who attempted to turn back the waves, but may equally be derived from its call.

p.138 **Sanderling** *Calidris alba*

Description: 19–22 cm (7½–8½ in). A shorebird that causes confusion when present on marshes particularly in summer plumage. In winter, it is palest of all waders: pale grey above, white below with distinctive *black patch at bend of wing*. In summer, upperparts spangled chestnut and black, head to breast heavily streaked chestnut forming a contrasting breast-band where it meets white underparts. Bill short, about three-quarters the length of head, and straight; legs black. Typically runs up and down beaches in small groups with the waves; also feeds among rocky pools. The short bill and overall shape is similar to a stint.

Voice: A sharp *quit-quit* repeated.

Habitat: Open shorelines, both rocky and sandy, but seldom on estuaries. Breeds among tundra.

Breeding: Four olive, lightly spotted-brown eggs laid in leaf-lined hollow beside tuft of vegetation. Incubation 23–24 days, by both sexes. Female sometimes lays second clutch which is incubated by male while she returns to incubate first-laid clutch.

Range: Breeds on high Arctic tundra of central Siberia, Canadian archipelago and north and east coasts of Greenland. A true globe spanner, Sanderling winter in northern Europe and on all the world's large landmasses south to Tierra del Fuego.

The ability of these tiny birds (weighing only about 50g) to fly from Cape Town to Greenland in a few brief weeks of spring is amazing. That they then may not find conditions suitable for breeding is doubtless compensated for by their ability to rear two broods concurrently when conditions are right.

p.140 Little Stint *Calidris minuta*

Description: 14–15 cm (5½–6 in). Tiny wader, about the same size as House Sparrow, and the standard stint from which all rarities must be distinguished. In summer, spangled chestnut and black above, white below, with warm streaking on sides of breast. On close approach, a clear supercilium can be seen to be *'split'*. Tertials extend almost to tips of primaries on folded wing. Legs and feet black. In juvenile, most frequent plumage on passage through Europe, is warmer than adult with less chestnut, less streaking and characteristic *white double 'V' on back*. In winter, grey above, white below with a little breast streaking.

Voice: High-pitched *tit*, repeated.

Habitat: Breeds on Arctic tundra pools and marshes. Outside breeding season frequents marshes, lakeside margins, estuaries, salt-pans, sewage-plants, and occasionally open shorelines.

Breeding: Four pale-olive, brown-speckled eggs laid in cup of grasses constructed in hollow. Incubation 20–21 days, by both sexes. There are cases of two clutches being laid by a single female that then incubates the first clutch while her mate takes on the second. Such tactics are well suited to the short breeding season in the high latitudes that this species inhabits.

Range: Breeds among high Arctic tundra from northernmost Scandinavia to eastern Siberia. Winters in India and Middle East, and across savannah Africa. Common spring and autumn migrant through most of Europe, with smaller numbers in winter mainly in Mediterranean.

The standard, small sandpiper from which all others must be distinguished. With an increasing number of Asiatic stints and American peep occurring as vagrants in Europe, a thorough familiarity with this species is essential if satisfactory identifications are to be made. The presumption is that all small sandpipers are Little Stints until proved otherwise.

p.140 **Temminck's Stint** *Calidris temminckii*

Description: 13–15 cm (5–6 in). Slightly smaller than
Little Stint and decidedly less common on
passage through Europe. In summer adult
has black, chestnut-fringed upperparts wit
streaked breast forming *distinct line* with
white underparts. Legs short and *yellow-
green;* bill black and three-quarters the
length of head. Juvenile and passage adult
are greyish olive above and much more
uniform and less scalloped than Little Stin
Bears more resemblance to Common
Sandpiper than to Dunlin-like Little Stint
Picks food from surface rather than
probing. In flight, shows white outer tail
like Common Sandpiper.

Voice: Sharp, rolling *prrit* in flight.

Habitat: Open tundra and similar landscapes
southwards at altitude. On passage, mostl
along margins of freshwater pools.

Breeding: Four greyish-olive, brown-spotted eggs lai
in scrape with a few grasses as lining.
Incubation 21–22 days, mainly by male.

Range: Breeds from Scandinavian mountains
(recently in northern Scotland) eastwards
across the tundra to Bering Straits. Winter
in China, Southeast Asia, India and across
the Sahelian zone of Africa. Scarce passage
migrant through Europe.

This species is often confused with other
pale-legged stints, though its similarity to
Common Sandpiper should quickly
eliminate both Least Sandpiper and Long-
toed Stint. It is usually a very tame bird
that ignores humans as it feeds busily alon
some marshy edge.

p.139 **Pectoral Sandpiper** *Calidris melanotos*

Description: 17–21 cm (6½–8 in). Slightly larger than
Dunlin and always much browner; may
recall diminutive Ruff. Upperparts brow
marked by bold, *double, white 'V' on back,*
more prominent on juvenile than summe
adult. Underparts white, but with heavily
streaked breast terminating abruptly *to*

form distinct band. Small head, with clear, pale supercilium isolating brown cap. Bill longer than head and slightly decurved. Legs shortish, like Common Sandpiper, and yellow. In flight shows narrow wingbar and dark central tail with white ovals.

Voice: Clear, but grating *kreep*.

Habitat: Breeds along rivers and marshes among taiga zone, rather than open tundra beyond tree line. On passage and in winter, on freshwater marshes, floods and coastal pools mostly with good growth of emergent vegetation.

Breeding: Four greenish, brown-blotched eggs laid in hollow lined with grasses. Incubation 21–23 days, by female.

Range: Most regular of all transatlantic vagrant waders to Europe. Breeds in eastern Siberia into Alaska and west Canadian archipelago. Winters mainly in South America.

The great circle route, from northwestern North America to the pampas of Argentina, follows a line eastwards out over the Atlantic, avoiding the Caribbean. It is therefore easy to see how these birds can get lost in mid-ocean and make a European landfall. The increasing frequency of these birds in July, and their more eastern distribution as vagrants, has led to speculation that they may now be breeding somewhere in northern Europe.

---

p.141 **Curlew Sandpiper** *Calidris ferruginea*

Description: 18–20 cm (7–8 in). Very similar to Dunlin, but marginally larger and decidedly *more elegant*. In summer, whole of underparts rich chestnut; upperparts spangled chestnut and black. In winter, grey like Dunlin above with faint breast-streaking. Juvenile scaly above, with black margins to grey feathers. Underparts white, with warm buff wash over breast. In all plumages, *small head on long neck, coupled with long, decurved bill and long legs* create an elegance never associated with Dunlin. In flight, one of only a few similar-sized waders with *clear white rump*.

Voice: A soft *chirrup*.

Habitat: High Arctic tundra pools in summer. In winter, frequents freshwater pools and marshes, salt-pans and estuaries.

Breeding: Three to four olive, brown-blotched eggs laid in cup placed in tussock. Incubation period unknown, but apparently performed by both sexes.

Range: Breeds only among coastal tundra in central and eastern Siberia. Winters along coasts from India to Australia and throughout savannah Africa. Regular double-passage migrant through Europe, more numerous in autumn.

The Curlew Sandpiper occurs in Europe in variable numbers each autumn, with adults passing through in July and August and juveniles in August and September. This pattern of occurrence probably indicates a first wave of failed breeders, followed by the season's juveniles and, at the tail end, a scattering of winter-plumaged adults. It may, however, indicate that either adult males, or more likely, adult females leave the breeding grounds while their partner rears the young.

p.139 **Purple Sandpiper** *Calidris maritima*

Description: 20–22 cm (8–8½ in). A dark, thickset, chunky wader marked by longish, pink-based bill and short yellow legs. In summer has brown margins to black feathers on upperparts, white underparts heavily streaked by lines of black arrowheads. In winter uniformly dark grey above, with streaking confined to breast and flanks. In flight, shows narrow white bar across dark wings and dark-centred tail. *Short legs, dark coloration* and rocky habitat are major features.

Voice: A twittering *weet-wet* among flocks in flight; mostly silent.

Habitat: High Arctic tundra coastlines, but also at altitude among mountains. In winter, found along rocky shorelines, locally on wave-washed jetties and groynes.

Breeding: Four pale-green, brown-blotched eggs laid in cup of grass. Incubation 21–22 days, mainly by male.

Range: Circumpolar along Arctic coastlines, though absent from large areas either side of Bering Straits. Seldom ventures further south than northwestern Europe, wintering along coasts of north and west Europe and eastern coasts of USA.

A tough little wader that breeds among the high Arctic wastes and winters as far north as ice-free shores can be found. Moves southwards only when forced to by harsh conditions, but is then locally plentiful along suitable shorelines of Britain and northwest France.

p.141 **Dunlin** *Calidris alpina*

Description: 16–19 cm (6½–7½ in). Commonest European shorebird and the standard small wader from which all others must be separated. Usually seen in flocks, busily feeding in typical hunched-up posture. In summer has broad brown margins to black feathers of upperparts, with broad *black belly-patch* and heavily streaked breast. In winter, grey above, white below with streaking on breast. Juvenile has buffy margins to feathers of upperparts, extensive breast streaking, and odd black feathers on belly. At all times, *longish, slightly decurved bill and hunched posture* are useful features. In flight, shows white wingbar and black-centred white rump.

Voice: A rasping *schreep* in flight.

Habitat: Breeds among tundra, in mountains and even temperate lowland marshes. Winters along shores and estuaries in vast flocks, as well as at inland lakes and marshes.

Breeding: Four green, brown-blotched eggs laid in cup of grasses placed in tussock. Incubation 21–22 days, by both sexes.

Range: Circumpolar on open tundra, but southwards among temperate mountains

and coastal marshes. Winters along temperate coasts, but does not regularly penetrate southern hemisphere.

A thorough knowledge of the plumages and structure of Dunlin is an essential for any northern-hemisphere birder with even the vaguest ambition of picking out Curlew Sandpiper, Little Stint, Knot and any number of rarer species. Positive identification is by no means simple as birds vary in size and pass through various stages between plumages.

---

p.141 **Broad-billed Sandpiper**
Limicola falcinellus

Description: 16–17 cm (6½ in). Something like a Dunlin in Snipe's clothing. In summer, black feathers of upperparts broadly edged buff and white creating highly contrasted appearance. *White, double 'V' marks the back,* and *crown is decidedly striped*. Bill long, Dunlin-sized, and distinctly decurved at tip. Breast heavily streaked with *chevrons extending along flanks*. Much duller grey above in winter, with only faint streaking at sides of breast on otherwise white underparts. There is a Sanderling-like black area at bend of wing, but head striping and decurved bill are the best features. In flight dark with narrow white wingbar.

Voice: A trilled *tir-eek*.

Habitat: Breeds among Arctic tundra and, at altitude, among northern mountains with pools and bogs. Winters along coastal marshes, salt-pans and on estuaries.

Breeding: Four pale-buffy eggs, heavily spotted reddish-brown, laid in cup placed in tussock among marshland. Incubation 21 days, by both sexes.

Range: Highly disjointed in coastal Siberia, but also a scarce and elusive summer visitor through Scandinavian mountains and open lowlands. Winters from Middle East to India and Southeast Asia. Passage migrant through eastern Mediterranean to, as yet, unknown wintering area in Africa.

This largely solitary wader is always difficult to locate and is, as a result, little known. It may well breed over a much wider area of Siberia than is thought and winter somewhere in Africa where it has been overlooked. The healthy Swedish and Finnish populations presumably pass through the Mediterranean, but are still largely missed.

p.142 **Ruff** *Philomachus pugnax*

Description: ♂ 27–31 cm (10½–12 in); ♀ 22–25 cm (8½–10 in). When breeding, male (Ruff) is spangled chestnut and black above, white below, with unmistakable breast, neck- and head-plumes that are erected in display. Slightly smaller female (Reeve) is spangled black and buff above with heavily barred breast and white underparts. In winter, both sexes scalloped above, the feathers neatly margined with buff, and white below. Juvenile similar, but with warm-buffy wash over breast. At all times *long neck, small head and medium-length bill* are structurally distinct from most other waders. Legs red, orange or yellow.

Voice: Mostly silent.

Habitat: Breeds on marshes and pools in tundra, as well as similar zones in mountains and temperate lowlands. Winters on freshwater marshes, floods and lakes.

Breeding: Four pale-green eggs, boldly blotched dark red-brown, laid in well-lined hollow among dense grasses. Incubation 20–21 days, by female alone.

Range: Widespread double-passage migrant and summer visitor to Europe. Breeds right-across Palearctic; winters sub-Saharan Africa, also India and locally in western Europe.

Like many of the grouse, Ruff gather at a communal lekking ground where males stake out a small territory which they defend with elaborate dances designed to show their head-plumes to greatest advantage. Females visit the lek only to mate, choosing the dominant male at the centre of the lek. Sometimes females queue for attention, while all around them rival males are doing their best to attract them. After mating, the males have nothing whatever to do with the eggs or brood.

---

p.143 **Jack Snipe** *Lymnocryptes minimus*

Description: 18–20 cm (7–8 in). Very similar to Common Snipe, but smaller and marked by much *shorter bill*. Even more secretive and shy than Snipe, keeping to dense cover and flying only when flushed, and then only low and for short distances. (Common Snipe tower into the sky and circle when disturbed.) Upperparts effectively camouflaged in brown and black with distinct creamy stripes. Underparts white with bold streaking on breast and flanks. Head boldly striped. Bill no more than one and a half times length of head; legs short and greenish yellow. In flight *lacks white on margins of wedge-shaped tail*.

Voice: Usually silent.

Habitat: Breeds among tundra and taiga marshes and bogs. On passage and in winter frequents well-vegetated swamps and marshes.

Breeding: Four greenish, brown-blotched eggs, laid in cup in grassy tussock. Incubation 24 days or more, by female alone.

Range: Breeds right across northern Palearctic from Fennoscandia almost to Bering Straits. Winters from northwestern Europe through Mediterranean and Middle East to India and Sahelian Africa.

Though it is a regular winter visitor to so much of Europe, Jack Snipe remains a highly elusive bird due mainly to its secretive habits. Even where locally numerous, it is seldom seen except when flushed and, even then, only briefly.

---

p.143 **Common Snipe** *Gallinago gallinago*

Description: 25–27 cm (10–10½ in). Medium-sized, well-camouflaged wader, marked by *very long bill*. Upperparts heavily barred and streaked, marked by bold creamy stripes.

Underparts buffy on breast, white on belly, both heavily streaked with chevrons. Head striped; bill some two and a half times length of head; legs shortish and yellow-green. When flushed, *towers high into the air* showing *white margins* to rounded tail.

Voice: Harsh *scarp*; also a repeated *chiper-chiper*.

Habitat: Marshes, bogs, swamps and fens, from tundra and taiga zones south to temperate climes. Indeed, almost any wetland with good growth of emergent vegetation.

Breeding: Four pale-green eggs, blotched and spotted dark red-brown, laid in cup placed in tussock surrounded by water or marsh. Incubation 18–20 days, by female.

Range: Circumpolar in north, where mainly a summer visitor. Also resident in South America and South and East Africa. Northern birds winter in India and Southeast Asia through Middle East and across most of temperate western Europe.

Snipe find their food by deep probing in soft, freshwater mud with their exceptionally long bills. They are seldom found on intertidal areas and are particularly prone to hard winters when a freeze-up prevents them from feeding. They are therefore highly mobile during the winter and may concentrate in enormous numbers at ice-free areas.

p.143 **Great Snipe** *Gallinago media*

Description: 27–29 cm (10½–11½ in). Slightly larger and decidedly *more chunky* than Common Snipe, with slightly, but noticeably *shorter bill*. Upperparts boldly barred and striped in brown and black, with creamy horizontal stripes and three bold white bars across folded wing. Underparts buffy on breast; white below, heavily barred dark brown. Head large, rounded and striped. Bill about twice length of head. In flight, corpulent shape is reminiscent of Woodcock, which is similarly barred, rather than streaked, below. When flushed, flies low before alighting, quite unlike Common Snipe's towering.

Voice: A croak when flushed, but often silent when not displaying.

Habitat: Flooded grasslands and marshes among wooded countryside. In winter mostly marshes, but also dry grasslands.

Breeding: Four grey-buff, brown speckled eggs laid in a well-lined hollow. Incubation 22–24 days, by female alone.

Range: Breeds from mountains of Scandinavia and from Baltic eastwards across Russia to central Siberia. Winters right across savannah Africa. In Europe, also breeds in eastern Poland.

This is one of the lekking waders, the male of which gather at a jousting ground and display, with chests held high and puffed out, while uttering various warbling, twittering and deep throbbing sounds. Territorial males soon sort out their mini-territories, but leks are often visited by other males that may hold a territory at another lek. Dominant males at the centre of the lek are most successful with the females.

---

p.143 **Woodcock** *Scolopax rusticola*

Description: 32–36 cm (12½–14 in). Medium-sized, chubby wader that is most active at dawn and dusk. Highly camouflaged and difficult to locate and see at rest. Upperparts heavily *barred* in buff, brown and black merge perfectly with forest debris. Underparts buffy, heavily barred brown. Crown has broad, dark-brown transverse bars. Legs short; bill less than twice length of head. In flight, *tubby shape, rounded wings and downward-pointing bill* are good features.

Voice: A high pitched *tissick* in roding over territory at dusk.

Habitat: Damp, often mixed woodlands, with moist patches or boggy ponds. More widespread in winter woodlands when damp patches more prevalent than in summer.

Breeding: Four buff, heavily blotched brown eggs,
laid in depression lined with leaves, often
against a tree. Incubation 20–23 days,
solely by female.

Range: Breeds right across Palearctic from
northern Spain to Japan with outposts in
Caucasus and Himalayas. Most are summer
visitors, though British birds and those of
adjacent Continent may be resident.
Widespread winter visitor to south and
west Europe.

One of those species that has to be
searched for, rather than encountered
casually. A spring visit in the early evening
to suitable habitat may be rewarded with
the sight of males roding overhead and
uttering their characteristic calls just as it
becomes really dark.

---

p.144 **Black-tailed Godwit** *Limosa limosa*

Description: 38–43 cm (15–17in). Medium to large
wader marked by long, straight, Snipe-like
bill. In summer, head, neck and breast
rufous with distinct dark barring on breast.
Remaining underparts white, with a few
black chevrons along flanks. Upperparts
spangled black and brown. In winter,
whole plumage greyish, lacking streaks;
whitish on belly. Always a larger, *less-
streaked, longer-legged and longer-billed bird*
than Bar-tailed Godwit. In flight, shows
distinctive black, *white-barred wing, white
tail with black terminal band,* and legs that
extend beyond tail tip.

Voice: Loud *reeka-reeka-reeka*.

Habitat: Flooded grassland; winters on marshes,
lakes and estuaries. Seldom on open
shorelines like Bar-tailed Godwit.

Breeding: Four greenish, brown-blotched eggs laid in
neat cup of grasses among tussocky, damp
ground. Incubation 22–24 days, by both
sexes.

Range: Breeds from Iceland across temperate
Europe and Russia to central Siberia. Also
breeds locally in eastern Siberia. Winters
from India to Australia, across Sahelian

Africa and in Mediterranean and western
Europe.

Vast numbers, perhaps a majority of the
world population, are trans-Saharan
migrants that winter in the western
Sahelian region at Lake Chad and the Niger
Inundation Zone. In autumn, birds fly the
Sahara from Morocco. In spring, a large
passage through Italy indicates a more
easterly route – a loop migration.

p.144 Bar-tailed Godwit *Limosa lapponica*

Description: 36–40 cm (14–16 in). Slightly smaller
than similar Black-tailed Godwit and
distinctly more marine outside breeding
season. In summer, adult has black
upperparts, boldly spangled with buffy
chestnut. Head and entire underparts, (not
just the breast), are warm rufous. Outside
breeding season, upperparts buffy-brown
and heavily *streaked* like a Curlew's. In all
plumages, bill is a little shorter than
Black-tailed Godwit's and *slightly uptilted*.
Legs shorter, with only the feet extending
beyond tail in flight; *lack of wing bar, and
multi-barred tail,* are diagnostic.

Voice: A brief *kirrick*.

Habitat: Open tundra pools and swamps in summer.
In winter open shores and estuaries.

Breeding: Four olive, brown-blotched eggs laid in
hollow lined with leaves among vegetation.
Incubation 20–21 days, by both sexes.

Range: Breeds in high Arctic from northern
Scandinavia right across Siberia. Winters
from Southeast Asia to Australia, through
Middle East, in Africa south to the Cape,
and widely in western Europe.

Winters in huge numbers at favoured sites
where they obtain their food by deep and
vigorous probing in oozy mud. When
their feeding grounds are covered by the
tide they flight, along with other waders,
to an undisturbed high-tide roost to await
lower water. Thus their feeding is quite
independent of clock time.

p.145 **Whimbrel** *Numenius phaeopus*

Description: 39–43 cm (15½–17 in). Similar to Curlew, but smaller, with *striped crown*. Dark grey-brown above, with narrow, pale-buff margins to feathers. Underparts white, with warm wash over breast; heavy streaks on breast graduating to line of chevrons along flanks. Head has dark lores, bold supercilium and distinct-striped crown. Bill twice length of head, *decurved towards tip, and shorter than that of Curlew*. In flight, shows similar white 'V' extending up back and lacks wingbar.

Voice: A whistled *whi-whi-whi-whi-whi-whi-whi*.

Habitat: Breeds in wooded tundra with lakes and marshes. Outside breeding season, frequents open shores, estuaries and marshes.

Breeding: Four olive-green, brown-blotched eggs laid in cup of grasses. Incubation 24–28 days, by both sexes.

Range: Circumpolar in north, extending from Iceland and Scotland to Siberia, Alaska and Canadian Arctic. Winters in southern hemisphere, but also locally in southern Iberia.

The American subspecies *N. p. hudsonicus* is recognizable in the field by its darker underparts and underwing and, particularly, by its lacking the white 'V' up the back.

---

p.145 **Slender-billed Curlew**
Numenius tenuirostris

Description: 36–41 cm (14–16 in). Small relative of Curlew and Whimbrel that teeters on verge of extinction. Streaked upperparts *lack crown stripes* of Whimbrel; underparts white with *distinct rows of spots rather than streaks*. Decurved bill finer and shorter than that of relatives. In flight shows white 'V' on back and white underwing.

Voice: Brief, high-pitched *coor-lee*.

Habitat: Breeds on marshy steppes and damp taiga; winters at coastal freshwater marshes.

Breeding: Four rufus-blotched, olive-yellow eggs laid in cup in tussock. Incubation unknown.

Range: Breeds central Siberia east of Caspian Sea; winters Mediterranean region.

Present breeding grounds unknown. Winters Morocco and Italy in tiny numbers. Europe's most endangered bird with world population of less than fifty.

p.145 **Curlew** *Numenius arquata*

Description: 51–61 cm (20–24 in). Large, brown wader with very long, decurved bill. Upperpart heavily streaked black and grey-brown. Underparts warm buff on breast, white on belly, and heavily streaked throughout, with chevrons along flanks. *Head streaked and very plain. Bill over three times length of head* and decurved. In flight, shows white 'V' extending up back. Juvenile Curlews have shorter bills and could be confused with Slender-billed Curlew.

Voice: A plaintive *coor-lee*; in display produces a bubbling, drawn-out call.

Habitat: Upland moors, heaths, damp meadows and marshes in summer. Shorebird in winter, mainly resorting to estuaries and shoreline.

Breeding: Four olive eggs, blotched dark reddish brown, laid in scrape among grasses. Incubation 26–30 days, mainly by female.

Range: Breeds right across northern and temperate Europe, through Russia and Siberia almost to Sea of Japan. Winters in coastal Africa and Asia, but also in northwestern Europe.

Although its calls are a familiar evocation of the countryside of Europe, its vast range, particularly in winter, makes it equally familiar throughout the Old World.

pp.146 & 150 **Spotted Redshank** *Tringa erythropus*

Description: 29–32 cm (11½–12½ in). Arctic version of Common Redshank. In summer, *black, with white spots* over wings and white bars on undertail. In winter, pale grey above, with fine black barring over wings. In flight, shows white 'V' extending up the back, uniform wings lacking bar, and feet extended well beyond tail tip. In all plumages, slightly larger, slimmer and more elegant than Common Redshank, with *longer red legs and longer and slimmer red-based bill*. Often feeds in deeper water, picking food delicately from the surface.

Voice: Explosive *choo-it*.

Habitat: Breeds among wooded Arctic tundra and on marshes in conifer forests. In winter and on passage haunts freshwater marshes, sheltered estuaries and lagoons; seldom found on open shorelines.

Breeding: Four olive, blotched-brown eggs laid in grass-lined hollow. Incubation period remains unknown, but male probably takes sole charge of eggs and rearing the young.

Range: Summer visitor to far north of Europe. Breeds from Fennoscandia eastwards across Eurasia to Bering Straits. Winters in China, India and across Sahelian zone. A few overwinter in Europe, mainly in Mediterranean.

Black birds, in full summer plumage, pass through temperate Europe in late spring and are nothing less than splendid. With a gap of no more than three or four weeks, they start to return southwards. Most of these early birds are presumed to be females that have laid their eggs and left their partners to incubate and care for their broods.

pp.146 & 150 **Common Redshank** *Tringa totanus*

Description: 26–30 cm (10–12 in). Common and conspicuous throughout most of Europe; in all plumages a medium-sized, brown wader with streaked breast and flanks, marked by long red legs. Red-based bill less than twice length of head. In flight, shows bold *white trailing edge to the wings*. Confusable only with more elegant Spotted Redshank and small-headed, long-necked Ruff. Often very noisy, particularly when breeding territory disturbed.

Voice: A melodic *tyew-yew-yew*; also a harsh *teuk* of alarm.

Habitat: Upland moors and lowland marshes and
floods. In winter frequents wide range of
habitats including rocky and muddy
shorelines, estuaries, floods and marshes,
lagoons, salt-pans, and damp coastal fields

Breeding: Four buffy, black-blotched eggs laid in nea
cup of grasses among long grass that forms
canopy over nest. Incubation 23–24 days,
by both sexes.

Range: Breeds right across whole of Palearctic, wit
an extension southwards to Tibet. In
Europe, range fragmented in the dry south
with largest numbers in the wetter north. I
winter frequents coasts of Asia and Africa,
but many can be found around North Sea.

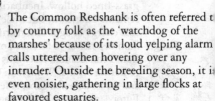

The Common Redshank is often referred t
by country folk as the 'watchdog of the
marshes' because of its loud yelping alarm
calls uttered when hovering over any
intruder. Outside the breeding season, it i
even noisier, gathering in large flocks at
favoured estuaries.

pp.147 & 150   **Marsh Sandpiper** *Tringa stagnatilis*

Description: 22–24 cm (8½–9½ in). Slim, elegant wader
with very long legs that extend well beyon
tail tip in flight. In summer, grey
upperparts with black anchors on feather
centres create a spotted effect. Underparts
white, with black streaking on breast and a
few chevrons on flanks. Slim shape, *delicate
rounded head, needle-like bill and very long
greenish legs* are the best field characters. In
winter, pale grey above, with dark near ber
of the wing, and unspotted white
underparts. Head plain white with only a
little pale grey on crown giving it a
somewhat bland look. Wades in water,
picking food delicately from the surface.

Voice: Distant *tu* and *tchik* notes.

Habitat: Freshwater marshes, lakes and pools amon
grassy steppes.

Breeding: Four buffy eggs, spotted and blotched
brown, laid in grass-lined hollow.
Incubation period unknown but performe
by both sexes.

Range: Breeds on Russian steppes eastwards across Siberia. In winter found mainly in savannah Africa and in India as well as Southeast Asia. A passage migrant through southeast Europe, and a vagrant westwards.

The occurrence of these birds in winter in West Africa, combined with their virtual absence to the north, is seen as indicating not so much a trans-Saharan crossing, but a diagonal crossing of several thousand miles of the world's most inhospitable desert.

---

pp.147 & 151 **Greenshank** *Tringa nebularia*

Description: 29–32 cm (11½–12½ in). A medium-sized, grey wader marked by long green legs. In summer, grey upperparts spangled or dotted with black. Underparts white, with heavy streaking on head and breast. In winter, grey above, with reduced streaking on head and breast. In all plumages, *long, green legs and long, slightly uptilted bill* are characteristic. Bill twice length of head, and longer and heavier than Marsh Sandpiper. In flight shows white 'V' extending up the back and feet that project beyond tail, but no wingbar.

Voice: A loud *tu-tu-tu*.

Habitat: Marshes and bogs among open moorland and conifer forests. Winters on marshes, floods and estuaries.

Breeding: Four buffy, brown-blotched eggs laid in neat cup, sited in marshland tussock or on dry ground near a broken-off dead branch. Incubation 24–25 days, mainly by female.

Range: Breeds from Scotland across northern Europe and through boreal zone of Siberia to Kamchatka. Winters throughout most of Old World southern hemisphere, as well as along shores of Mediterranean and European Atlantic.

This is a common double-passage migrant through Europe that seldom occurs in large flocks. It is most at home among freshwater marshes and will use even tiny waters as stop-overs. Its characteristic call is among the first learned by would-be wader watchers.

pp.148 & 151 **Green Sandpiper** *Tringa ochropus*

Description: 22–24 cm (8½–9½ in). A medium to small
dark-backed wader that appears black abov
in flight. Easily confused with Wood
Sandpiper, but distinguished by having
*only white speckles on dark greenish-brown
upperparts*. Underparts white, clearly
streaked on breast. Head shows broad
supercilium that extends to, *but not beyond,
eye*. Bill about one and a half times length
of head; green legs comparatively short. In
flight shows white rump, wings uniformly
dark above and below.

Voice: A rising *tluit-weet-wit* alarm call.

Habitat: Breeds among conifer-forest marshes and
bogs. Outside breeding season frequents
edge of marshes, drainage ditches and
streams with high banks.

Breeding: Four olive-coloured eggs, spotted reddish
brown, laid in old nest of another species i
a tree. Incubation 20–23 days, mainly by
female.

Range: Breeds right across boreal zone of Palearct
from Scandinavia to Sea of Japan. In winte
found in India, China and northern
savannah Africa, as well as in temperate ar
northern Europe. On passage occurs
throughout Europe.

These are generally solitary birds that
characteristically rise, with loud calls, from
marshland drainage ditch. This habitat is
shared by few other waders and none use it s
regularly. Its ecological replacement in Nor
America is aptly called Solitary Sandpiper.

pp.148 & 151 **Wood Sandpiper** *Tringa glareola*

Description: 19–21 cm (7½–8 in). Medium to small
wader marked by slim elegance. Grey-
brown upperparts *heavily speckled with whit*
making it much paler than Green
Sandpiper at rest, though it can appear
surprisingly dark in flight. Prominent
supercilium extends well behind eye; bill about
one and a half times length of head. Breas
heavily streaked, belly white. Legs yellow,

and longer than those of Green Sandpiper. In flight shows white rump and pale underwing. Compared with Green Sandpiper, a slimmer, longer-necked and longer-legged bird, with paler upperparts.

Voice: A trilled *whit-whit-whit*.

Habitat: Breeds among marshes and lakes in conifer forests. Outside breeding season haunts freshwater marshes and lake margins.

Breeding: Four pale-green, brown-blotched eggs laid in grass-lined hollow. Incubation 22–23 days, mainly by female.

Range: Breeds across boreal zone of Palearctic from Scandinavia to Bering Straits. Winters in savannah Africa, India, and from Southeast Asia to Australia. Common passage migrant through Europe, particularly in autumn.

Huge numbers gather in southern Europe in autumn, feeding voraciously to put on fuel in the form of fat in preparation for flying the Sahara. Some individuals virtually double their weight in a few short weeks.

pp.149 & 151 **Common Sandpiper** *Actitis hypoleucos*

Description: 18–21 cm (7–8 in). A small to medium-sized wader that bobs continuously in tumbling streams in summer. Upperparts olive-brown, with inconspicuous black streaks. Underparts white with heavy streaking that terminates abruptly to form a breast-band. *A wedge of white between breast and wing* is a diagnostic field mark. Bill is one and a half times length of head; legs short and green. The continuous bobbing, wagtail-like action of this bird distinguishes it from most other waders except Wood and Green Sandpipers which do bob, but not continuously. Shows narrow white wingbar in strangely *stuttering, shallow-winged flight*.

Voice: Whistling, high-pitched *swee-swee-oo*.

Habitat: In summer frequents fast-running streams and upland lake shores. Outside the breeding season, freshwater marshes, lake and pool margins, and estuaries.

Breeding: Four cream-coloured, chestnut-spotted eggs, laid in shallow cup of grasses placed beneath tussock. Incubation 20-23 days, b both sexes.

Range: Summer visitor to whole of north and temperate Palearctic from Spain to Kamchatka. Winters from Australia through Asia to sub-Saharan Africa.

The jerking, stiff-winged flight action, as well as the continuous bobbing when at rest, makes this one of the easiest of all sandpipers to identify, no matter how it is seen. Only its close American relative, Spotted Sandpiper, is at all confusable.

p.149 Terek Sandpiper *Xenus cinereus*

Description: 22–24 cm (8½–9½ in). Medium-sized, gre and white sandpiper, with short, orange legs and long, upcurved bill that is quite unlike any other wader. In summer, upperparts grey with black 'braces' and black at bend of wing. *Legs orange and short; bill long, upcurved and red based*. The combination of short legs and long bill accentuates length of body. Winter plumage similar but black 'braces' are lost In flight, shows white trailing edge to win like Common Redshank.

Voice: A whistling *wik-a-wik-a-wik*.

Habitat: Breeds among marshes in boreal zone. Winters on mud flats and estuaries.

Breeding: Four buff-coloured eggs, blotched reddish-brown, laid in hollow, frequently on small island. Incubation 23–24 days, by both sexe

Range: Breeds across northern Palearctic from Finland eastwards to Bering Straits. Decidedly scarce on passage in Europe. Winters on coasts from Nigeria and South Africa eastwards through Middle East and Asia to Australia.

The European breeding range is centred o Finland at Oulu where it is nevertheless decidedly scarce. It is also rare on passage, even in the eastern Mediterranean and in North Africa.

p.152 **Turnstone** *Arenaria interpres*

Description: 22–24 cm (8½–9½ in). Medium to small-sized wader of stocky build, with short legs and bill. Shows remarkable feeding technique of turning over stones, seaweed and other debris to obtain marine animals sheltering beneath. Also practises same technique on dry land, and even visits coastal bird tables. In summer, chestnut and black above, white below with *complex facial pattern* of black and white. In winter, loses chestnut and becomes greyish brown with less complex facial pattern. Short, pointed, black bill slightly upturned; legs orange.

Voice: Rapidly repeated *tuk-a-tuk*.

Habitat: Coastal tundra and adjacent river islets; in winter, all manner of shorelines from sheltered estuaries and coastal marshes to wave-driven rocky shores. Rare away from coast.

Breeding: Four greenish, blotched-brown eggs laid in scrape lined with grasses and leaves, usually on small island. Incubation 22–23 days, by both sexes.

Range: Circumpolar along Arctic coastlines as far north as ice-free land exists. In Europe extends southwards through coastal Scandinavia to Denmark. In winter found along almost all the world's coastlines, including most of ice-free Europe.

These chunky waders are among the world's greatest travellers and can be found even on the most remote and isolated islands. They are also highly adaptable, turning over all manner of objects in their search for food and even taking bread thrown to gulls, and shoreline carrion.

p.152 **Wilson's Phalarope** *Phalaropus tricolor*

Description: 24–27 cm (9½–10½ in). Larger and more terrestrial than the other phalaropes. In summer, female is banded grey and chestnut above, with *broad, dark-chestnut eye-stripe that extends to nape* and continues in a band down side of neck. Underparts white, with warm wash on foreneck. Male a paler version of female. In winter, upperparts pale grey with only the faintest of grey marks behind eye; underparts white. *Bill long, and even thinner* than Red-necked Phalarope's, and virtual lack of head markings in winter distinguishes it from Grey Phalarope. More inclined than other phalaropes to wade rather than swim on freshwater marshes. Shows white rump and trailing feet in flight.

Voice: Harsh croaks in flight.

Habitat: Marshy pools and lakeside margins at all seasons.

Breeding: Four buffy, brown-spotted eggs laid in grass-lined hollow adjacent to water. Incubation 20–22 days, by male alone.

Range: Breeds in western Canadian and American mountains and plains; also in eastern Canada where it is increasing and spreading. Winters in South America. Vagrant and increasingly regular in Europe.

First identified in Europe only in 1954, Wilson's Phalarope is now a regular vagrant every autumn mainly to Britain and Ireland, with between 4 and 12 each year. Also occurring with more frequency in spring. In pale winter plumage, it could be confused with Marsh Sandpiper, but much shorter-legged than that bird.

---

p.153 **Red-necked Phalarope** *Phalaropus lobatus*

Description: 17–19 cm (6½–7½ in). Small, delicately built wader that habitually swims buoyantly, both on marshes and at sea. In summer, female brown-black above marked by two, *straw-coloured 'V's over back*. Head grey, with rust-red extending from eye and nape to breast and enclosing white chin. Breast grey, belly white, *bill one and a half times length of head and very thin* and needle-like. Male similar, but duller. Winter adult grey and brown above, not uniform pale grey, with dark crown and dark comma through eye. Juvenile warm brown and black above with two bold 'V's on back and large dark-eye comma. Shows bold wingbar in flight.

Voice: A quiet *tyit*.

Habitat: Breeds among tundra pools and marshes and, locally, at more southerly sites. Winters at sea, usually well out of sight of land.

Breeding: Four pale-green, brown-blotched eggs laid in cup placed in marshland tussock. Incubation 18–20 days, by male alone. Female may lay a second clutch with another male.

Range: Circumpolar in Arctic zone. In Europe breeds in Iceland, Scottish islands, and Scandinavian mountain chain and northern tundra. Winters off Arabia, Ecuador and New Guinea. European birds make long overland flight to Arabia.

These small swimming waders pick tiny food particles from the surface of the sea and often form large flocks at suitably rich feeding grounds. In summer, they swim over marshes, often spinning to create an upwelling that brings food to the surface.

p.153 **Grey Phalarope** *Phalaropus fulicarius*

Description: 19–21 cm (7½–8 in). Similar to Red-necked Phalarope, but distinctly stockier and with *shorter, thicker bill*. Female in summer has chestnut-red underparts extending from throat to tail. Head white, with black crown, eye-stripe and chin. Upperparts black, broadly edged buff. Male slightly duller. In winter, uniform pale grey above, white below, with dark comma through eye. Juvenile dark above with narrow, buff feather margins, and lacking any pale stripes or 'V's. Crown and eye-comma much less boldly marked than Red-necked.

Voice: High-pitched *priip*.

Habitat: High Arctic tundra pools and coastal marshes in summer. Winters at sea.

Breeding: Three to four pale-green, brown-blotched eggs laid in cup in marshy tussock.

Incubation 19 days, solely by male. Often semi-colonial.

Range: Circumpolar in high Arctic north of range of Red-necked Phalarope. Called Red Phalarope in North America. In Europe breeds only in Iceland in small numbers; otherwise no more than passage migrant most often seen following autumn gales. Winters on coasts of Chile, Mauritania and South Africa.

Role reversal during the breeding cycle is particularly well developed among Arctic waders, though in none more so than in the phalaropes. The female is more boldly coloured and takes the initiative in courtship. If there is a surplus of males, she will lay two clutches of eggs to satisfy the paternal needs of both mates. Egg production is, however, very draining and i is an effective tactic for the male to take on rearing responsibilities.

SKUAS (STERCORARIIDAE)

Five or six species; largely confined to Arctic and Antarctic regions. Three species breed in Europe and one other is a regular passage migrant. Skuas are medium-sized gull-like seabirds that can be – and are – confused with brown immature gulls, but they fly with all the power and agility of falcons. They are robust in build, with powerful bills and long, pointed wings. The legs are relatively short, the feet fully webbed. While all species are generally brown, the smaller ones also exhibit a pale colour phase with white underparts. All species, to a greater or lesser extent, show a white flash in the wing at the base of the primaries. The smaller species also show extended central tail feathers in spring adults, though these are frequently broken off by autumn and are absent from juveniles. Skuas are pirates that pursue other seabirds and force them to drop or disgorge their food. When chasing potential victims their flight is fast and full of menace as they twist and turn with consummate agility as their victim seeks to escape with its hard-won meal intact. Occasionally a victim is seized by a wingtip and toppled into the sea. Migration, over the sea, can often be seen from coastal promontories. The exact status of the southern breeding skuas and, in particular, the number of species involved remains a subject of argument and debate.

---

p.156 **Pomarine Skua** *Stercorarius pomarinus*

Description: 43–53 cm (17–21 in). More robust and heavily built than Arctic Skua, but without the breadth of wing of Great Skua. Pale phase brown above and white below, with prominent brown *band across buffy washed chest* that accentuates barrel-chested structure. Dark phase brown above and below. Black cap is more obvious in pale birds, and both phases show prominent white wing-flash. Spring adults have *elongated and twisted tail feathers* quite unlike other skuas. Juvenile more heavily barred on belly than juvenile Arctic.

Voice: Harsh *wish-yo, wish-yo*; generally silent at sea.

Habitat: Breeds among high Arctic tundra. Winters at sea, often well out of sight of land.

Breeding: Two buffy, brown-spotted eggs laid in depression on dry tundra. Incubation 27–28 days, by both sexes.

Range: Circumpolar, but completely absent as a breeder from Europe. In winter moves southward over world's major oceans reaching Cape of Good Hope and Australasia. A double-passage migrant along western coasts of Europe including the Channel and the seas between Scotland and Iceland.

The first half of May sees a regular up-Channel passage of Pomarine Skuas that is visible from adjacent shores. Flocks are generally small, however, and the birds seldom pause during their journeys. By the second half of May the birds are passing through the Baltic. In autumn, passage is more leisurely, and individuals may pause for several days where good feeding opportunities present themselves.

---

p.156   **Arctic Skua** *Stercorarius parasiticus*

Description: 38–48 cm (15–19 in). By far the most commonly seen skua through most of Europe. Pale-phase birds are brown above, white below, with incomplete breast band that is often no more than a smudge either side of breast. Dark-phase birds are uniformly brown above and below. Both phases show white wing-flashes. Adult has two *central tail feathers extending* to a point. Juvenile heavily barred, but with pale belly-patch. More lightly built and *less barrel chested* than Pomarine, but much heavier than Long-tailed.

Voice: High-pitched *kee-ow* and hard *tuk-tuk*; silent at sea.

Habitat: Breeds among Arctic tundra, but also southwards along coastal moorland. Winter off coasts of most of world's large oceans.

Breeding: Two greenish, brown-blotched eggs laid in depression among grass or moss. Incubatio 24–28 days, by both sexes.

Range: Circumpolar in Arctic. In Europe, breeds along coasts of Scandinavia, Scotland and Iceland. Elsewhere, mainly a double-passage migrant along western coasts.

Birds that winter in the Red Sea and Persia Gulf overfly Europe from their northern breeding grounds. Their regular presence i the eastern Mediterranean supports this overland route. Strangely, there is little evidence that Pomarine Skuas, that winter in the same areas migrate overland.

---

p.157   **Long-tailed Skua** *Stercorarius longicaudus*

Description: 36–56 cm (14–22 in). Smallest and most lightly built of the skuas, with large part o overall length consisting of *extended tail feathers*. Pale grey-brown above, with *contrasting dark cap* and dark flight feathers, and only a tiny white wing-flash. White underparts, washed yellow around head, contrast with dark underwing. Summer adult has long extended central tail feathers. In rare dark phase, bird identified on build and size. Juvenile barred like other juvenile skuas, but more buff below, short extended tail feathers and lighter build. Much more *tern-like* than any other skua.

Voice: A tern-like *kree* at breeding grounds; silent at sea.

Habitat: Breeds on open tundra and in other tundra-like areas at altitude in mountains to the south. Winters at sea.

Breeding: Two olive, brown-blotched eggs laid in hollow among lichens or moss. Incubation, starting with the first egg, 23–25 days by both sexes. The eggs are rested on adult's feet.

Range: Circumpolar in high Arctic in summer. In winter ranges southern Atlantic and Pacific; absent from Indian Ocean and Australasia. In Europe breeds in Scandinavian mountain chain; otherwise only a scarce passage migrant along North Sea and Atlantic coasts.

Although piratical like other skuas, this bird frequently catches small fish for itself. In summer it turns its attention to small mammals and its breeding success depends entirely on the population of lemmings. In a poor lemming year birds may not even attempt to breed.

---

p.157 **Great Skua** *Stercorarius skua*

Description: 56–61 cm (22–24 in). Large, bulky, powerful, brown seabird, virtually as large as Great Black-backed Gull. Warm brown above, liberally streaked with buffy white. Warm brown below, with streaking confined to breast and sides of neck. Large head, with darker cap and dark around eye, and surprisingly small bill. In flight shows bold white wing-flashes and *wedge-shaped tail*. Broad-based wings and deep chest give 'heavy' impression that is instantly banished as this powerful pirate goes to work. Quite capable of downing birds as large as Gannet.

Voice: A nasal *skeer* and hard *tuk-tuk*.

Habitat: In summer frequents coastal moorland and hillsides near large seabird colonies. Winters at sea; will follow ships.

Breeding: Two olive, brown-spotted eggs laid in hollow, usually on a ridge or similar vantage point. Incubation 28–30 days, by both sexes

Range: Endemic to Europe, breeding only in Iceland Faeroes and Scottish islands. In winter range over Atlantic as far west as coastal North America and southwards to Equator.

Though this is the only large skua to occur in Europe, there are increasingly reports of bird showing the characters of South Polar Skua. Such birds are greyer brown, with little or no streaking above or on the breast, and have a dark cap highlighted by a golden wash on the nape. To date no sight records have been accepted, though three older specimen records are judged to be this species.

GULLS AND TERNS (LARIDAE)

90 species; worldwide. Twenty-two species breed in Europe and a further five are visitors. Gulls and terns are long-winged, mostly grey or white, seabirds with webbed feet. They are excellent fliers and many, particularly the terns, search for food from the air. Others are buoyant swimmers and effective plunge-divers. Gulls are mostly larger with long, round-tipped wings that are held bowed in flight. Most are coastal rather than pelagic, finding their food along the shoreline. This semi-scavenging lifestyle has been easily adapted to scavenging near man, and the populations of many species have boomed as birds have learned to feed on rubbish tips and agricultural land, and by following the plough. Gulls are long-lived and slow to mature, passing through several immature, mainly brown, plumages before

reaching adulthood. Such birds were, not so
long ago, regarded as difficult to identify and
often ignored as a result. Today's criteria
make identification relatively
straightforward enabling major rarities to be
picked out from the more abundant common
species. Terns are generally smaller and
lighter in build, with long pointed wings.
Typical terns haunt coastlines where they
dive spectacularly into the sea for food.
Marsh terns, as their name implies, frequent
freshwater marshes, though they are also seen
at sea, where they delicately pick food from
the surface. All terns have pointed bills, short
legs and black caps that are partially lost in
winter. All members of the family are
gregarious throughout the year.

pp.158 & 166 **Mediterranean Gull** *Larus melanocephalus*

Description: 37–40 cm (14½–16 in). Medium-sized,
pale-grey gull that is whiter than any other
similar-sized species. Summer adult pale
grey above with *white wingtips*. Black head
elongated rather than rounded, with
prominent, broken, white eye-ring. Bill
red, *heavy and droopy;* legs red. In winter,
black hood is replaced by dark smudge
through eye and over nape. In flight, wings
are pale and white, not black tipped. First-
winter birds show same droopy bill and
head markings as winter adult, but have
pale-grey saddle and dark wings marked by
prominent pale mid-wing panel. Tail has
broad black terminal band. This wing
pattern more closely resembles Ring-billed
than Black-headed Gull. As birds mature
they lose most of the black in wing, though
second-summer birds still show a few black
spots on tips of the outer primaries.
Voice: Plaintive *kee-er* or *kee-ow*.
Habitat: Breeds on freshwater marshes, lakes and
deltas. In winter frequents coastal marshes
and shorelines.
Breeding: Three grey-buff eggs, spotted and streaked
with brown, laid on nest of grasses, usually
on an island in lagoon or marsh. Incubation
23–25 days, by both sexes.

Range:

Virtually confined to Europe with colonies in Mediterranean and Black Seas. More numerous in east than west. Also colonies in eastern Germany and southern England

This gull first colonized England during the late 1960s, when isolated individuals paired with Black-headed Gulls among large colonies of that species. It has since become established and now breeds in small numbers in pure pairs. In winter it can now be found in quite large flocks at favoured sites, and individuals are widespread.

---

pp.159 & 166 **Little Gull** *Larus minutus*

Description: 27–29 cm (10½–11½ in). Tiny gull that feeds by picking food from the water's surface in the manner of a marsh tern. Summer adult has black hood with dark red bill and legs. Upperparts pale grey with white wingtips lacking black; *underwing uniformly dark grey*. Underparts white. In winter, black hood is replaced by pale grey crown and black spot behind eye. First-winter birds have similar head pattern, but are marked by inverted *black 'W' across wing* and lower back, and a black tail-band.

Voice: A nasal *kee-arr* and a staccato *kek-kek-kek*.

Habitat: Marshes, floods and lakesides during breeding season. In winter and on passage frequents similar areas as well as more open fresh waters and coasts.

Breeding: Three buffy, brown-blotched eggs laid in substantial nest of reeds among marshy vegetation. Incubation 23–24 days, by both sexes.

Range: Breeds from Baltic eastwards across Siberia to Sea of Japan. In Europe largely confined to Finland, but extending westwards through Baltic states, Swedish islands, Denmark and Holland. Whole population moves westwards to winter around European shores, especially Mediterranean, frequently some distance from land.

This gull's complex movements are little understood, but they involve even eastern

Siberian birds migrating westwards to at least the Caspian and probably the Black Sea and Mediterranean. Certainly, numbers passing through the English Channel — mostly along French shores — can only be a small fraction of the world population. Most birds probably fly overland and are seen only at somewhat localized feeding grounds.

pp.165 & 169   **Sabine's Gull** *Larus sabini*

Description: 32–34 cm (12½–13½ in). A small, neat, ocean-going gull. Adult grey above and white below, marked in summer by slate-grey hood, bordered black. In winter, hood becomes smudge on nape. Bill black, tipped yellow; legs black. Shows neat row of white mirrors on black wingtips. In flight, *black outer primaries contrast with white innerwing and grey coverts* and back. Tail notched. Juvenile barred brown above, but shows similar flight pattern as adult.

Voice: Tern-like, high-pitched, raucous calls.

Habitat: In summer frequents tundra marshes, pools and deltas. Winters at sea.

Breeding: Three olive-green, brown-blotched eggs laid in grassy tussock on marshy island. Incubation 23–26 days, by both sexes.

Range: Circumpolar in north, though absent from Europe and western Siberia. Western Canadian and Greenland birds cross Atlantic in autumn and are quite numerous from Biscay southwards. Winters off South and West Africa.

Autumn gales sometimes bring individuals or flocks of these American gulls northwards to the Western Approaches and even into the Channel and southern Irish Sea. Occasionally they may be seen from land and, exceptionally, inland under duress. They were named after Edward Sabine who discovered them in 1818 while he was a member of James Ross's expedition in search of the Northwest Passage.

pp.159 & 166 **Black-headed Gull** *Larus ridibundus*

Description: 35–38 cm (14–15 in). Very common, medium-sized gull throughout most of Europe. Summer adult has chocolate-brown hood with faint white eye-ring, red bill and red legs. Upperparts pale grey with black wingtips at rest; underparts white. In winter, hood replaced by dark dot behind eye. In flight shows prominent *white forewing;* underwing shows dark primaries only. First-winter birds have black trailing edge to wing, and dark greater coverts separated by pale-grey mid-wing panel, and pale grey saddle. Even in this plumage a white forewing is evident.

Voice: Loud *kee-ar* and angry *kuk-kuk-kuk*.

Habitat: Breeds on marshes, islands in large lakes, upland moors and bogs. Winters on coasts, estuaries, harbours, marshes, lakes, reservoirs and grasslands, sewage-works and rubbish tips.

Range: Breeds right across temperate Palearctic from Iceland to Kamchatka southwards to Mediterranean and Caspian Sea. Winters from Azores to Japan with huge numbers in western Europe.

This abundant gull is so familiar inland in winter that it comes as something of a surprise to learn that this habit is only a little over 100 years old. Black-headed Gull find ideal wintering grounds around large cities, where the combination of rubbish tip and large reservoirs is perfectly suited to their feeding and roosting needs. Many bird may therefore never see the sea during the whole of their lives.

pp.160 & 166 **Slender-billed Gull** *Larus genei*

Description: 41–45 cm (16–17½ in). Decidedly scarce and localized gull that shares its major field mark with Black-headed Gull, but lacks both summer hood and winter head markings of that species. Pale grey above and white below, with prominent *white forewing* and black-tipped primaries like winter Black-headed Gull. Plain, *unmarked face*, elongated head, with *sloping forehead, and long, pointed red bill*. In all plumages appears long necked. First-winter birds show white forewing, pale mid-wing panel, and black tail-band. Weight-forward, long-necked appearance and lack of head markings are major features at all times.

Voice: A nasal *kaar* like a tern.

Habitat: Coastal lagoons, estuaries, marshes at all times.

Breeding: Two to three creamy-buff, brown-blotched eggs laid in depression with little lining. Incubation 22 days, by both sexes.

Range: Largely confined to a broad area extending eastwards from Mediterranean to Caspian and beyond. Scarce in southern Europe with decline in west. Largest numbers now centred on Black Sea. Vagrant northwards from Mediterranean across Europe.

The highly fragmented range of this gull indicates a declining species that was once more widespread. In Europe it breeds only at a handful of outstanding Mediterranean wetlands, but numbers remain highly variable. Surprisingly large numbers still exist in the Persian Gulf and on the Ukrainian shores of the Black Sea.

pp.160 & 166 **Audouin's Gull** *Larus audouinii*

Description: 48–52 cm (19–20½ in). Medium-sized gull, larger than Black-headed, but smaller than Herring. Adult has pale-grey upperparts with extensive black wingtips marked by small white mirrors. Elongated head accentuated by *large, droopy red bill* marked, in summer, by black band; grey legs. First-winter birds are brown and buff with very broad, black tail-band and pale 'U'-shaped rump. In all plumages, *outer wings decidedly narrow* and pointed, and large head and droopy bill quite obvious.

Voice: Hoarse, braying *kee-ow*.

Habitat: Coastal lagoons and deltas, and particularly isolated rocky islands. Essentially coastal at all times.

Breeding: Two to three buffy, black-blotched eggs
laid in hollow with scant lining of seawee
Incubation 21–25 days, by both sexes.

Range: Confined to Mediterranean with major
concentrations around Balearics and nearb
coasts of Spain; around Corsica and Sardin
and coasts of North Africa, Aegean, and
Cyprus. Winters in same areas, though sor
birds move to Atlantic coasts of Morocco.

Audouin's Gull was once regarded as a
highly endangered European endemic, wit
a world population of less than 1,000 pair
Today we are better informed and know of
the splendid populations in the Ebro Delt
and the Islas Chafarinas off the coast of
Morocco, which have added several
thousands of pairs to the total. Neverthele
it remains a decidedly scarce bird that cou
easily be threatened once more.

---

pp.161 & 166 **Ring-billed Gull** *Larus delawarensis*

Description: 46–51 cm (18–20 in). Typical grey-backed
gull, with black wingtips and white mirror
Most easily confused with Common Gull,
though fierce expression more reminiscent o
Herring Gull. Summer adult grey above an
white below, with yellow legs, and yellow
bill marked by black band. *Eye pale* and set
strongly built, elongated head, quite differe
to rounded, gentle head of Common Gull.
winter, crown and nape spotted brown. Firs
winter birds, black or dark across wings wit
very bold, clear-cut, pale mid-wing panel.
Crown, *nape, breast and throat heavily spotted,
is black-banded tail*. In this plumage it is
closer to Mediterranean than Common Gull
The pale eye, which aids the fierce expressio
is not present in sub-adults.

Voice: Loud *kok;* generally closer to Herring Gull
than mewing of Common Gull.

Habitat: Coasts, harbours, mud flats.

Breeding: Two or three, brown-blotched, buffy eggs
laid in nest of grasses. Incubation 23–25
days, by both sexes.

Range: Breeds both sides of border between Cana
and USA, from Washington through Grea

Lakes to Newfoundland. Winters southern and coastal USA. A scarce but increasingly regular winter and passage migrant to Europe, particularly to southwest England in early spring.

First observed in Europe in March 1973 and increasingly identified ever since. This increase in European records coincided with a boom in numbers in eastern North America, but was also doubtless due to improved skill with gull identification and the associated effort put into scanning large flocks of gulls in search of the unusual.

pp.161 & 167 **Common Gull** *Larus canus*

Description: 38–43 cm (15–17 in). Similar to Herring Gull in plumage, but with distinctly lighter build and more benign expression. Adult pale grey above, white below; wingtips black, with large white mirrors virtually forming a bar. Bill and legs both yellow. Small, *rounded head and small bill produce gentle look* more like Kittiwake than the fierce expression of Herring Gull. In winter, head and nape liberally spotted. First-winter birds dark-winged with far from obvious pale central panel (compare with first-winter Ring-billed and second-winter Herring), and black tail-band.

Voice: High-pitched, mewing *kee-aa*.

Habitat: Breeds on marshes, lakes and deltas among tundra, taiga and temperate landscapes. Winters along coasts and estuaries, but more frequently inland on fields than most other species.

Breeding: Three pale-green, brown-blotched, eggs laid in well-built nest of grasses on an island in lake or pond, sometimes on shingle or even in small tree. Incubation 22–27 days, by both sexes.

Range: Virtually circumpolar in north, though absent from eastern half of North America, where it is called Mew Gull, and Greenland. In Europe, breeds from Iceland to Scotland and Scandinavia southwards

through northern France, Holland and
Germany. Abundant winter visitor to coas
of Britain and Ireland, and North Sea.

A remarkably adaptable gull that follows
ships, scavenges the shoreline and plunge
dives, but it is equally at home on urban
playing fields and rural pastures. It even
visits rubbish tips, though it is much less
frequent than other gull species.

pp.162 & 167   **Lesser Black-backed Gull** *Larus fuscus*

Description: 51–56 cm (20–22 in). Structurally very
similar to Herring Gull, but with coloratio
of Great Black-backed. Adult *dark slate-gre*
above and white below, with red-spotted
yellow bill and yellow legs. Scandinavian
birds (*L. f. fuscus*) are black above and show
no contrast between mantle and wingtips.
Icelandic and northwest European birds
(*L. f. graellsii*) have paler mantle that
contrasts with black wingtips. In winter he
and nape heavily spotted. First- and second
winter birds are much darker than Herring
Gull of similar ages, *lack pale inner primary*
patches of Herring, and show dark band alo
trailing edge of wing. Adult confusable on
with much larger Great Black-backed.

Voice: Loud *kyow-kyow* and *kee-aa* like Herring
Gull, but rather more nasal.

Habitat: Breeds on low-lying coastal islands, tund
and upland moors. In winter frequents
coasts, salt-pans and inland grassy fields.

Breeding: Two to three olive-green, brown-speckled
eggs laid in hollow lined with grasses.
Incubation 25–29 days, by both sexes.
Highly colonial.

Range: Breeds from Iceland to Britain and
northern France eastwards through Baltic
to central Siberia. Mostly a summer visit
though increasingly present in western
Europe in winter.

The systematics of the Herring Gull
complex are nothing less than confusing
and the subject of continued debate amon
ornithologists. The Lesser Black-backed

Gull can be regarded as the easternmost representative of this complex which, starting with the European Herring Gull, extends eastwards around the world, becoming gradually darker mantled, and terminating in Europe (again) with a very dark Lesser Black-backed. Such a complex is called a 'ring' species though, to be fair, things are not as simple as that.

p.164 & 168 | **Iceland Gull** *Larus glaucoides*

Description: 51–57 cm (20–22½ in). Scarce, but regular, winter visitor to northern Europe. Adult pale grey above and white below, marked by pink legs, rounded head, *dark eye* and small, red-spotted bill. *Wingtips white,* rather than black like Herring Gull. Confusable only with Glaucous Gull, which is similarly a winter visitor to the north, but Glaucous larger, with much heavier and longer head, larger bill, and particularly fierce expression. First-winter birds are creamy-brown, almost fawn, and best separated from similar-aged Glaucous Gulls by size, head and bill shape, and by all-dark bill. Wings extend well beyond tail at rest.

Voice: A shrill *kyow*, higher pitched than Herring Gull.

Habitat: Breeds on high Arctic rocky coasts, usually well sheltered in deep fjords. In winter frequents all manner of coastlines including harbours.

Breeding: Two to three olive-buff, brown-spotted eggs laid in loose collection of grasses and seaweeds on cliff ledge. Incubation period and role of the sexes has not been described.

Range: Breeds coastal Greenland and adjacent coasts of Baffinland and Canadian archipelago. Winters over nearby seas, wandering across Atlantic to Iceland, Scotland and northern North Sea.

Despite its name this bird does not breed in Iceland, which the Glaucous does, and is far less frequent in Europe than that bird. The Glaucous and Iceland Gulls, are frequently referred to as the 'white-winged gulls'.

pp.164 & 168   **Glaucous Gull** *Larus hyperboreus*

Description: 58–69 cm (23–27 in). A large, 'white-winged gull', almost as large as Great Bla[ck-]backed Gull, and equally as fierce. Adult pale grey above and white below, marked [with] pink legs, large, red-spotted yellow bill, a[nd] *white (not black) wingtips*. Coloration and wingtip pattern distinguish it from all ot[her] gulls save Iceland. Glaucous has larger he[ad] with *heavier, longer bill, and a particularly f[ierce] expression*. Wingtips only just extend beyo[nd] tail at rest. Heavily spotted head in winte[r.] First-winter birds buffy with pale wingti[ps,] dark-tipped pink bill, and similar head a[nd] bill shape to adult.

Voice: Harsh *kyow*, like Herring Gull, though mostly silent in winter.

Habitat: Breeds along Arctic coastlines on islands and inland cliffs as well as islands in lake[s] and rivers. In winter frequents all coastlines, including harbours, but ventu[res] inland to rubbish tips where individuals may become quite regular.

Breeding: Two to three pale-olive, brown-blotched eggs laid in large nest of seaweed and other available material, usually in well-sheltered spot. Incubation 27–30 days, [by] both sexes.

Range: Circumpolar in north though, in Europe confined to Iceland. A scarce winter visit[or] to northern Europe. Winters across Nort[h] Atlantic south to England, northern Fra[nce] and shores of the North Sea.

This gull is much more frequent than Iceland Gull in Europe, with some birds returning to the same location each win[ter] for several successive years. Though mor[e] numerous in Scotland than further south[,] the most famous individual spent a number of winters at Cley in Norfolk, where it was affectionately known as 'George'. When it eventually failed to return one winter, but was replaced by a buffy first-winter bird, its successor was immediately christened 'Boy George', a pop star of the period.

pp.163 & 167 **Yellow-legged Gull** *Larus cachinnans*

Description: 55–67 cm (21½–26½ in). Recently classified as separate species from Herring Gull. Adult slightly *darker above* than Herring Gull, and *yellow (not pink) legs,* but otherwise virtually identical. First- and second-winter birds show only a hint of paleness on inner primaries, and a bolder, pale mid-wing panel than Herring Gulls of the same age.

Voice: Loud ringing and laughing calls like Herring Gull.

Habitat: Coasts with cliffs, harbours, estuaries, coastal marshes.

Breeding: Two to three pale-green, brown-blotched eggs laid on cliff ledge or shoreline scrape. Incubation 28–30 days, mainly by female.

Range: Breeds from southern Portugal through Mediterranean to Black Sea and eastwards across southern Siberia. Most winter in Mediterranean, though there is a northwards movement across eastern Europe in autumn that regularly reaches North Sea and southern England.

The recent recognition of this group of southern 'Herring Gulls' as a separate species goes some way towards bringing order to the whole Herring Gull complex. At much the same time, a population resident on the Turkey–Armenian border was similarly accorded specific status as the Armenian Gull (*L.armenicus*).

pp.163 & 167 **Herring Gull** *Larus argentatus*

Description: 53–59 cm (21–23 in). Large gull. Adult pale grey above, white below, marked by red-spotted, yellow bill and *pink legs*. Large head, pale eye and heavy bill create a fierce expression. In flight shows black wingtips marked with white mirrors. In winter, head and nape heavily streaked. First- and second-winter birds are brown, with dark trailing edge of wing broken by *pale patch on inner primaries* that is not present on similar-aged Lesser Black-backed Gulls.

Voice: Loud *kyow-kyow* and laughing *hah-hah-ha*
        noisy throughout the year.
Habitat: Coastal, breeding on cliffs and offshore
        islands, though also on islands in lakes and
        on boggy moorlands. Mostly coastal in
        winter, though also inland on rubbish tips
        and reservoirs.
Breeding: Two to three pale-green, brown-blotched
        eggs laid on cliff ledge, in scrape among
        dunes or in scruffy nest on a building.
        Incubation 28–30 days, mainly by female
        Highly colonial.
Range: Common and widespread in north and
        western Europe. Circumpolar in north,
        from Iceland and Britain through
        Scandinavia, eastern Siberia and northern
        Canada. More widespread in winter with
        large numbers moving westwards to
        temperate European coasts.

        The dramatic population boom enjoyed by
        the Herring Gull can be largely attributed
        to its ability to live alongside man and
        exploit the opportunities he creates. Urban
        man creates reservoirs to service his
        personal and industrial needs and rubbish
        tips to dispose of his waste. The
        combination has proved perfect for these
        adaptable gulls that also find industrial
        fishing, with its associated waste, a highly
        attractive source of more natural food.

pp.162 & 167 **Great Black-backed Gull** *Larus marinus*

Description: 63–69 cm (25–27 in). Huge gull with
        massive head and bill. Adult black above,
        white below. Bill yellow, with bold red
        spot; legs flesh-pink. Distinguished from
        Lesser Black-backed, the only confusable
        species, by black not dark-grey upperparts
        with no contrast between wing and
        wingtips, and by *huge size,* particularly of
        head and bill. First-winter birds are
        mottled black and white, significantly paler
        than first-year Lesser Black-backed, with
        more prominent black trailing edge to
        secondaries, and pale inner primaries
        forming distinct patch. Stands much taller

than any other European gull and, in flight, appears slightly weight forward.

Voice: Deep *awk* and *uk-uk-uk*.

Habitat: Essentially marine. Breeds on rocky coastlines and offshore islands usually adjacent, though not within, other large seabird colonies. Winters on coasts and at sea, but also frequents rubbish tips near coasts or estuaries.

Breeding: Two to three olive, brown-speckled eggs, laid in large nest of seaweed and sticks on rocky stack. Incubation 26–30 days, by both sexes.

Range: Confined to North Atlantic, breeding in northeast North America, Greenland, Iceland, Britain and Ireland, and Scandinavia. Winters over adjacent seas.

In summer this is the major predator on the seabird colonies alongside which it nests. Species such as Puffin and Manx Shearwater nest in burrows for protection, the latter even coming to land under a cloak of darkness. Evidence of Great Black-backed predation is easily found as nesting sites may be littered with prey skins turned inside out.

p.164 & 168 **Ross's Gull** *Rhodostethia rosea*

Description: 29–31 cm (11½–12 in). Small and dainty gull. Summer adult grey above and pink below, marked by clear-cut black ring around white head and neck. Head rounded; bill short and black; legs red. In winter, both neck-ring and pink underparts lost; it is then grey above and white below, with only a *black dot behind eye*. A broad white trailing edge to wing shows in flight, and tail is *wedge-shaped*. First-winter birds show black 'W' across wings, with white trailing edge and black-tipped, wedge-shaped tail. Only adult and first-winter Little Gulls are confusable, but wedge-shaped tail is diagnostic.

Voice: Tern-like *ke-wa* and *a-wow, a-wow*.

Habitat: Breeds on pools, marshes and rivers in remote tundra. Winters at sea on edge of pack ice.

Breeding: Three olive, brown-blotched eggs, laid i
nest of grasses and other vegetation plac
on small islet in a marsh, often among
Arctic Terns. Incubation about 21 days,
both sexes.

Range: Breeds only in northeastern Siberia, witl
three sites in northern Canada and
Greenland. Winters in Arctic seas with
regular passage off Alaska. Decidedly ra
visitor to Europe, mainly in farthest nor

With no more than one or two reports e
year, this is the gull that, when it comes
from the cold, sets the telephone wires
humming. Sadly, most occur in the far
north in Scotland, with a majority even
farther away in Shetland. A speculative
to find the bird should be timed for late
January and start at Lerwick Harbour.

pp.165 & 169 Ivory Gull *Pagophila eburnea*

Description: 40–43 cm (16–17 in). An all-white, Arc
gull, grey-white above and white below,
with small, rounded head and short,
yellow-tipped bill. In flight, all white, w
square-cut tail. First-winter birds have
smudgy, dirty-looking face, wing covert
spotted black, and black tips to white
primaries. In flight shows black trailing
edge to outerwing and black band on tai
Legs short and black. Somewhat *dove-lik*
at rest.

Voice: A harsh *kree-kree* and tern-like *kaar*.

Habitat: Breeds on bare tundra, broad sea-cliffs a
inland cliffs protruding through ice.
Winters at sea among pack ice.

Breeding: One to two buff, brown-spotted eggs lai
in large nest of seaweed and other availab
material, placed on the ground or on bro
upper ledge of cliff. Incubation 24–26 d
by both sexes.

Range: Breeds in highest Arctic from Canada an
Greenland to islands of Siberia. Winters
pack ice. Wanders southwards to
northernmost Europe with an average of
one per year to Britain, mostly Shetland,
but has reached Switzerland and Italy.

Ivory Gulls spend most of their lives at sea, though they seldom alight on water. In winter, they frequent dense pack ice, often in association with seals and polar bears, and feed on carrion. They will also accompany Eskimos on seal-hunting trips for similar reasons. Long-stay individuals in Europe attract vast numbers of admirers.

p.165 & 169 **Kittiwake** *Rissa tridactyla*

Description: 38–43 cm (15–17 in). Highly successful, cliff-nesting, sea-going gull. Grey above, white below, with pure, *ink-pot black wingtips*. Adult has small, rounded head with benign face, dark eye, small yellow bill and black legs. In flight shows *pale rear wing* that accentuates black wingtips. In winter has black smudge over crown. First-winter birds have *inverted black 'W' across wings* and bold line across hind neck. Long, narrow wings apparent in all plumages.

Voice: A ringing *kitti-week*, repeated.

Habitat: Breeds in huge colonies on precipitous sea cliffs. At other times ranges well out to sea, but one of the few truly pelagic gulls, but also frequents shorelines and harbours.

Breeding: Two buffy, brown-speckled eggs laid in well-built nest constructed on tiny ledge on large cliff. Incubation 25–30 days, by both sexes.

Range: Circumpolar in north. In Europe found along northern and western coasts, particularly in Iceland, Britain and Ireland, and northern Scandinavia. Winters over North Atlantic and North Pacific. Also penetrates western Mediterranean.

This is the gull that swarms over the great seabird colonies of northern Europe and is also the noisiest member of those communities. It occupies the tiniest of ledges on the sheerest of cliffs in quite amazing numbers. It has experienced a population boom during the past 100 years due, almost certainly, to the increase in deep-sea fishing.

p.170 **Lesser Crested Tern** *Sterna bengalensis*

Description: 38–43 cm (15–17 in). Medium-sized, pa
grey tern, about the *same size as Sandwich*
Tern, but darker grey above. Grey above
and white below, with prominent black c
that terminates in ragged crest on nape.
Bill thin, tapered, and warm yellow in colo
legs black. In flight shows darker outer
primaries than Sandwich. In winter, blac
cap confined to hind crown. First-winter
birds show dark secondaries bordered by
white bars.

Voice: A scratchy *kriik* similar to Sandwich Ter
but less strident.

Habitat: Breeds on low-lying coastal islets and on
similar islands in coastal lagoons and del
Winters along coasts and also well offshc

Breeding: One, occasionally two, creamy, brown-
spotted eggs laid in bare scrape among si
or shingle. Incubation 21–26 days, by be
sexes.

Range: Breeds from Red Sea and Persian Gulf
eastwards across tropical Asia to norther
Australia. A recent arrival in Europe tha
has established a colony in the Ebro Del
a single bird was regular in Britain durir
the late 1980s and the1990s. Winters ov
tropical Old World seas.

During a 'live' television birdwatch
programme on the Farne Islands, off
northeast England, viewers were stagger
to see a Lesser Crested sitting happily
among a dense colony of Sandwich Terns
So, unannounced and previously unseen,
Lesser Crested had started to breed in
Britain. Elsie, as this bird was called,
returned every year until at least 1997 a
reared hybrid young with her Sandwich
Tern partner.

p.171 **Sandwich Tern** *Sterna sandvicensis*

Description: 38–43 cm (15–17 in). Medium to large
tern that is considerably *whiter* than alm
all other European terns. Upperparts pa
grey, with no more than a hint of darkne

on outer primaries; underparts white. Crown has black cap ending in ragged crest on nape. Bill long, thin and *black with yellow tip* that is difficult to see, especially in flight. In winter, black cap confined to hind crown. Juvenile much more scaly on back and wing coverts than other juvenile terns. In flight, size and whiteness are major features.

Voice: A loud *ker-rick*, like the sound made by a rusty door hinge.

Habitat: Offshore islets and islands among coastal marshes and lagoons. Winters along shorelines as well as in harbours and estuaries.

Breeding: Two buffy, brown-speckled eggs laid in bare scrape among sand or shingle, also among vegetation on uninhabited islands. Incubation 20–24 days, by both sexes.

Range: Breeds both sides of Atlantic extending eastwards through Mediterranean and Black Seas to Caspian. Winters southwards as far as Argentina and South Africa. In Europe largest numbers are concentrated around Britain and Ireland, North Sea and western Baltic. Absent in winter, though a few can be found in Mediterranean at this time.

This is the most gregarious of all European terns, forming tightly packed colonies of substantial size. 'Dreads', in which the birds rise *en masse* and circle overhead for no apparent reason, are common. Dreads frequently precede a complete abandonment of a colony that seems well established. Such colonial fickleness remains unexplained.

p.172 **Common Tern** *Sterna hirundo*

Description: 30–36 cm (12–14 in). Adult pale grey above and white below, marked by neat black cap, black-tipped *orange-red bill,* and short red legs. In flight, long pointed wings show *translucent inner primaries,* and tail deeply forked. Major confusable species is Arctic Tern, so much so that the two are often referred to as 'Comic Terns'. Adult Arctic greyer below showing contrasting white 'cheek' between grey neck and black cap, fully translucent wings, and a blood-red b Adult Common Tern sometimes lacks bla tip to bill, but bill always orange-red rath than blood-red. First-winter Common Te shows prominent *dark leading edge to wing* and dark-grey trailing edge, creating *pale mid-wing panel*. Similar-aged Arctic Terns have white trailing edge and are easier to identify than adults.

Voice: Strident and harsh *key-arr* and *kirri-kirri*

Habitat: Breeds along low-lying coasts, on flat uninhabited islands, among marshes and islands in major rivers, pools and lakes. Winters along coasts, but frequently on passage inland.

Breeding: Two to three creamy, brown-blotched eg laid in bare scrape among sand or shingle Incubation 20–23 days, mainly by femal Forms loose colonies.

Range: Circumpolar in northern temperate regie with isolated colonies in tropics. Comme summer visitor to coasts, lakes and rivers Europe from Mediterranean to North Ca of Norway.

The 'common' tern through most of temperate Europe, being outnumbered b the Arctic Tern only in the far north. Th are highly expert fishermen that dive fro considerable heights to catch their prey, often after hovering above the waves. Mature birds average one successful dive out of three.

p.170   **Caspian Tern** *Sterna caspia*

Description: 48–56 cm (19–22 in). Huge, long-legge tern marked by long and *heavy red bill*. Upperparts grey, underparts white, with large head marked by black cap that terminates on nape in ragged crest. Bill long, deep, red, and an outstanding field mark in all conditions. Long legs are bla In winter, cap becomes mottled white an first-winter birds show dark trailing edge to secondaries.

Voice: Loud, harsh *kraagh*.

Habitat: Breeds on marshes and particularly offshore islets. Outside breeding season found along coasts, estuaries, salt-pans and lagoons, but also inland along large rivers.

Breeding: Two to three black-speckled, creamy eggs laid in depression in sand or shingle. Incubation 20–22 days, by both sexes.

Range: Cosmopolitan, found in all the world's faunal zones. In Europe breeds through Mediterranean and in Jutland. Winters over large areas of Africa including inland at Niger Inundation Zone.

In any group of terns loafing on a sandbar, the Caspian stands head and shoulders above all others. In fact it is much the same size as a Herring Gull, though the black cap and red bill can be seen at long range. It is equally impressive in the air when diving, often from considerable height, into the sea in pursuit of fish.

p.172 **Arctic Tern** *Sterna paradisaea*

Description: 30–39 cm (12–15½ in). Similar to same-sized Common Tern, which it replaces at higher latitudes. Upperparts grey, underparts greyish white divided by white 'cheeks'. Clear-cut black cap. Bill *blood-red,* lacking black tip; legs red and very short. In flight, *whole wing is translucent,* and tail deeply forked. At rest, tail-streamers extend beyond folded wings; in Common Tern tail and wings are roughly equal. Juvenile and first-winter birds show *white trailing edge to wing* in flight and less dark leading edge at rest.

Voice: A harsh *key-rr*, a briefer version of Common Tern's call.

Habitat: Breeds on low-lying offshore islets and shingle bars; inland only along tundra rivers and adjacent lakes and marshes. More maritime than Common Tern. Winters along coasts and over open oceans.

Breeding: Two buffy, brown-blotched eggs laid in bare scrape among shingle. Incubation 20–22 days, by both sexes. Colonial.

Range: Circumpolar in far north extending as far
ice-free land exists. Also southwards to
temperate England and Holland. The
dominant tern in Iceland, where Commo
Tern is absent. Winters in southern ocean
as far as coast of Antarctica.

This bird covers 35,000 km (22,000 mile
each year on migration alone, and probab
well over twice, possibly three times, tha
distance when deviations and feeding
flights are included. The oldest recorded
bird lived 34 years and must have covere
minimum of nearly 2 million kilometres
(over 1 million miles).

p.173 **Roseate Tern** *Sterna dougallii*

Description: 32–40 cm (12–16 in). Though similar in
overall measurements to both Common a
Arctic Terns this is a significantly smalle
bird marked by extremely long tail-
streamers that boost its length. Much
whiter than either Common or Arctic, wi
pale grey upperparts similar in colour to
much larger Sandwich Tern. Underparts
white, not grey, and washed with *pale pin*
in summer. Cap black; bill black,
sometimes with reddish base; legs red. A
rest and in flight, smaller size, whitish
coloration and *highly extended tail-streame*
are all obvious features. Juvenile has blac
leading edge to wing like Common Tern
and white trailing edge like Arctic Tern;
upperparts heavily scaled like juvenile
Sandwich.

Voice: Shrill *kee-a* and *pee-pee-pee*, similar to
Common Tern.

Habitat: Breeds on coastal islands, often in compa
with Common or Arctic Terns. Winters
mainly on coastal seas.

Breeding: One to two creamy, brown-speckled egg
laid in hollow among rocks or in bare
scrape. Incubation 21–26 days, by both
sexes.

Range: Widespread throughout much of the
world and on all major continents. In
Europe breeds only in Britain and Irelan

and in northwestern France; these birds winter in tropical West Africa, especially Ghana.

This beautiful tern is in decline throughout its range and probably numbers less than 1,000 pairs in Europe. Individual pairs and small colonies are often severely harassed by Common Terns where the species breed together, but Roseate will also practise piracy on other terns, even the much larger Sandwich Tern.

p.173 Little Tern *Sterna albifrons*

Description: 23–26 cm (9–10 in). Smallest of the 'sea' terns. Grey above, white below, with black cap broken by prominent *white forehead*. Long, black-tipped bill and legs, both yellow. In flight, *wings very narrow*, almost swift-like, and beaten fast, much less gracefully than larger 'sea' terns. Juvenile scaly above with prominent black leading edge to wing, but best identified by size and narrow wings.

Voice: A shrill *kirri-kirri-kirri*.

Habitat: Shingle and sandy coasts as well as shingly rivers and lakeside shorelines. Winters along coasts and locally at large inland floods.

Breeding: Two to three olive, brown-blotched eggs laid in simple scrape among shingle, only a little above high-tide mark. Incubation 19–22 days, by both sexes.

Range: Widespread throughout Old World, but mostly in Eurasia and Far East. Summer visitor to Europe, breeding along coasts from Mediterranean to Baltic, but absent from Iceland and Norway. Also inland along major rivers such as Loire, Po and Danube. Winters along coasts of Africa, but inland at Niger Inundation Zone; passes through central Europe as well as Atlantic coasts on passage.

A serious decline in numbers in Europe has been attributed to the lack of undisturbed beaches in summer. A highly mobile human population can destroy a colony during a single sunny weekend and only by encouraging birds away from beaches as soon as they arrive can colonies be protected. They are also prone to attacks by aerial and terrestrial predators including Little Owls and Kestrels.

---

p.174 **Gull-billed Tern** *Gelochelidon nilotica*

Description: 35–39 cm (14–15½ in). A very pale, larger tern marked by distinctive bull-necked appearance. Upperparts very pale grey, underparts white, making this one of the *'whitest' of all European terns,* even paler than Sandwich Tern. Black cap extends to nape; bill black, heavy and stubby; legs black and relatively long. In flight, heavy head, *stubby bill and thick neck* create bull-necked appearance unlike any other tern. In winter, black cap is replaced by black comma through the eye making it the palest of all European terns.

Voice: A harsh *ack-ack* almost duck-like quacking.

Habitat: Marshes and shallow lagoons, salt-pans, coasts and especially drying-out floods and adjacent bare ground. Unlike other marsh terns it feeds mostly over dry ground and is thus more robustly built.

Breeding: Three brown-speckled, creamy eggs laid in hollow with token lining of grasses. Incubation 22–23 days, by both sexes.

Range: Widespread in northern hemisphere on coasts of North America, Europe and through central-southern Siberia. Winters mainly in southern hemisphere. Decidedly fragmented European range, mainly in Mediterranean, but also in Jutland.

The ability of this summer visitor to make long overland journeys, even across the Sahara, may account for the paucity of records along the North Sea and Channel coasts. The Danish and German populatio has, however, suffered a serious recent decline and the species is now only a vagrant in southern England.

p.174 **Black Tern** *Chlidonias niger*

Description: 23–26 cm (9–10 in). Most common and widespread of the marsh terns. Summer adult *black* to slate-grey, with grey wings, white undertail coverts, and forked tail. Small bill and short legs both black. In winter, grey above, white below, with black crown and white forehead. A *smudge of black projects across breast side* from wing, absent in otherwise similar White-winged Black Tern. Black on ear coverts extends below eye, and white on sides of nape to top of eye, not well below and well above as in White-winged Black. Juvenile has mottled and barred grey upperparts and grey rump, not marked saddle and white rump of White-winged Black. Characteristically hunts by swooping erratically to pick insects from surface of water.

Voice: High-pitched *kik*.

Habitat: Marshes, lagoons, river backwaters and floods with strong growth of emergent vegetation. Outside breeding season utilizes rivers, reservoirs, lakes, salt-pans and inshore waters. Generally more maritime than other marsh terns.

Breeding: Three buffy, brown-spotted eggs laid on platform of aquatic vegetation usually placed among emergent growth. Incubation 14–17 days, mainly by female.

Range: Widespread in Europe extending eastwards to central Siberia; also throughout temperate North America. European birds winter along coasts of West Africa as well as along Nile.

The criteria for identifying winter-plumage marsh terns have been well developed and are now widely understood. Nevertheless great care should be exercised in ensuring that the salient points are well seen. This particularly applies to mixed groups at rest. The presence of a 'tear drop' shape at the base of the black cap and its exact shape is particularly useful, being absent in Whiskered, present in Black and highly accentuated in White-winged Black.

p.175 **White-winged Black Tern**
Chlidonias leucopterus

Description: 22–24 cm (8½–9½ in). Nothing less than
beautiful in black and white summer
plumage. Whole body *black,* broken only
by white undertail coverts. *Wings white* at
rest, but showing black underwing coverts
in flight. The black and white flashing
pattern as a flock of these birds hunts low
over a marsh is simply spectacular, and
unmistakable. Winter adult, much like
Black Tern, but crown shows less black, tail
notched rather than forked, and *lacks smudge
at sides of breast.* Overall effect of a whiter
tern as it flies towards you. Juvenile has
black saddle, contrasting with grey
innerwing coverts and *white rump.* Red legs
may be useful feature.

Voice: Harsh and loud *keer.*

Habitat: Breeds on marshes, lagoons and floods, with
good growth of emergent vegetation. On
passage and in winter also utilizes reservoir
and lakes; mostly found over fresh water.

Breeding: Three buffy, brown-blotched eggs laid on
platform of vegetation among emergent
vegetation. Incubation 14–17 days, mainly
by female.

Range: Breeds from eastern Europe eastwards
across southern Siberia to Sea of Japan.
European birds pass through eastern
Mediterranean, occasionally wandering
further west, to winter over savannah
Africa.

These essentially 'eastern' marsh terns
regularly wander westwards across Europe
as far as Britain, where juveniles are of
annual autumn occurrence. They are,
however, nowhere numerous along the
coasts of North Africa and it is presumed
that the huge numbers that winter in the
western Sahelian zone as far as Senegal
make a diagonal southwestern crossing of
the Sahara. These birds are certainly
abundant along the Nile Valley in autumn
and equally so over the Rift Valley lakes of
East Africa where they are the dominant
marsh tern in winter.

p.175 **Whiskered Tern** *Chlidonias hybridus*

Description: 26–29 cm (10–11½ in). Slightly larger than other marsh terns and decidedly more like typical tern in appearance. Upperparts pale grey and, in summer, virtually the same grey below. Head marked by typical tern black cap, with *white cheeks contrasting with cap and grey underparts*. Dark-red bill, heavier than in other marsh terns; legs dark red. In winter pale grey above and white below, with speckled crown and black nape horseshoe extending to eye. Lacks dark shoulder smudge. Notched tail white, not grey as in other marsh terns. Juvenile shows mottled black saddle, grey wings and white tail with narrow, black terminal band. In all plumages it is *paler than other marsh terns* and in winter can only be confused with White-winged Black. At this time the nape shows a *regular black 'cap'*, quite unlike the marked 'commas' of the other two marsh tern species.

Voice: Discordant *tank*. Considerably more vocal than other marsh terns.

Habitat: Breeds on marshes, lakes and particularly on flooded rice-fields. On passage and in winter frequents wide range of fresh waters, though still favouring marshes.

Breeding: Three blue-green, brown-blotched eggs laid on floating platform of aquatic vegetation among emergent growth. Incubation 18–20 days, by both sexes.

Range: Widespread throughout Old World from Europe to China and Africa to Australia. European birds are summer visitors, wintering over savannah Africa from the Sahel and through East Africa to the Cape of Good Hope, where it winters alongside the resident population.

There is considerable evidence to support the assumption that many west European Whiskered Terns make a double crossing of the Sahara to and from their winter quarters in West Africa. Numbers in Mali, Chad and Ghana are locally impressive and must account for a significant proportion of the west European population.

AUKS, GUILLEMOTS AND PUFFINS
(ALCIDAE)

22 species; mostly confined to higher
latitudes of the northern hemisphere. Six
species breed in Europe and one other has
occurred as an exceptional vagrant. These
are small to medium-sized seabirds that
swim and dive with consummate ease, but
which are poorly equipped for both flight
and walking. Though no species, save the
extinct Great Auk, has actually lost the
power of flight, they are more or less the
northern equivalent of the penguins of the
southern hemisphere. Auks have small
heads, compact bodies and short wings, and
they are mostly black (or dark) above and
white below. They have short tails, webbed
feet, and stubby to quite-large bills, the
latter often highly coloured. The legs are
set well back on the body, useful for
swimming, but unsuited to progress on
land. Like the penguins they use their
wings to 'fly' underwater, and progress in
the air is marked by rapid wingbeating low
over the water surface. These are pure
seabirds, though some smaller species make
quite long journeys over land to reach their
breeding sites. Food is obtained by diving.

p.176 **Common Guillemot** *Uria aalge*

Description: 40–44 cm (16–17½ in). Medium to large
seabird that gathers on narrow cliff ledges
to breed. *Dark brown,* virtually black,
above and white below, marked by dark
breast-band and *sharply pointed bill.* In
winter, dark breast lost and white extends
to sides of face. Some birds have white eye
ring and white line extending over ears.
These are called the bridled form and are
more numerous in the north than in the
south of the species range. Generally seen
in small groups on the sea, or flying low
over water. Sharply pointed bill is main
field mark.

Voice: Utters various groaning and moaning
noises during the breeding season.

Habitat: Sheer cliffs with narrow ledges near rich feeding grounds in summer. In winter found offshore, but also well out of sight of land over continental shelf.

Breeding: One highly variable blue or green egg, variably blotched black or brown, laid on bare cliff ledge. Incubation 28–35 days, by both sexes. Highly colonial.

Range: Circumpolar, though absent from harshest areas of Siberia and Canadian archipelago. In Europe, confined to coasts of Iceland, Britain and Ireland with a few in northwestern France, western Portugal and Spain, Norway, and a few sites in Baltic. Winters near colonies, though European birds do extend as far south as Gibraltar.

Guillemots crowd together literally cheek by jowl on their narrow nesting ledges. Their eggs are particularly tapered in shape to spin, rather than roll, when disturbed. Nevertheless, many do tumble to destruction. The highly variable colouring of the eggs may aid individual recognition in what are highly crowded and often chaotic conditions. Before they can fly the youngsters leap to the sea where their parents continue to tend them.

---

p.176 **Brünnich's Guillemot** *Uria lomvia*

Description: 40–44 cm (16–17½ in). The Arctic replacement of the Common Guillemot to which it is very similar in both structure and coloration. Bill shorter and thicker, and marked by clear *white line along basal half of cutting edge*. In winter, white of the face does not extend to eye. Lacks flank-streaking of Common Guillemot and appears more hunch-backed both swimming and flying.

Voice: Growls like Common Guillemot at breeding colonies.

Habitat: Breeds on sheer cliffs, choosing narrower ledges than Common Guillemot, where upwelling creates rich open waters. Winters well out to sea, usually further from land than Common Guillemot.

Breeding: One highly variable, white, buff, green or
blue egg, marked by variable lines, spots
and blotches of brown and black.
Incubation 28–35 days, by both sexes.
Range: Circumpolar in high Arctic, though absent
from much of Canadian archipelago. In
Europe, breeds in Iceland and northern
Norway. Seldom wanders south of Faeroes;
an exceptional vagrant to temperate
Europe.

Despite their clear similarity to Common
Guillemot, Brünnich's are heavier chested,
more bulky birds capable of deeper dives
and longer flights. They occupy narrower
ledges, often so narrow that only one
member of the pair can perch at a time,
and they do not crowd together so closely
as Common Guillemot. They have
occurred on only 24 occasions in Britain,
mostly found dead along the tideline,
though more recent occurrences have been
of live, tickable individuals mainly in the
far north of Scotland and the islands.

p.176 **Razorbill** *Alca torda*

Description: 39–43 cm (15½–17 in). A black and
white auk that is numerous at northern
seabird colonies. Similar to Common and
Brünnich's Guillemots, but black rather
than brown-black above, and with *larger,
deeper and laterally compressed bill marked
by a vertical white line*. In winter, white
extends to face and hind crown. At all
times bill shape is best feature, even in
flight. Also has longer tail than the
guillemots, and feet do not extend in
flight.
Voice: Various growling calls during breeding
season; silent at sea.
Habitat: Frequents cliffs during breeding season;
particularly with jumble of fallen rocks an
crumbling landslides. Winters at sea,
usually inshore, but also out of sight of
land.
Breeding: One white or buffy egg, spotted and
blotched with dark brown, laid in hole or

crevice among rocks. Incubation 25–39 days, by both sexes. Variation in incubation period so large that checking seems necessary.

Range: Confined to North Atlantic coasts. In Europe, breeds from Iceland, Britain and Ireland to Scandinavia, including Baltic, south to northwestern France. Winters within this range, but also southwards to Morocco and western Mediterranean.

Well over half the world population of Razorbills breeds around the coasts of Britain and Ireland. It catches mainly small fish by diving from the surface and will continue hunting even with a bill-full of horizontally held prey. Sand-eels are the dominant prey in most areas and their seasonal absence is a disaster.

p.177 **Black Guillemot** *Cepphus grylle*

Description: 33–35 cm (13–14 in). In summer, an all-black auk, marked only by bold, *white, oval wing-patches* and red legs. In winter, mottled and barred grey above, with white wing-patches still relatively obvious. Bill sharply pointed like Common Guillemot, but decidedly shorter. Seldom found far from land, except in Arctic where it frequents pack ice.

Voice: A thin whistle uttered only in summer at breeding grounds.

Habitat: Breeds along cliff and other rocky coastlines; often, but not always, associated with colonies of other seabirds. Winters mainly near breeding colonies, but also ranges among pack ice some distance from land.

Breeding: Two white eggs, washed blue-grey or buff and spotted black or brown, laid in rock crevice, scree, or among boulders often, but not always, at the foot of a cliff. In Arctic may nest 1 km (⅔mile) or more inland. Incubation 21–25 days, by both sexes.

Range: North Atlantic and North Pacific. In Europe breeds in Iceland, Ireland, Scotland, and all coasts of Scandinavia including

islands of Denmark. Winters around breeding areas.

Black Guillemots differ from the other auks in being bottom feeders; they are, therefore confined to shallow water. They feed mainly on small fish, though the more northern populations take a larger proportion of crustaceans.

p.177 **Little Auk** *Alle alle*

Description: 20–22 cm (8–8½ in). The only *tiny auk* of the Atlantic. Stocky, black and white seabird, about the size of Starling. In summer, black above extending over head and breast, and white below. In winter, breast, neck and sides of head are white with almost complete white collar at nape. Flies fast on whirring wings. *Stubby bill* accentuates dumpy character.

Voice: Chattering calls at breeding colonies; silent at sea.

Habitat: Breeds on high Arctic cliffs and screes, usually along coast, but also among inland mountains. Winters at sea.

Breeding: One pale green-blue egg, sometimes spotted and scrawled with brown, laid in rock crevice on bed of small pebbles. Incubation 28–31 days, by both sexes. Colonial.

Range: Confined to North Atlantic at highest latitudes, where it is abundant; only a scarce, weather-driven migrant to temperate European shores. In Europe a tiny colony may still persist on Grimsey Island, Iceland. Abundant in Spitzbergen. Winter visitor to North Sea and coasts of Iceland and Norway.

One of the candidates for the title of the world's most abundant bird. Arctic colonies are huge and spectacular, with thousands and thousands of birds returning to their rocky colonies. Despite such numbers, it is only rarely seen from the shore, even in northern Europe. Occasional autumn 'wrecks' may bring them to land in large numbers.

p.177 **Puffin** *Fratercula arctica*

Description: 29–31 cm (11½–12 in). Small, chunky, black and white seabird marked by large colourful bill and upright stance. Upperparts black, underparts white, with white 'face' surrounded by black. *Conical bill vertically striped* in orange, yellow and grey; legs red. In winter, 'face' becomes dirty grey and bill reduced in both size and colour. Flies on short, whirring wings, swims and dives easily, and frequently loafs on grassy cliff tops.

Voice: A deep *arr-arr* while breeding.

Habitat: Breeds on grassy cliff tops, often on offshore islands, and particularly where grassy landslips have created predator-free environment. Winters at sea, though not truly pelagic.

Breeding: One white egg laid in burrow excavated in soft grassy cliff top, though rabbit burrows are also adopted. Incubation 40–43 days, by female alone.

Range: Confined to North Atlantic. In Europe breeds in Iceland, Britain and Ireland, northwest France, and coasts of Norway. In winter found around breeding areas, but ranging at sea as far south as Morocco and Canary Islands.

Its easy, waddling walk, coupled with its upright stance and plumage reminiscent of a waiter in black tie uniform, creates a comical appearance. Off-duty birds stand around in groups just like waiters before the lunchtime rush.

SANDGROUSE (Pteroclididae)

16 species; confined to temperate and tropical areas of Old World. Two species breed in Europe and another is a rare visitor from the east. These are medium-sized, ground-dwelling birds of dry, or semi-desert landscapes. They resemble pigeons, but are torpedo shaped, with long pointed wings and tapered, often extended,

pointed tails. The legs are remarkably
short and well feathered.

They are generally sandy brown above,
merging well with their background and
difficult to see on the ground. The
underparts and head are often well marked
and the main means of identification. They
fly fast in small groups and are best seen at
dawn and dusk when they fly to water.
When breeding, birds soak their breast
feathers, which are specially shaped for the
purpose of carrying water back for their
young to drink, or to cool their eggs. The
sexes are dimorphic.

p.180 **Black-bellied Sandgrouse**
Pterocles orientalis

Description: 33–35 cm (13–14 in). Medium-sized,
short-legged and stocky. Male is brown
above, heavily spotted with pale orange.
Grey head has rich orange-red throat and
foreneck. Narrow, black breast-band
separates grey above and pink below, with
extensive *black belly*. Tail pointed, though
not extended. Female buff above, with
extensive black barring and mottling over
head terminating in narrow, black breast-
band. Belly black. In flight, both sexes
show black belly contrasting with white
underwing coverts and black flight feather

Voice: A deep, laughing *churr-ow* that fades away
to nothing.

Habitat: Dry, open landscapes with scant vegetatio
steppes, semi-deserts, stony wastes.

Breeding: Two to three buff, brown-blotched eggs
laid in bare hollow. Incubation 21–22 day
by both sexes.

Range: Breeds across southern Mediterranean
eastwards through Turkey to Middle East
and southern Siberia. In Europe confined t
Portugal and Spain. Mostly resident,
though Siberian birds winter in Pakistan
and adjacent northwest India.

A suitable water-hole will attract these
birds at both dawn and dusk, usually at
quite precise times on a daily basis. Over

most of their Iberian range such water-holes
are now much more abundant than
formerly due to the creation of huge
reservoirs. As a result it is much more
difficult to predict their gatherings.

---

p.180 **Pin-tailed Sandgrouse** *Pterocles alchata*

Description: 31–33 cm (12–13 in). Long extended tail
feathers mask overall size, which is slightly
smaller than Black-bellied Sandgrouse.
Male yellow-green above, spotted pale
yellow, with brown at bend of wing.
Orange head, marked black through eye
and on throat. Narrow, black breast-bands
separate green, fawn and white areas of
neck, breast and belly. Underparts white;
tail long and extended. Female heavily
blotched and barred buff and black with
more complex pattern of black bars and
colours on neck and breast. In flight, *white
belly and underwing* create completely
different pattern to Black-bellied
Sandgrouse. Extended central tail feathers
are additional feature.

Voice: Loud *quet-tar* is somewhat crow-like; also a
cackled *kack-kack-kack*.

Habitat: Arid plains, dry stony areas, dried-out
muddy margins, semi-desert.

Breeding: Three buffy, brown-speckled eggs laid in
bare hollow. Incubation 19–21 days, by
both sexes.

Range: Resident from Mediterranean through
Middle East to southern Siberia, though
some eastern birds do move southwards to
Pakistan and Arabia. In Europe confined
to Spain and adjacent border areas of
Portugal and to the stony La Crau area of
southern France.

A glance at the distribution maps confirms
that the two European sandgrouse share
similar ranges and must, therefore, be
ecologically rather than geographically
distinct. Pin-tailed prefers low-lying, flat,
sandy, bare areas, rather than the rolling,
stony uplands with vegetation favoured by
Black-bellied.

PARROTS (PSITTACIDAE)

316 species; confined to tropics. A single species has been introduced to Europe and has established a feral population around London, England. These are small to medium-sized birds that are mostly brightly coloured in both male and female. Many species are green and merge well with the foliage of rainforests, but others may be quite dull. They have hooked bills like birds of prey, though they function as fruit-openers rather than flesh-tearers. One species, however, has made the transfer and is a dedicated carrion-eater. The strong feet have well-developed claws with two toes pointing forwards and two backwards; and like the woodpeckers, they are expert climbers among the trunks and branches of trees. Most nest in tree holes and lay white eggs. They fly fast on long, pointed wings, and many species have extended central tail feathers. Parrots are mostly highly gregarious and very noisy. Many species are widely kept as pets.

p.181 **Rose-ringed Parakeet** *Psittacula krameri*

Description: 37–43 cm (14½–17 in). The *only European parrot;* established around London in the 1960s. Green above, yellow-green below; extremely *long, extended green tail* makes this species unmistakable. Large, hooked bill bright red. Male has clear black neck-ring that becomes rosy on nape, lacking in the female.

Voice: Screaming *keeo-keeo*.

Habitat: Suburban parks, gardens and orchards in Europe, but open country and even city centres in native range.

Breeding: Three to four white eggs in tree hole, often a disused woodpecker hole. Incubation 22–24 days, by female alone.

Range: Resident across Sahelian zone of Africa and locally through Middle East to Indian subcontinent. Feral populations established in southeast England, Belgium, Holland and northwestern Germany.

Feral populations in Europe have now survived several severe winters and must be regarded as well established. They often come to bird feeders in suburban gardens, which helps them through the winter, but they face severe competition from Starlings for nest holes. By laying their first eggs in January they may get a head start over their rivals. Though this species frequently called Ring-necked Parakeet, many other parakeets have rings around their necks; Rose-ringed is its name in its native India.

CUCKOOS (CUCULIDAE)

125 species; worldwide. Two species breed in Europe and a few others are extremely rare vagrants from east and west. Cuckoos are small to medium-sized birds of decidedly slender build, with long graduated tails, short legs and stubby, decurved bills. They have long wings and characteristic, shallow-beat mode of flying that is particularly obvious in the European species. Plumage is highly variable, though many are prominently barred on the underparts. Most are arboreal and feed mainly on insects. The two European species are summer visitors that utter loud, highly characteristic calls. That of the Common Cuckoo, a distinct *cuc-oo* has given its name to the whole family. While several species are brood parasites, the majority build their own nests and rear their own young.

---

p.182 **Great Spotted Cuckoo** *Clamator glandarius*

Description: 38–41 cm (15–16 in). Medium-sized cuckoo. Adult grey-brown above, liberally spotted with white. Underparts white, with *yellowish wash* over neck and breast. Grey head extends to *obvious crest* at hind crown, and long, graduated tail has white margins. Short, decurved bill and short legs are slate-grey. Juvenile much more finely marked, with brown upperparts spotted white, yellow-buff underparts, and black cap that extends below eye. In flight all ages have long, pointed wings and tail, but fly slowly with shallow wingbeats. Juvenile has rich-chestnut primaries.

Voice: Harsh, raucous chattering *kittera-kittera* repeated.

Habitat: Orchard and park-like country with scattered trees and scrub. Also open woodlands and forest margins. Particularly fond of olive and cork groves.

Breeding: Maximum 18 pale blue-green, spotted-brown eggs, to mimic eggs of host, laid in three series of five to six, in nests of Azure-winged Magpie, Magpie and Carrion Crow, usually one per nest, but occasionally up to three. Incubation 12–14 days, by the host.

Range: Widespread resident across Sahelian zone of Africa, with summer populations in Mediterranean and southern Africa, where it is locally common and obvious. In Europe confined to Iberia, southern France, western Italy and northeastern Greece.

Unlike the Common Cuckoo, the Great Spotted only rarely removes one of its host eggs when laying its own. When hatched the chick does not eject the host's eggs or young and is reared alongside its host's own brood. Such a system works because the hosts of Great Spotted are themselves large and quite capable of rearing one or two extra youngsters.

---

p.183 **Common Cuckoo** *Cuculus canorus*

Description: 32–34 cm (12½–13½ in). Adult grey above with grey head and breast, and black *barring on white underparts. Tail long and graduated; wings long and narrow.* Bill, eye-ring and short legs yellow. Juvenile mottled and barred brown and black above and on head and breast, with brown-on-white barring below. A small percentage of adult females rich chestnut, barred black above, and barred buffy and white below. Chestnut uppertail heavily barred. This rare colour form is called the hepatic phase or morph.

Cuckoos fly with shallow beats of their wings and are somewhat hawk-like in shape. When arriving at a perch they seem to have great difficulty in folding their wings, and even when settled, often seem ungainly.

Voice: Clear *cuc-oo*, repeated; female also utters bubbling trill.

Habitat: Highly varied from marshes and moorlands to woods and fields. Absent only from highest mountains, densest forests and remotest islands.

Breeding: 1–25 eggs, average eight to nine, are highly variable and closely mimic those of host. Females are host specific laying all, or most, of their eggs in those of single species, one per nest. Incubation 12–13 days (as short a period as many small birds), by the host.

Range:  Widespread and familiar summer visitor throughout Europe, breeding right across Palearctic from Britain to Bering Straits and Japan, extending southwards to China. In Europe absent only from Iceland, Crete and Cyprus. Winters in southern Africa and Indochina.

In utilizing a wide variety of small passerine hosts to rear their young, cuckoos produce eggs that closely match those of their hosts. Females are thus host specific, though males are not or are, at best, location and habitat specific. If both sexes were host specific, the Common Cuckoo would show a strong tendency to speciate.

PIGEONS AND DOVES (COLUMBIDAE)

290 species; worldwide. Six species breed in Europe. Pigeons and doves are small to medium-sized birds with short bills on small, rounded heads. They have stocky, rounded bodies, longish, square or graduated tails, short legs, and long, pointed wings. They fly fast and strongly, and several species perform lengthy migrations. Most species are brown or grey in overall colour, though some tropical

species are predominantly green and a few
boast elaborate plumes. While most
European species are predominantly
terrestrial, others are purely arboreal. They
feed on seeds and fruit, and they drink with
a peculiar sucking action that does not
involve lifting the head to swallow. They
nest on cliffs or in trees and the young are
fed on 'pigeon's milk' produced in the
adult's crop.

---

p.184   **Rock Dove** *Columba livia*

Description: 31–35 cm (12–14 in). A stocky, grey dove
True Rock Dove is pale-grey above marked
by bold, *black, double wingbar* and clear-cut
white rump. Iridescent green slash marks
sides of neck. Head and underparts darker
grey than upperparts. In flight, double
wingbar and white rump obvious.

Voice: Repeated *oo-roo-coo*.

Habitat: Cliffs or remote islands and high
mountains; also tall city buildings, urban
railway bridges, city squares, rubbish tips
parks.

Breeding: Two white eggs laid in nest of twigs on cliff
or cave ledge; feral birds use buildings,
bridges and dovecotes. Incubation 17–19
days, by both sexes.

Range: Resident in many parts of the world from
Eurasia to India and across North America
Also more locally in Africa, south America
and Australasia. Original natural range
obscure.

Formerly domesticated for food and
subsequently bred for racing, the Feral
Pigeon, as it is known, is a highly successful
species that is often abundant where food
provided by tourists in city centres. Their
numbers are regularly augmented by
escapee racing pigeons and perhaps by true
Rock Doves. Many feral birds have reverted
to more natural habitats where they breed
freely with wild stock to form variably
plumaged hybrids. Truly wild birds may be
sought at the most remote sites, but may no
longer exist in Europe.

p.184 **Stock Dove** *Columba oenas*

Description: 31–35 cm (12–14 in). A medium-sized, grey pigeon similar to Rock Dove. Uniformly dark grey above and below, with green neck-slash and dull-pinkish wash over breast. Shows two tiny black wingbars both at rest and, on the inner wing, in flight. Rump uniform grey, not white. In flight whole of *wing shows broad black margins,* which facilitate identification even at long range.

Voice: A monotonous *coo-roo-oo*.

Habitat: Highly variable from open woodland and parkland with large, old trees, to sea and inland cliffs bordered by agricultural land. In winter, also occupies more open farmland.

Breeding: Two white eggs laid in nest of loosely gathered twigs, tree hole or large, trunk-hung nest box erected for owls; also in cliff crevice or hole, or even in rabbit burrow. Incubation 16–18 days, by both sexes.

Range: Breeds across temperate Western Palearctic extending eastwards to south-central Siberia. West European birds resident; those from Germany eastwards are summer visitors.

A strangely localized breeding bird that feeds mainly on seeds and grain on agricultural land, sometimes in association with the larger and more numerous Wood Pigeon. Despite its ability to exploit a variety of land forms, it is nowhere abundant and nowhere the dominant pigeon species.

p.185 **Wood Pigeon** *Columba palumbus*

Description: 39–43 cm (15½–17 in). Adult has grey upperparts, with narrow, white margin to bend of wing. Small head has pale eye, white at base of bill, and bold *neck-slash of white* over green. Underparts dull pink shading to dirty white on belly. In flight, shows *bold white bar across* (not along) wing. Juvenile similar, but lacks green and white

neck-slash. Gregarious when not breeding
forming huge feeding flocks.

Voice: An endlessly repeated *coo-coo-cu-coo*.

Habitat: Woodland, copses and shelter belts, with
easy access to open farmland and grazing.
Also in city parks and squares.

Breeding: Two white eggs laid on flimsy platform of
twigs placed in tree. Incubation 17 days,
both sexes.

Range: Breeds across most of western Palearctic,
with isolated populations in Tibet and
Hindu Kush. Eastern birds move southwe
in winter.

This is the largest and most widespread o
European pigeons, with a population
estimated at several million pairs.
Agricultural change, particularly wastefu
mechanized harvesting, has created perfec
feeding conditions for Wood Pigeons, wh
the planting of lowland forests during the
second half of the twentieth century
produced a pigeon's nesting paradise. Bir
find plentiful food on our fields and perfe
nest sites deep in our new plantations. In
many areas they are now regarded as a
serious agricultural pest, best controlled
spring rather than autumn shooting.

p.185 **Collared Dove** *Streptopelia decaocto*

Description: 29–32 cm (11½–12½ in). Highly successf
and confiding dove that spread right acro
Europe during the second half of the
twentieth century. Upperparts buffy grey
brown with pinkish head and bold, *black
neck-slash*. Underparts pinkish, fading to
grey-brown on belly. Neat, rounded
featureless face and longish, white-
margined tail. *Undertail has the distal half
pure white,* which shows well in flight.

Voice: A plaintive *weer* of greeting and a
monotonous *coo-coo-cuc-coo*, repeated *ad
nauseum*.

Habitat: Suburban gardens and parks; rural
farmsteads, particularly with free-range
fowl; town parks. Elsewhere among palm
groves and in dry brushland.

Breeding: Two white eggs laid on flimsiest of twig platforms placed at no great height in a tree. Incubation 14 days, by both sexes. Multi-brooded.

Range: Resident right across Europe from Faeroes to Greece, northwards to Scandinavia and eastwards to Urals. Also from Persian Gulf eastwards through India to China. Still spreading westwards and becoming established in Spain and Portugal.

The dramatic spread northwest across Europe started in Balkans in the 1930s, reached Britain in 1955, and has continued as far as the Faeroes and, more recently, to Portugal. Whether or not these birds will make the final leap across the Atlantic is a matter of conjecture, but in the absence of the now extinct Passenger Pigeon, there seems to be a vacant niche for such a granivorus species.

p.185 **Turtle Dove** *Streptopelia turtur*

Description: 26–29 cm (10–11½ in). Small dove. Upperparts scaly, with black feathers broadly edged rusty-chestnut, creating a turtle-shell pattern. Crown grey; neck and breast pinkish fading to grey on belly. Bold neck-slash of several black and white lines. In flight tail shows terminal white outer margins above and narrow white tip below. In flight at any distance *warm brown upperparts* distinguish it from similar-sized Collared Dove.

Voice: A deep purring *roor-rr*.

Habitat: Broken countryside, with mixture of open ground and trees, wind breaks and open woodland. Winters among similar broken land in acacia grassland of savannah Africa.

Breeding: Two white eggs laid on platform of twigs placed in low tree or bush. Incubation 13–14 days, by both sexes.

Range: Summer visitor across Mediterranean and most of temperate Europe as far north as southern Scotland and central Denmark, eastwards across Russia to south-central

Siberia. Also breeds in North Africa and northern Sahelian zone. Whole population winters in Sahelian zone.

The decline of this delightful dove, which produces one of the most characteristic sounds of summer, can be attributed fairly and squarely to the absurd practice of shooting spring migrants as they make their European landfall. It is easy to blame the Italians and the Maltese, but the practice extends from one end of Mediterranean to the other. Just when is the EC going to do something about this senseless slaughter?

p.185   **Laughing Dove** *Streptopelia senegalensis*

Description: 25–27 cm (10–10½ in). Small dove, with pinkish-brown upperparts, chestnut back, and *pale-blue wing coverts*. Head is featureless pink fading to white on belly; breast is prominently and neatly streaked black. In flight, wings show chestnut, blue and black, and the long tail has bold black and white corners.

Voice: A laughing *poo-poo-pooo-poo-poo*.

Habitat: Over much of its range frequents dry scrub though will readily take to gardens where available. In Europe, frequents parks and buildings.

Breeding: Two white eggs laid on platform of twigs placed in tree, bush or on ledge of building. Incubation 12–14 days, by both sexes.

Range: Widespread and common resident in savannah Africa through Middle East to Pakistan and India. In Europe only in Istanbul, and no more than a vagrant to neighbouring Greece and Bulgaria.

Formerly known as Palm Dove in Europe, which was inappropriate, and still called Little Brown Dove in India, which is inaccurate. Called Laughing Dove throughout Africa after its calls, which are a characteristic sound of the bush. Just why it has not spread farther into Europe is a mystery.

BARN OWLS (TYTONIDAE)

12 species; worldwide. One species breeds in Europe. Barn owls are medium-sized, nocturnal birds of prey, marked by a large and prominent facial disc lacking ear tufts and a largely hidden, hooked bill. The legs are long and feathered, and the toes are long, powerful and armed with fearsome claws. The outer toe is reversible. The wings are long and rounded and the flight feathers have soft margins to facilitate silent flight. In the air the body tapers towards the rear from the broad, flat face. Most are coloured in buffs and browns, and several species exhibit two distinct colour phases. Most inhabit grassland and woodland, but the Barn Owl *Tyto alba* also frequents buildings. They hunt low over the ground like a harrier and take mainly small mammals.

---

p.188 **Barn Owl** *Tyto alba*

Description: 33–36 cm (13–14 in). Western and southern birds *T. a. alba* are *pale orange-buff spotted with grey and black above;* underparts and prominent facial disc white. Eastern birds *T. a guttata* are more heavily spotted grey and black above, and orange-buff below with neat rows of black spots; *facial disc white.* In flight, the flat face creates a large-headed appearance, with body tapering towards tail. Quarters hunting grounds like a harrier, often during daylight.

Voice: Variety of shrieks, hisses and snoring calls.

Habitat: Farms and woods with plenty of rough ground rich in small mammals; also uses buildings as nesting and roosting sites.

Breeding: Four to seven white eggs laid in tree hole or on large ledge or upper floor of barn, or derelict house. Also more recently in specially erected nest boxes in barns and on poles. Incubation 32–34 days, by female alone.

Range: Virtually cosmopolitan, present on all the world's great landmasses as well as many quite small islands. Widespread resident

right across Europe. Absent only from Canada and from most of former Soviet Union and China, where winters are too harsh.

This is probably the world's most widespread bird, widely resident. No less than 37 distinct subspecies have been described.

OWLS (STRIGIDAE)

130 species; worldwide. Twelve species breed in Europe. Owls vary in size from small to large, from the tiny Pygmy Owl to the huge Eagle Owl. They are perfectly adapted nocturnal predators, though not all owls are night-time hunters. They have flat faces with both eyes facing forwards to provide binocular vision; asymmetrical ears to aid prey location; soft margins to the flight feathers of wing and tail to enhance silent flight; strong feet with fearsome talons and the outer toe reversible to grasp and kill prey; and a powerful hooked bill, much of which is hidden beneath facial feathers. They are large-headed, short-necked birds with rounded wings and short tails. Most perch upright and are clothed in mottled shades of brown or grey to merge with their background during the hours of daylight. The Snowy Owl is white to merge with its ice-covered habitats. Prey, which varies from insects and worms to birds, mammals and fish are swallowed whole. Undigested fur and bones are ejected from the mouth in the form of pellets, the examination and analysis of which produces an accurate picture of prey taken by particular species and individuals.

p.188   **Snowy Owl** *Nyctea scandiaca*

Description: 53–66 cm (21–26 in). Large, *white owl*. Female marked by rows of large black spots forming bars above and below; face and breast white. In both sexes, smallish, rounded head and lack of obvious neck, coupled with bulky, formless body creates seal-like appearance. Smaller male is all white with black bill, yellow eyes, and a few black spots at tips of wing feathers. In flight, large rounded wings and short tail obvious.

Voice: Harsh barking and mewing, and a deep repeated *hoo*.

Habitat: Open tundra with rocks; alpine wastes. In winter frequents similar areas as well as other open landscapes.

Breeding: Four to ten white eggs laid in bare scrape. Incubation 32–37 days, by female alone.

Range: Circumpolar in tundra zone. In Europe breeds only in Scandinavian mountain system and in Lapland. Usually wanders southwards in small numbers in winter, but seldom outside Scandinavia.

The Snowy Owl is largely dependent on the supply of lemmings, though it will also take rabbits, hares and large birds. In a 'lemming year' these owls lay larger clutches, rear larger broods, and follow the rodents southwards when they erupt. In North America an 'owl year' sees large numbers of Snowy Owls as far south as the US border. In Europe they wander only as far south as Stockholm and Oslo. They colonized the Shetland Isles between 1967 and 1975, and non-breeding females remain present at this site.

p.189 **Scops Owl** *Otus scops*

Description: 18–20 cm (7–8 in). Tiny, difficult to see, and located by highly characteristic call. Upright, thin, grey or brownish owl, marked by prominent *ear tufts, clear facial disc* and surprised expression. Camouflage is highly effective, though once found the bird allows a close approach, particularly in daylight.

Voice: A repeated *poop-poop-poop* that continues for minutes at a time.

Habitat: Towns and villages with old buildings and trees; also in more open farmland with copses and buildings.

Breeding: Four to five white eggs laid in hole in tree or building. Incubation 24–25 days, by female alone.

Range: Breeds right across southern and eastern Europe extending eastwards through Turkey and Middle East to south-central Siberia. Mostly a summer visitor to southern Europe, but resident in southernmost parts of Mediterranean.

This owl's call is as much a part of summer nights in Mediterranean as the chattering and reeling of cicadas, and listening for it is the best method of locating what would otherwise be a highly elusive species. It responds to tapes and will approach closely after dark. Care should be taken not to disturb individual pairs more than once, especially in areas where travelling birders are abundant. Numbers are declining in many parts of Europe.

p.189   **Pygmy Owl** *Glaucidium passerinum*

Description: 16–17 cm (6½ in). Tiny owl with small, *rounded head, double facial disc and bold eyebrows;* facial features far less marked than in similar, but larger, Little Owl. Upperpart lightly speckled, underparts lightly streaked. Often sits at an angle, rather than upright, and has characteristic habit of *cocking and waving tail* in a jerky movement. Hunts at dawn and dusk and flies direct, rather than bounding woodpecker-like as Little Owl.

Voice: Repeated, piping *du-du-du.*

Habitat: Extensive conifer forests in mountains of central Europe and at lower levels in north.

Breeding: Four to six white eggs laid in tree hole, usually an old woodpecker hole but also a nest box cleared of debris. Incubation 28–30 days, by female alone.

Range: From central Europe and Scandinavia eastwards across Palearctic to northern Japan. Vagrant away from breeding areas.

For its weight this is one of the most ferocious of all avian predators, quite capable of taking rodents heavier than itself. It also takes birds of its own size, often caught in flight. Like a shrike it builds up caches of food items, particularly in winter, to tide it over when hunting conditions are poor. Up to 200 food items have been counted at a single cache.

---

p.190 **Tawny Owl** *Strix aluco*

Description: 36–40 cm (14–16 in). Medium-sized, but chunky and well-built owl, with large rounded head marked by prominent facial disc, *dark eyes and no ear tufts*. Mostly barred and streaked in tawny brown, but also in paler grey-brown. Shows flat head and large, rounded wings in flight.

Voice: A deep and quivering *hoo-hoowoohoohoo*; also a shrill *kee-wick*.

Habitat: Towns, gardens, parkland, deciduous woods and broken farming countryside.

Breeding: Two to four white eggs laid in tree hole or building. Incubation 28–30 days, by female.

Range: Widespread and common resident across most of Europe, eastwards to western Siberia though absent from northern Scandinavia. Also resident in Himalayas eastwards through China.

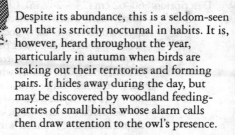

Despite its abundance, this is a seldom-seen owl that is strictly nocturnal in habits. It is, however, heard throughout the year, particularly in autumn when birds are staking out their territories and forming pairs. It hides away during the day, but may be discovered by woodland feeding-parties of small birds whose alarm calls then draw attention to the owl's presence.

---

p.189 **Hawk Owl** *Surnia ulula*

Description: 34–41 cm (13½–16 in). Medium-sized, diurnal owl that often perches quite *openly during the day*. About the same overall size as Tawny Owl, but a smaller bird marked by significantly *longer tail*. Basically slate-grey above with pale scapulars; white-barred grey below. Facial disc has *prominent dark side-burns,* frowning eyebrows and fierce yellow eyes. In flight shows short, pointed wings and long tail.

Voice: Hawk-like *ki-ki-ki* and bubbling *pru-lu-lu-lu*.
Habitat: Open conifer forests with areas of
regenerating birch.
Breeding: Three to ten white eggs laid in bare tree
hole. Incubation 25–30 days,
predominantly by female.
Range: Circumpolar in northern boreal zone and
absent from treeless Greenland and Iceland.
In Europe confined to Fennoscandia with
occasional southward irruptions that
seldom cross Baltic Sea.

Frequently seen in relatively open areas,
perched atop a conifer where it regularly
flicks its tail. Though a ferocious hunter
quite capable of pursuing and killing other
birds in flight, it more often takes rodents
captured with a shrike-like drop-and-
pounce technique. Exceptionally rare
vagrant to Britain, with birds of both
American and European origins.

p.190 **Ural Owl** *Strix uralensis*

Description: 60–62 cm (23½–24½ in). Closely related to
Tawny Owl, which it replaces among
northern forests. Equally nocturnal in
habits, but larger and paler than Tawny.
Upperparts streaked and barred buff and
brown; underparts creamy with clear-cut
dark streaking. Large, rounded head has
dark eyes set in *plain, heart-shaped facial
disc* bordered by narrow black line. In
flight, broad and rounded wings and
relatively *long tail* produce hawk-like
impression.
Voice: A clear *hoo-hoo-hoo-hoo* that increases in
volume.
Habitat: Mainly conifer forests, though also mixed
woods and wooded heaths and bogs.
Breeding: Three to four white eggs laid in tree hole or
rock crevice. Incubation 27–29 days, by
female alone.
Range: Resident in northern boreal zone of
Palearctic from Sweden and Finland to
Siberia and Japan. Also in mountains of
former Yugoslavia, in Carpathians, and in
northwestern China.

The propensity of this species to winter and breed in open areas of farmland, and among farm buildings, towns and even cities, may account for its apparent increase in numbers. It is far less confined to conifers than Great Grey Owl and often has areas of open water in its territories.

p.190 **Great Grey Owl** *Strix nebulosa*

Description: 65–70 cm (25½ 27½ in). Large, dark, grey owl of northern forests; often hunts during the day and may seek to drive off intruders with dramatic, head-on flights. Heavily streaked above and below. Most obvious feature is *huge facial disc* consisting of series of rings around yellow eyes with double white 'nose' bands. Dense, insulating plumage enhances size and apparent bulk, but it weighs only half as much as the similar-sized Eagle Owl.

Voice: A series of deep hoots, *ho-ho-ho*, that gradually die away to nothing.

Habitat: Strictly a bird of extensive conifer forests.

Breeding: Three to five white eggs laid in old nest of another species placed high in a conifer. Incubation, 28–30 days, by the female.

Range: Circumpolar, mostly in high Arctic boreal zone. In Europe breeds regularly only in northernmost Sweden and through most of Finland.

Outside the breeding season these owls disperse widely through northern conifer forests, often moving considerable distances south of their normal range. Sometimes, when the population of prey species crashes, they may wander to the forest margins and even beyond in search of food. They nevertheless remain vagrants further south.

p.190 **Eagle Owl** *Bubo bubo*

Description: 60–75 cm (23½–29½ in). Huge, brown owl that is among the most powerful of all avian predators. Heavily barred brown and black above, heavily streaked below. Large, plain facial disc with prominent *orange-yellow eyes and bold ear tufts*. In flight resembles huge, dark Tawny Owl.

Voice: Deep, far-carrying *hoo-hu* repeated.

Habitat: Wilderness areas of forest and mountain with broken land, gorges and rocky screes mostly with little or no human disturban

Breeding: Two to three white eggs laid in cave or roc crevice on rocky hillside, or in old nest of another species. Incubation 34–36 days, b female alone.

Range: Resident right across Palearctic and Oriental regions from Morocco to Sea of Japan and southern India. In Europe present in most mountain and densely forested areas of south and east; also, more locally, in Belgium and Germany.

This fearsome predator hunts at dawn and dusk taking a wide variety of mammalian and avian prey according to availability: coastal birds may kill Puffins and other auks; woodland birds take Capercaillie an Goshawk; and wetland birds take duck an even fish. Even an adult fox has been recorded as prey.

p.191 **Long-eared Owl** *Asio otus*

Description: 34–37 cm (13½–14½ in). A medium-sized, nocturnal owl, marked by orange facial disc and *prominent ear tufts*, and most often seen sitting in a remarkably *thin, upright posture*. Heavily streaked above and below. In flight shows orange patches in outer wing.

Voice: A low *oo-oo-oo*; young produce a rusty-hinge-like call in the nest.

Habitat: Wide variety of mainly open landscapes with woods, tree clumps, avenues and plantations. In some areas has definite association with conifers.

Breeding: Four to five white eggs laid in old nest of another species in tree or bush. Incubatio 25–30 days, by female alone.

Range: Circumpolar from edge of boreal zone southwards. Northern birds move southwards for the winter. In Europe, widespread but scarce south of Arctic Circle

with definite movement from northeast to southwest in winter.

This is one of the most difficult of all European birds to track down and see, though it is often very confiding once found. In winter, migrants often form communal roosts. A sure knowledge of its calls is the best means of location.

p.191 **Short-eared Owl** *Asio flammeus*

Description: 36–39 cm (14–15½ in). A long-winged, diurnal owl of marsh and moorland. Buffy, heavily streaked breast. Clear-cut, *plain facial disc with yellow eyes* surrounded by black 'bags' create a surprised look. In flight, long, narrow wings and quartering flight reminiscent of a harrier.

Voice: Deep *boo-boo-boo*, also a high-pitched *kee-aw*.

Habitat: Marshes, rough-grazing, floods and damp open moorland.

Breeding: Four to eight white eggs laid in hollow among rough grass. Incubation 24–28 days, by female alone.

Range: Circumpolar in tundra, boreal and steppe zones of Holarctic; also in southern South America. Mostly a summer visitor migrating southwards, often very long distances, to winter in Africa and Asia. In Europe mainly confined to north, though more widespread in winter.

The long-distance migrations of this essentially northern owl are doubtless responsible for its colonization of several parts of South America and the Caribbean island of Jamaica. Some birds regularly cross the Sahara, and Siberian birds range as far south as southern India.

p.189 **Little Owl** *Athene noctua*

Description: 21–23 cm (8–9 in). Small, grey-buff owl, boldly spotted white above, with pale underparts heavily streaked with black. Well-marked facial disc with *bold eyebrows* and piercing *yellow eyes* create fierce expression. Stands upright atop rock or po and flies with bounding action. Active during daylight and one of the easiest of a European owls to see.

Voice: A whistled hoot; also a sharp *kee-oo*.

Habitat: Wide variety of open country broken by copses, woods, farms, old buildings and rocky outcrops.

Breeding: Three to five white eggs laid in tree hole, hole in building. Incubation 28–29 days, by female alone.

Range: Breeds right across temperate zone of Palearctic from Portugal to northern China also southwards to central Sahara and Middle East. Introduced to Britain in late nineteenth century and has since spread.

Although declining in several areas, notably Austria and Switzerland, this remains one of the commonest of all European owls and, in most places, the easiest to locate. It regularly sits atop roadside fence and telegraph posts and wil allow a relatively close approach before flying off with its characteristic woodpecker-like undulating flight. It feed by pouncing on small mammals, large insects and worms augmented by the occasional small bird.

---

p.191   **Tengmalm's Owl** *Aegolius funereus*

Description: 24–27 cm (9½–10½ in). A shy, nocturnal, forest-dwelling owl, about the same size a Little Owl. Grey-buff above with large, whitish spots and bold 'braces'. White below with bold dark streaks on breast an flanks. Head seems too large for body and is marked by *bold, heart-shaped facial disc* and piercing yellow eyes with dark 'eye bags'.

Voice: A rapid *po-po-po-po-pop*.

Habitat: Found among open conifer forests from taiga to temperate hills and mountains. Also clearings in more densely forested country, especially spruce, and in mixed woodland.

Breeding: Three to six white eggs laid in tree hole, often the old nest of Black Woodpecker, or a nest box. Incubation 26–36 days, by female alone.

Range: Circumpolar in boreal and taiga zone and known as Boreal Owl in North America. In Europe breeds through Fennoscandia and among hills and forests of central Europe from eastern France eastwards to Carpathians and southwards to Greece, where it is very local.

The erection of suitably sized nest boxes has enabled these owls to increase and spread among the hills and forests of southern Belgium. Sadly regularly robbed by egg collectors. One female robbed of her eggs flew 700 km (435 miles) eastwards and successfully reared a brood that same season in Germany – a remarkable reaction to losing her clutch.

NIGHTJARS (CAPRIMULGIDAE)

76 species; worldwide. Only two species breed in Europe and another two are exceptional vagrants. Nightjars are small to medium-sized nocturnal birds that feed exclusively on the wing on flying insects, predominantly moths. Cryptically camouflaged in shades of brown, black and buff and are all but impossible to find and see on the ground among broken stems and leaves. Indeed, many species are very similar in plumage, with only white patches on outer wing and tail tip to aid identification. Some species have extended wing feathers during the breeding season that are used in display. In flight, wings are long and pointed and, in most species, tail is long and broad. Like owls, the flight feathers have soft margins to deaden sound and the birds enjoy completely silent flight. They fly low over lightly vegetated broken ground, with easy changes of direction, to catch their prey in their huge, swallow-like gapes. Legs are short and weak. Strangely their eggs, which

are laid on ground, are white and rely on t
highly camouflaged sitting bird to avoid
detection. Nightjars frequently rest on ro
and tracks at night, and these are often th
best places to locate them.

p.192 **European Nightjar** *Caprimulgus europaeu*

Description: 25–28 cm (10–11 in). The only nightjar ov
most of Europe. Medium-sized nocturnal
bird, with characteristic *churring call, long,
pointed wings and long tail,* both marked wit
bold white patches in male. Extremely wel
camouflaged in shades of brown, buff and
grey (*see* Red-necked Nightjar for plumage
distinctions). A summer visitor active at
dawn and dusk and otherwise seen only wh
accidentally flushed.

Voice: Long, drawn-out, churring song similar t
the noise created by vibrating the tongue
the mouth; variable in pitch and volume.
Also claps wings in display.

Habitat: Heaths, forestry drives, coppiced and burne
out woodland, and regenerating scrub.

Breeding: Two white eggs, lightly spotted with grey
brown, laid in bare scrape among woodla
or heathland litter. Incubation 18 days, b
both sexes.

Range: Summer visitor right across temperate
Europe from Iberia and Ireland eastwards
central-eastern Siberia. The whole
population winters in savannah Africa.

The old country name of Goatsucker deriv
from the erroneous view that nightjars
sucked the milk from domestic stock after
dark. The association with domestic anima
doubtless arises from its pursuit of insects,
which are attracted to stockyards, pens and
other areas where animals concentrate.

p.192 **Red-necked Nightjar** *Caprimulgus ruficol*

Description: 30–32 cm (12–12½ in). Slightly larger th
European Nightjar and generally paler,
though these are fine points. Best identifi
by *sandy-rufous areas on nape and throat* and

distinctive *white chin*. Shape and habits closely resemble more widespread bird. Song completely different.

Voice: A long repeated *ko-tok, ko-tok, ko-tok* quite distinct from churring of European Nightjar, though similarly uttered at dawn and dusk.

Habitat: Dry scrub, open pinewoods, semi-desert with trees.

Breeding: Two white eggs laid in bare scrape. Incubation period and role of sexes are unknown.

Range: Confined to Iberia and northwestern North Africa, and thus a Western Palearctic endemic. Winters in Sahelian Africa at Niger Inundation Zone, but also probably elsewhere.

Though said to be numerous in Spain, this is often a difficult bird to see. The best tactic is to locate birds by their calls and then drive slowly along little-used roads and tracks with headlights blazing watching for resting birds. With care they may continue resting in the headlights.

SWIFTS (Apodidae)

70 species; worldwide. Four breed regularly in Europe and a further four are exceptional vagrants. Swifts are mainly small to medium in size and most aerial of all birds. They feed, drink, sleep and mate on wing and come to land only to lay their eggs and rear their young. All have long, sickle-like wings, slim bodies, short, square or forked tails, and tiny bills backed by a huge gape. They feed exclusively on flying insects. They are among fastest fliers in the world and cover many thousands of kilometres per year. Most species are black or dark, often uniformly so and confusing as a result. Some have white patches, mostly on rump or underparts. Legs are short and feet small. The four toes in many species all face forward and are suited to clinging, rather than walking or perching. All swifts have a

large salivary gland and use saliva to glue their rudimentary nests together. Some tropical species construct their nests entirely of saliva, which is the basis of bird's-nest soup and highly regarded in t east. Perhaps if it was known that this delicacy is nothing more than swift spit i would lose some of its magic.

---

p.202 **Common Swift** *Apus apus*

Description: 16–17 cm (6½ in). An *all-black*, swallow-like bird, with torpedo-shaped body and forked tail, that flies on long, narrow, *sickle shaped wings*. Most aerial of all birds, with flicking wingbeats and stiff-winged glide Gregarious, forming 'screaming' parties over town and suburban breeding ground Never perches on wires like swallows and martins.

Voice: High-pitched screaming.

Habitat: Any area with adequate supplies of flying insect food; often congregates in large numbers over fresh waters and marshes during poor weather. Breeds in towns and suburbs, but also in large cities and, occasionally, along coastal cliffs.

Breeding: Three white eggs laid inside a building offering entrance hole, but still sometime in cliff hole or cave crevice. Incubation 14–20 days, by both sexes.

Range: Summer visitor to most of Europe, save mountains and tundra of Scandinavia and Iceland, extending eastwards across Siber to northern China. Winters in Africa sou of Sahara.

Swifts arrive late in spring and depart ea in autumn. Over most of temperate Euro they thus spend only the months from M to July at their breeding grounds. During that period they are among the most obvious of all summer visitors, though during poor weather they will move long distances ahead of weather fronts. Radar studies have proved that Swifts cat-nap o the wing and that they do spend much o their lives airborne.

p.202 **Pallid Swift** *Apus pallidus*

Description: 16–17 cm (6½ in). Very similar to Common Swift and separated from that more widespread bird only with great care and good views. Long, narrow wings, torpedo-shaped body and forked tail shared with Common Swift, but paler and more sandy overall, with difficult-to-see *white throat*. Contrast between dark-brown body and pale inner wings creates *dark 'saddle'* on back. Wing coverts also paler than primaries.

Voice: High-pitched screaming.

Habitat: Towns and cities and other areas frequented by Common Swift, but generally more concentrated along coasts.

Breeding: Two white eggs laid in hole in building, or occasionally in cliff hole or cave crevice. Incubation 14–20 days, by both sexes.

Range: Summer visitor to Mediterranean coasts extending eastwards as far as Persian Gulf. Winters in African Sahelian zone.

Pallid Swifts return earlier in summer and are often more abundant than Common Swifts along Mediterranean coasts. They should, however, be identified with care, especially by birders visiting from temperate north who are unaccustomed to bright Mediterranean light. Even Common Swifts can appear brown in good light and also show a small white bib when their mouths are bulging with food for their young.

p.202 **Alpine Swift** *Apus melba*

Description: 20–22 cm (8–8½ in). Considerably larger than other European swifts, with slower beats of longer wings. Overall shape and structure much as Common Swift; but plumage brown not black, and broken by *white belly and throat* separated by narrow, brown breast-band. Gregarious, forming large feeding flocks and dense colonies.

Voice: Loud chittering, quite unlike screaming of other swifts.

Habitat: Cliffs, gorges, sea cliffs, buildings, towns and bridges, mostly at comparatively low altitudes despite its vernacular name.

Breeding: Three white eggs laid on platform of grasses and feathers placed in rock crevice or hole in building or bridge. Incubation 17–23 days, by both sexes.

Range: Summer visitor through southern Europe eastwards to Turkey, Middle East and India where it is resident. Winters in South and East Africa, where there are also scattered breeding populations. Irregular further nor

Though clearly a swift, it does bear a superficial similarity to a Hobby with whi it may be confused by the uninitiated, or a great distances. Its somewhat stiff-winged flight is, however, quite distinct from the supple, deep wingbeats of the falcon.

p.202 **White-rumped Swift** *Apus caffer*

Description: 14 cm (5½ in). Smallest European swift, with characteristic long, narrow, stiffly he wings and torpedo-shaped body. Whole plumage black, broken by *white, horseshoe shaped rump*, white chin and pale face. A dark-blue wash, particularly on body and wing coverts, is visible only at close range Deeply forked tail, coupled with narrow white rump distinguishes from vagrant Little Swift *A. affinis*.

Voice: A low-pitched twittering.

Habitat: Broken rocky country with caves, but als increasingly in more open country with road bridges and culverts.

Breeding: Two to three white eggs laid in old nest o swallow, usually Red-rumped Swallow. Incubation 21–25 days, by both sexes.

Range: Widespread breeder over much of sub-Saharan Africa, with recently established outposts in Morocco and Spain where it i scarce summer visitor. Winters in savann Africa.

First discovered in Europe among sea clif of Atlantic Andalucia in southern Spain a misidentified as Little Swift, which nests commonly in northern Morocco. Later correctly identified as this species with nearest known (at the time) breeding colony nearly 3,000 km (1,860 miles) to south. Arrives late and takes over Red-rumped Swallow nests to breed. It is extending slowly northwards to central Spain, though it is still decidedly rare in rest of Europe.

KINGFISHERS (ALCEDINIDAE)

90 species; worldwide. Only one breeds in Europe, though two others do so as near as western Turkey. These are mainly small to medium-sized colourful birds with large, robust bills and small, weak legs and feet. Wings are short and rounded and whirr rapidly in fast flight. While many kingfishers feed on fish caught by a hovering-diving technique, others shun water entirely and hunt shrike-like over dry country. While fish-eating species have long, pointed bills, dry-ground specialists have short, heavily built, strong bills. All species have two outer toes largely fused and joined to the inner toe for nearly a third of its length. Most nest in holes and lay white eggs.

p.192 **Common Kingfisher** *Alcedo atthis*

Description: 15–16 cm (6–6½ in). The only European kingfisher and quite unmistakable, even when only glimpsed. Vivid pale *blue above and orange-red below,* marked by bold face pattern and long, pointed bill. Most often seen as fast-flying blue flash low over water.

Voice: Hard, metallic *chee* or *chee-kee.*

Habitat: Unpolluted rivers, streams, marshes and lakes. Also on coasts in arid areas, and on coasts and estuaries in hard winters.

Breeding: Six to seven white eggs laid at end of tunnel excavated by birds themselves in earthen bank of river or stream. Incubation 19–21 days, by both sexes.

Range: Resident over most of temperate Europe, though birds breeding from Poland

eastwards move away during winter.
Breeding extends right across Palearctic t
Japan, southwards through Asia to Sri
Lanka and Papua New Guinea.

This bird sits patiently on a riverside perc
watching for passing small fish. Sometime
it plunges directly, but most often it hove
over the water before diving head first to
catch its prey in its bill. Fish are carried t
favoured perch before being knocked
senseless and swallowed head first.

BEE-EATERS (MEROPIDAE)

24 species; tropical, Old World. Only one
is a summer visitor to Europe and another
rare vagrant. This is a highly colourful
family of predominantly gregarious birds
that feed on bees and wasps caught in the
air. They are slim and long-winged, with
several species having extended tail
feathers. In the air they are exceptionally
graceful, gliding and diving with
consummate ease. Prey is caught in long,
thin bill and stings are removed by beatin
the insect on a perch. On migration they
frequently fly very high and their presenc
may be detected only by their high-
pitched, liquid calls.

p.193 **European Bee-eater** *Merops apiaster*

Description: 27–29 cm (10½–11½in). A *rainbow of a bi*
marked by chestnut cap merging with
yellow back, yellow chin and blue
underparts. Central tail feathers are
extended to form streamers. Distinctive
slim shape apparent in all plumages; flies
on long, sharply pointed wings.

Voice: Loud, liquid *quip-quip*, repeated
continuously among flocks.

Habitat: Open, wooded and park-like country ofter
near water.

Breeding: Four to seven white eggs laid at end of
tunnel, excavated by the birds themselves

in earthen or sandy bank in dense colonies. Incubation 20 days, by both sexes.

Range: Breeds right across warmer parts of Western Palearctic, extending eastwards to Iran and adjacent Siberia. In Europe mainly a southern and eastern summer visitor, with occasional overshooting to more temperate areas. Winters in western and southern Africa and breeds in South Africa.

A small colony was established and successfully bred in a gravel pit in Sussex in 1955. Though this is regarded as a freak, once in a lifetime experience, Bee-eaters now breed regularly in Paris area and sporadically further west in Normandy and Brittany. Numbers overshoot every spring and further breeding in Britain should not be discounted.

ROLLERS (CORACIIDAE)

11 species; mainly warm, tropical Old World. A single species is a summer visitor to Europe. Rollers are medium-sized, heavily built, perching birds with large heads and strong, broad-based bills. The legs are short and weak. The wings are broad and rounded and they fly strongly. The name derives from their display flights, which involve acrobatics that show their boldly coloured plumage to advantage. Most are clothed in bright colours, with blue predominating especially in flight. They hunt shrike-like, by glides and pounces from a prominent perch and are therefore frequently seen on roadside poles. They are usually solitary, though numbers will gather at brush fires.

p.193 **European Roller** *Coracias garrulus*

Description: 30–32 cm (12–12½ in). Medium-sized, stocky, highly colourful and quite unmistakable bird, frequently seen perched on roadside telegraph pole. Back pale chestnut-brown; *rest of plumage a vivid turquoise-blue.* In flight shows black and blue wings.

Voice: Harsh, chattering *kraak*.

Habitat: Parkland, groves, broken ground with shrubs and belts of trees, open pine wood

Breeding: Four to five white eggs laid in hole in tre bank, derelict building or rock crevice. Incubation 18–19 days, by both sexes.

Range: Summer visitor to warmer parts of West Palearctic from Spain to Poland eastward to central Siberia and Afghanistan. Decidedly more widespread in eastern th western Europe. Winters exclusively in eastern Africa.

A decline during the twentieth century h been variously attributed to climatic char and to changing land use, both of which have affected the food supply. In central Spain suitable hunting territories have be converted to breeding sites by erecting ne boxes on telegraph poles. Though primar intended for Lesser Kestrels, Rollers have taken well to these new opportunities.

HOOPOES (UPUPIDAE)

One to three species; confined to Old Wo One species breeds in Europe. Systematis are divided in whether to regard all hoop as belonging to a single species, or wheth to split those of India and Africa from the nominate Eurasian form to create two separate species. All share a similar struct and plumage, though they differ in basic coloration and size. Hoopoes are medium sized, perching birds that find most of th food on the ground. Despite their short le they walk well. They use a long decurved bill to pick and probe in the manner of a ground wader. They vary in colour from a pale buff-brown to almost chestnut-brow and are marked by a bold, erectile, black-tipped crest and by bold black and white wingbars that are particularly obvious in flight. Flight is deeply undulating like a woodpecker's, but also quite erratic.

p.193 **Hoopoe** *Upupa epops*

Description: 27–29 cm (10½–11½ in). A medium-sized, sandy-fawn bird marked by prominent, black-tipped, *erectile crest* and bold *black and white barred wings* shaped like table-tennis bats. Feeds on ground, probing and picking with long, decurved bill. Quite unmistakable.

Voice: Repeated *poo-poo-poo* from which it is named.

Habitat: Park-like groves, gardens, broken and dry agricultural land, and orchards.

Breeding: Five to eight greyish eggs laid in tree hole, rock crevice or hole in building, which quickly becomes foul due to lack of nest sanitation. Incubation 16–19 days, by female alone.

Range: Widespread through warm and temperate Palearctic, Oriental and Ethiopian regions. Most European and Palearctic birds are summer visitors as far north as Channel and Baltic shores. Small numbers winter in southern Iberia.

The slow decline of this charismatic species began over 150 years ago and thus cannot be blamed on modern agricultural chemicals – or not entirely anyway. But since they feed mainly on ground-dwelling insects and their larvae, the more widespread use of pesticides may have added to the trend.

WOODPECKERS (PICIDAE)

210 species; worldwide, except Madagascar and part of Australasia. Ten species breed in Europe and two more are extreme transatlantic vagrants. Woodpeckers and wrynecks are small to medium-sized arboreal birds well-adapted to climbing and boring holes in trees. They have strong legs and feet with two toes pointing forwards and two backwards to aid tree climbing. The tail feathers have particularly strong shafts and, with the feet, form a firm triangular basis for attacking trees. The bill forms a sharply

pointed and strongly built chisel, and the
exceptionally long and prehensile tongue
be extended to search out wood-boring
insects and their larvae. The wings are
rounded, and in most species, flight is dee
undulating. The sexes are similar, though
males often have patches of colour, mainly
red, on the crown. Their excavation of a n
nest hole each season, often in a living tre
creates nest sites for many other hole-nest
species. Wrynecks lack both the strong bi
and tail of woodpeckers; they feed on the
ground and by probing among bark. They
are cryptically coloured, whereas most
woodpeckers are boldly patterned.

p.197 **Wryneck** *Jynx torquilla*

Description: 15–16 cm (6–6½ in). Small, woodpecker-l
bird that feeds mainly on the ground, but
shares woodpecker's foot structure and tree
clinging capacity. Heavily camouflaged, w
bars and stripes of grey, buff and brown above
Barred below on throat and breast, but pal
on belly with lines of chevrons. Peculiar
triangular-shaped head, with short, pointe
bill. Flies directly with *long, square-cut tail*
prominent feature. Easily overlooked both
the ground and among bushes.

Voice: Loud *kee-kee-kee* repeated soon after arrival
spring, but then silent and difficult to loc

Habitat: Parkland, orchards, groves, riverside
tangles, heaths.

Breeding: Four to six white eggs laid in tree hole,
usually in deciduous tree but also in nest
box or rock crevice. Incubation 12–14 d
mainly by female.

Range: Summer visitor right across temperate a
boreal Palearctic from Spain to Japan. In
Europe breeds as far north as tree line,
though it abandoned Britain during
twentieth century. Winters from India t
China, and across Sahelian zone of Africa

The strong neck-twisting characteristic,
from which this bird is named, is seen on
when a bird is trapped for ringing and b
those fortunate enough to witness a

territorial display. Like a Robin, the head is pushed back (or forwards) to expose the breast in the most elaborate contortions.

---

p.196 **Grey-headed Woodpecker** *Picus canus*

Description: 25–26 cm (10 in). Similar to and closely related to Green Woodpecker, but slightly smaller and with *plain grey head* marked only by narrow moustachial streak and loral line. Male has red forehead. Upperparts green, with yellow rump; underparts grey and unbarred.

Voice: A flute-like, laughing *ku-ku* repeated five to eight times; also drums, unlike Green Woodpecker.

Habitat: Hill and mountain forests as well as riverine and other smaller woodlands. Avoids competition with Green Woodpecker among conifers, where that species does not occur.

Breeding: Four to five white eggs laid in specially excavated tree hole. Incubation 17–18 days, by both sexes.

Range: Breeds right across Palearctic in boreal and temperate zones as far as Japan, China and Java. In Europe, resident from northwestern France across central and eastern Europe, but largely absent from areas near coasts and from Mediterranean.

A glance at the world range of this species shows it to be far more widespread in Asia, its presumed origins. Having colonized westwards, it faced competition with Green Woodpecker west of Urals and succeeded only by occupying upland and marginal woodland not utilized by that species. It remains essentially a bird of Continental-type climate found either at altitude, or in the east of our region.

---

p.196 **Green Woodpecker** *Picus viridis*

Description: 30–33 cm (12–13 in). Large woodpecker, frequently observed feeding on the ground. Upperparts green with pale greenish yellow rump; underparts pale grey-green.

Both sexes show *red crown and black face,* but male has red centre to black moustachial streak lacking in female. Juvenile mottled green and yellow above, and heavily barred black and white on hea and underparts.

Voice: Loud, yaffling laughs *keu-keu-keu*.

Habitat: Wide variety of deciduous woodland, usually with adjacent open and agricultur country; also orchards, parks and groves.

Breeding: Four to nine white eggs laid in specially excavated tree hole. Incubation 18–19 day by both sexes.

Range: Virtually a western Palearctic endemic. Resident over most of Europe, except Ireland and much of Scandinavia.

Although it feeds and breeds among trees this is a species that has found its place by also feeding on the ground in search of an and their larvae. As a result, it often forag quite long distances from the nearest woodland. Its presence is often detected b its loud laughing calls.

---

p.198 **Great Spotted Woodpecker**
Dendrocopos major

Description: 22–24 cm (8½–9½ in). Medium-sized, black and white woodpecker, marked by large *white ovals on back,* a feature shared only with Syrian and Middle Spotted Woodpeckers. Complex head pattern has broad *black line extending from nape to bill,* a feature lacking in other species which, as a result, have a whiter, more open-faced appearance. Male has tiny red patch on rea of crown, lacking in female, and red undertail. Juvenile has red crown.

Voice: Loud, high-pitched, *tchack*; also far-carrying, hollow drumming.

Habitat: Wide variety of woodlands from taiga and pure conifers to mixed and purely deciduous, as well as Mediterranean evergreens and groves.

Breeding: Four to seven white eggs laid in hole excavated in a tree. Incubation 16 days, mainly by female.

Range: Resident across Palearctic from Iberia to Japan southwards to Caucasus and through China. In Europe absent only from Iceland, Ireland, northern Scandinavia and southern Greece.

This is the standard pied woodpecker over most of Europe and the one with which other species should be compared. Its adaptability is evident from its wide choice of habitat, but it also comes to gardens and feeds freely at bird tables where it is often aggressive.

---

p.198 **Syrian Woodpecker** *Dendrocopos syriacus*

Description: 22–23 cm (8½–9 in). Very similar to Great Spotted Woodpecker, but *lacks cheek-stripe* of that species creating more *open-faced appearance* in all plumages. At a glance seems white headed, with extended black, zig-zag moustachial streak. White wing-patches less extensive and squarer than in Great Spotted. Juvenile has red crown, but bordered black and with some streaking on underparts; beware confusion with Middle Spotted Woodpecker.

Voice: Variety of hard calls, including *schik*, *churr* and *kwick-kwick*, all less piercing than Great Spotted's; also drums.

Habitat: Open woods, parks, gardens and particularly villages and farmsteads.

Breeding: Four to seven white eggs laid in tree hole. Incubation 9–14 days, by both sexes.

Range: Resident in central and southeast Europe from the Czech Republic eastwards through Turkey to Middle East.

Though its name derives from the country where it was first described, this woodpecker is neither widespread nor common there. It did, however, expand its range considerably during the twentieth century, colonizing much of southeastern Europe where it was previously unknown. The causes remain a mystery, though its ability to live happily alongside man may be significant.

p.199 **Middle Spotted Woodpecker**
Dendrocopos medius

Description: 20–22 cm (8–8½ in). Slightly smaller th
Great Spotted Woodpecker, but similarl
marked in black and white, with *white o*
on wings. Red crown and white face lacki
prominent black moustache, create *pale-
headed effect*. Flanks finely streaked;
undertail pale pink. Folded wings show
more *black and white barring* than other
'oval-backed' woodpeckers.

Voice: A repeated *qua-qua*; also drums.

Habitat: Mainly deciduous forests, especially thos
containing hornbeam, but also in mixed
oak-spruce forests. Usually at low altitud

Breeding: Four to eight white eggs laid in excavate
hole in tree. Incubation 11–14 days, by
both sexes.

Range: Virtually endemic to western Palearctic.
Resident across most of central, tempera
Europe from France to Ukraine and from
coastal Turkey to Middle East.

This is a far less robust species than Grea
Spotted, with a significantly smaller bill
that is used for probing rather than
chiselling. It spends more time in the
canopy and on the trunks of dead trees a
is seldom seen on the ground. It is thus
to co-exist with its more powerful and
widespread relative.

p.199 **White-backed Woodpecker**
Dendrocopos leucotos

Description: 24–26 cm (9½–10 in). Significantly larg
than Great Spotted Woodpecker and lac
white ovals on back. One of only two
'ladder-backed' woodpeckers in Europe.
Male has red crown, but otherwise simil
head pattern to Great Spotted. Female h
black crown and is very similar to femal
Great Spotted. Underparts finely streake
undertail pale pink. In flight, *white back*
extends upwards from rump.

Voice: A sharp *juk-juk* similar to Great Spotted
also drums.

Habitat: Mainly upland deciduous woodland, but also in mixed and pure conifers provided there are sufficient dead or dying trees.

Breeding: Three to five white eggs laid in excavated hole. Incubation 10–11 days, by both sexes.

Range: Resident from central Europe eastwards to Japan and Kamchatka, with outlying populations in Pyrenees, Formosa and China. In Europe breeds from Scandinavia to Alps eastwards.

This is one of the most elusive and, therefore, most sought after European birds, with declining populations in many areas. There is no doubt that its preference for dead and dying trees, with plentiful rotting, fallen timber, is at odds with modern forestry practice. Its future lies in remote mature woodlands, or specifically unmanaged ones.

---

p.199 **Lesser Spotted Woodpecker**
Dendrocopos minor

Description: 14–15 cm (5½–6 in). Small woodpecker, with barred, *ladder-back* appearance, that spends most of its time among the canopy and is generally elusive. Male has red crown; female buffy. Underparts, especially flanks, finely streaked. Face buffy, creating a rather *scruffy* appearance.

Voice: High-pitched *kee-kee-kee* similar to call of Wryneck; drums on dead branches much more rapidly than other woodpeckers.

Habitat: Wide range of woodland from taiga and pure conifers to Mediterranean groves and scrub.

Breeding: Four to six white eggs laid in tree hole, usually in damaged or dead branch or trunk, sometimes on underside of bare branch. Incubation 14 days, by both sexes.

Range: Resident right across Palearctic from Britain to Japan. In Europe breeds from northern Scandinavia to southern Italy and from Portugal eastwards.

Feeds much higher among smaller branches than any other woodpecker and easily overlooked among winter tit flocks. Also nests higher than other woodpeckers,

excavating its hole in relatively thin outer
branches as well as on damaged tree trunk
Essentially a prober rather than a hacker. I
is best located by its calls in early spring,
before Wryneck arrives.

p.197 **Three-toed Woodpecker**
Picoides tridactylus

Description: 21–22 cm (8–8½ in). Though basically
black and white, this is not a true pied
woodpecker. Upperparts black, broken by
white back, and *virtually devoid of barring.*
Underparts white, heavily barred on flank
Distinctive dark *head pattern of black with
white lines,* not white with black lines. Ma
has yellow on crown, lacking in female.
Three, rather than four, toes.

Voice: A quiet *tuk-tuk*, much less vocal than pie
woodpeckers; drums slowly.

Habitat: Conifer forests, often near water or where
fire has created open areas with dead trees

Breeding: Three to five white eggs laid in tree hole.
Incubation 14 days, by both sexes.

Range: Circumpolar in taiga and boreal zones. In
Europe, breeds across Fennoscandia as well
in montane forests of Alps and Carpathians

This is the only European woodpecker wi
three toes; the rest have four. It is a scarce
and elusive bird that spends much of its
time systematically feeding quietly on a
chosen tree. It is far less vocal than other
woodpeckers, making location that much
more difficult.

p.197 **Black Woodpecker** *Dryocopus martius*

Description: 45–47 cm (17½–18½ in). Largest Europe
woodpecker and, in flight, similar in size
and appearance to Rook. *Uniformly black*
with long tail and red crown in male and
hind crown in female. Appears somewhat
ragged in flight.

Voice: Loud *kee-arr* and chattering *kwick-kwick-
kwick* that are highly distinctive and far
carrying.

Habitat: Extensive, mature, conifer forests with
stands of deciduous trees, predominantly
beech, often in hilly or mountain regions.

Breeding: Four to six white eggs laid in specially
excavated hole in large tree, usually
deciduous. Incubation 12–14 days, by both
sexes.

Range: Resident across Palearctic from Spain to
Japan and Kamchatka. In Europe breeds in
lowland Fennoscandia southwards through
much of temperate Europe. Widespread in
former Yugoslavia and Greece, but with
only isolated populations in mountains of
Spain and Italy. Absent from Britain.

But for its distinctive, far-carrying calls, this
would be a difficult bird to locate at all
times. In winter, it forms communal, tree-
top roosts and has a distinctive roosting call.
Its large holes, excavated anew each season,
are widely adopted by owls after use.

LARKS (ALAUDIDAE)

80 species; mostly confined to Old World.
Nine species breed in Europe. These are
mainly small, ground-dwelling birds of
brown and buff streaked plumage, with
relatively few distinguishing features. The
sexes are similar. Larks have mainly short
bills, but they vary from the thin and weak
to the stout and powerful. They walk well,
often hunched close to the ground, and are
gregarious when not breeding. They have
fine, distinctive songs and many perform
high-flying, song-flights over their
territories. They mostly inhabit open
country, often in more dry and arid areas.
Several are distinctly desert orientated
where they are the dominant bird family.

p.206 **Calandra Lark** *Melanocorypha calandra*

Description: 18–20 cm (7–8 in). Large, stocky lark with
heavy, conical bill, large rounded wings and
short tail. Greyish buff above with broad,

darker streaking; white below with lightly streaked breast. At rest, large head and bo. *black breast-crescent* are most obvious features. In flight, large floppy wings with dark underwing can be recognized even at great distance. Closer approach reveals distinctive *white trailing edge to wing*.

Voice: Sky Lark-like stream of liquid chattering notes of considerable virtuosity, broken by discordant notes and mimicry uttered in high, circling flight. Contact note a nasal *kreet*.

Habitat: Open grassland and arable fields, dry stony areas and wasteland.

Breeding: Four to five, brown-speckled white eggs laid in neat cup of bents on the ground, sheltered by vegetation. Incubation 16 days, by female, though male may take some part.

Range: Resident through Mediterranean eastward through Middle East to south central Siberia. Vagrant northwards.

Although resident, birds form winter flocks, often in association with Corn Buntings, that wander nomadically over their breeding range and occasionally venture beyond. Thus they are mainly winter visitors to Romania. There has bee a significant decline detected in many part of Europe, probably linked to changing agricultural practice.

p.206 **Short-toed Lark** *Calandrella brachydactyla*

Description: 13–15 cm (5–6 in). Fawny buff or greyish buff above, with some light streaking; white and unstreaked below. Pale, *stubby bill* and, in eastern subspecies, a clear dark moustachial streak widening to form *smudgy patch at sides of breast*, are good field marks. Western subspecies is less well-marked, but has rufous cap. Feeds gregariously on ground and shows distinctive *torpedo shape in flight*. Tertials cover primaries at rest.

Voice: A harsh *chirrip*; song an extended repetitio of variable phrases in high flight.

Habitat:	Dry open ground with sandy or stony wastes and scant vegetation; dried out marshes and saltings; poor grazing.
Breeding:	Three to five variably coloured eggs, speckled with brown or grey, laid in well-lined cup on the ground, sheltered by tussock. Incubation 13 days, by female.
Range:	Summer visitor to warm temperate areas of Palearctic from Spain to eastern Siberia. In Europe, essentially Mediterranean. Winters in Sahelian zone of Africa and plains of northern India.

This highly migratory lark occurs in large numbers on passage through Mediterranean and, as a result, frequently overshoots in spring and wanders northwards in autumn. It is annual in Britain, especially at well-watched offshore islands, with between 10 and 20 records per year. Most records are of single birds.

p.206 Lesser Short-toed Lark
Calandrella rufescens

Description:	13.5–14.5 cm (5½ in). Similar to Short-toed Lark, but distinctly darker and greyer, with extensive *streaking on breast* and flanks. Streaking is diagnostic difference between the species, but when Lesser Short-toed turns its head to one side the breast feathers may merge to form a patch similar to that of more widespread Short-toed Lark. Long *primary projection* visible at close range.
Voice:	A harsh rolled *prrt*; song is more musical, with extended phrases, than Short-toed and uttered in a lower-level song-flight.
Habitat:	Decidedly drier country, with scant vegetation, than Short-toed; steppes, semi-desert and arid pastures.
Breeding:	Three to four creamy, brown-speckled eggs laid in cup beside grassy tussock. Incubation period unknown, by female with help from male.
Range:	Arid areas from Mediterranean eastwards to steppes of Kazakhstan. European birds replaced eastwards by recently split Asian

Short-toed Lark *C. cheleensis*. Resident.
Vagrant northwards.

Although this bird roams widely in flock
during the winter its occurrences as a
vagrant northwards usually involve singl
birds. During the late 1950s, no less tha
42 individuals were seen in three flocks i
Ireland, including a single flock of 30 in
Kerry.

p.206 **Crested Lark** *Galerida cristata*

Description: 16.5–17.5 cm (6½–7 in). Widespread an
common Sky Lark-type bird marked by
distinctly *spiked crest*. Upperparts grey-bі
heavily streaked; underparts creamy witl
fine streaking on breast. Tail short with
rufous outer feathers. Bill longish
and distinctly decurved. Confusable only
with geographically restricted Thekla La

Voice: Song similar to Sky Lark, but less melodi
and with shorter phrases. Call a distinctiv
wee-weeoo.

Habitat: Dry, open country, arable fields and
pastures, coastal dunes and bare wastelan
around farms and villages.

Breeding: Three to five whitish, buff-speckled eggs
laid in neat cup on the ground. Incubatiо
12–13 days, by female.

Range: Resident across southern Palearctic as fai
northern China and southwards through
northern Africa and Middle East. In
Europe breeds throughout the Continent
but does not reach either Britain or
Scandinavia.

No less than 28 distinct subspecies of
Crested Lark have been described, mainly
differing in the colour tone of plumage,
which varies from warm rufous to a cold
grey. Most subspecies have evolved amon
the resident populations of the west and
south, including four in Europe. Birds frо
Siberia are migratory and more uniform
over large areas as a result of the mixing о
individuals that long migrations tend to
encourage.

p.206 **Thekla Lark** *Galerida theklae*

Description: 15.5–16.5 cm (6–6½ in). To be
distinguished from Crested Lark only with
the greatest of care and with good extended
views. Like Crested, grey-buff and streaked
above; creamy and streaked below; and
marked by *spiky crest*. Major identification
points are *shorter bill, bolder streaking
(especially on breast) that extends to nape,* and
usually a *ragged, multi-pointed crest*. Similar
short tail with rufous outer feathers. A grey,
rather than rufous, underwing is a negative
feature that identifies Crested positively,
but is difficult to see and leaves only doubt
when rufous not seen.

Voice: Musical song uttered in Sky Lark-like
continuous stream, usually in prolonged
song-flight.

Habitat: Open ground and rocky hillsides, usually at
some altitude. Shuns farmland and human
dwellings.

Breeding: Three to six off-white, buff-speckled eggs
laid in neat cup on the ground. Role of sexes
and duration of incubation are undescribed.

Range: Resident in Spain and Portugal northwards
along Mediterranean coast to France. Also
through North Africa. An isolated
population exists in Ethiopia.

Despite everything that has been written on
the separation of Crested and Thekla Larks,
the best features remain the Thekla's boldly
spotted breast streaking and small bill. All
other features are nothing more than
confirmatory at best, misleading at worst.

p.207 **Wood Lark** *Lullula arborea*

Description: 14.5–16 cm (5½–6 in). Slightly smaller
than similar Sky Lark, but much *shorter tail*
creates characteristic shape in flight.
Upperparts heavily streaked black, buff and
brown; underparts creamy white with fine
streaks confined to breast. A bold, pale
supercilium extends to nape, isolating crestless
cap, and there is a bold *black and white mark
at bend of wing.*

Voice: A flute-like, descending *lu-lu-lu-lu-lu* that
fades away, uttered in high circular flight
and as bird descends to its perch high in a
tree, or on a wire.

Habitat: Parkland, groves, open woodland, heaths
with trees.

Breeding: Three to five creamy, brown-spotted eggs
laid in cup on the ground. Incubation
12–16 days, by female alone.

Range: Breeds throughout temperate and
Mediterranean Europe extending eastward
through European Russia and Turkey to
adjacent Middle East. Southern and weste
birds are resident.

The slow decline and contraction of range
of this bird during the twentieth century
may be no more than a highly sensitive
reaction to climatic change. In Britain,
where populations have been assessed or
monitored longer, there was a marked
decline in the early nineteenth century
followed by an increase from 1920 to
1950, followed by another period of
decline in the 1980s and a further recover
in the 1990s.

p.207 **Sky Lark** *Alauda arvensis*

Description: 17–18 cm (6½–7 in). Heavily streaked bu
brown and black above with *small crest* tha
extends from hind crown. Creamy buff
below with streaking on breast and flanks
Lacks clear-cut supercilium. *Tail long with
white outer feathers.* In flight shows narrow
white trailing edge to wing like Calandra La
which is quite different in shape.

Voice: Prolonged musical warbling and trilling
uttered in high, hovering display-flight;
call a liquid *chirrup.*

Habitat: Grassland, grazing pastures, plough,
heaths, moors, coastal marshes.

Breeding: Three to four greyish eggs, blotched with
brown, laid in neat cup of bents on the
ground. Incubation 11 days, by female.

Range: Widespread and common over much of
Europe. Breeds right across Palearctic fro
Britain and Spain to Japan and Kamchatk

In Europe, southern and western birds are resident; eastern birds migrate south and west in vast numbers to Britain, Ireland, France and Spain.

The song of the Sky Lark is legendary and has been the inspiration of poets and composers for centuries. Towards the end of the twentieth century its numbers showed a catastrophic decline in western Europe, which has been attributed to the effectiveness of both insecticides and selective weed-killers causing literal starvation to millions of birds. The Sky Lark is also a culinary delicacy in France. Will the French ever be persuaded to abandon the obnoxious slaughter they perpetrate on this species every year?

p.207 **Shore Lark** *Eremophila alpestris*

Description: 16–17 cm (6½ in). A high alpine and Arctic breeding species that winters along shorelines. Grey-buff upperparts and pale-buff underparts lightly streaked on flanks; outer feathers of tail white. Easily identified by *yellow face marked by black-breast crescent, black loral area, and black lateral crown-stripes* that terminate in 'horns' at rear of crown. This bold head pattern is somewhat reduced in winter. Crouches low to the ground, shuffling along, and is difficult to see without flushing.

Voice: Distinctive *tseep*, rather like a wagtail.

Habitat: Bare mountain plateaux and open tundra wastes. In winter along shingle and sandy shorelines with scant vegetation.

Breeding: Three to four greenish-grey, brown-spotted eggs laid in loose cup of grasses sheltered by tussock. Incubation 10–11 days, by female alone.

Range: Circumpolar in tundra zone and to the south in steppe country and among high mountains. Northernmost birds are summer visitors. In Europe breeds only among high mountains of Scandinavia and mountains of Balkans. Winter visitor to shores of North Sea, mostly in small numbers.

In North America, where it is known as Horned Lark, this species breeds from the high Arctic tundras of the Canadian archipelago southwards to southern Mexico and is absent only from the boreal forest zone. It occupies a wide range of habitats that are used, in the Palearctic, by other larks that are absent in the Nearctic.

---

p.207   **Dupont's Lark** *Chersophilus duponti*

Description: 17–18 cm (6½–7 in). A highly elusive, ground-dwelling lark that is exceptionally difficult to locate and just as difficult to flush. Streaked above in shades of brown and black, with buffy, neatly streaked breast and white belly. *Head rounded, with pale, central crown-stripe and long, decurved bill.* Legs are long, and bird invariably runs rather than flies to avoid danger. Its secretiveness, specialized habitat, long, decurved bill and lack of crest distinguish it from other species.

Voice: Nasal, Greenfinch-like calls; twittering song.

Habitat: Extensive stands of feather-grass, with isolated clumps of vegetation separated by bare narrow pathways, usually on flat or gently sloping land. Roams cereal fields in winter.

Breeding: Three to four whitish eggs, heavily spotted with brown, laid in depression lined with available material and hidden in tussock. Incubation period and role of sexes are unknown.

Range: Confined to North Africa from Morocco to Egypt and a large area of eastern Spain. Some wandering in winter.

As recently as the early 1980s this bird was not known to breed in Europe and was regarded as a Moroccan speciality. Today it breeds over large areas of central and eastern Spain south to the Mediterranean coast, and it is regarded as relatively abundant. It seems amazing that it could have been overlooked for so long, but even more amazing that this loath-to-fly bird could have colonized Spain from North Africa.

SWALLOWS AND MARTINS
(HIRUNDINIDAE)

80 species; worldwide. Five species breed
in Europe and another is the rarest of rare
vagrants. These are highly aerial birds that
catch all their food on the wing and are
among the most masterful of all fliers.
Several species perform huge migrations,
from one end of the earth to the other,
covering more miles than all but a handful
of other species. They are small birds with
long, pointed wings and square-cut or
forked tails. They are streamlined and
have tiny bills backed by large insect-
grabbing mouths. The feet and legs are
short, weak, and used only for perching.
Many species gather mud to form their
nests, but may otherwise never come to the
ground. They are highly gregarious, some
forming dense nesting colonies, others
feeding and roosting communally. They
also perch on wires and many species have
adapted to nest on man-made structures.
Many species are brown, or brown and
white; others are black and white, often
with patches of red.

---

p.202 **Sand Martin** *Riparia riparia*

Description: 11–12 cm (4½ in). Smallest of the European
swallows and a highly gregarious summer
visitor. *Brown above, white below,* marked by
distinctive *brown breast-band* that is not
always easy to see in birds overhead. Shows
forked tail, fluttery flight and lacks white
rump. Only Crag Martin is similarly
brown, but that is a chunky bird with
triangular wings, a more gliding flight and
uniform buffy-brown underparts.

Voice: Confiding twittering.

Habitat: Frequents lakes, marshes and reed-beds
with abundant insect food. Breeds in sandy
cliffs, both inland and coastal.

Breeding: Four to five white eggs laid at end of
specially excavated tunnel in sand cliff, and
in dense colonies occupied year after year.
Incubation 14–15 days, by both sexes.

Range: Circumpolar from tundra southwards to warm temperate zone. In Europe found throughout Continent eastwards across Siberia to Bering Straits and China. A resident population is found from Hindu Kush to western China. Most winter in savannah Africa.

Although nesting in 'natural' sites, compared with many of its close relatives, Sand Martins have undoubtedly benefited from the creation of quarries for sand and gravel, especially with the post-war boom in the use of concrete. The catastrophic decline in the 1960s was a result of drought in their major winter quarters in Sahelian Africa, a decline first made apparent by a drop in the numbers ringed.

p.203 **Crag Martin** *Ptyonoprogne rupestris*

Description: 14.5–15 cm (6 in). Slightly larger and distinctly *chunkier* than similarly brown Sand Martin. Brown above, *paler buff-brown below*, with row of *white spots in spread tail* the only distinctive field mark. Broad-based triangular wings, less fluttering and more *gliding flight*, thickset body and notched, not forked, tail are better features.

Voice: A thin *trrit* and *chwee*.

Habitat: Cliffs and gorges in upland areas, but often at sea level in winter.

Breeding: Three to five red-spotted white eggs laid in deep cup of mud plastered to wall of cave, or beneath an overhang, on a steep cliff, but away from full sunlight. Incubation 13–17 days, by female.

Range: Breeds through Mediterranean eastwards through Turkey and Middle East to Himalayas and northern China. Central Asian birds are summer visitors. In Europe most birds are resident or make only local movements.

This is the only resident European swallow. It is closely related to the Rock Martin of Africa, with which the former Pale Crag

Martin is now regarded as conspecific, and the Dusky Crag Martin of India. The latter are often more associated with buildings than the European species.

---

p.203 **Swallow** *Hirundo rustica*

Description: 16–22 cm (6½–8½ in). One of the most abundant and obvious of all summer visitors to Europe. Black, washed metallic blue above, with white to pale pinkish underparts. *Dark red and black face* produces dark-headed appearance from below. *Tail deeply forked,* with longer tail-streamers in male than female. Long, angular wings indicate aerial expertise.

Voice: Confiding chattering and twittering.

Habitat: Frequents wide range of landscapes rich in insects, particularly marshes and other wetlands. Breeds in villages and farmsteads, and winters in similar areas.

Breeding: Four to five reddish-spotted white eggs laid in shallow mud cup constructed against wall, or on shelf or ledge inside building. Incubation 11–19 days, by female alone, though some males may take a brief stint.

Range: Circumpolar, breeding from beyond Arctic Circle southwards to North Africa, Middle East and China. Breeds throughout Europe, save Iceland; winters in sub-Saharan Africa.

The confiding nature of the Swallow and its use of buildings in which to nest has endeared it to all country dwellers. Some birds do still nest in caves, but the limited availability of such sites must have made this species a very rare bird indeed prior to our constructing suitable alternatives.

---

p.203 **Red-rumped Swallow** *Hirundo daurica*

Description: 17–18 cm (6½–7 in). Superficially similar to Swallow, but with stouter, more *torpedo-shaped body* and *longer, inward-turning tail-streamers.* Similar flight, but with more extensive gliding. Upperparts metallic black broken by *pinkish rump-patch*

and narrow collar. Underparts rufous
pink, with *faint streaking* in juvenile and
autumn adults. The *lack of dark face* and
throat distinguishes it from Swallow at all
times.

Voice: A confiding, but harsh chirrup; song a
twittering, noticeably shorter than
Swallow's.

Habitat: Rocky and open country usually near wate

Breeding: Three to five red-speckled white eggs laid
in flask-shaped nest stuck to horizontal ro
of cave or culvert. Incubation 14–15 days,
by both sexes.

Range: Summer visitor from Mediterranean
eastwards through Middle East to China
and Japan. Resident in India and in drier
areas of sub-Saharan Africa. In Europe,
widespread in Iberia and Greece, but more
locally distributed in between.

The northwards spread of this swallow
through Europe has been associated with
widespread use of culverts and bridges
constructed of concrete, the rough
undersurfaces of which offer perfect nestin
sites. Whether there are other factors
involved is unknown.

p.203 **House Martin** *Delichon urbica*

Description: 12–13 cm (4½–5 in). Chunky, black and
white swallow that nests in densely packe
colonies on building exteriors. Black abov
with blue-metallic sheen visible at close
range, marked by *broad white rump.*
Underparts pure white. Wings broad based
and not as pointed as in Swallow; tends to
glide more than that bird. Tail notched
rather than forked.

Voice: Clear *chirrup* quite unlike other swallows;
song a low chattering.

Habitat: Towns and villages; also over water.

Breeding: Four to five white eggs laid in ball-shaped
nest of mud attached to eaves of a buildin,
with only a narrow entrance hole at the to
Nests are often plastered together;
invariably colonial. Incubation 13–19 day
by both sexes.

Range: Summer visitor right across Palearctic, from beyond Arctic Circle southwards to Himalayas. Breeds throughout Europe, save Iceland where it is only the rarest of summer visitors. Has, on occasion, also bred in South Africa.

The largest colonies of House Martins can be found in southern Europe where hundreds of nests may be crammed together under a bridge or beneath the elaborate eaves of a church. On migration, Swallows and Sand Martins roost communally in reed-beds, but it has long been open to debate as to where House Martins roost when away from their colonies. There are records of many (17 or more) emerging from a single nest, so perhaps passing birds bed-and-breakfast with 'friends' along the way.

PIPITS AND WAGTAILS
(MOTACILLIDAE)

54 species; worldwide, but mostly in Old World. Eight species breed in Europe and several others are irregular migrants or vagrants. These are small, slimline, mostly ground-dwelling birds with long tails that are frequently wagged. Pipits are predominantly brown and buff with variable amounts of streaking and closely resemble the more bulky robust larks. Wagtails are mostly larger, longer tailed and more boldly marked in black, white, grey and yellow. All species have long legs and are good walkers. They fly well with a typically undulating action and are gregarious outside the breeding season. Being largely insectivorous most species are, to a greater or lesser extent, migratory. While most wagtails are relatively straightforward to identify, many pipits pose serious identification problems, particularly to the beginner, but also to the most experienced observer when faced with a single off-course vagrant.

p.208 **Richard's Pipit** *Anthus novaeseelandiae*

Description: 18 cm (7 in). Largest European pipit
comparable in size with Tawny Pipit, but
much darker and more heavily streaked.
Upperparts *olive-brown with heavy streaking;*
underparts washed with buff-brown on
heavily streaked breast and flanks. Shows
white lores, black moustachial streak, long
yellow-red bill and long pink legs. Stands
upright like Tawny Pipit, which is less
streaked above even in first-winter
plumage.

Voice: Loud Sparrow-like *shreep.*

Habitat: Damp grasslands, especially near coast on
migration in Europe.

Breeding: Four to six olive-brown eggs laid in neatly
lined cup on the ground well hidden
among grass. Incubation period and role of
sexes unknown.

Range: Breeds from eastern Siberia southwards
through China, Asia to Australia and New
Zealand; also in India and Southeast Asia,
and in savannah Africa. Siberian and
Chinese birds are migrants. In Europe, a
regular autumn migrant in small numbers.

The majority of Richard's Pipit population
are resident and the occurrence of birds,
sometimes in small flocks, in Europe is
generally regarded as a long-distance
westwards movement of eastern Siberian
birds. Some birds do winter in the Sahelian
zone of Africa, and the great circle (i.e.
shortest) route between, say, the Sea of
Okhotsk and the Niger Inundation Zone
does pass through central Europe.

---

p.208 **Tawny Pipit** *Anthus campestris*

Description: 16–17 cm (6½ in). Largest breeding pipit in
Europe and distinctive in all plumages.
Breeding adult *sandy-brown, lightly
streaked above,* with row of *dark spots across
wing;* underparts *unstreaked white.* Head
shows dark lores and fine moustachial
streak. Juvenile more heavily streaked
above and with *fine streaking on breast.*

Long legs and longish bill. *Stands upright* and runs well.

Voice: A clear *tseep*, more like a wagtail than other pipits; song in descending flight a *chivee-chivee-chivee*.

Habitat: Dry, sandy wastes with scrub, vineyards and other dry areas with scant vegetation.

Breeding: Four to five brown-blotched white eggs laid in depression lined with grasses and hair and sheltered by tussock. Incubation 13–14 days, almost exclusively by female.

Range: Summer visitor from Europe eastwards across steppes to eastern Siberia. Winters in Sahelian Africa, Arabia and India. In Europe, absent from Iceland, Britain and Ireland, and Scandinavia, save for southernmost Sweden. Scarce in France, Germany and over much of eastern Europe.

This is a regular, if scarce, passage migrant through Britain that has surprisingly never managed to breed, despite giving its name to the melodramatic 1940s British film *The Tawny Pipit*. The choice of subject, which showed the effects of the appearance of a rare bird on local people, was unfortunate in selecting the wrong bird. Only ten years later Bee-eaters were actually breeding in Sussex.

p.208 **Red-throated Pipit** *Anthus cervinus*

Description: 14–15 cm (5½–6 in). Very similar to Meadow Pipit and Scandinavian subspecies of Rock Pipit, but with more contrasting, *darker streaking* than either. Upperparts boldly streaked black on buff and brown; underparts creamy with *bold streaking* extending to flanks. In summer face and throat dullish *rusty red;* in winter and on passage a *creamy bib* is prominent. Legs pink as Meadow Pipit, but unlike Rock Pipit.

Voice: A distinctive thin *tseep*, higher and longer than similar call of Tree Pipit.

Habitat: Breeds on wet tundra; on migration frequents marshes and damp grasslands as well as other, drier short-grass areas.

Breeding: Five to six grey-buff, brown-speckled eggs laid in cup of grasses placed in tussock. Incubation by female alone for unknown period.

Range: Breeds across Palearctic tundra from northern Scandinavia to Bering Straits and westernmost Alaska. Winters in savannah Africa and in China and Southeast Asia.

Although it winters across the Sahelian zone of Africa, it is much more common in the east than in the west. This distribution is reflected on passage where it is scarce in western Europe but relatively common in the central and eastern Mediterranean.

p.209 **Water Pipit** *Anthus spinoletta*

Description: 15–16 cm (6–6½ in). Readily identified by grey-brown or grey-buff *unstreaked upperparts* and bold, *white supercilium*. In summer, breast washed warm creamy buff in winter, white with clear-cut, black streaking. Legs dark. The combination of unstreaked back and distinct habitat preference ensures identification.

Voice: A clear *weest*.

Habitat: In summer, high, bare, mountain plateaux with rocks and low vegetation. In winter frequents inland marshes, often watercress beds, as well as estuaries.

Breeding: Four to six grey, brown-spotted eggs laid cup hidden among low vegetation. Incubation 14 days, by female alone.

Range: Summer visitor to mountains of central and southern Europe and Siberia. Widespread in winter on lowland wetlands over much of western and southern Europe.

Although only comparatively recently split from Rock Pipit, the complex relationship in this group of pipits remains a problem. North American and eastern Siberian birds are now recognized as a separate species, Buff-Bellied Pipit *A.rubescens*. They occupy a different habitat and show distinct plumage characters, though closer to Water Pipit than Rock Pipit.

p.209 **Rock Pipit** *Anthus petrosus*

Description: 15–16.5 cm (6–6½ in). A very dark pipit that is *coastal in habits* at virtually all times. Two distinct subspecies occur; both have *dark legs* and are *dark olive-brown with darker streaking above*. The British subspecies, *A. p. petrosus*, is grey-buff with dark streaking below, and lacks clear supercilium. The Scandinavian subspecies *A. p. littoralis*, shows *pale supercilium*, creamy-buff on breast, white belly, and clear black stripes extending only from upper breast to flanks. Scandinavian birds are thus paler and more clearly marked than British ones.

Voice: A clear *weest*.

Habitat: Rocky coasts and coastal marshes.

Breeding: Four to six grey, brown-spotted eggs laid in neat cup of grasses sheltered by rock or grass. Incubation 14–15 days, by female.

Range: Confined to coasts of Britain, Ireland and Scandinavia and adjacent parts of Russia. Winters along coasts from southern Scandinavia to Portugal and Gibraltar. British birds are resident.

While the darker British Rock Pipits are relatively easy to distinguish, birds from Scandinavia can easily be confused with the more abundant Meadow Pipit, especially darker-grey-type birds. Leg colour is then the best field mark, though the calls are quite distinctive.

p.209 **Tree Pipit** *Anthus trivialis*

Description: 14–16 cm (5½–6½ in). Clean-cut, well-marked version of Meadow Pipit. Upperparts olive-buff, with *clear dark streaking;* underparts *white* with pale-buff wash and *clean streaking over breast and flanks*. Fine moustachial streak, pale-pink legs and white outertail feathers are features shared with Meadow Pipit. Perches in trees and wires, and most obvious during song-flight.

Voice: Harsh *teez*; song a loud trill terminating with drawn-out *see-see-see*.

Habitat: Open woods with clearings, parks, groves and heaths with trees.

Breeding: Four to six brown, grey or reddish eggs, speckled brown, laid in neat cup of grasses on the ground. Incubation 12–14 days, by female alone.

Range: Summer visitor right across northern and central Palearctic southwards to plateaux Tibet and Middle East. Winters in India and in Sahelian savannah of East Africa. In Europe, widespread away from coasts of Mediterranean, and Atlantic coasts of Spain, Ireland and Iceland.

Most obvious in spring when in song-flight it reaches high in the sky before parachuting down, singing as it descends, to alight on a tree, bush or wire. Though non-breeder in Mediterranean, large numbers of birds pass through on passage

p.209 Meadow Pipit *Anthus pratensis*

Description: 14–15 cm (5½–6 in). Buffy olive, or buffy brown, with clear or obscure streaking above. White below with *warm-buff wash over breast and flanks, both streaked black. Leg pinkish;* outertail white. Forms loose winter flocks that feed on the ground. Sometimes perches on fence posts and wires.

Voice: High-pitched *eest* or *tissip*.

Habitat: Breeds on coastal marshes, heaths, hilly moors, inland wetland margins to open tundra. Winters in similar areas, especially coasts.

Breeding: Three to five variably coloured eggs, spotted brown, laid in neat cup of grasses depression among vegetation. Incubation 11–15 days, by female alone.

Range: Widespread and locally abundant. Breeds from eastern Greenland and Iceland across northern and temperate Europe to Urals. Winters in south and west Europe to North Africa and Middle East.

Vast numbers of these birds head southwestwards every autumn to winter among the marshes and along the

shorelines of south and west Europe. It is often the most abundant bird along the shorelines of England in winter.

---

p.210 Grey Wagtail *Motacilla cinerea*

Description: 18–20 cm (7–8 in). Largest and *longest-tailed* European wagtail and the one most closely associated with water. Summer male blue-grey above, yellow below. Grey extends over head, which shows narrow, white supercilium and moustachial streak, and distinctive *black bib*. Tail long, with white outer feathers; *legs pink* (all other wagtails have black legs). Female and winter male lack white moustache and black bib. Underparts often show little yellow, save on undertail.

Voice: High-pitched, metallic *dzit*, song *zee-zee-zee*.

Habitat: Mostly fast-running streams, but also other areas where fresh water runs fast.

Breeding: Four to six buffy eggs, streaked darker, laid in nest of grasses, leaves and moss in hole in bank, bridge or riverside wall. Incubation 11–14 days, by female.

Range: Breeds across Palearctic from Portugal to Kamchatka southwards to Himalayas. Absent from much of eastern Europe and Russia west of Urals. Eastern birds are migrants.

Takes readily to man-made structures that convert still or slow-flowing water to fast-moving torrents or rapids. Thus it frequents mill races, weirs and lake outflows. Outside the breeding season it also utilizes ponds, lakes, canals and other still waters.

---

p.211 Pied Wagtail *Motacilla alba*

Description: 17–18 cm (6½–7 in). In summer, adults have *black crown and large bib* enclosing clear, white face, black wings with double white wingbar and white central panel, greyish-white underparts, and black tail with white outer feathers. Male British

subspecies *M. a. yarrellii* has *black back,*
female slate-grey. Continental subspecies
M. a. alba known as White Wagtail has
pale-grey back. Both lose black chin in
winter and show only a broad, black breast
band. Juvenile and first-winter *yarrellii* may
have backs as pale as *alba*.

Voice: Harsh *chis-ick*; song a twitter incorporating
call notes.

Habitat: Open country, often, but not invariably,
near water.

Breeding: Five to six brown-speckled, grey eggs laid
in nest of grasses, leaves and moss placed in
hole in wall, bank, tree or among stems of
creeper. Incubation 12–14 days, by female
though the male may help.

Range: Breeds right across Palearctic from Iceland
to Bering Straits and western Alaska. Also
southwards across Asia from Iran to China.
Western European birds are resident; those
of Iceland, Scandinavia and eastern Europe
are summer visitors that migrate to the
Sahelian zone of Africa.

The adaptability of this familiar bird has
enabled it to abandon watersides in many
parts of its range where it is now frequently
seen around farmyards, gardens and
agricultural land. In the north and in
mountain districts it replaces the House
Sparrow around buildings that are
unoccupied during the winter.

pp.212 & 213 **Yellow Wagtail** *Motacilla flava*

Description: 16–17 cm (6½ in). Summer visitor to
marshes and damp fields that varies
enormously in colour according to
subspecies. All slim, elegant and long-
tailed, with *yellow underparts* in male, paler
in female. *Back varies from yellowish green to
brown and slate-grey.* Most distinctive is
colour and pattern of male head in summer.
M. f. flava of north-central Europe has
blue-grey head, white supercilium and
yellow throat. *M. f. flavissima* of Britain has
yellow head with pale-yellow supercilium.
M. f. iberiae of Spain and Portugal has

blue-grey head with white supercilium, dark ear coverts and white throat. *M. f. cinereocapilla* of Italy has blue-grey head, no supercilium, dark ear coverts and white throat. *M. f. thunbergi* of Scandinavia has slate-grey crown, no supercilium, black ear coverts and yellow throat. *M. f. feldegg* of Greece has black head, no supercilium and yellow throat. *M. f. beema* of the Caspian has grey head with white supercilium and throat. *M. f. pygmaea* of Egypt has grey crown, black ear coverts and white throat. There are other subspecies extending eastwards across Eurasia, all with different head patterns, some of which occur on passage through eastern Europe.

Voice: A loud *tsweep*.

Habitat: Damp meadows and drying floods.

Breeding: Five to six grey, brownish-speckled eggs laid in neat cup of grasses hidden in tussock. Incubation 12–14 days, mainly by female.

Range: Summer visitor across Palearctic from Morocco to western Alaska, southwards to northern China and Tibetan Plateau. Winters in India, Southeast Asia and savannah Africa.

Spring males of the various subspecies are relatively straightforward to identify, though both Grey Wagtail and the rare Citrine Wagtail also have yellow underparts. With many females and juveniles, subspecific identification is often impossible.

---

p.210 **Citrine Wagtail** *Motacilla citreola*

Description: 16–17 cm (6½ in). Superficially like Yellow Wagtail but distinctly *shorter tailed.* Adult male has yellow head and underparts and *black nape that fades to slate-grey on back.* Female has paler-grey crown and back, paler-yellow face and breast, and white underparts. Juvenile brownish-grey above and white below, with buffish wash over breast and flanks and well-marked supercilium and ear coverts. In all plumages a *bold, white, double wingbar* is diagnostic.

Voice: Metallic *tsreep*, like Yellow Wagtail, but harsher.

Habitat: Osier thickets along rivers and coasts in tundra zone and along rivers and in marshe in steppe and hill regions.

Breeding: Four to six buff-grey, brown-speckled eggs laid in grass-lined cup in hollow or bank, sheltered by tussock or rock. Incubation 14–15 days, by both sexes.

Range: Summer visitor to tundra of central Siberi and from western Russia across steppes to China and Tibetan Plateau. Expanding range westwards to Europe from Russia, and regular migrant in southeast. All bird winter in India and Southeast Asia.

The expansion of its range westwards sees progressively more of these birds wandering to Europe as far west as Irelan There are already isolated examples of males hybridizing with Yellow Wagtails and it cannot be long before it is fully established as a breeding European bird i Poland or Slovakia.

WAXWINGS (BOMBYCILLIDAE)

3 species; boreal zone of northern hemisphe One species breeds in Europe and another h occurred once. Waxwings are Starling-sized arboreal birds, with a prominent crest and a 'cross' expression. They live predominantly among the boreal forests. They have stocky bodies, short tails and fly on Starling-like pointed wings. Indeed the similarity to a Starling, especially in flight, is remarkable. The feathers are soft and silky and predominantly a greyish-cinnamon in colo Their name is derived from the wax-like tip to the secondaries. From time to time large numbers of birds leave their native forests a occur in more open landscapes to the south These irruptions – called Waxwing years – are triggered when high populations coinci with a failure in the crop of rowan and othe berries. During these years they scour the hedgerows, often in substantial flocks.

p.216 **Waxwing** *Bombycilla garrulus*

Description:	17–18 cm (6½–7½ in). Stocky, rotund bird of Arctic forests marked by *short tail and pointed wings* reminiscent of Starling. Whole *body pale-pinkish brown* with *bold crest* extending from hind crown. A black line extends from upper mandible, through eye, rising towards nape, giving face a distinctly 'cross' expression; black bib. The folded wing shows small patches of red, white and yellow; grey tail has broad, yellow terminal band.
Voice:	High-pitched *scree*; song is trilling mixed with chirrups.
Habitat:	Northern margins of boreal forests with conifers mixed with birches and other hardy deciduous species. During irruptions frequents berry-bearing hedgerows.
Breeding:	Five to six pale-blue eggs, finely marked black, laid in tree nest of twigs and grasses. Incubation 14–15 days, by female alone.
Range:	Virtually circumpolar in northern boreal zone, though absent from eastern half of Canada. In Europe breeds only in northern Norway and Sweden, though more widespread in Finland. Winters southwards in Scandinavia southwards to central-eastern Europe.

The periodic irruptions to northwestern Europe may bring several thousands of these birds as far west as Britain, where substantial flocks may occur near the east coast. Exceptional irruptions may take birds as far west as Ireland. Sadly, such large-scale movements are, at best, once or twice in a birder's lifetime.

DIPPERS (CINCLIDAE)

5 species; temperate regions of Eurasia and New World. A single species is found in Europe. Dippers are small stocky birds with chubby bodies, short, cocked tails and strong legs and feet. The wings are comparatively short, but flight is fast and low. These are

totally aquatic birds that swim, dive and wade in tumbling hill streams. Their cocked-tail shape creates downward pressu as water flows over their back, enabling them literally to walk underwater on the riverbed. They feed on aquatic insects and their larvae, and they hold territories that may be several kilometres long but only tw or three metres wide.

p.216 **Dipper** *Cinclus cinclus*

Description: 17–18 cm (6½–7 in). Chunky waterbird, dark, with *white breast and short, cocked tail* reminiscent of an overlarge Wren. Apart from white throat and breast-patch, entire plumage dark chocolate. Wings short and whirred in flight; tail short and frequently cocked. British subspecies *C. c. gularis* differs from nominate Continental birds i having warm-chestnut area below white gorget. Wades and dives with ease in fast-flowing waters.

Voice: Sharp, hard *zit-zit*.

Habitat: Fast-flowing streams with exposed boulde and shingle banks, also weirs and lake outflows.

Breeding: Four to five white eggs laid in domed nest constructed of grasses placed in hole or crevice in riverside bank, often among exposed roots. Incubation 15–18 days, by female alone.

Range: Essentially Palearctic from Portugal acros Europe to Urals and mountains of central-southern Siberia and western China. Though mostly resident, more northerly birds migrate to winter in Finland and adjacent areas of Baltic to Denmark.

Being totally confined to streams, these birds hold long, but exceedingly narrow territories. Making contact with them ma therefore involve a long walk along the banks of a suitable stream. Most would-be Dipper-watchers save their legs by stoppi at every bridge and scanning up and dowr stream, encouraged by the presence of 'whitewash' on prominent boulders.

WRENS (TROGLODYTIDAE)

60 species; all but one confined to New World. A single species is found in Europe. These are very small to medium-sized birds, mainly clothed in cryptic shades of brown, buff and grey and heavily barred or streaked. They have short, thin, often decurved bills, short, rounded wings, and mostly short, cocked tails. The legs are strong and often relatively long. Most wrens are shy, spending much time among dense thickets, often low to the ground. This secretiveness coupled with their dull, camouflaged plumage accounts for their fine, loud songs. Indeed, they are among the world's greatest singers. Most nest in holes, or construct domed nests with a side entrance hole, and many are polygamous.

p.217 **Wren** *Troglodytes troglodytes*

Description: 9–10 cm (3½–4 in). Very small bird; dark plumage and *cocked tail* facilitate identification. Upperparts warm chestnut-brown *heavily barred,* especially on short, cocked tail. Mottled face shows *clear, pale supercilium* and dark eye-stripe. Underparts dull buff, *heavily barred* on flanks and undertail. Bill short and thin.

Voice: Harsh *tac*, often quickly repeated; song bright and melodic, terminating in an extended wheeze.

Habitat: Woods with strong undergrowth; parks, gardens, heaths and moors and even grass-covered sea cliffs.

Breeding: Five to six, red-spotted white eggs laid in domed nest constructed of grass, moss and leaves, in hole in bank or tree, rock or wall crevice, or hole in building. Incubation 14–17 days, by female alone.

Range: Circumpolar. In North America confined to boreal forests, migrating southwards in winter. In Palearctic occupies wider range of land forms from Europe to central-southern Siberia, northwards to China, Japan and Kamchatka. Absent from central and northern Siberia. One of Europe's most

widespread and abundant birds occupying a wide range of vegetated habitats. Most European birds are resident, but Scandinavian and northern Russian birds are only summer visitors.

This is the only wren to have colonized the Old World from its native America, where it is known as the Winter Wren. As a result it has been able to utilize a wide range of habitats that in America are occupied by other, competing wrens. It has spread westwards as far as Iceland and the remote Faeroes.

ACCENTORS (Prunellidae)

12 species; temperate regions of Palearctic. Two breed in Europe. Accentors are small, dull-coloured birds that spend much of their time on the ground, shuffling around in search of food. They characteristically adopt horizontal posture and hop rather than walk frequently flicking their wings. The bill is short and thin, which alone picks them out from other small ground feeders that, being seed-eaters, have chunky thick bills. Most species are found at high altitude, and make only short altitudinal movements in winter. Though similar in build, behaviour and plumage, they are easily distinguished by head pattern. The sexes are similar.

p.217 **Hedge Accentor** *Prunella modularis*

Description: 14–15 cm (5½–6 in). Also frequently called Dunnock. A small, ground-dwelling bird that shuffles around picking small food items from forest floor with *thin, pointed bill*. It is tame and has become a garden and hedgerow bird in many parts of its range. Upperparts rich chestnut-brown heavily streaked black. *Face grey,* with streaked-brown crown and mottled-brown ear coverts. *Grey breast* fades paler on belly, and flanks show bold *chestnut streaks*.

Voice: A flat, jingling warble; call note is a thin *tseep*.

Habitat: Undergrowth in woods, gardens and beneath hedges; scrubby hillsides.

Breeding: Four to five bright-blue eggs laid in cup of twigs and grasses placed low in dense bush. Incubation 12–13 days, by female alone.

Range: Virtually endemic to Western Palearctic. Breeds right across Europe in temperate and boreal zones as far as Urals, though absent from Mediterranean and eastern steppes. Scandinavian and east European birds are summer visitors.

The only species of accentor that has 'escaped' from the mountains and spread to lowland habitats. As a result it faces no competition from other accentors and has occupied a wide range of land forms from conifer forests to suburban gardens. Formerly called Hedge Sparrow, as well as Dunnock, the nineteenth-century name Hedge Accentor is well established and particularly apt since it would otherwise be the only member of its small family not called 'Accentor'.

---

p.217 **Alpine Accentor** *Prunella collaris*

Description: 17–19 cm (6½–7½ in). Larger than more widespread Hedge Accentor, but behaves in typical accentor fashion, feeding low on ground, shuffling along and picking food from among short vegetation. Upperparts chestnut, heavily streaked black, with bold, white, double wingbar. Head and breast grey with neatly enclosed, *black and white-spotted gorget*. Remaining *underparts heavily streaked rich chestnut,* much more extensive and obvious than in Hedge Accentor. Thin, yellowish bill.

Voice: Liquid *chirrup*; song like Hedge Accentor, but louder and more melodic.

Habitat: Breeds above tree line among rocky hillsides with scant vegetation. Winters among similar bare areas at lower altitude.

Breeding: Three to four pale-blue eggs laid in neat, grassy cup hidden in rock crevice. Incubation 14–15 days, by both sexes.

Range: Breeds in high mountains of Spain, Italy,
         the former Yugoslavia and in the Alps and
         Carpathians. Also from Turkey eastwards
         Tibetan Plateau, western China and Japan
         In Europe, wanders short distances in
         winter, sometimes to lowlands quite dista
         from breeding range.

         In summer this bird's dull coloration and
         inconspicuous behaviour make it difficult
         to find, but in winter it frequently comes
         the tables of ski resorts to search for
         crumbs. Probably seen by more skiers tha
         birders every year.

CHATS AND THRUSHES (TURDIDAE

310 species; worldwide, save New Zealand
where introduced. Twenty-three species
breeding in Europe and several more are
regular or irregular visitors, or vagrants.
These are small to medium-sized ground
arboreal birds, many of which show mark
sexual dimorphism. Juveniles are general
spotted. They frequent both wooded and
open country, feeding on insects, worms
and berries. They are well-proportioned
birds, with well-developed wings and tai
and are capable of strong flight. Many
species are migratory. Some are only
summer visitors to their breeding range,
while others are partial migrants. Most ar
solitary, though some of the larger thrush
form substantial flocks in winter. Most ar
highly territorial and the thrushes are
among the world's finest singers. Many
species, particularly among the wheatear
show highly variable plumage and are
difficult to identify.

p.220   **Rufous Bush-robin** *Cercotrichas galactote*

Description: 14–16 cm (5½–6½ in). Generally more
               difficult to find than to identify.
               Upperparts pale sandy cream with clear,
               dark eye-stripe and *bold pale supercilium.*

Underparts white, washed with buff over breast. *Long tail rich rufous, tipped bold black and white, and frequently cocked*. Legs long and strong. Feeds on ground, often in open near bushes, but disappears into cover when disturbed.

Voice: A pleasant twittering song uttered from perch or in song-flight; call a harsh *tec*.

Habitat: Dry or drying riverbeds with oleanders and other bush cover; cactus belts; overgrown gullies.

Breeding: Four to five brown-speckled white eggs laid in loose cup placed low in bush or cactus. Incubation 13 days, by female alone.

Range: Late-arriving summer visitor to Mediterranean eastwards through Middle East. In Europe confined to Iberia, Montenegro and Greece. Winters in Sahelian Africa where it also breeds.

This is the only bush-robin to have penetrated Europe from its origins in Africa. The group – which includes all members of the genus *Erythropygia*, in which the Rufous Bush-robin is placed by some authorities – is widespread south of the Sahara. A long, rusty-black, or black and white tipped tail is shared by several species.

---

p.220 **Robin** *Erithacus rubecula*

Description: 13–15 cm (5–6 in). A small, chubby bird, khaki on crown and upperparts, with medium-length *tail frequently cocked. Face and breast bright orange-red;* belly whitish. Juvenile heavily barred brown and buff over head and underparts with brown mantle heavily spotted buff. Upright posture on longish legs, together with pounce-and-stop behaviour and tail-cocking, identify.

Voice: Hard *tac-tac*; song high-pitched, slow warbling with trills.

Habitat: Woodland, scrub and gardens.

Breeding: Five to six brown-speckled white eggs laid in neat cup of grasses placed in low bush, on ledge in a building, or in open-fronted nest box. Incubation 12–15 days, by female alone.

Range: Widespread in Europe extending eastward to Urals and beyond to adjacent Siberia. European birds from Germany westwards are resident or partial migrants; eastern and northern birds are summer visitors, wintering south as far as North Africa.

Over most of its range, the Robin is a secretive bird of woodlands, but in Britain and other parts of western Europe it has become a tame and confiding bird of suburban gardens and open hedgerows. There it comes readily to bird tables, occupies nest boxes, and may even be habituated to feeding from the hand.

---

p.220 **Thrush Nightingale** *Luscinia luscinia*

Description: 16–17 cm (6½ in). Similar to Nightingale but *less brown on body and less rufous on tail*. Upperparts grey-brown; tail warm brown. Lacks any distinguishing features on head save a narrow, pale eye-ring. Underparts dull white, with grey-brown *mottling on breast and flanks*.

Voice: Song loud, with *peu-peu-peu* introduction of Nightingale, followed by equal variety and virtuosity. Main differences are inclusion of some hard notes, similar to Great Reed Warbler, and lack of crescendo of Nightingale. Sings equally at night.

Habitat: Damp undergrowth in woodland and dense, waterlogged thickets along rivers and among marshes.

Breeding: Four to five mottled creamy-rufous eggs laid in cup hidden among debris on the ground. Incubation 13 days, by female alone.

Range: Replaces Nightingale from eastern Europe eastwards to south-central Siberia. Summer visitor to southern Scandinavia and Denmark eastwards through Poland to Romania. Winters in eastern Africa south of Sahara, where it is called Sprosser.

In the areas of eastern Europe where the ranges of Nightingale and Thrush Nightingale overlap, the present species occupies wetland habitats, the Nightingale dry heaths. Both species are tolerant of tall trees provided that the canopy does not inhibit the growth of a dense understorey.

---

p.220 **Nightingale** *Luscinia megarhynchos*

Description: 16–17 cm (6½ in). A warm-brown bird acknowledged as one of the world's greatest songsters. Upperparts *uniform warm brown*, broken only by narrow eye-ring and *bright rufous tail*. Underparts buffy cream.

Voice: Song starts with plaintive *peu-peu-peu*, continues with rich melodic warbling of remarkable virtuosity, terminating in a crescendo. Call notes a duet of a whistle and a harsh *keek*.

Habitat: Dry woodlands and heaths, thickets and copses; sometimes near water in the western parts of its range.

Breeding: Four to five grey-blue eggs, marked light reddish, laid in cup on the ground hidden among ivy or natural debris. Incubation 13–14 days, by female alone.

Range: Summer visitor to south and temperate Europe extending eastwards around Black Sea to south-central Siberia. Overlaps with Thrush Nightingale in eastern Europe. Winters in Sahelian Africa.

While it is fashionable to compare the song of the Nightingale with that of the Blackcap, and even to put its reputation down to its propensity to sing at night when all around is quiet, there can be no doubt that this is the finest singing bird in Europe, perhaps in the world.

---

p.221 **Bluethroat** *Luscinia svecica*

Description: 13–15 cm (5–6 in). A neat, perky, Robin-like bird that feeds on the ground, usually under cover of dense thickets. Male has *bright-blue throat bordered by black and red breast-bands*, bold white supercilium, and *rusty patches at sides of uppertail*, particularly obvious in flight. A spot in the centre of the blue 'throat' is red in Scandinavian subspecies *L. s. svecica*, and white in Continental subspecies *L. s. cyanecula*. Female lacks boldly coloured breast markings, which are replaced by black *moustachial streak* against white background terminating in broad *spotted necklace* on upper breast.

Voice: Harsh *tac-tac*; song a high-pitched, metallic warble of discordant notes.

Habitat: Scrub-covered tundra; marshy or damp thickets; reed-beds with adjacent scrub.

Breeding: Five to seven greenish eggs, speckled reddish, laid in cup hidden on the ground or in base of bush. Incubation 14–15 days by female alone.

Range: Summer visitor to localized areas of Spain and France, eastwards through temperate and northern Europe, to huge area of north central and southern Siberia as far as Bering Straits, and a few spots in western Alaska. Winters across Sahelian Africa, Arabia, northern India and Southeast Asia.

While this bird is usually secretive and shy, quickly disappearing into the deep shadow of dense thickets when disturbed, during the early summer males will sit openly singing atop a marshy bush or even perched on a telegraph wire.

p.222 **Red-flanked Bluetail** *Tarsiger cyanurus*

Description: 13.5–14.5 cm (5½ in). A highly secretive Bluethroat-like chat. Male *metallic blue above* and white below, with *orange-rufous flanks*. Female brown above, buffy below, marked by white chin, *orange flanks and blue tail*. Short, buffy supercilium and pale eye-ring are additional features. Behaves like Bluethroat and frequently *cocks tail*.

Voice: Harsh *tic-tic*; pleasant warble of repeated phrases.

Habitat: Breeds among damp waterside thickets in conifer forests; winters among waterside parkland.

Breeding: Five to seven white eggs, sometimes speckled brown, laid in cup hidden among roots or in bank. Incubation by female alone for unknown period.

Range: An eastern species that breeds across east and central Siberia, Japan and northern China, as well as in Himalayan chain. Winters in China. It has spread westwards across northern Russia to Finland. Exceptional vagrant elsewhere in Europe.

This boldly coloured little chat caught the imagination of all European birders as soon as it appeared in colour in a post-war field guide. It has since taken on a magical quality, especially in Britain where only ten have ever been recorded. In November 1993 a single individual was responsible for one of the largest twitches ever and was seen by well over 2,000 birders.

p.222 **Black Redstart** *Phoenicurus ochruros*

Description: 14–15 cm (5½–6 in). A small black chat with red tail. Male *black, paler below, with greyish cap, white patch on wing, and rust-red tail* that shimmers. Female uniform dark grey-brown with *rust-red tail*. In winter, male resembles female, but with white wing-patch. Outside Europe highly variable plumage, often with red underparts.

Voice: Call is *tsip* or *tic-tic-tic*; song is a quiet squeaky warble.

Habitat: Cliffs, gorges, burnt ground; city and other industrial wastelands.

Breeding: Four to six white eggs laid in cup on ledge or in crevice among rocks. Incubation 14–16 days, by female alone.

Range: Breeds across most of Europe, except Scandinavia, eastwards to Turkey and the Caucasus to central-southern Siberia and western China. Birds from northern France eastwards are summer visitors, wintering in North Africa.

In Germany this species replaces the Robin as the common garden chat and is called the 'House Redstart' as a result. Elsewhere it frequents cliffs and burned-over hillsides. In England it first colonized bombed sites in the 1940s and has since moved on to railway sidings, power stations and other industrial sites.

---

p.222 **Common Redstart** *Phoenicurus phoenicuru*

Description: 13.5–14 cm (5½ in). A slim, summer visitor that perches on the lower, shaded branches of trees, *tail shimmering,* before pouncing to the ground to catch food. M grey on crown and back; rufous-orange below. *Grey crown separated from black face narrow, white supercilium.* Tail and rump *bright rufous-red.* Female brown above, bu below, with rufous-red rump and tail and pale eye-ring.

Voice: A soft *hooeet-tuc-tuc*; song is a metallic jingle.

Habitat: Mature deciduous woodland margins, parkland, orchards and groves, as well as stony areas with walls and bushes.

Breeding: Six to seven pale-blue eggs laid in neat cu in tree hole or broken stump, or in crevic in rocks or wall. Incubation 11–14 days, female.

Range: Summer visitor from Europe to central-eastern Siberia extending through Middl East. In Europe absent from Iceland, Ireland, southern Iberia and Greece. Wh population winters in Sahelian Africa.

The decline of the Common Redstart has been attributed to modern forestry techniques in which old trees, offering plentiful nest holes, are removed along w insect-rich dead and dying trees. Drough in its winter quarters may also be involve

---

p.223 **Whinchat** *Saxicola rubetra*

Description: 12–13 cm (4½–5 in). Perches upright and openly atop low vegetation like related Stonechat. Upperparts heavily streaked black and buff, with distinctive *broad wh supercilium* and moustachial stripe all but enclosing uniformly dark ear coverts. Ch throat, breast and flanks warm orange-bu belly white. Dark *tail shows white patches either side at the base.* Female a washed-out version of male.

Voice: Sharp *tic-tic*; song a squeaky warble.

Habitat: Heaths, open moors, wasteland and, on migration, among crops with fences.

Breeding: Five to seven pale-blue eggs, finely speckled brown, laid in cup placed on the ground and sheltered by bush. Incubation 13–14 days, by female.

Range: Largely absent from Mediterranean, but otherwise widely spread summer visitor throughout Europe eastwards to central Siberia; winters in Sahelian zone of Africa.

The bold white supercilium and lack of a black bib distinguish the Whinchat from the otherwise similar and closely related Stonechat, which also has the endearing habit of sitting atop a low bush where it can easily be seen. Nevertheless, beginners frequently mistake one for the other.

---

p.223 **Stonechat** *Saxicola torquata*

Description: 12–13 cm (4½–5 in). Small, upright chat that perches openly atop gorse or other bush. Male dark, virtually black above, narrowly streaked buff, and marked by uniform *black head and bold white half-collar.* Breast warm orange-red, fading to white on belly. A white patch across tertials and *white rump* are obvious in flight, but generally obscured when perched. Female similar, but paler, with broader brownish stripes on upperparts and pale margins to head feathers that create a scaly effect; also lacks white half-collar.

Voice: Metallic *chack-chack*; song a jingling warble.

Habitat: Heaths and wasteland with gorse and other shrubs; in winter often along coasts.

Breeding: Five to six pale-blue eggs, lightly speckled brown, laid in neat cup placed on the ground under bush. Incubation 14–15 days, by female alone.

Range: Breeds across Palearctic from Portugal to eastern Siberia and Japan, southwards through western China to Himalayas. Also

in sub-Saharan Africa. Birds from Germ
eastwards are summer visitors, though
probably do not leave Europe or, at leas
no further than North Africa.

A serious decline in numbers over many
parts of the Stonechat's range can be
attributed to the ploughing of marginal
land and heaths. It remains relatively
common among Mediterranean scrub, b
increased afforestation represents anoth
growing threat.

p.224 **Pied Wheatear** *Oenanthe pleschanka*

Description: 14.5–15 cm (6 in). Black and white. M
has *white crown* extending to nape, wash
grey in spring. Remaining upperparts
black, with white rump and tail and lor
shanked, black, terminal 'T'. Face, chin
upper breast black, forming distinct bre
band against white underparts washed
buffy on lower breast. The *black of face a
breast is joined to black of wing and back.*
Female brown above and below fading t
white on belly; shows faint pale
supercilium and tail pattern as male.

Voice: A harsh *zack-zack*; song a liquid warbli
with mimicry.

Habitat: Dry rocky hillsides with scant vegetatic

Breeding: Three to six blue-green eggs, speckled r
brown, laid in cup with twiggy entranc
platform, in hole in bank or rock crevic
beneath a rock. Incubation 13–14 days,
female alone.

Range: Summer visitor to extreme southeast of
Europe. Breeds from coasts of Romania
Bulgaria eastwards across steppes to ari
central-southern Siberia. Whole popula
winters in East Africa.

Only comparatively recently has the Cyr
Pied Wheatear *O. cypriaca* been recogniz
as a separate species, rather than a subsp
of the Pied. This is quite remarkable as
males differ in coloration, females are to
different, the songs differ and even the r
of the sexes in incubation are distinct.

p.224 Black-eared Wheatear *Oenanthe hispanica*

Description: 14–15 cm (5½–6 in). Highly variable
wheatear marked by narrow, black tail-
band forming a *long-shanked 'T'*, and *black
wings*. Body colour varies from rich sandy in
western *O. h. hispanica*, to virtually white in
eastern *O. h. melanoleuca*. Male *hispanica* has
either black mask and white throat, or
black face extending to throat; female
hispanica has unmarked head, dusky mask,
or dusky face extending to throat. Some
male *melanoleuca* have black mask on face,
with greyish crown in spring and hint of
warmth on breast. Female *melanoleuca* is
brownish above with plain face and warm
wash over breast. Tail pattern, *lack of black
back, lack of prominent supercilium, and at least
a hint of sandy coloration,* distinguish it from
other wheatears.

Voice: Song a series of warbled, grating notes; call
a harsh *zerrk*.

Habitat: Dry, stony hillsides and arid plains; on
migration also among agricultural areas.

Breeding: Four to five pale-blue eggs, speckled reddish
brown, laid in cup beneath stone or in hole.
Incubation 13–14 days, by female alone.

Range: Summer visitor throughout Mediterranean
eastwards through Turkey to Middle East.
Winters in Sahelian Africa.

In the black-throated form, the Black-eared
Wheatear bears a strong resemblance to
vagrant Desert Wheatear, which is also sandy
or white-bodied, but has a pure black tail.

---

p.225 Black Wheatear *Oenanthe leucura*

Description: 17–19 cm (6½–7½ in). Large, chunky, *all-
black wheatear,* marked by white rump and
undertail, and by black 'T' on white tail.
Size and plumage precludes confusion with
any other European wheatear. Sexes similar.

Voice: Call note a quiet *pee-pee-pee*; song a quiet
melodic warble ending in a chatter.

Habitat: Rocky hillsides and screes; sea cliffs.

Breeding: Three to six pale-blue eggs, speckled
brown, laid in cup placed in hole in a wall

or rock crevice. A small wall of stones is constructed across the entrance. Incubatic 14–18 days, by female alone.

Range: Endemic to Western Palearctic. Resident Iberia and adjacent Mediterranean France and North Africa east to Tunisia.

This bird could be confused with vagrant White-crowned Black Wheatear *O. leucopy* of North Africa which lacks white crown first-winter plumage. This is, however, a smaller bird with completely white (or virtually white) outer-tail feathers.

p.225 **Isabelline Wheatear** *Oenanthe isabellina*

Description: 16–17 cm (6½ in). Both sexes strongly resemble female Northern Wheatear, wi *sandy-brown upperparts and pale-cream underparts*. Shows *pronounced supercilium,* dark lores and no hint of a mask, but bes identified by structure. Always stands *sl* and *upright*, with longer legs and shorter tail than Northern Wheatear. Tail has broad terminal black band and short shanked 'T'.

Voice: Warbling song includes mimicry; call a loud *wheet*.

Habitat: Dry, bare areas of stones and sandy waste sometimes on hillsides, but also among poor grassy lowland plains.

Breeding: Four to seven pale-blue eggs laid in cup grasses placed in burrow, usually of a rodent. Incubation 12 days, by female alone.

Range: Summer visitor to extreme southeastern Europe, from Greece eastwards through Turkey and Middle East to China. Winte in Sahelian Africa, Arabia and in Pakista and adjacent India.

Though it is easily confused with female Northern Wheatear by the beginner, this bird soon becomes relatively straightforward to identify. Its shape and behaviour are quite distinctive and, to th more experienced eye, creates a quite different impression.

p.225 **Northern Wheatear** *Oenanthe oenanthe*

Description: 14–15.5 cm (5½–6 in). Male has *grey crown and back,* marked by prominent *black mask* through eye and black wings. Throat and breast pale orange, but belly white. Tail shows broad black terminal band and a regularly proportioned 'T'. Female brown above, creamy white below, with hint of a mask. Juvenile much warmer coloured than female, with bold supercilium and dark ear coverts.

Voice: Harsh *chack-chack*; a scratchy warble uttered in display flight.

Habitat: Open moorland, dry heaths, coastal dunes and shingle, dry chalklands and open tundra, and rocky hillsides.

Breeding: Five to six pale-blue eggs laid in bulky cup of vegetation placed in rodent hole, or rocky crevice. Incubation 14 days, mainly by female.

Range: Circumpolar in north, though absent from much of northern Canada. Widespread summer visitor to much of Europe from Iceland to Finland, Portugal to Turkey. Somewhat localized in intensively farmed areas of western Europe. Winters in Sahelian Africa.

The migrations of the Northern Wheatear rival those of the Arctic Tern in terms of endurance and distance. Birds from eastern Canada and Greenland still fly eastwards through Europe to Africa, while those of western Canada and Alaska fly in exactly the opposite direction across Siberia to reach the same destination. Both show the Northern Wheatear's directions of colonizing from its Afro-European origins.

---

p.226 **Rock Thrush** *Monticola saxatilis*

Description: 18–20 cm (7–8 in). Male boldly coloured, with *blue head, throat and back,* black wings; and *rufous tail and underparts.* Female brown above, heavily scaled buffy below. Similar to female Blue Rock Thrush, but with *warm wash on breast and flanks and rufous*

tail. Both sexes perch openly, are often sti
for long periods and show short tails in
flight.

Voice: Hard *chak*; song a flute-like warble often
flight.

Habitat: Rocky mountain slopes with walls and
shrub cover, but down to sea level in the
east. Along coasts only on migration.

Breeding: Four to five pale-blue eggs laid in hole
among rocks or in wall. Incubation 14–1
days, by female alone.

Range: Summer visitor to Mediterranean and
southern Europe. Breeds right across
southern Europe and eastwards through
Turkey to southern Siberia and northern
China. All birds winter in Sahelian and
East Africa.

The Rock Thrush is a secretive bird that i
easily overlooked both when breeding an
on migration. Its exploitation of lowland
habitats in the eastern parts of its range
may be owed to the absence of the Blue
Rock Thrush with which it competes in
the west.

p.226 **Blue Rock Thrush** *Monticola solitarius*

Description: 20–21 cm (8 in). Male *dark blue marked
by black wings,* but appears uniformly
dark, or even black, at any distance. Fem
slate-grey above and heavily barred below,
lacking any warm colours. Frequently
perches atop exposed rock and remains
static for long periods. In flight, short ta
and pointed head, bill and wings *resemble
Starling.*

Voice: Song resembles fluty warble of Blackbird
call a hard *chak-chak.*

Habitat: Open rocky hillsides with huge boulders
broken cliffs, from sea level to considerab
altitude. Also around ruins in many parts
range.

Breeding: Four to five pale-blue eggs laid in cup
placed in hole or crevice among rocks.
Incubation 12–13 days, by female alone.

Range: Breeds right across southern Palearctic fr
Portugal to Japan and China. Extreme

western and eastern populations are resident; birds from central parts of range move southwards to winter from East Africa to Malaysia. In Europe, resident in Mediterranean region; widespread in Spain, but distinctly coastal elsewhere.

Though attention is usually attracted by its song, this bird may still be difficult to locate. Scanning large rocks silhouetted against the skyline will usually produce decent views, but also watch for a bird that is Starling-like in flight.

p.226 **Ring Ouzel** *Turdus torquatus*

Description: 23–25 cm (9–10 in). Blackbird-like. Male all-black marked by yellow bill; bold *white breast-crescent* and *silvery wings* form pale panel at rest, but are particularly obvious in flight. Female browner with less clear-cut breast-crescent, but equally *silvery wings*.

Voice: Deep, harsh *chook-chook*; song repeats phrases.

Habitat: Rocky hillsides and moors mostly at altitude and frequently above tree line. More widespread on passage when it frequents bushy scrub and brambles and even open woodlands.

Breeding: Four to five pale-blue, brown-blotched eggs laid in neatly constructed cup placed in bush or against bank. Incubation 13–14 days, mainly by female.

Range: Virtually endemic to Western Palearctic. Summer visitor to mountains and hills of Scandinavia, Britain, Spain, France and eastwards through Alps and Carpathians to former Yugoslavia. Winters in Spain, North Africa, Greece and Turkey.

This upland 'Blackbird' arrives early, departs late, and is very shy and easily overlooked on migration. Its deep calls often betray its presence from deep inside a thicket or bramble patch. The silvery wings may frequently be the only visible field mark to distinguish it from the more abundant Blackbird.

p.227 **Blackbird** *Turdus merula*

Description: 24–27 cm (9½–10½ in). Male all *black, marked by yellow bill and eye-ring*. Female dark brown, with lightly mottled breast and yellowish base to bill.

Voice: Hard *chak*; harsh chatter of alarm; song a fluty warble.

Habitat: A wide variety of land forms from forests and woods, to parks, gardens, heaths, orchards, hedgerows and open grasslands.

Breeding: Four to five pale-blue eggs, liberally blotched rufous, laid in neat mud-reinforced cup placed in bush, tree, or ledge of building. Incubation 11–17 days, by female alone.

Range: Breeds right across Europe, through Turkey to Himalayas and hills of peninsular India and China. Successfully introduced to Australia and New Zealand. Common and widespread, European birds are resident in west, but only summer visitors from Poland eastwards.

The ability to exploit a wide variety of habitats in addition to its natural woodland base, coupled with the equal ability to produce and rear up to four broods of young each year, has made this thrush one of Europe's most abundant and successful birds.

p.227 **Song Thrush** *Turdus philomelos*

Description: 22–24 cm (8½–9½ in). Medium-sized, heavily spotted thrush. Brown above and white below, washed with *buff on breast*. Heavily *spotted below* and on face and lacking any distinctive facial markings. Similar to larger and greyer Mistle Thrush.

Voice: A *chuk* call note; song a variety of mostly melodic phrases repeated three, sometimes four, times.

Habitat: Woodland, parks, groves, orchards, gardens and hedgerows. Frequently feeds on grassland.

Breeding: Four to six pale-blue, black-speckled eggs laid in sturdy cup of grasses lined with mud

often placed against trunk of a tree.
Incubation 11–15 days, by female alone.

Range: Breeds across Europe eastwards to central
Russian Siberia. In Europe, resident in south
and west, but only a summer visitor from
most of Germany eastwards. Numerous
winter visitor to Iberia and Mediterranean.

The number of Song Thrushes wintering in
Spain may be confirmed by visiting any
food market, where bundles of these birds
are offered for sale at incredibly cheap
prices. Just how the supposedly uniform
laws of the European Community can be
flouted in this way remains a mystery.

---

p.227 **Redwing** *Turdus iliacus*

Description: 20–22 cm (8–8½ in). Smaller than Song
Thrush, but similarly brown above and
spotted below. Head shows prominent *pale
supercilium* and dark moustachial streak. A
flash of chestnut lines flanks and extends to
underwing coverts.

Voice: A soft *tseep* and harsh *chok*; song repeats
fluty notes four or five times.

Habitat: Scrubby areas of birch, willow, alder and
dwarf conifers in taiga and tundra zones;
winters on grasslands, flooded fields and
along hedgerows.

Breeding: Four to five brown-speckled, pale-blue eggs
laid in cup placed against trunk of a tree or
in low shrub. Incubation 11–15 days, by
female.

Range: Summer visitor right across Palearctic from
Iceland to far eastern Siberia in tundra and
boreal zones. Virtually the whole
population winters in Europe, widely
spread from Britain to Turkey eastwards.

The autumn influx of Redwings sees large
flocks of birds scouring the hedgerows
stripping the berry crop, often in company
with Fieldfares, Song Thrushes and
Blackbirds. By mid-winter, when the berry
crop is exhausted, they turn their attention
to damp and flooded grassland, where
animate food is often abundant.

p.227 **Fieldfare** *Turdus pilaris*

Description: 24–27 cm (9½–10½ in). Large, well-mark
thrush. Rich, *dark-chestnut back and wings
separate grey head from grey rump.* Underpar
white, with wash of orange-buff on breas
heavily barred with black chevrons. Tail
black and accentuates grey rump, which
the major in-flight field mark.

Voice: Harsh *chack-chack*; song consists of melc
chuckles.

Habitat: Upland scrub of birches near tree line,
woodland clearings; in winter frequents
damp fields, hedgerows and arable farml

Breeding: Five to six pale-blue, spotted-brown eg;
laid in cup lined with mud placed in for
a tree. Incubation 11–14 days, by femal
alone.

Range: Breeds from eastern France across most
Europe, through northern Siberia virtua
to Bering Straits. In Europe, mostly
resident; Scandinavian and Russian bird
are widespread visitors to all parts from
Spain eastwards.

Along with several other typical
Scandinavian species, the Fieldfare bega
colonize Britain during the late 1960s.
Thirty years later the colonization had
progressed no further than a handful of
pairs. Yet just across the North Sea, the
Netherlands boasted a true colonization
with upwards of 700 breeding pairs.

p.227 **Mistle Thrush** *Turdus viscivorus*

Description: 26–28 cm (10–11 in). Largest of the
European thrushes. *Grey-brown* upperpa
not warm brown of Song Thrush, coupl
with creamy, *heavily spotted underparts* an
large size are best features. At rest, wing
show pale central panel; in flight, *tail ha
bold white outer margins.* Distinctive,
undulating flight.

Voice: Harsh, dry *churr*; song a fluty, melodic
whistling less varied than Blackbird.

Habitat: Open woodland, parks, groves, orchards
gardens.

Breeding: Four to five pale-blue, spotted-brown eggs laid in cup placed in major fork of a tree. Incubation 12–15 days, by female.

Range: Breeds over most of Europe eastwards to central, southern Siberia. Scandinavian and birds from Poland eastwards are summer visitors that move south and west in winter.

This is one of the earliest breeders. Singing in February it is known as the Stormcock by country people. It lays its eggs in March, when the trees are still bare, and hides its nest in the major fork of a tree at no great height from the ground.

WARBLERS AND CRESTS (SYLVIIDAE)

300 or so species; worldwide, though mostly confined to Old World. Thirty-six species breed in Europe and several more are irregular visitors or vagrants. These are mainly small, highly active birds with thin, insect-eating bills. They forage among vegetation, but while some are decidedly woodland orientated, others inhabit scrub, others marshland, and others still parks and orchards. Mostly they are somewhat drably coloured in shades of brown and buff, green and grey. The sexes are similar, except among the scrub-based *Sylvia*. Some species, or species groups, offer the greatest of all identification challenges. Many European species are highly migratory and are among the most accomplished of all bird singers. Although, quite naturally, individual species differ in their habitat preferences the Sylviidae can generally be divided into the marsh-dwelling *Locustella* and *Acrocephalus*, the scrub-dwelling *Sylvia*, the woodland-dwelling *Phylloscopus*, and the tree- or bush-dwelling *Hippolais*.

p.230 **Fan-tailed Warbler** *Cisticola juncidis*

Description: 9–11 cm (3½–4½ in). Tiny, *heavily streaked bird, marked by short, rounded tail*, that would be hard to locate and identify but for its characteristic display and calls. Flies high in *bouncing flight* as if suspended on a piece of elastic, while uttering *zit-zit-zit* calls. When perched shows bold cream and black streaked upperparts, finely streaked crown and thin *decurved* bill.

Voice: Repeated *zit-zit-zit*.

Habitat: Damp marshy vegetation, but also in extensive dry cereal fields.

Breeding: Four to six pale-blue, sometimes speckled, eggs laid in neatly woven, purse-shaped nest of grasses suspended among tall grasses or cereals. Incubation 10 days, by both sexes.

Range: Largely resident in Mediterranean, sub-Saharan Africa, and from India through Southeast Asia and China. In Europe, widespread in Iberia, Italy and Greece.

The twentieth-century spread of this little bird both northwards and eastwards through Europe has been well documented. From coastal Mediterranean it spread northwards along the west coast of France to the Channel. It has occurred in Britain and Ireland, but has not yet managed to breed there.

p.230   **Cetti's Warbler** *Cettia cetti*

Description: 13.5–14.5 cm (5–5½ in). A featureless bird of marshland margins, easily distinguished by its *dark coloration*. Small warbler with dark-chestnut upperparts and longish, rounded tail. Underparts dirty white, washed with grey-brown on flanks. Lacks head markings. Secretive, but with explosive call.

Voice: Sudden, loud *chetti-chetti-chetti*.

Habitat: Marshland edges with thick, tangled bushes over water; riverside margins.

Breeding: Four to five chestnut eggs laid in untidy cup placed in base of bush. Incubation 16–17 days, by female alone.

Range: Breeds from Iberia through Mediterranean to Kazakhstan. Resident in west; summer

visitor from Turkey eastwards. In Europe, breeds through western France north to Britain and along coasts of Mediterranean.

Cetti's Warbler spread northwards from Iberia through France to southern England during the second half of the twentieth century, probably as a result of climate change. In England, on the edge of its range, it is susceptible to harsh winters and has been wiped out locally by severe and prolonged snow storms only to make a full subsequent recovery.

---

p.230 **Grasshopper Warbler** *Locustella naevia*

Description: 12–13 cm (4½–5 in). Small warbler; upperparts *darkly streaked brown and black;* underparts buffy brown *lightly streaked on flanks and undertail.* Head shows faintest supercilium; tail well-rounded. Secretive, usually located by calls.

Voice: Continuous reeling, likened to sound of fisherman's reel being wound in.

Habitat: Low, scrubby, waterside thickets, but also similar tangles in drier areas such as heaths and young plantations.

Breeding: Four to six brownish-speckled white eggs laid in cup hidden near the ground among dense vegetation. Incubation 13–15 days, by both sexes.

Range: Summer visitor to most of temperate Europe eastwards to central and southern Siberia. Winters in India and locally in Africa. In Europe, absent from Mediterranean and most of Scandinavia, but otherwise widespread from northernmost Spain to southern Finland, and from Ireland to Romania.

One of three 'reelers' to breed in Europe; the others are Savi's and River Warblers, both of which have plain, unstreaked backs and are more or less confined to aquatic habitats. The Grasshopper Warbler is difficult to locate when it is not singing, but given good views identification is straightforward.

p.232 **River Warbler** *Locustella fluviatilis*

Description: 13.5–14 cm (5½ in). Upperparts unstreak
                olive-brown, with only short, narrow
                supercilium; underparts buffy on breast a
                flanks, with *fine streaking on sides of neck an*
                breast. Most obvious features are boldly
                barred undertail coverts and *small primary*
                projection. Best located and identified by
                song.

Voice: A distinctive soft chuffing, like a distant
         steam train, consisting of two fast notes
         followed by two slow notes uttered in
         continuous reeling.

Habitat: Thickets in damp pastures or in dense w
           woodland.

Breeding: Five to six brown-speckled white eggs la
            in cup hidden by vegetation on the grou
            Incubation 11–12 days, female taking th
            larger share.

Range: Virtually endemic to western Palearctic.
         Europe, summer visitor to wetlands from
         eastern Germany and Romania eastward
         through Russia to just beyond Urals.
         Winters in eastern Africa; passage migra
         through southeast Europe.

         A highly secretive, skulking bird that is
         virtually impossible to locate when it is n
         singing. Once located great patience is
         required to obtain satisfactory views. Tho
         most birds are olive-brown, a proportion a
         dark brown and therefore confusing.

p.232 **Savi's Warbler** *Locustella luscinioides*

Description: 13–14 cm (5–5½ in). Marked by plain,
                unstreaked, rich, *uniform-brown upperpar*
                with no more than a hint of a pale
                supercilium. Underparts white, washed
                buffy on flanks. Tail distinctly rounded;
                much shorter and less dagger-like than R
                Warbler. When singing atop a reed, wh
                throat is often obvious.

Voice: Very like reeling of Grasshopper Warbl
         but faster and distinctly lower pitched.
         Uttered in short bursts, rather than
         continuous reeling.

Habitat: Reed-beds.

Breeding: Four to five white, brown-speckled eggs, laid in substantial nest low down among reeds. Incubation 10–12 days, female taking the larger share.

Range: Breeding summer visitor right across temperate Europe, but more numerous in east, extending eastwards to Kazakhstan. Winters only in central Sahelian region of Africa.

During the twentieth century, this elusive warbler enjoyed a significant north and west expansion of range that saw it colonize much of France and eventually southern England. Until the mid-nineteenth century it had bred in England from where a specimen was sent to the Dutch ornithologist Coenraad Temminck, who failed to recognize it as new to science. Thus it fell to the Italian Paolo Savi to describe this bird first in 1824, otherwise we would have a Temminck's Warbler to add to our Stint, Horned Lark, and so on.

p.232 **Moustached Warbler**
Acrocephalus melanopogon

Description: 12–13 cm (4½–5 in). Strongly *contrasting* upperparts, with broad streaks of rufous-brown and black. *Crown black,* bordered by broad, *white, square-cut supercilium* with clear black eye-stripe. Underparts white, broadly washed with warm buff on flanks. Frequently cocks tail when alarmed.

Voice: Song similar to Sedge Warbler, but lacks jarring rattles. Introduced by melodic ascending *tu-tu-tu-tu* not dissimilar to that of Nightingale.

Habitat: Reed-beds and other emergent vegetation.

Breeding: Five to six green-washed white eggs, spotted with green, laid in cup well hidden among aquatic vegetation. Incubation for 13–14 days, by female, sometimes with help from male.

Range: Highly localized resident along Mediterranean coasts; seldom common.

Summer visitor to Ukraine and inland along course of Danube as far as Austria. Also summer visitor to Caspian region, wintering in northwestern India.

Throughout its Mediterranean range, where it is resident, this is a decidedly scarce and elusive bird save only in the Albufera Marsh of Mallorca where it is nothing less than common. A recent estimate suggested that 5,000 to 7,000 pairs were present in this marsh, which must represent a significant proportion of the European population.

---

p.231 **Aquatic Warbler** *Acrocephalus paludicola*

Description: 12–13 cm (4½–5 in). Highly contrasting stripes of golden buff and black cover back and wings. Head shows *golden crown-stripe, black lateral stripes and golden-white supercilium,* creating unique pattern. Some Sedge Warblers are contrastingly striped and may even show a crown-stripe, but they are never marked like an Aquatic.

Voice: Harsh, jarring notes similar to Sedge Warbler's, but briefer and lacking variety Sedge.

Habitat: Marshes with thick growth of sedges; reed beds on migration.

Breeding: Four to six buffy-speckled, white eggs laid in domed cup well hidden in dense shrub. Incubation for 12–15 days, by female alone

Range: Virtually endemic to Western Palearctic. A decidedly scarce and localized summer visitor to marshes of eastern Europe, from German Hungary and Poland eastwards to Urals, with an isolated outpost beyond. Winters in Niger Inundation Zone and perhaps elsewhere in western Sahelian zone of Afric

The decline of this species in Europe has brought it to the endangered level. The largest population is now confined to eastern Poland, especially the Biebrza Marshes where perhaps 1,000 pairs survive Its regular occurrence along the English south coast in autumn is confirmed as a result of intensive ringing programmes.

p.231 Sedge Warbler *Acrocephalus schoenobaenus*

Description: 12–13 cm (4½–5 in). Upperparts heavily streaked brown and black, more contrasting buffy brown and black in first-winter plumage. Head shows *bold, creamy-white supercilium* contrasting with dark crown and eye-stripe. Underparts white, washed tawny-rufous on flanks. Rump unstreaked rufous-brown.

Voice: Chatter of harsh and melodic notes, often produced in song-flight and continuing for lengthy periods.

Habitat: Reed-beds, wetland thickets and marginal vegetation, more varied than Reed Warbler.

Breeding: Five to six green-washed eggs, speckled buff, laid in deep cup supported by aquatic vegetation of reeds or bushes. Incubation 13–14 days, mainly by female.

Range: Widespread and locally common summer visitor to much of temperate Europe, though absent from Iberia and much of Mediterranean as well as hills of Scandinavia. Extends eastwards to central Siberia. Winters in savannah Africa.

This is the standard, streaked, marshy warbler from which other, scarcer or more localized species must be distinguished. Its bold supercilium is a major field mark; only Moustached Warbler shows a similar (even bolder) feature.

p.232 Paddyfield Warbler *Acrocephalus agricola*

Description: 12–13 cm (4½–5 in). Upperparts rufous-brown and unstreaked, showing very *short primary projection*. Head marked by bold *white supercilium*, dark eye-stripe and tendency to raise feathers of crown to form peak above eye. Underparts heavily washed creamy buff, but white on throat and centre of belly. Long *tail is frequently cocked*, even as bird sits upright clinging to aquatic vegetation.

Voice: Decidedly pleasant warble, lacking harsh notes of Marsh Warbler.

Habitat: Margins of lakes and ditches with reeds ar
           sedges, but also among damp meadows
           with tall grasses.

Breeding: Four to five pale-green eggs, blotched wit
           darker green or grey, laid in cup of grasses
           suspended between reeds or other stems.
           Incubation about 12 days, by female.

Range: Localized summer visitor to extreme
           southeast of Europe, from coasts of Bulgar
           and Romania eastwards to south central
           Siberia. Winters in India; decidedly rare
           west of breeding grounds, though over 20
           have been recorded in Britain and Ireland

           Although similar to several other
           unstreaked *Acrocephalus* warblers, such as
           Reed, Marsh, Blyth's Reed and Savi's, this
           is one of those birds that is best separated
           by 'jizz' rather than plumage details. Its
           propensity to sit upright, raise its crown
           feathers and cock its tail picks it out as
           different. Plumage features, especially the
           bold supercilium, then confirm its identit

---

p.233   **Blyth's Reed Warbler**
        Acrocephalus dumetorum

Description: 12–13 cm (4½–5 in). A plain-backed
              warbler distinguished from Reed and
              Marsh warblers with care. Upperparts
              olive-brown, marked by pale eye-ring,
              peaked crown, and *short primary projection*.
              Virtually no supercilium. Underparts
              white, lightly washed grey-buff on breast
              and flanks; dark-grey legs. Habitually *cock
              tail* as it moves through vegetation. First-
              winter birds warmer coloured, more like
              Reed Warbler.

Voice: Slow, melodic warbling, with mimicry like
              Marsh Warbler, but repeating phrases two
              four times like Song Thrush. Highly vocal.

Habitat: Wetland margins with trees, scrubby
              thickets and woody debris.

Breeding: Five to six green-washed eggs, spotted lig
              brown, laid in deep cup hidden among
              thick vegetation. Incubation 12–14 days;
              role of sexes varies according to their
              relationships with other mates.

Range: Summer visitor from Finland eastwards to central Siberia, extending southwards to Caspian and Kazakhstan. Winters in Pakistan, India and Burma.

Although it is increasing in numbers and spreading westwards in Finland and Sweden, it remains a decidedly rare bird elsewhere in Europe despite its east-west migrational axis. Of the accepted records for Britain (less than 40 at the time of writing) most have been trapped or found dead, indicating the difficulties of positive identification in the field when this bird is not singing.

---

p.233 **Marsh Warbler** *Acrocephalus palustris*

Description: 12–13 cm (4½–5 in). Upperparts uniform *olive*-brown, with pale supercilium that extends a little behind eye; underparts white with no more than a hint of warmth along flanks. Sloping, *forehead is steeper* than similar Reed Warbler, and bill is slightly shorter and less dagger-like. Wings show *long primary projection,* unlike Blyth's Reed Warbler, and tertials have pale tips. *Legs pale flesh,* not dark like the two other confusable species.

Voice: Melodic with much mimicry and trills, but also incorporating harsh Reed Warbler-like notes.

Habitat: Damp ditches with bushes, hedgerows with adjacent damp areas; much less aquatic than Reed Warbler.

Breeding: Four to five pale-blue eggs, laid in cup hidden low among bushes. Incubation 12 days, by both sexes.

Range: Virtual Western Palearctic endemic. Widespread summer visitor to north and eastern Europe, from borders of France eastwards through southern Sweden and northern Greece to Urals and just beyond. Winters in eastern Africa. Maintains a toe-hold in southern England.

The pleasant, melodic and highly varied song, which contains Reed Warbler-like harsh, jarring notes and much mimicry, but lacks phase repetition of Blyth's Reed Warbler, is the best means of identification It is never as rufous as Reed, nor as olive as Blyth's, and it shows pale legs and long wings; it is found in drier habitats, but beware out-of-habitat migrants.

p.233   **Reed Warbler** *Acrocephalus scirpaceus*

Description: 12–13 cm (4½–5 in). The standard, uniform marshy warbler. Upperparts rufous-brown with decidedly *rufous rump;* underparts *washed rufous-buff* on breast and flanks. Sloping forehead accentuates *long, dagger-like bill*. Shows only faint supercilium long primary projection and dark legs.

Voice: Harsh, grating notes broken by jarring phrases; lacks variety of Sedge Warbler, particularly sweeter notes.

Habitat: Decidedly aquatic, mostly in large reed-beds; also along reed-fringed dykes. Migrants may occur in dry scrub.

Breeding: Four to five green-washed eggs, liberally blotched olive-green, laid in deep cup lashed to several reeds above water. Incubation 11–12 days, by both sexes.

Range: Widespread summer visitor to most of temperate Europe eastwards to Kazakhstan Winters in Sahelian and East Africa. In Europe absent only from Iceland, Ireland, northern Britain and most of Scandinavia.

The song is distinguished by the complete lack of any sweet or melodic notes, by its slow delivery, and by the lack of any loud strident phrases. It just goes on and on.

p.233   **Great Reed Warbler**
Acrocephalus arundinaceus

Description: 18–20 cm (7–8 in). The largest European warbler. Similar to Reed Warbler, but *much larger,* about the size of a Song Thrush. Upperparts warm buffy brown, marked by prominent, but short, pale supercilium and long, rounded tail. Underparts washed buffy on breast and belly. *Head large, bill long and dagger-like,* and wings short and rounded. Sits singing atop reeds and flies like Song Thrush.

Voice: Loud, strident, harsh rattles, repeating phrases *curra-curra-curra, jag-jag-jag.*

Habitat: Reed-beds with open water, reedy lake margins.

Breeding: Four to six pale blue-green eggs, spotted black, laid in deep cup lashed to reeds. Incubation 14–15 days, by both sexes.

Range: Summer visitor right across temperate Palearctic from Portugal to Japan and China. Winters across savannah Africa and in Southeast Asia. In Europe, absent from Britain, Ireland, Iceland and Scandinavia, though regularly overshoots in spring.

Though regular in spring, and nesting only a short distance southwards in northern France, there has never been a single case of breeding in Britain. Males do occasionally sing for several days and may take up territories, but their sudden silence invariably indicates departure rather than the arrival of a mate though the 1990s saw several 'possible' breeders.

---

p.234 **Olivaceous Warbler** *Hippolais pallida*

Description: 12–14 cm (4½–5½ in). Pale olive-grey warbler with plain face, marked by *white eye-ring,* sloping forehead, and long, dagger-like bill. Upperparts grey-brown; underparts white; legs dark bluish. Short wings, with *small primary projection,* and distinctive plump body are subtle, but useful, features.

Voice: Loud harsh notes interspersed with melodic phrases reminiscent of Sedge Warbler. Hard *chak-chak.*

Habitat: Bushes and thickets, riversides, gardens, orchards and groves; also in semi-desert and oases.

Breeding: Three to four greyish, black-speckled eggs laid in neat cup placed among outer branches of bush. Incubation 12–13 days, by female.

Range: Summer visitor to southwest and southeast Europe, breeding from Mediterranean

eastwards to Turkey and Middle East as fa as Afghanistan. Also in central Sahara, where resident in semi-desert. Winters in Sahelian and East Africa.

There are several well-marked subspecies of this warbler. The western *H. p. opaca* is more olive and longer billed than the smaller, grey-brown eastern *H. p. elaeica*, which is also shorter winged and shorter tailed. The central-Saharan subspecies *H. p. pallida* (and *reiseri* and *laeneni*) are also smaller than *opaca*, but they are additionally much paler. These three major groups may be recognized as separate species in the future.

p.234 Olive-tree Warbler *Hippolais olivetorum*

Description: 15–16 cm (6–6½ in). Largest and greyest the *Hippolais* warblers, virtually the *size of Great Reed Warbler*. Upperparts grey; underparts white, washed greyish on flan Huge *yellow dagger-like bill* accentuated b sloping forehead; short supercilium exten just behind eye. Legs bluish. Wing has lo primary projection and prominent pale mid-wing panel.

Voice: Slow, grating calls reminiscent of Great Reed Warbler, though lacking loud strident quality.

Habitat: Bushy hillsides, groves and orchards; sometimes in damp valleys.

Breeding: Three to four pinkish, lightly spotted bla eggs laid in deep cup placed in bush. Incubation about 13 days; role of the sexe unknown.

Range: Confined to southeast Europe and adjace Turkey in summer. Winters in southeast Africa.

A secretive warbler that is difficult to loc and identify. However, a Great Reed Warbler-type song issuing from a dry, bush-covered hillside or olive grove is certainly this species. Once seen, the hug yellow bill and large size are the most prominent features.

p.235 **Icterine Warbler** *Hippolais icterina*

Description: 13–14 cm (5–5½ in). One of two predominantly yellowish *Hippolais* warblers. Upperparts pale olive-green, marked by large bill and sloping forehead, short supercilium, prominent *pale mid-wing panel* and long primary projection. *Underparts yellow; legs bluish*.

Voice: A mixture of chattering and melodic notes with each phase repeated. Similar to Marsh Warbler, but more strident and rapid.

Habitat: Bushy thickets, gardens, hedgerows, woods.

Breeding: Four to five pinkish-purple eggs, spotted black, laid in deep cup placed in bush or tree fork. Incubation 13 days, by both sexes.

Range: Summer visitor from northern and central France eastwards across most of temperate Europe to Urals and beyond. Winters in South Africa. Replaced westwards in Europe by similar Melodious Warbler.

This is one of a pair of 'yellow' *Hippolais* warblers. The other, the similar Melodious Warbler, has a more rounded head; shorter primary projection which is apparent in flight from the more rounded wing; it lacks a mid-wing panel and has flesh-coloured, not bluish, legs.

p.234 **Melodious Warbler** *Hippolais polyglotta*

Description: 12–13 cm (4½–5 in). Upperparts yellow-green with *short, rounded wing* and rounded crown. Face appears plain and bill medium in length. *Underparts yellow; legs pale flesh* occasionally bluish. Lacks distinguishing features of Icterine Warbler of eastern Europe.

Voice: Song distinctly quicker and more melodic than Icterine Warbler, though with extended chattering. Does not repeat phrases like Icterine, and only seldom mimics other species.

Habitat: Riverside thickets, hedgerows and woodland clearings with shrub layer.

Breeding: Four to five pinkish, black-spotted eggs
laid in cup placed in fork of bush.
Incubation 12–13 days, by female alone.
Range: Breeds in Iberia, France and Italy, as well as
in Morocco and Tunisia. Winters in West
Africa.

Although the two species of 'yellow'
Hippolais warblers are almost entirely
separated geographically, they have
overlapped in eastern France for many
years. The Melodious Warbler continues an
eastward extension of its range with a
recent colonization of Holland, Germany
and Switzerland. Birds have been recorded
singing in Denmark, and perhaps even
Britain will soon be occupied.

p.235 **Marmora's Warbler** *Sylvia sarda*

Description: 12 cm (4½ in). Similar to more widespread
Dartford Warbler. Upperparts slate-grey;
underparts slate-grey becoming paler, almost
white, on belly and with a few white
speckles on throat. *Large head and long tail*
are features shared with Dartford Warbler,
but grey underparts of Marmora's
distinguish. Young Dartfords also grey
below and may be confused with Marmora
in late spring and summer.
Voice: Song an extended Whitethroat-like chatter
but rather sweeter.
Habitat: Maquis generally more than a metre (3 ft)
tall near sea, or on rocky hillsides.
Breeding: Three to four white, spotted-reddish eggs
laid in cup near the ground among dense
prickly ground cover. Incubation 12–15
days; female takes the larger share.
Range: Breeds only in western Mediterranean on
Balearic Islands and in Corsica and
Sardinia. Mostly resident, though some
winter in Tunisia.

The reported occurrences of this species
along the Mediterranean coasts of Spain
are the result of spring overshooting or
misidentification. Quite remarkably a
male established a territory in Yorkshire,

England in May 1982 and sang for two months to the delight of 1,000 or more birders. This incredible record – the first for northern Europe – was regarded as a one-off until others were reported in 1992 and 1993.

---

p.235 **Dartford Warbler** *Sylvia undata*

Description: 12–13 cm (4½–5 in). Male slate-grey above with brown wings, *very long, often cocked tail*, large head and boldly red eye. *Underparts vinous-brown* with white speckles on throat. Female similar, but paler with dirty-pink underparts fading to white on central belly. Juvenile greyish below. Highly secretive when not singing.

Voice: Song a grating Whitethroat-like chatter uttered from top of bush or in flight.

Habitat: Maquis, heaths with gorse.

Breeding: Three to four reddish-spotted, white eggs laid in cup hidden among dense vegetation near the ground. Incubation 11–13 days, mainly by female.

Range: Breeds in Iberia, south and western France, southern England, southern Italy and Corsica and Sardinia. Also along coasts of Morocco and Algeria. Mostly resident, but some winter through North Africa.

This is one of the very few resident warblers of Europe. It winters as far north as England, where hard winters reduce its numbers dramatically. It has recently colonized Menorca in the Balearics, where it has replaced Marmora's Warbler. These two similar species manage to co-exist in both Corsica and Sardinia.

---

p.236 **Spectacled Warbler** *Sylvia conspicillata*

Description: 11.5–12.5 cm (4½–5 in). Like a *small Common Whitethroat*. Male has brown upperparts, with distinctly *rufous wings* (much more so than in Whitethroat), grey head with *dark lores*, and white eye-ring. Rump and tail grey. Underparts pinkish

becoming greyish behind the prominent
white throat. Female has brownish head
and lacks dark lores, but has equally bold
rufous wings. Scarce and elusive.

Voice: Song similar to Whitethroat, but less
grating; call a harsh rattle.

Habitat: Dwarf maquis scrub in arid plateaux and
rocky hillsides; also among *Salicornia* scru[b]
on dried-out floods and thickets.

Breeding: Four to five whitish, olive-speckled eggs
laid in well-hidden cup near the ground.
Incubation 12–14 days, by both sexes.

Range: Endemic to Western Palearctic. Summer
visitor to western Mediterranean, winteri[ng]
in North Africa. In Europe, in Spain,
coastal France, Italy, Corsica and Sardinia.
Also in Cyprus and Israel where largely
resident.

This is truly a bird of the maquis and oth[er]
uniform low vegetation, avoids trees and
spends most of its time out of sight amon[g]
deep cover. Though locally common it is
difficult to locate.

p.236   **Subalpine Warbler** *Sylvia cantillans*

Description: 11.5–12.5 cm (4½–5 in). Small, scrub
warbler. Male has slate-grey upperparts,
contrasting with *orange-red underparts* fadi[ng]
to white on belly and separated only by
thin, white moustachial streak. Eye
prominently red. Female greyish, with
brownish wash over wing, and white
underparts, extending to throat, washed
pale orange on flanks. Pale eye-ring is
useful feature.

Voice: A Whitethroat-like warble that lacks har[sh]
chattering of that bird; call a hard *tec-tec*.

Habitat: Maquis with trees, walls, rocky outcrops
and hedges.

Breeding: Three to four buffy-spotted white eggs la[id]
in cup placed in low vegetation. Incubati[on]
11–12 days, by female alone.

Range: Summer visitor endemic in Mediterranea[n]
from Portugal to western Turkey; also in
North Africa. Winters across Sahelian
Africa.

Though it ranges to considerable altitudes this warbler is equally at home along coasts wherever suitable broken habitat exists. The presence of trees, rocks or bushy thickets, to break up the pure maquis, seems an essential requirement.

p.237 **Sardinian Warbler** *Sylvia melanocephala*

Description: 12.5–14 cm (5–5½ in). Wherever it occurs this is usually the most common of the *Sylvia* warblers. Male grey above, with *black cap* that extends below prominent *red-ringed eye* to white throat; underparts washed grey. The longish tail has white outer feathers and tips, particularly obvious as it flies away, and is frequently cocked. Female brown above with grey head, darker on ear coverts; underparts washed buff. Generally skulking among dense ground cover except when singing.

Voice: Scolding rattle; song a chattering warble uttered from prominent song post atop a low bush or shrub.

Habitat: Varies from low maquis to groves, scrub, woods with ground cover, and even well-kept gardens.

Breeding: Three to four whitish eggs, washed in various colours and speckled with brown, laid in neat cup placed near the ground among dense vegetation. Incubation 13–14 days, by both sexes.

Range: Western Palearctic endemic, largely resident in Mediterranean and North Africa, but a proportion of birds migrate southwards as far as central Sahara. Some eastern populations are total summer visitors.

Its ability to adapt to a wide variety of different habitats has ensured that this attractive little warbler outnumbers all other members of its genus virtually wherever it occurs. As the Mediterranean coast is progressively developed for tourism, Sardinian Warblers can be found nesting on building sites, in hotel grounds, and in suburban-style gardens.

p.237 **Rüppell's Warbler** *Sylvia rueppelli*

Description: 13.5–14.5 cm (5½ in). Male grey above and white below, marked by *black head* broken b distinctive white moustachial streak and a boldl red eye, creating head pattern similar to ma Reed Bunting. Female warmer grey above and washed dirty pink below; dark, not blac head shows white moustachial streak with dark speckling on throat. Both sexes have white outer tail and red legs.

Voice: Whitethroat-like chattering warble broke by hard *chak-chak-chak* alarms.

Habitat: Maquis-covered plains and hillsides, with low scrub in more arid environments.

Breeding: Four to five whitish eggs, heavily spotted and speckled with various colours, laid in cup among thick, thorny scrub. Incubatio about 13 days, by both sexes.

Range: Summer visitor to southeast Europe, from southern Greece to Crete and south and west Turkey. Regular migrant through Cyprus. Winters in eastern Sahelian Afric

One of the easiest of all *Sylvia* warblers to identify, though not to locate. Its preferei for uniformly low growths of thorny Mediterranean scrub, either on hillsides c lowlands, should help the birdwatcher to pick out suitable areas.

p.237 **Orphean Warbler** *Sylvia hortensis*

Description: 14.5–16 cm (5½–6½ in). Large *Sylvia* warbler, reminiscent of an overgrown Sardinian Warbler. Male grey above, with *black cap* that extends below *prominent yellow eye*. Underparts white with pale-yellowish wash along flanks. Female similar, but has grey head with dark lores Legs grey.

Voice: Melodic warbling with repeated Song Thrush-like phrases; hard rattling *tac-tac* call note.

Habitat: Maquis-covered hillsides with tall thicke like growth; olive groves and densely vegetated gardens, and among scrub in p forests and along riversides.

Breeding: Four to five white, brown-spotted eggs laid in cup placed among outer branches of bush or tree. Incubation for 12–14 days, mainly by female.

Range: Summer visitor through Mediterranean eastwards through Turkey and Middle East to Kazakhstan. Winters across Sahelian Africa to Persian Gulf and India.

An elusive, skulking species that spends much time low down among dense vegetation. Best located when singing, though even then not as obvious as many other *Sylvia* warblers.

---

p.238 **Barred Warbler** *Sylvia nisoria*

Description: 14–16 cm (5½–6½ in). A large, *chunky* warbler. Summer adult grey above, marked by far from obvious double wingbar. *Yellow eye* stands out against uniform grey head. Underparts *regularly barred from chin to undertail*. Short, stout bill reminiscent of Garden Warbler, as is first-winter plumage which is paler above, *lacks yellow eye* and has *barring confined to undertail*. White outer tail in all plumages.

Voice: Song a mixture of melodic and rattling phrases; call a hard *chak*.

Habitat: Woodland clearings and regenerating areas, shelter belts, thickets and hedgerows in dry countryside, usually with thorny shrubs.

Breeding: Four to six grey-speckled, white eggs laid in cup placed in fork of thorny bush. Incubation 12–15 days, by both sexes.

Range: Summer visitor from eastern Europe across southern Siberia to south-central Asia. Whole population winters in East Africa. In Europe, breeds in Po Valley of Italy, through former Yugoslavia north to Denmark, and from southern Sweden eastwards.

A straight line drawn between its breeding range in, say, Poland and its wintering range in East Africa, would indicate passage through the Mediterranean. In fact, this is a decidedly scarce bird even in the eastern Mediterranean with most European birds moving eastwards before turning south via Lebanon and Syria.

p.238   **Lesser Whitethroat** *Sylvia curruca*

Description: 13–14 cm (5–5½ in). Typical skulking *Sylvia* warbler, with harsh chattering song and call note. Adult grey-brown above with grey head marked by *distinctive darker mask*. Underparts white, with no more than wash of buff on flanks. First-winter has brownish head with reduced mask. In all plumages, white throat less pronounced than in Common Whitethroat.

Voice: A rattle on a single note; call a hard, metallic *chak*.

Habitat: Dry thickets and tall scrub with trees; heaths, hedgerows.

Breeding: Four to six olive-blotched, white eggs laid in cup placed in bush among thick cover. Incubation 10–11 days, by both sexes.

Range: Widespread summer visitor over most of temperate Europe except southwest, from England eastwards across Europe and Siberia almost to Pacific. Winters largely from Arabia to India, though some winter in Sahelian Africa.

A well-marked subspecies *S. c. althaea* is darker on the back and crown and breeds among mountains from the Taurus to the Himalayas. Known as Hume's Lesser Whitethroat, it is a prime target for separate species status and does not interbreed where its range overlaps nominate *curruca*. It is a vagrant westwards, as is the equally distinctive sandy Desert Lesser Whitethroat *S. c. minula* of Central Asia.

p.239   **Common Whitethroat** *Sylvia communis*

Description: 13–15 cm (5–6 in). Adult brown above, with bold *rusty margins to flight feathers* producing diagnostic wing-patch. Underparts warm buff. Male has grey crown extending to ear coverts, with clear *white throat* often puffed up. Female has less obvious white throat and brownish, not grey, head. Buffy legs.

Voice: A scratchy, warbled song often uttered in bouncy display-flight; call a harsh rattle.

Habitat: Heaths, woodland clearings, scrub, overgrown corners, hedgerows, young plantations.

Breeding: Four to five pale-blue eggs, speckled olive, laid in neat cup of grasses placed among bushes or tall grass. Incubation 13–15 days, by both sexes.

Range: Widespread and locally common summer visitor throughout whole of temperate Europe. from Iberia to east-central Siberia, south to Turkey and Kazakhstan. Winters over savannah Africa. In Europe extends northwards beyond Arctic Circle along coasts of Norway and Sweden, but also breeds as far south as Crete.

A catastrophic decline in the numbers of Whitethroats arriving in Europe in the spring of 1965 was attributed to the disastrous drought in the Sahelian wintering grounds in Africa. In fact, based solely on the Whitethroat catastrophe, ornithologists could have been the first to break the news of famine to the world.

p.239 **Garden Warbler** *Sylvia borin*

Description: 13–15 cm (5–6 in). A warbler virtually devoid of field marks. Upperparts greyish olive-brown marked only by *pale eye-ring;* underparts washed buffy. Short, *stout bill* and general stockiness are best features and separate from similar, but larger-billed, *Hippolais* warblers.

Voice: Sweet, sustained, melodic chattering, like Blackcap, but lacking the loud notes of that species. Call a hard *chuk*.

Habitat: Woodland with extensive undergrowth, thickets, hedgerows with brambles and vines.

Breeding: Four to five white, brown-blotched eggs laid in cup hidden among dense ground

vegetation of grasses and low shrubs.
Incubation 11–12 days, by both sexes.

Range: Summer visitor to most of Europe, save
Mediterranean coasts, eastwards to central
Siberia. Ranges as far north as northern
Norway southwards to southern Spain.
Winters throughout savannah Africa.

Despite its name, this is not a regular
garden bird. While it tolerates treeless area
(unlike the Blackcap), it is also found
among woods and forages among tall trees
as frequently as the Blackcap. In fact, there
is little difference between the species in
food taken.

---

p.239 **Blackcap** *Sylvia atricapilla*

Description: 13–15 cm (5–6 in). A large, well-built
warbler. Male *grey above, paler grey below*,
with plain grey face marked by *dull black
cap* that extends to eye. Female and first-
winter birds brown-grey above with dark,
rusty cap. Bill shortish, but not thick and
stubby like Garden Warbler. Grey
coloration coupled with bulk and size are
major features.

Voice: A melodic, virtuoso performance with
warbling broken by loud, flute-like notes.
Regarded by some as rival to Nightingale.
Call a hard, metallic *tac-tac*.

Habitat: Woodland with strong undergrowth layer;
thickets, hedgerows and orchards with tall
trees. Often in gardens in winter.

Breeding: Four to six variably washed eggs, spotted
and blotched laid in cup placed in tree or
scrub. Incubation 10–16 days, by both
sexes.

Range: Summer visitor to most of Europe,
breeding eastwards to Urals and a little
beyond. Winters in three distinct areas of
savannah Africa, as well as in North Africa
Mediterranean and Atlantic coasts north to
England and Denmark.

The ability of this warbler to survive the
often quite harsh winters of northern Europe
is owed, in part, to its readiness to exploit

gardens. Though it seldom comes to feeders, it will take spilt food and probably benefits from the slightly higher temperatures found around villages and towns.

p.240 **Greenish Warbler** *Phylloscopus trochiloides*

Description: 10–11 cm (4–4½ in). Small and Chiffchaff-like, with olive-green upperparts marked by *single, narrow, white wingbar*. A *bold white supercilium* extends well beyond eye, bordered by narrow black eye-stripe. Bill thin and short, with pale lower mandible; legs generally brown. Underparts white. Compare with Arctic Warbler, which shares single narrow wingbar.

Voice: A loud *chu-wee*; song a brief, high-pitched, wren-like warble ending in a flourish or rattle.

Habitat: Wide variety of deciduous and coniferous woodlands and wooded scrub. More catholic in winter.

Breeding: Four to five white eggs laid in domed nest of grasses hidden on the ground among vegetation, usually against a bank. Incubation 12–13 days, by female alone.

Range: Summer visitor to northeastern Europe from Baltic Germany and Finland eastwards to central Siberia and southwards to Himalayas. Vagrant westwards. Winters exclusively in India, Burma and adjacent Southeast Asia.

An Asiatic species that has expanded westwards, but which still migrates southeast to winter in its natal area. As a result Greenish Warblers are decidedly scarce west of their breeding range in Europe. There are some 200 records for Britain; surprisingly most are in autumn.

p.240 **Arctic Warbler** *Phylloscopus borealis*

Description: 11.5–12.5 cm (4½–5 in). Resembles Willow and Greenish Warblers, but larger. Upperparts yellow olive-green, with single *narrow white wingbar*; underparts white. A narrow *white supercilium, extending to nape, terminally upswept.* A black eye-stripe, wide behind eye, merges with dark-mottled ear coverts. Longish bill yellowish; legs pale pinkish. Occasionally shows short, narrow second wingbar.

Voice: Harsh *zik*; song a pleasant trilling rattle resembling Lesser Whitethroat.

Habitat: Conifer forests with undergrowth of scrub birch and willow in boreal zone and southwards among mountains.

Breeding: Six to seven white speckled-reddish eggs laid in domed nest of grasses hidden on the ground. Incubation 11–13 days, by female alone.

Range: Summer visitor to extreme northeastern Europe, from northern Scandinavia right across Palearctic conifer forests to Bering Straits and western Alaska. Winters in Southeast Asia in Indonesia.

The extraordinary migrations of this 10 g bird cover up to 13,000 km (8,000 miles) from Arctic Norway to, at least, Peninsular Malaysia. It is a vagrant to most of Europe that has occurred in Britain less than 200 times. An average of about four are now recorded each year.

p.242 **Pallas's Warbler** *Phylloscopus proregulus*

Description: 8.5–9. cm (3½ in). Tiny, crest-like, somewhat *tubby Goldcrest-like build,* and a combination of all the features found on *Phylloscopus* warblers make this Asiatic waif one of the easiest of all rare birds to identify: olive-green upperparts marked by bold, *double wingbar;* clear *yellow rump*-patch; broad, yellow supercilium; bold *black eye-stripe;* and *black lateral crown stripes and yellow central crown-stripe.* Bill dark and tiny. Underparts white washed yellow on flanks. Flits and hovers like Goldcrest.

Voice: Song consists of medley of sweet notes, each repeated four or five times; call a soft *tweet* unlike explosive monosyllable of Yellow-browed Warbler. Also a loud *ch-weet.*

Habitat: Coniferous forests in summer; migrants occur in woods and scrub.

Breeding: Five to six white, reddish-spotted eggs laid in domed nest placed among twigs near trunk of substantial conifer. Incubation period and role of sexes unknown.

Range: Breeds in north-eastern Siberia and northern Japan, as well as from Himalayas eastwards to eastern China. Winters from northern India to Malaysia and south and east China. Vagrant to Europe.

The increasing frequency with which this tiny bird is found, mainly in late autumn, in Europe is almost certainly due to the ever-increasing army of highly skilled and aware birders that is now on the look out for such birds. As a result Pallas's Warbler is now regarded as a regular wanderer rather than the extreme rarity it was only 25 years ago.

p.242 **Yellow-browed Warbler**
Phylloscopus inornatus

Description: 9.5–10.5 cm (3½–4 in). Tiny, Goldcrest-like, Siberian warbler, with clear distinguishing marks that separate from related Chiffchaff. Olive-green upperparts; white underparts. Wing shows *bold, white, double wingbar*, accentuated by black margins to coverts and tertials. A *bold yellow supercilium* extends broadly behind eye; *black eye-stripe similarly well marked*. Ear coverts heavily mottled. Legs pale flesh.

Voice: Explosive monosyllabic *tswee*; song a somewhat plaintive repetition of call note, terminating in a buzzing.

Habitat: Conifer and mixed forests, but mainly among birch and willow scrub, usually in lowlands but at altitude in Himalayas. Migrants occur in available vegetation.

Breeding: Four to five white, reddish-spotted eggs laid in neatly domed nest placed on the ground against bank. Incubation 11–14 days, by female alone.

Range: Summer visitor across Siberia to Bering Straits. Winters across India, Southeast Asia and southeastern China. Scarce autumn visitor to Europe. Hume's Leaf Warbler *P. humei* from central Asia and China has been recently split from Yellow-browed an will doubtless soon be added to the British and European lists.

This bird is now a regular, if scarce autumn visitor to western Europe, and its occurrences have been explained either by population explosions following successful breeding seasons, or by reverse migration in which birds set out in exactly the opposite direction to their normal migration route. I the case of far northeastern birds, however, a great circle route to India would bring then as far as Omsk in western Siberia.

p.240　**Bonelli's Warbler** *Phylloscopus bonelli*

Description:　11–12 cm (4½ in). Similar to Chiffchaff, bu decidedly '*washed out*'. Crown and back pale greyish, becoming distinctly coloured *yellowish green on wings and tail,* with *pale-yellow rump and wing panel;* underparts white. Head *greyish-white* with faint supercilium and *prominent dark eye*. Washed out, virtually featureless face, contrasts wit colourful wings and rear end. Legs dark.

Voice:　Loud *hooeet;* song a trill on a single note, like a brief Wood Warbler song, but lacking a flourish at the end.

Habitat:　Conifer and deciduous woodland with dense canopy and only light ground cover; also birchwoods among hills.

Breeding:　Five to six white, brown-speckled eggs, lai in domed nest placed on the ground again bank. Incubation 12–13 days, by female alone.

Range:　Western Palearctic endemic being confine to southern and western Europe, east to western Turkey and North Africa. Winter in Sahelian Africa.

This species has recently been split into Western Bonelli's Warbler *P. bonelli* of Hungary westwards, and Eastern Bonelli's Warbler *P. orientalis* of the Balkans and Turkey. Eastern birds have a more pronounced face pattern and even brighter coloured wings.

---

p.242 **Wood Warbler** *Phylloscopus sibilatrix*

Description: 12–13 cm (4½–5 in). Larger than either similar Chiffchaff or Willow Warbler and much brighter in colour. Upperparts *yellow-green*, with marked *yellow supercilium* and yellow mid-wing panel. Underparts bright *yellow on chin and breast*, with *glistening white belly* and undertail. Legs pinkish.

Voice: A quiet *peu*; song starts with series of *sit* notes accelerating into sibilant trill uttered in display-flight from one tree to another beneath canopy.

Habitat: Mature beech, or other deciduous woods, with little or scant undergrowth.

Breeding: Five to seven white, reddish-speckled eggs laid in domed nest well hidden by low vegetation on the ground. Incubation 12–14 days, by female.

Range: Summer visitor to much of temperate and northern Europe eastwards across Russia to beyond Urals. Winters among forests of West Africa and forested savannahs to east. In Europe absent from Iberia and much of Mediterranean, though extending well north of Arctic Circle in Scandinavia.

The migration patterns of this warbler are concentrated over the central Sahara, with comparatively few birds passing through the eastern Mediterranean and even fewer through the west. Most of the population funnels through Italy to winter in the forests of Zaire.

---

p.241 **Chiffchaff** *Phylloscopus collybita*

Description: 10.5–11.5 (4–4½ in). Widespread summer visitor over most of Europe, that is a common winter resident in the west and the Mediterranean. A species pair with the Willow Warbler, the separation of which is an essential skill of a Euro-birder. Chiffchaff is olive-green above, buffy white below

with a *short, pale supercilium* that extends
beyond the eye, *dark legs* and a relatively
short primary projection. first winter bird
in autumn are brighter showing yellow in
the wing and yellow washed underparts,
much more like a Willow Warbler.

Voice: Song a repetitive *chiff-chaff-chiff-chaff-chif,*
call a distinctive monosyllabic *hooet.*

Habitat: Deciduous woods, but in conifers in centr
and eastern Europe, also tree heaths and
copses with strong ground cover.

Breeding: Four to nine white, purplish-speckled egg
laid in domed nest hidden against small
bank. Incubation 13–14 days, by female.

Range: Widespread summer visitor right across
northern Palearctic from Portugal almost
Bering Straits, southwards through Italy,
and locally in Middle East. Over most of
Siberia found in boreal zone. Common
winter resident around Mediterranean and
in Atlantic Europe; also winter migrant t
Sahelian Africa, and from Arabia to
northern India.

Compared with the Willow Warbler, the
Chiffchaff is smaller, scruffier, shows less
yellow and has a shorter, less clear-cut
supercilium. A glimpse of dark legs
confirms its identity. Some vagrant easter
subspecies are brown and buff and may
show a pale wingbar.

p.241 **Willow Warbler** *Phylloscopus trochilus*

Description: 10.5–11.5 cm (4–4½ in). Similar to
Chiffchaff, though slightly larger.
Upperparts yellow-green; underparts *wh
washed yellow. Bold yellow supercilium exten
well behind eye* and well-marked dark eye-
stripe joins ear coverts. *Pale legs* and long
primary projection. First-winter birds pa
yellow-green above and yellow below, *m
brighter* than any Chiffchaff.

Voice: Two syllable *hoo-eet* call; song a sweet
descending trill.

Habitat: Woods with clearings, birch scrub, heath
with invading trees. In winter from fores
to tree savannahs.

Breeding: Six to seven reddish-speckled, white eggs laid in domed nest set against bank or hummock on the ground. Incubation 13–16 days, by female alone.

Range: Widespread and often abundant summer visitor across whole of Palearctic from Ireland to Bering Straits. Generally more northerly than Chiffchaff, though with much overlap. Winters throughout sub-Saharan Africa.

The decline of this species was a feature of the late 1980s and was attributed to the continued drought in the Sahelian zone of Africa. While these birds do not typically winter in the Sahelian zone, it is believed that the region is a major spring feeding area, whose unavailability had a disastrous effect on birds moving north. No doubt, given time, populations will adapt and recover, but by then yet more human/natural disasters may await them.

p.243 Goldcrest *Regulus regulus*

Description: 9 cm (3½ in). Along with closely related Firecrest, this is *Europe's smallest bird*. Upperparts dark olive-green with black wings broken by bold, white, *double wingbar;* underparts washed buffy on flanks. *Plain face shows prominent eye* and faint moustachial streak; crown has black-bordered crest – yellow and red in male, pure yellow in female. Juvenile has plain, virtually grey face.

Voice: Very high-pitched *zi-zi-zi-zi-zi*; song similar but terminates in a flourish.

Habitat: Breeds among conifers; also found in deciduous woods with spruce, usually in winter.

Breeding: Seven to ten white, brown-speckled eggs laid in a neat woven cup suspended from outer tips of conifer, usually spruce. Incubation 14–17 days, by female.

Range: Breeds across Palearctic from Ireland to Japan; also southwards in the Himalayas and mountains of western China. Southern birds are resident, but northern

Scandinavian and Russian birds migrate south across Europe. Generally more northerly than Firecrest.

The Goldcrest weighs between 4 and 8 grams, yet it is capable of flying non-stop across the North Sea and probably much further. Even when foraging its use of energy is prodigious as it flits constantly among vegetation, with much hovering in search of small insects and spiders.

p.243 Firecrest *Regulus ignicapillus*

Description: 9 cm (3½ in). A species pair with related Goldcrest. Upperparts yellow-green and *much brighter than Goldcrest;* underparts whitish with yellow-buff wash. Black wings with white, double wingbar similar to Goldcrest, but *head boldly marked* by black moustachial streak, black eye-stripe, white supercilium, and black lateral crown stripes enclosing red and yellow crest in male, yellow crest in female. Juvenile has plainer face, but marked by bold, white supercilium.

Voice: Very high-pitched *zit-zit-zit*; song similar terminating abruptly and lacking flourish of Goldcrest.

Habitat: Conifer woods, but also among thickets and mixed woodlands.

Breeding: Seven to eleven pale-buffy eggs, speckled brown, laid in cup suspended from tip of high conifer branch. Incubation 14–15 days, by female.

Range: Endemic to Western Palearctic from southern England to Morocco eastwards western Russia. Resident in south and west; summer visitor from Germany eastwards.

An expansion of range, which brought birds to southern England as early as 196 seems to be somewhat erratic since good years and poor years occur randomly. By 1990 as many as 100 pairs may have bred but this may simply have been an artificially high peak.

FLYCATCHERS (MUSCICAPIDAE)

110 species; Old World. Five species breed
in Europe. These are small birds adapted
to catching insects in flight, though they
are equally adept at a shrike-like perch-
and-pounce technique. The legs are short
and adequate for perching; the short bill
with a broad base and a flattened profile
backed by a large gape is ideally adapted
to catching flying insects. The plumage is
highly variable; the sexes may or may not
be similar, but juveniles are mostly spotted
or barred. They perch, often quite openly,
for long periods, making occasional sallies
to grab their food, often with an audible
snap of their bill. While some species
return to the same perch, others move
from perch to perch after each aerial hunt.
Insects are the major food source, but
spiders are frequently picked from the
branches or trunk of a tree. These are
predominantly arboreal birds occurring in
a wide variety of woodland and savannah-
type country.

p.244 **Spotted Flycatcher** *Muscicapa striata*

Description: 13.5–14.5 cm (5½). A somewhat
nondescript, streaked-brown bird, but
easily identified by its behaviour.
Upperparts brown, with buffy margins to
wings forming pale central panel; crown
and throat streaked; face plain with pale
eye-ring. Underparts *white, finely streaked on
breast and flanks*. Sits upright making
occasional sallies to catch passing insects
before returning, *usually, to same perch*. Large
wings obvious in flight. Juvenile heavily
spotted above, barred below.

Voice: Weak *tsee*.

Habitat: Woodland clearings and margins, parks,
orchards, groves and gardens.

Breeding: Four to five pale-blue eggs, blotched reddish,
and placed in shallow cup or platform resting
on ledge of building, in an open nest box or
against trunk of a tree. Incubation 11–15
days, by female.

Range: Summer visitor from Europe to central
Siberia; in Europe, absent only from Icelar
and high, barren mountains. Winters over
sub-Saharan Africa.

The provision of open-fronted nest boxes
out of direct sunlight and away from the
prevailing wind will regularly attract thes
birds to open woodland, farmsteads and
gardens. They can be attached to a tree or
wall. An old kettle, with the lid hole facin
vertically, is equally acceptable.

---

p.244 **Red-breasted Flycatcher** *Ficedula parva*

Description: 11–12 cm (4½ in). Adult summer male
grey-brown above, with grey head and
prominent, *white eye-ring. Chin and throat
bright orange-red;* remaining underparts
white, with warm wash along flanks.
Female lacks grey head and red throat, bu
has prominent pale eye-ring on otherwise
plain face. Both sexes, as well as juveniles,
have *white outer feathers on basal half of
frequently cocked black tail.*

Voice: A pleasant medley of clear, fluty notes
ending on descending scale like Willow
Warbler; call a hard *dzit.*

Habitat: Damp deciduous woodland, with tangles
undergrowth often growing in water.
Frequents bush country in winter.

Breeding: Five to six white, reddish-spotted eggs lai
in cup placed in tree hole, rock crevice or
against trunk of a tree. Incubation 11–15
days, by female alone.

Range: Breeds from central Europe eastwards
across boreal zone of Siberia to Bering
Straits; also southwards through Caucasu
Carpathians, and mountains of former
Yugoslavia. Rare in the west. Winters in
India and Southeast Asia.

A less than typical flycatcher that seldom
perches openly and prefers to feed high in
the canopy of trees. It is easily overlooked
though, when seen, its cocked tail with it
white patches is an obvious diagnostic
feature.

p.244 **Semi-collared Flycatcher**
Ficedula semitorquata

Description: 12–13 cm (4½–5 in). The standard male
Semi-collared is black and white with a
*white half-collar, white-based outer-tail
feathers,* extensive white patch on the
closed wing, *small white patch on primaries,*
and a *row of white spots across 'shoulder'.*
Female brown above and white below,
with less white in wing, but also shows
*white primary patch and row of white
spots across the shoulder.* The presence of
some, or even all, these features does
not, however, make for certain
identification. *See* Collared and Pied
Flycatchers.

Voice: Repeated *see-see-see-see-oo*, very similar to
Collared Flycatcher but faster: also a hard
tak.

Habitat: Deciduous woods, often on hillsides, but
also in wet lowlands.

Breeding: Five to six pale-blue eggs laid in cup placed
in tree hole. Incubation 13–14 days, by
female.

Range: Summer visitor to southeast Europe,
Caucasus and southern Caspian. Winters in
East Africa in western Kenya and Rwanda.

One of three black and white flycatchers
that, with the exception of well-marked
adult males, should be separated with the
greatest of care. There is considerable
plumage variation and even the best
characters may or may not be present in
both males and females.

---

p.245 **Collared Flycatcher** *Ficedula albicollis*

Description: 12–13 cm (4½–5 in). Adult male black
above with complete *broad, white collar,*
prominent *white patch at base of bill,* bold
*white wing-patch, and small white patch on
primaries. Outer tail narrowly edged white;
rump greyish.* Female grey-brown with
extensive white in wing and small white
patch on primaries; very similar to female
Pied and Semi-collared Flycatchers.

Voice: A *sit-sit-sit-sueeri*, higher pitched than song of Pied Flycatcher.

Habitat: Mature forests of oaks and other deciduous trees as well as parks and orchards.

Breeding: Six to seven pale-blue eggs laid in tree hole. Incubation 12–14 days, by female alone.

Range: Summer visitor from eastern France, across Germany to Russia as far as Urals. Breeds north of Semi-collared though ranges overlap in Albania.

While adult male is easily identified in summer, other plumages create problems and should be approached with caution. Virtually all features of the female and juvenile Collared can be found on similar-aged Pied and Semi-collared. A clear combination of most, if not all, features is required for certain identification.

---

p.245 **Pied Flycatcher** *Ficedula hypoleuca*

Description: 12–13 cm (4½–5 in). Male black above, white below, with *tiny white patch at base of bill. White patch across wing is neither as bold nor as extensive, as the 'collared' flycatcher's* and shows no more than tiny mark on the closed primaries. *White in outer tail is bold* than in the other species. Female very similar to female collareds, but with less white in wing, particularly the primaries. First-winter birds like female, but can show line of
pale spots on median coverts like female Semi-collared.

Voice: Song a repeated *zee-chi* terminating in a trill; call a *whit*.

Habitat: Mature deciduous forests mostly of oak, also mixed forests, but in pure conifers only where nest boxes provided.

Breeding: Four to seven pale-blue eggs laid in cup placed in tree hole. Incubation 12–13 day by female.

Range: The most widespread and abundant of the three black and white flycatchers, breeding across temperate and northern Europe from hills of central Spain to Alps and Britain eastwards to Urals and beyond. Winters in

West Africa. Regular passage migrant through Mediterranean.

Visitors to eastern Europe should be well aware that this species is still the dominant black and white flycatcher in most woodland as well as on passage through the eastern Mediterranean.

LONG-TAILED TITS (AEGITHALIDAE)

Seven species; across Eurasia and into Nearctic. A single species breeds in Europe. Though related to the true tits (Paridae) these birds form a distinct group that share Asiatic origins, small size, and notably long tails that often double their overall length. They are tubby-bodied, have short, pointed bills and are largely gregarious. They feed on small insects and their larvae, gleaned from the foliage and bark of trees. Unlike the true tits they construct quite elaborate dome-shaped nests with a side entrance, and do not use holes.

p.248 **Long-tailed Tit** *Aegithalos caudatus*

Description: 13.5–14.5 cm (5½ in). A black and white bird marked by *tail that is equally as long as body*. Basic plumage pattern consists of black back and primaries, with variable amounts of white in tertials, creating broadly striped effect. Underparts white. Several distinct subspecies occur with variable amounts of dull pink on wings and underparts. Many show broad black supercilium and white coronal stripe, but others have pure white or grey heads with more extensive white in wings. Despite such variation, the species is easily identified at all times.

Voice: A thin *see-see-see* as well as a rattling *tsirrrrup*.

Habitat: Woodlands, scrub, gardens, hedgerows and parks, with extensive bush cover. Avoids tundra and uniform boreal forest.

Breeding: Eight to twelve red-spotted, white eggs laid in neatly woven oval nest with side entrance hole. Incubation 12–14 days, b female.

Range: Resident across temperate Palearctic fro Portugal and Ireland to Japan and Chin Absent from Mediterranean islands, sav Corsica.

The nest is a remarkable structure, decorated with mosses and lichens boun together with spiders' webs. As the larg brood grows towards maturity, the nest expands to accommodate the growing chicks. Often older brothers and sisters play a part in feeding the young.

BABBLERS (Timaliidae)

282 species; Old World, but single spe in the Nearctic. One species breeds in Europe. This is a highly diverse family mainly dull-coloured birds that spend much of their time on or near the grou among dense cover. They vary from sm to medium in size and many have long tails and short, rounded wings. Bill variation, from the broad and conical (parrotbills) to the long and decurved (scimitar babblers), indicates an adapta to a wide range of foods and habitats. N are highly gregarious and noisy, but equally have the habit of fading away i cover when disturbed. The single Euro species belongs to the subfamily Panurinae, the parrotbills, which are largely confined to Southeast Asia and extensive stands of bamboo.

p.249 **Bearded Tit** *Panurus biarmicus*

Description: 16–17 cm (6½ in). Adult male rich, *ruf chestnut* marked by blue-grey head, *blac moustache* and yellow eye. Wings marke black and white; *tail long* and rounded. Female similar, but with brownish head and lacking moustache. Overall tubby shape, coupled with coloration, long tail and reed-based habitat are diagnostic. Flies low over reed tops on whirring wings, calling.

Voice: Distinct *pting-pting*, repeated.

Habitat: Reed beds.

Breeding: Five to seven brown-speckled, white eggs laid in untidy cup of reed leaves placed low down among reed debris over water. Incubation 12–13 days, by female.

Range: Resident across much of temperate Europe, though restricted to reed-beds and therefore decidedly local. Also eastwards from Kazakhstan to Sea of Japan. Sometimes irrupts to non-breeding areas.

The periodic irruptions of these gregarious little birds often brings them to quite small patches of reeds where they do not breed. This is the result of a season of high breeding success and usually occurs in autumn. Such irruptions frequently lead to the colonization of new areas as happened in western England in the 1960s and 1970s.

PENDULINE TITS (REMIZIDAE)

10 species; Eurasia, North America and Africa. A single species breeds in Europe. Penduline tits are small birds with short, thin Goldfinch-like bills, though they are more akin to the true tits in terms of behaviour. They frequent scrubby, bushy areas and feed busily among the foliage of shrubs and trees. They frequently use their feet to grasp food and their thin bills to prise open hard shells. They also reach for food with their feet, a habit shared with the peculiar, but related, Verdin of the USA and Mexico. In fact, authorities are divided about the relationship of the family to other families and, indeed, relationships within the family itself. They do, however, share the ability to construct a penduline nest of woven materials with an entrance near the top.

p.250   **Willow Tit** *Parus montanus*

Description: 11–12 cm (4½in). Northern replacement
Marsh Tit. Nominate, west European bird
are, like Marsh Tit, brown above, buffy
below, marked by *dull (not glossy) black ca*
and large black bib. Cheeks dirty white.
Overall impression is of a *scruffy bird*.
Northern subspecies *P. m. borealis* grey
above and white below. All plumages sho
diagnostic *pale mid-wing panel*.

Voice: A harsh buzzing *erz-erz-erz* and high-
pitched *zi-zi-zi*.

Habitat: Deciduous, coniferous and mixed woods,
often with damp or wet patches, as well a
dry conifer woods up to tree line in
mountains.

Breeding: Six to nine white, speckled-reddish eggs
laid in specially excavated hole in rotten
tree stump. Incubation 13–15 days, by
female alone.

Range: Resident from Britain to Kamchatka in
boreal zone as well as in more temperate
climes within Europe. Absent from
southern Europe, except mountain areas.

The need to excavate its own nest hole in
rotten tree or stump restricts this bird to
mature and mostly unmanaged woodlan
It can, however, be persuaded to use nest
boxes provided they are filled with a blo
of expanded polystyrene that the bird ca
then excavate.

p.250   **Sombre Tit** *Parus lugubris*

Description: 14 cm (5½ in). Resembles both Marsh an
Willow Tits, but *significantly larger*.
Upperparts brownish-grey; underparts
white, washed buffy on flanks. *Black cap,*
washed brown with large black bib enclose
white cheeks. Cap and bib both more
substantial than either confusable species
Shows pale mid-wing panel and chunky

Voice: Variety of calls including harsh *chaar*; *zi*
zi, and other repeated discordant notes.

Habitat: Open woodlands of oak, beech and coni
as well as copses and orchards.

Breeding: Five to seven red-spotted, white eggs laid in tree hole. Incubation 12–14 days, by female.

Range: Virtually endemic to Western Palearctic. Resident through former Yugoslavia and Greece, as well as parts of Bulgaria and Romania and thus very much a southeastern European species. Also eastwards through Turkey to Iran.

Generally solitary, this large tit is best looked for among trees bordering archeological and similar sites with rocks and bushes, and among rocky, well-vegetated hillsides.

p.250 **Siberian Tit** *Parus cinctus*

Description: 13–15.5 cm (5–6 in). Large tit with grey-brown upperparts marked by *brown-washed black cap* and extensive, *scruffy bib*. Underparts white with distinct *rufous-washed flanks*. Wings show pale mid-wing panel, though not as bold as Willow Tit which shares its range and is thus the only confusable species.

Voice: Slow *chee-ee*, or *chick-a-cheo-ee-ee*, or *dee-deer* notes.

Habitat: Mixed birch and conifers in boreal zone.

Breeding: Six to ten red-spotted, white eggs laid in tree hole. Incubation for 14–15 days, by female alone.

Range: Breeds from northern Scandinavia across conifer forests of Siberia to Bering Straits, central Alaska and adjacent Canada. Resident, and mostly unknown away from breeding areas, though some do wander southwards within conifer forests in winter.

The southward wanderings of juvenile Siberian Tits, which take them several hundred kilometres or more south of their breeding range, show an irruptive pattern similar to that of crossbills and Nutcracker. They may begin as early as July and usually move in small flocks that may appear as far south as Helsinki and St Petersburg. They often associate with Willow Tits.

p.251 **Great Tit** *Parus major*

Description: 13.5–14.5 cm (5½ in). Well marked, wi
green upperparts, blue and yellow in wing
with single white wingbar. Underparts
yellow with black central breast-stripe; in m
breast-stripe widens between legs and jo
large black bib. *Black cap* extends along
of ear coverts to enclose white cheeks.
Substantial bill.

Voice: Highly vocal and variable; most commo
call a distinctive *teecha-teecha-teecha.*

Habitat: Woods, hedgerows, copses, orchards,
groves, gardens, and scrub.

Breeding: 8–13 white, spotted-reddish eggs laid i
neat cup of mosses and hair placed in tre
hole or nest box. Incubation for 13–14
days, by female.

Range: Widespread resident across Palearctic ar
Oriental regions almost as far as Austral
Absent only from highest mountains, In
Gangetic plain, central Asian deserts, ar
high Arctic tundra. Widespread and
common in Europe.

Common member of winter tit flocks, a
frequent visitor to garden bird-feeding
stations, where it is often the most
aggressive species.

NUTHATCHES (SITTIDAE)

22 species; Eurasia and North America.
Three species breed in Europe and anoth
is the rarest of transatlantic vagrants.
Nuthatches are small birds, usually well
marked with blue in the plumage, that
climb easily both up and down trees and
rock faces. The bill is long and sharply
pointed and used both to probe and to
hack, woodpecker-like, for food. The tai
short and the legs are long and strong, b
characteristics important aids to climbin
They feed on insects extracted from bark
and rock crevices but, as their name
implies, they are quite capable of hackin
open hard nuts to obtain the kernel insi

Though mostly hole nesters, all species use mud in one way or another to modify their nests, while some species construct a pure mud nest in the manner of a swallow. They are mostly resident.

p.252 European Nuthatch *Sitta europaea*

Description: 13.5–14.5 cm (5½ in). Upperparts *pale blue* marked by *extended black eye-stripe,* long heavy bill and short tail with black and white outer feathers. In west and central European birds, *S. e. caesia, underparts are rich buff* with chestnut flanks; in Scandinavian birds, *S. e. europaea,* underparts lightly streaked with deep chestnut on flanks. Flies in undulating woodpecker manner.

Voice: A whistled *wit-wit-wit* and trilling *tsirr;* song a repeated loud single whistle.

Habitat: Deciduous forests, groves, gardens, parks.

Breeding: Six to nine white, spotted-reddish eggs laid in tree hole with entrance plastered with mud to form correct-sized entrance. Incubation 14–18 days, by female.

Range: Widespread resident throughout temperate Europe extending across Palearctic to Pacific and southwards through China to India.

The name Nuthatch derives from 'Nuthack', which refers to the species' habit of placing a hard nut in the fork or crotch of a tree and hammering it woodpecker-fashion to obtain the kernel. It also scours the bark of trees in its search for insects, climbing upwards and, equally, head-first downwards.

p.252 Krüper's Nuthatch *Sitta krueperi*

Description: 12 cm (4½ in). Small nuthatch, closely related to Corsican Nuthatch. Upperparts pale grey-blue with *black cap, white supercilium* and marked black eye-stripe. Underparts white with *rufous-orange chest-patch* and undertail coverts. Short, uptilted bill.

p.253 **Wallcreeper** *Tichodroma muraria*

Description: 16–17 cm (6½ in). Grey above, with bla
wings and tail. Bright-*crimson wing cover*
that are exposed as the wings are continuousl
flicked. Dark face in summer, pale in wir
Bill long and decurved. In flight, *wings*
ping-pong-bat shape and tail is short and
white margined. Climbs rocks with
consummate ease.

Voice: A soft, high-pitched *zee-zee-zee* that is
surprisingly quiet for a bird that freque:
gorges with noisy, fast-flowing streams
torrents.

Habitat: Mountain cliff faces and gorges in sumr
in winter descends to quarries and often
buildings including churches in mount
towns and even cities.

Breeding: Three to four white eggs, sparsely spott
red, laid in rock cleft or crevice, often n
water or in damp conditions, with narre
predator-proof entrance. Incubation 18-
days, by female alone.

Range: Breeds across southern Palearctic from
northern Spain and most European
mountains to central-southern Asia.
Winters nearby at lower altitudes, but
occasionally wanders some distance.

One of Europe's most elusive and sough
after birds. Mostly seen at regular, lowl
wintering sites, or as a long-stay vagran
abandons its high-level breeding groun
in October, irrespective of weather
conditions, and it is thus more a true
migrant than many other mountain bir
It is, nevertheless, somewhat erratic in
appearances and may abandon a regular
wintering site for no apparent reason.

TREECREEPERS (CERTHIIDAE)

5 species; temperate Holarctic. Two spe
are resident in Europe. Treecreepers are
small, arboreal birds with heavily streak
brown and black upperparts and white,
pale buff, underparts. They have short,

strong legs marked by large feet and claws, well suited to climbing the trunks and major branches of trees. The bill is long and decurved, and an ideal probe for collecting small insects and spiders from among bark and crevices. The tail is medium to long and has strong feather shafts that, in being used as a climbing aid, become increasingly pointed by abrasion. They share the unendearing habit of climbing out of sight to the far side of a tree trunk when aware of being observed.

p.253 **Eurasian Treecreeper** *Certhia familiaris*

Description: 12–13 cm (4½–5 in). Small tree climber with well-camouflaged, heavily streaked brown and black upperparts and *white underparts*. Long, fine, decurved bill and *prominent white supercilium*. Confusable only with Short-toed Treecreeper which has buffy flanks and supercilium.

Voice: Thin *tsee-tsee-tsee*, similar to a crest.

Habitat: Wide variety of woodlands from pure deciduous to pure conifer. In south and west Europe in upland conifers; elsewhere in parks, orchards, groves and large gardens.

Breeding: Five to six white eggs, finely speckled reddish, laid in neat cup hidden behind piece of loose bark, sometimes between planks of a garden shed or suchlike. Incubation 14–15 days, by female alone.

Range: Resident across Palearctic from Ireland to Japan, with a separate population in Himalayas and adjacent mountains of central Asia. In Europe confined to mountains in Spain, France and Italy; more widespread to north and east. Some local movements in winter.

The jerky, tree-climbing technique of this species takes it spiralling up the trunk of one tree before flying off to the foot of the next. It can climb upside down along horizontal branches and is a regular member of nomadic tit flocks that roam the woods of winter.

strong, was marked below are used claws,
well suited to climbing the trunks and
major branches of trees. The bill is long and
decurved, and an ideal probe for collecting
small insects and spiders from moss, bark
and crevices. The tail is... and its... in...
and just among techniques that in being
used as a climbing aid, become increasingly
pointed by abrasion. They use the
woodpecker's habit of climbing up of tree
so the bird does not make such even of
being observed.

1630 Eurasian Tree Creeper *Certhia familiaris*

Description 12.5–14cm – Tiny small tree climber
with well-camouflaged, richly streaked
brown and black upperparts and near
pure white underparts. Bill rather curved and
with short... Tree creeper which has
tiny flanks and superciliaries.

Voice Thin reedy *tseee*, similar to a crest

Habitat Wide variety of woodlands from pine
and oak to... In such and
west Europe in upland conifers, else where
in... such as orchards, groves and larger
gardens.

Breeding Five to six white eggs, finely speckled
reddish, laid in nest cup hidden behind
bark or loose bark, sometimes between
planks of a garden shed or suchlike.
Incubation Two... days, by female alone.

Range Two subspecies Palearctic from Ireland to
Japan, with European population in...
Himalayas and other... mountains of
Central Asia. In Europe confined to
mountains in Spain, France and Italy, more
widespread to north and east. Some local
movements in winter.

The Jerkey-type climbing technique of this
species takes it spiralling up the trunk of a
one tree before flying off to the foot of the
next. It... can climb upside down along
horizontal branches and is a regular
partaker of nomadic tit flocks that roam the
woods of winter.

prey, usually on the ground. Unusually, the
create 'larders' of surplus prey by impaling
them on thorns or barbed wire. They have
strongly built, hooked bills, heavy heads, a
most have long tails. The legs and feet are
well proportioned, not heavily built and
taloned like diurnal and nocturnal birds of
prey which grasp their prey. Some tropical
species, particularly in Africa, are highly
gregarious and others utter the duet calls t
are the characteristic sounds of wildlife filn
Most temperate species are rather silent.

p.254 **Red-backed Shrike** *Lanius collurio*

Description: 16–18 cm (6½–7 in). Male has *grey crown*
marked by *black mask through eye, chestnut
back* and wings, grey rump, and black tai
edged white at base. Underparts white.
Female *brown above,* with grey wash over
crown and rump, and hint of a mask
through the eye. Underparts buffy, boldly
marked with dark crescents. Juvenile
resembles female, but additionally marke
with crescents on upperparts.

Voice: Harsh *chak-chak*; song a quiet chatter wit
some mimicry.

Habitat: Open country with thickets, heaths; scru
covered wasteland; orchards and groves
with neglected corners or hedges.

Breeding: Five to six variably coloured, brown-
spotted eggs laid in cup in thick bush.
Incubation 14–16 days, by female alone.

Range: Summer visitor from northern Spain acro
temperate Europe northwards to Gulf of
Bothnia and south to Crete; absent from
extreme west of Europe. Extends eastwar
to Urals and western Siberia. Whole
population winters in southeast Africa.

The serious decline of this species in Brit
from 300 pairs in the mid-twentieth
century to virtual extinction by the end,
paralleled elsewhere in Belgium, Hollanc
northern Germany, Denmark and Sweder
In some areas this has been attributed to
habitat destruction, though climatic fact
also seem to be involved.

p.254 **Lesser Grey Shrike** *Lanius minor*

Description: 19–21 cm (7½–8 in). Similar to slightly larger Great Grey Shrike, with grey upperparts marked by black wings and *shorter black and white tail*. Black facial *mask extends to forehead and shows no white supercilium*. Underparts washed pale pinkish, but beware warm light on Great Grey creating same effect. Juvenile scaled with crescents above and below, and shows dark mask through eye not extending to forehead.

Voice: Hard *chak*; various chattering and whistled notes together with mimicry in song.

Habitat: Open, bushy country with trees, fields, gardens and woodland margins.

Breeding: Five to six pale-green eggs, spotted olive-brown, laid in bulky cup of twigs and grasses placed in tree. Incubation 15–16 days, entirely or mainly by female.

Range: Summer visitor to southern Europe with a definite southeastern bias. Breeds locally on Mediterranean coasts of Spain and France eastwards through Italy and Balkans, and from central Europe to central-southern Siberia. Winters in southwest Africa.

The autumn migration of this species passes through Greece and Egypt. In spring a more easterly route is followed making this a decidedly rare bird in the Mediterranean basin. Its patchy distribution in western Europe no doubt indicates colonization from the east.

p.254 **Great Grey Shrike** *Lanius excubitor*

Description: 23–25 cm (9–10 in). Largest of the shrikes and marked by *significantly longer tail* than other species. Grey crown and back, with *black mask through eye bordered above by narrow white supercilium*; black wings and black, white margined tail. Underparts pure white. Perches on bushes and posts when white breast visible at long range. Juvenile is barred buffy below.

Voice: Harsh *chak-chak*; song a chattering of harsh and sweet notes.

CROWS, MAGPIES AND JAYS
(Corvidae)

107 species, worldwide save New Zealand, some 41 species breed in Europe. These birds are the largest of the passerines, though they vary in size from medium to decidedly large. They are marked by large, powerful bills and strong legs, well adapted to both walking and perching. While the typical crows are predominantly black, the jays and magpies are more colourful, with bold plumage patches or of blue. Many crows therefore present a considerable identification problem, in which size and shape are useful factors. These birds are intelligent and adaptable birds, capable of living alongside man and exploiting his activities in developed areas. Some become remarkably bold, raiding and nesting very close to busy areas. The diet of omnivorous birds that will tempt of a wide variety of foods.

p.35 Jurassian Jay (Garrulus glandarius)

Description   Up to 35 cm (14 in). Greyish-brown, pink marked by blue and white wing patch, crown, belly, rump, etc. Black wings with a patches of white and strong of blue and a velvet-black bill, black throat, tail and a undertail. In flight long tail, rounded wings and a white rump are good features. Generally solitary or in pairs.

Voice   Harsh raw and other carving and guttural notes.

Habitat   Deciduous, conifer and mixed woodland, from lowland to high mountain forests. Also in more open parkland and gardens and even city parks.

Breeding   Five to seven pale-green eggs, blotched built in nest of twigs, built on high tree. Incubation 16–18 days, by both sexes.

Range   Widespread resident right across Palearctic from Portugal to Japan and northwards through China to Himalaya. In northern

CROWS, MAGPIES AND JAYS
(CORVIDAE)

107 species; worldwide, save New Zealand. Some 11 species breed in Europe. These birds are the largest of the passerines, and they vary in size from medium to decidedly large. They are marked by large, powerful bills and strong legs, well adapted to both walking and perching. While the typical crows are predominantly black, the jays and magpies are more colourful, with bold plumage patches often of blue. Many crows therefore present a considerable identification problem, in which structure and range are crucial factors. These are highly intelligent and adaptable birds capable of living alongside man and exploiting his activities in a wide variety of ways. Some become remarkably confiding and nestlings easily survive as pets. They are omnivorous birds that will adapt to a wide variety of foods.

p.258 **Eurasian Jay** *Garrulus glandarius*

Description: 33–36 cm (13–14 in). Whole *body brownish pink* marked by black and white streaked crown, black moustache, black wings with patches of white and stripes of blue and black, black tail, and *white rump* and undertail. In flight, *long tail, rounded wings* and white rump are good features. Generally solitary or in pairs.

Voice: Harsh *skaa* and other cawing and grating notes.

Habitat: Deciduous, conifer and mixed woodlands from lowlands to high mountain forests. Also in more open parkland and groves, gardens, and even city parks.

Breeding: Five to seven pale-green eggs, speckled buff, laid in nest of twigs placed high in a tree. Incubation 16–17 days, by both sexes.

Range: Widespread resident right across Palearctic from Portugal to Japan and southwards through China to Himalayas. In Europe,

absent only from Iceland, the mountains and far north of Scandinavia, and from Danube plain.

Though more often heard than seen, this is by no means a difficult bird to locate. It is more often seen flying than perching, and in autumn it may make long flights to woods and copses of oak in search of acorns, which it carries away to bury as a reserve food supply. Following the last ice age 10,000 years ago, oak forests spread northwards at a rate of nearly 2 km (1¼ miles) per year as a result of this acorn-burying habit of Jays.

---

p.258 **Siberian Jay** *Perisoreus infaustus*

Description: 30–32 cm (12–12½ in). A round-winged, long-tailed relative of Eurasian Jay, pale grey above, with dusky face; *rufous-orange wing-patches, rump and tail*. Breast grey; *belly orange-rufous*. In flight; rufous-orange tail, wing-patches and underwing coverts are prominent features on an otherwise dull-coloured bird.

Voice: A hard *kook-kook* and *chair*.

Habitat: Conifer forests and adjacent birchwoods, especially dense stands of natural, unexploited spruce and pine.

Breeding: Three to four pale-bluish eggs, spotted brown, laid in large nest of twigs and bark placed high in conifer, usually close to the trunk. Incubation 19 days, by female alone.

Range: Resident of far north across boreal Palearctic from Norway to Kamchatka. In Europe confined to mountains of southern Scandinavia, extending to lowlands north of Arctic Circle.

This is a highly elusive forest bird that seldom strays far from its native patch and has the habit of melting away into the forest when disturbed. It is generally solitary. In winter it may be emboldened to frequent the neighbourhood of farms and other buildings.

p.259   **Red-billed Chough** *Pyrrhocorax pyrrhocorax*

Description: 36–41 cm (14–16 in). Black, crow-like
bird, easily confused in the air with
Jackdaw and Alpine Chough.
Distinguished from latter only by *longer,
red, decurved bill*. Gregarious, forming
acrobatic flocks that seemingly fly for
pure enjoyment. *Waisted wings and
large square-cut tail shared with Alpine
Chough*.

Voice: High-pitched *caw* or *caar*, plus a lower *cuf*
from which it is named.

Habitat: Mountain cliffs and gorges usually, but no
always, at lower altitudes than Alpine
Chough. Also sea cliffs.

Breeding: Three to four pale-green eggs, blotched
brown, laid in bulky nest of sticks placed
cliff hole or crevice. Incubation 17–23 da
by female.

Range: Resident of sea cliffs and mountains of
south and western Europe, from Spain
eastwards through Mediterranean to Turk
and Middle East, and widely through Asi
plateaux from Himalayas to northern
China. Also resident along coasts of
Atlantic Europe.

It would appear that cow-pats, which
harbour populations of insect larvae, are
essential to the Chough's survival. The
bird's decline in several parts of its range
Europe can therefore be attributed to the
practice of keeping domestic stock,
particularly cattle, indoors during the
winter.

p.259   **Nutcracker** *Nucifraga caryocatactes*

Description: 30–33 cm (12–13 in). Resembles a small,
dark Jay with similar rounded wings, but
distinctly shorter tail. Whole *body dark
brown, evenly spotted white*. Black cap and
black wings; black tail tipped white with
prominent *white undertail coverts*. Bill
distinctly pointed. Gregarious.

Voice: Variety of harsh caws and croaks and,
particularly, a high-pitched *chair*.

Habitat: Conifer forests in mountains of south-central Europe and in lowland boreal forests.

Breeding: Three to four brown-spotted, blue eggs laid in nest of twigs lined with grass and lichens placed on conifer branch near the trunk. Incubation 17–19 days, by female alone.

Range: Widespread resident of montane and boreal conifer forests of northern and eastern Europe, from southern Sweden across boreal Palearctic to the Bering Straits, and among mountains of south-central Europe, Himalayas and eastern China.

The Nutcracker occasionally erupts from northern breeding forests and may then occur in forested areas hundreds of miles outside its normal range. Rarely, such eruptions reach more open landscapes and birds may occur in gardens and even cemeteries.

p.259 **Jackdaw** *Corvus monedula*

Description: 32–34 cm (12½–13½ in). Medium-sized, all-black crow, marked by *short bill, distinct grey nape and white eye*. In flight shows rounded wings and gregarious acrobatics of choughs, but has distinctly longer tail.

Voice: High-pitched *kyaa*, clear *chock*.

Habitat: From mountain cliffs and gorges to coastal cliffs and tall buildings, usually churches, in towns and cities. Feeds on agricultural land.

Breeding: Four to six brown-spotted, pale-blue eggs laid in cup of twigs constructed in hole in a cliff, tree or building, or in a chimney. Incubation 17–18 days, by female alone.

Range: Largely resident from Europe across Turkey and Russia to central Siberia. Far northern birds move southwards in winter to mix with resident populations.

Takes a wide variety of foods usually found on the ground, though it is not averse to joining the tree-top caterpillar feast of early summer. It eats many terrestrial invertebrates, as well as seeds, fruit and

Range:

Resident of wilderness areas throughout Europe, from Iceland to Portugal eastwar to Siberia, Bering Straits and most of Nor America; also southwards to Himalayas, Pakistan, Iran and North Africa. Largely absent from lowland northwestern and central Europe.

This is a powerful predator with a fearsome bill considerably larger than th of most birds of prey. It will kill mammalian prey, but it is not above scavenging and will compete with larger birds over a carcass. It is extremely wary man, not without due cause, and has disappeared from lowland Europe as a direct result of persecution.

STARLINGS (STURNIDAE)

111 species; Old World. Three species breed in Europe. Starlings are small to medium-sized birds that walk well with somewhat waddling gait. They are aggressive, adaptable and curious, and gi the impression of being the 'wide boys' o the bird world. They have longish legs a bills and many have short tails creating a distinctive silhouette in flight. Though their plumage is highly variable, many have a metallic gloss of blue or green ove their darker parts. Most are highly gregarious outside the breeding season a some form truly huge roosting flocks. Th are hole nesters.

p.261 **Common Starling** *Sturnus vulgaris*

Description: 20.5–22.5 cm (8–9 in). Dark-plumaged bird marked by *long bill, short tail and pointed wings.* Summer adult *black, washed with metallic green,* with a few buffy spots confined to back and undertail. Bill yello legs red. In winter becomes *more spotted* w buff, particularly on head and breast. Juvenile buffy, gradually moulting to

winter plumage during autumn with head
the last to change colour.

Voice: Wide variety of chuckles and whistles,
clicking and mimicry.

Habitat: Woodland, parks, groves, marshes, cities,
towns, villages, rubbish tips.

Breeding: Five to seven pale-blue eggs laid in messy
nest of vegetation constructed in hole in a
tree or building, or in any other hole
available. Incubation 12–15 days, by both
sexes.

Range: Widespread and common, breeding
throughout Europe, except in Iberia,
southern Italy, Greece and Mediterranean
islands; extends eastwards through Turkey
and former USSR to Pacific. Winters in
south and west through Iberia,
Mediterranean and Middle East to northern
India. Introduced to North America, South
Africa and Australasia.

This is a highly successful species that
spread right across North America to the
detriment of many native species after
being introduced by a nineteenth-century
idiot. Vast winter flocks form regular roosts
in city centres, marshes and woods, where
the local hawks and falcons are assured a
regular supper.

p.261 **Spotless Starling** *Sturnus unicolor*

Description: 21–22 cm (8–8½ in). Very similar to
Common Starling, but black, *lacking both
metallic green gloss and buffy spots*. Bill yellow;
and legs pink, not dark red. In winter
shows a few buffy spots on body.
Gregarious, but never in such large flocks as
Common Starling.

Voice: Similar to Common Starling, with wide
variety of chuckles, whistles and wheezing
notes, with some excellent mimicry.

Habitat: Towns, ruins, agricultural land.

Breeding: Four to five pale-blue eggs laid in nest of
grasses placed in hole in tree or building.
Incubation 10–15 days, mainly by female.

Range: Virtually endemic resident of Europe,
expanding eastwards into southern France,

Range: Resident right across Palearctic from
Portugal to Sea of Japan, southwards
through Middle East to Indian subcontine
Introduced to North and South America,
South Africa and Australia. Widespread
resident throughout Europe, but absent fro
Iceland and Scandinavian mountains.

The House Sparrow's absence from
Sardinia, where it is replaced by the Spani
Sparrow, is seen only as a hiccup in its
colonization of Europe. Elsewhere in the
central Mediterranean it has colonized an
hybridized with that bird to form the
distinctive subspecies *P. d. italiae*.

p.264 **Spanish Sparrow** *Passer hispaniolensis*

Description: 14–15.5 cm (5½–6 in). Male has *chocolate
crown* extending to nape with narrow,
broken, white supercilium and *white
cheeks* enclosed by large black bib. *Bib
extends to breast and continues as black
chevrons along flanks*. Upperparts streaked
chestnut and black with distinctive buffy
braces. Female like female House Sparrow
but far paler in buffy grey with *pale
braces, a bold supercilium, and faint flank-
streaks*.

Voice: Various *chirrup* calls, deeper and richer tha
House Sparrow.

Habitat: Olive and citrus groves, bushy heaths and
scrub, often along watercourses and amon
rocky countryside.

Breeding: Three to six whitish eggs, heavily blotche
and spotted grey, laid in untidy ball of
vegetation and feathers placed in tree or c
telegraph pole. Incubation 11–14 days, b
both sexes, though female plays the large
role.

Range: Breeds through Mediterranean to Turkey,
eastwards to Kazakhstan. Resident in wes
but only a summer visitor in eastern part
of its range. Winters widely in North
Africa, Arabia and Pakistan.

While it is invariably outnumbered by th
House Sparrow, the Spanish Sparrow may

be locally more abundant. Where the House Sparrow is absent, as in Sardinia, these birds will happily build their nests in occupied buildings; elsewhere, faced by competition, they build in trees, on telegraph poles and in the large nests of vultures, birds of prey, and, especially, White Storks. In the latter they often form mixed colonies with House Sparrows and regularly hybridize.

---

p.265 **Tree Sparrow** *Passer montanus*

Description: 13.5–14.5 cm (5½–6 in). This sparrow avoids competition with House Sparrow mainly by adopting a more rural habitat. Sexes similar with *rich-chestnut crown* and nape, *small black bib,* and neat *black comma prominent on white cheek.* At any distance, *white half-collar* is particularly prominent feature, more so than cheek-comma.

Voice: Distinct, abrupt *chup*.

Habitat: Mature tree belts, orchards and groves, copses and parks in west, but also among buildings in east.

Breeding: Four to six pale-grey, brown-spotted eggs laid in untidy nest of grasses placed in hole in tree or building. Incubation 11–14 days, by both sexes.

Range: Resident throughout temperate Europe and right across Palearctic to Japan, China and Indonesia. Boreal and tundra breeding birds are summer visitors, and some European birds move southwards to winter in Greece and Turkey.

Where its range overlaps that of the House Sparrow, this is a bird of the countryside. Where that more aggressive bird does not occur, the Tree Sparrow occupies a niche around buildings and even in town and city centres. It is, for example, the common sparrow of Kathmandu City in Nepal. Its catastrophic decline in numbers, particularly in England during the 1990s, paralleled by the House Sparrow, is difficult to explain.

Conical *bill bright red*. Female buffy with
black mark through eye, and black wings
and tail. Bright-red bill and rump are be
features.

Voice: A descending, liquid twittering; plus
various chirps.

Habitat: Waterside vegetation, including reeds,
bushes, and so on.

Breeding: Four to seven white eggs laid in ball-sha
nest, with tube-shaped side entrance,
placed in emergent or waterside vegetati
Incubation 13–14 days, by both sexes.

Range: Natural resident in India and Southeast
Asia south to Java. Introduced in Spain a
in Po Valley in Italy.

Breeding was first recorded in central Sp
in 1974, with subsequent spread to the
River Guadiana, where it now has its ma
stronghold. It was introduced to Italy an
well established by 1983. Subsequent ha
winters reduced the population, but it ha
since recovered.

FINCHES (FRINGILLIDAE)

124 species; worldwide. Nineteen species
breed in Europe. Finches are small to
medium-small, predominantly arboreal
birds that have stout, conical bills ideally
suited to cracking the seeds on which the
rely for food. Mostly food is taken on the
ground, though many species take large
quantities of insect larvae from among
vegetation during the breeding season. So
species take seeds from trees and are more
less exclusively arboreal as a result. Severa
such birds have extremely large and
powerful bills and heads, and one group h
crossed mandibles with which to extract
conifer seeds from cones. Finches often bo
quite colourful plumage, especially in the
male, with bold marks of white that enha
flock cohesion. They are good fliers and
while some perform elaborate song-flights
others are long-distance migrants. They
build cup-shaped nests in trees and bushe

p.266 **Chaffinch** *Fringilla coelebs*

Description: 14.5–16 cm (5½–6 ½ in). Male has blue-grey crown, bold, *double, white wingbar, white outer-tail feathers*, deep-pink breast, and steel-blue bill. Female brown above and creamy buff below, with *white wingbars and outer tail*. Shuffles along ground in loose feeding flocks, showing white in flight.

Voice: Loud *pink-pink*; pleasant descending song terminates in flourish.

Habitat: Woodland clearings and margins, hedgerows, gardens, parks and orchards.

Breeding: Four to five pale-blue eggs, scrawled dark pink, laid in delicate cup of grasses, camouflaged with lichens and mosses and placed in low bush or shrub. Incubation 11–13 days, by female.

Range: Widespread resident across temperate and southern Europe northwards to southern Scandinavia. Most Scandinavian and Russian birds, east to central Siberia, are summer visitors that pour westwards in autumn. Replaced in northeast by closely related Brambling.

While the Chaffinch is a common European resident over large areas of Europe, its numbers are augmented by a huge influx of northern and eastern birds in winter. Flocks arrive throughout October and many hundreds, or even thousands, can be seen from a single well-sited watchpoint heading westwards early in the morning.

p.266 **Brambling** *Fringilla montifringilla*

Description: 14–15 cm (5½–6 in). Similar in shape and behaviour to Chaffinch, but with quite distinct plumage. Summer male has *black head and back, orange chin and underparts*, bold orange areas in wing, and *white rump*; in winter, black head and back boldly mottled with buff, creating scaly effect. Female has brown cap, grey nape, streaked black and brown upperparts, and orange

p.267 **Goldfinch** *Carduelis carduelis*

Description: 11.5–12.5 cm (4½–5 in). A dainty, well-marked finch with *crimson face and black and yellow wings*. Upperparts brown with black cap and crimson and white face. Underparts warm buff. The yellow in black wings is obvious both at rest and in flight. Juvenile lacks face pattern, but not yellow and black wings. Gregarious, forming single-species flocks.

Voice: A sweet tinkling warble uttered in a hurry.

Habitat: Woodland margins, orchards, groves, gardens, wasteland with good growth of thistles.

Breeding: Four to seven black-spotted, blue eggs laid in neat little cup placed at outer edge of bush or shrub. Incubation 13–14 days, by female.

Range: Common and locally abundant resident right across Europe to southern Scandinavia, eastwards to central Siberia and southwards to eastern Mediterranean, Iran and Himalayas. Only northernmost Finnish and Siberian birds are migrants.

Known as 'charms', flocks of Goldfinches roam wasteland and hedgerows feeding on weed seeds on the ground and on those of thistles that are extracted by their thin (for a finch) tweezer-like bills. Just occasionally an individual will be caught by thistle burrs and be unable to escape.

p.268 **Citril Finch** *Serinus citrinella*

Description: 12 cm (4½ in). A Canary-like finch. Male has *yellow face and grey hind crown* and nape, bold yellow bar in wing, and yellow rump and breast. Female similar, but with yellow on head confined to bib and forehead. Similar to related Serin, but never as streaked or as yellow in wing.

Voice: Sings in aerial display like Serin uttering musical twitter; call a *tsoo-oo* and a hard *twit*.

Habitat: Open rocky areas at or above tree line in high mountains; also in open lowlands in Corsica.

Breeding: Four to five reddish-speckled, pale-blue
eggs laid in neat cup placed high in a tree.
Incubation 13–14 days, by female alone.

Range: Resident, European endemic in mountains
of central and northern Spain, France,
Switzerland and Austria. Descends to
lowlands in winter. Also in Corsica and
Sardinia.

Birds resident in Corsica, Sardinia, Elba
and Capraia are placed in the separate
subspecies *S. c. corsicana*. They differ in
coloration, size, calls and in regularly
breeding among both mountains and
lowlands, despite the presence of their close
relative and competitor the Serin. The case
for regarding these Mediterranean island
populations as a separate species is hotly
debated.

---

p.268 **Siskin** *Carduelis spinus*

Description: 11.5–12.5 cm (4½–5 in). Male yellow and
black, heavily streaked above with *black cap
and bib*. White underparts heavily streaked
black, and black wings show yellow
wingbar and broad yellow tips to tertials.
Female similar, but with less yellow on face
and lacking black bib. Essentially arboreal,
feeding acrobatically like a tit.

Voice: A wheezing *tsu tsu-weet*; song a musical
twitter terminating in a buzz.

Habitat: Breeds among conifers of northern boreal
forests and among mountain forests to
south, with clear preference for spruce. In
winter often near water with good growth
of alders.

Breeding: Three to five pale-blue, reddish-speckled
eggs laid in nest of twigs lined with grasses
and placed at end of high conifer branch.
Incubation 11–14 days, by female.

Range: Summer visitor or resident in northern and
eastern Europe, and winter visitor to south
and west. Breeds from Scotland eastwards
through Scandinavia and northern Russia to
Japan; also among high mountains of
Europe to Caucasus. Winters in Europe,
Japan and China.

Breeding: Four to five pale-blue, speckled-reddish eggs laid in cup placed in fork of a tree. Incubation 10–13 days, by female.

Range: Circumpolar, breeding from Ireland and Britain eastwards to Scandinavia, through boreal Russia to Bering Straits and across Alaska and northern Canada to Greenland Winters southwards including most of temperate Europe from France eastwards. Absent from Mediterranean.

The redpoll complex is nothing less than that: a fascinating problem for the taxonomist, a headache for the ordinary birder. In the Common Redpoll several well marked subspecies include the small dark Lesser Redpoll (*C. f. cabaret*) of Britain, Ireland and central European mountains; th Mealy Redpoll (*C. f. flammea*) of northern Europe, which is larger and much paler; an the Greenland Redpoll (*C. f. rostrata*) of Greenland, which is much larger, but as da as *cabaret*. Compare with Arctic Redpoll, which is accorded specific status.

---

p.269 **Arctic Redpoll** *Carduelis hornemanni*

Description: 12–13 cm (4½–5 in). Similar to Common Redpoll, but *much paler* with greyish-buff, heavily streaked upperparts, dark eye-stripe, red cap, small black bib, white wingbar and, significantly, *bold white rump Underparts white,* with fine streaking confined to flanks. Behaviour much the same as Common Redpoll.

Voice: Similar nasal quality as Common Redpoll

Habitat: Dwarf vegetation of birch and willow among open tundra in summer; more extensive birch and alder stands in winter.

Breeding: Four to five pale-blue, reddish-speckled eggs laid in cup of twigs and roots placed on or near the ground among vegetation o rocks. Incubation 11–12 days, by female alone.

Range: Northern tundra replacement of Common Redpoll. Circumpolar from northernmost Scandinavia across northern Siberia, Alask and Canada to Greenland. One of the mos

northerly breeding passerines in the world. Erratic winter visitor southwards.

Great care should be taken in identifying this species away from its Arctic breeding grounds, as the Mealy subspecies of the Common Redpoll *C. f. flammea* of northern Europe is also considerably paler than other subspecies of that bird. The white rump is diagnostic, though Mealy Redpoll often shows a distinctly pale rump.

p.271 **Two-barred Crossbill** *Loxia leucoptera*

Description: 14–15 cm (5½–6 in). Similar to other crossbills. Male red, with *relatively thin crossed bill*, and black wings marked by *bold, double, white bar*. Female greenish with similar bill and wing markings. The white wingbars would make for relatively straightforward identification were it not that some first-winter male and juvenile Common Crossbills also show this feature. Fortunately, Two-barred also shows *white tips to tertials* (not prominent in first-winter and juveniles) which, coupled with thinner bill, aid identification.

Voice: A clear *chiff-chiff*, less metallic than Common Crossbill.

Habitat: Conifer forests, especially of larch.

Breeding: Four pale-blue, purple-spotted eggs laid in cup placed on conifer branch. Incubation 14–15 days, by female alone.

Range: Circumpolar in boreal zone from eastern Finland across Siberia and from Alaska across northern Canada. Largely resident; vagrant elsewhere.

The Finnish population averages some 500 pairs, but may be substantially larger during good seasons. At such times birds may breed in Norway and Sweden, and exceptionally they have done so in Germany. Like the Common Crossbill, numbers sometimes erupt south and west, mostly coinciding with that species, and may reach Britain, where there are over 130 records.

Common Crossbills cannot be taken as a
increase in actual numbers. Following an
irruption in 1982, during which over 10
individuals were reported, breeding took
place in north and east England from 19
to 1985.

---

p.272 **Trumpeter Finch** *Bucanetes githagineus*

Description: 13–14 cm (5–5½ in). A small, large-
headed desert finch, with *large stubby bil*
Male *pinkish around face, breast and on fol
wing,* with bold red bill and rump. Fem
brown above and buff below, with plain
featureless head, warm-yellow bill, and
more than a *pink flush in folded wing.* Th
large head and bill on a tiny bird are be
features.

Voice: High-pitched nasal buzzing.

Habitat: Bare, arid wastes, dry gullies, semi-deser

Breeding: Four to six pale-blue, lightly speckled eg
laid in cup placed in rock crevice or bene
a stone. Incubation 11–14 days, by fema
alone.

Range: Breeding resident across northern Sahara
Middle East. Colonized southern Spain i
the 1960s.

The Trumpeter Finch colonized the area
Almeria in southern Spain where it foun
natural home in a dry valley used to mak
'paella westerns'. Its subsequent
wanderings northwards, as far as Britain,
are unlikely to encounter similar conditi
and most vagrants occur on sandy beache

---

p.272 **Common Rosefinch** *Carpodacus erythrin*

Description: 14–15 cm (5½–6 in). Male streaked bro
and buff above, white below, marked by
reddish head and breast, pink rump and
double pinkish wingbar. Female streake
buffy above, white below, with double
wingbar and *plain featureless face* that is
distinct from well-marked face of Hous
Sparrow. Both sexes show clear silvery-
white bill.

Voice: Call a clear *tu-ick*; song consists of several piping notes.

Habitat: Swampy wetlands and ditches with bushes and thickets; also around upland villages in Turkey and elsewhere.

Breeding: Four to five blue eggs, lightly spotted and streaked brown, laid in cup placed low in bush. Incubation 12–14 days, by female alone.

Range: Summer visitor from southern Norway and Baltic coasts to eastern Germany and Denmark, and eastwards across Russia to Pacific. Also in Turkey, Caucasus, Himalayas and western China. Winters in India and eastern China. Vagrant and spreading westwards.

This species is now so regular in Britain that it is regarded as a local, rather than a national, rarity; it has bred regularly in Scotland since 1982 and in England since 1992. It is still highly localized, but capable of establishing itself virtually anywhere in the country.

p.272 **Snow Finch** *Montifringilla nivalis*

Description: 17–19 cm (6½–7½ in). Brown streaked upperparts, with *plain grey head marked* only by *small black bib*, bold black and white wings, and broad white margins to black tail. In flight, *whole inner wing white* contrasting with mainly black primaries and brown back. Bill black in summer, yellow in winter.

Voice: Repeated *sitti-char*; a nasal *tsweek*.

Habitat: Bare rocky slopes; mountain slopes over 2,000 m (6,000 ft), though rather lower in winter.

Breeding: Four to five white eggs laid in cup placed in hole in rock or building. Incubation 13–14 days, by both sexes.

Range: Resident of highest mountain slopes in northern Spain, Pyrenees, Alps, central Italy, locally in former Yugoslavia and Greece eastwards through Turkey and Caucasus to central Siberia. Not a true migrant; relatively few records away from mountains.

Along with the Alpine Accentor, this is
of the elusive, high-altitude species of
Europe, but it is regularly seen in snow-
areas among ski resorts and along roadsi
For the sight of two high-value species i
seems a small price to pay to take a skiin
holiday and not bother with hiring the g
or setting foot on the snow.

---

p.273 **Pine Grosbeak** *Pinicola enucleator*

Description: 20–22 cm (8–8½ in). A small to mediun
sized, crossbill-like bird, marked by *dir*
pink plumage in male, with *double white*
wingbar on black wings. Pinkish confine
to head, breast, flanks and rump. Female
has *orange wash* rather than pink of male
Heavy, conical, uncrossed bill.

Voice: Pleasant, liquid *tee-tu, tee-tee-tu* calls; son,
rich warble.

Habitat: Conifer forests as well as mixed woodlan
with birches.

Breeding: Three to four greenish-blue eggs, spotte
and blotched black, laid in cup of twigs
placed in conifer or birch. Incubation
13–14 days, by female alone.

Range: Circumpolar resident in boreal zone from
mountains of Scandinavia across Russia a
Siberia to Alaska and northern Canada; a
southwards through Rocky Mountains.
Wanders a little in winter, but remains
within conifers.

Although it will visit gardens in villages
and towns in winter to feed on berries, th
is a highly conservative species that is
decidedly restricted to conifer forests. It
and does take a wide variety of foods
including birch and juniper seeds, but on
when conifers are available nearby.

---

p.273 **Bullfinch** *Pyrrhula pyrrhula*

Description: 14–15 cm (5½–6 in). Decidedly solitary,
woodland finch. Chunky, thickset bird
marked by short, but *powerfully deep bill*.
Male grey above, with black cap, wings a

tail broken by square-cut *white rump*. Underparts *vivid pink*. Female shares same overall pattern, but *vinous-pink* above, pinky buff below.

Voice: A soft *heu*; poor disjointed song.

Habitat: Woods, hedgerows, scrub, orchards, thickets and, in eastern Europe, conifer forests among hills.

Breeding: Four to five pale-blue eggs, lightly spotted black, laid on twiggy nest placed in dense bush. Incubation 12–14 days, by female alone.

Range: Widespread through most of Europe, breeding across Palearctic from northern Iberia to Scandinavia, Turkey and eastwards across boreal Siberia to Kamchatka. Some winter movements take birds to areas around Mediterranean, where they do not breed.

This is a decidedly shy species found solitarily or, more often, in pairs. It is loath to fly long distances away from cover. It depends largely on the crop of ash seeds in western Europe, and when this food source runs out in late winter it regularly resorts to the fruit buds of orchards; as a result it is widely regarded as a pest.

p.273 **Hawfinch** *Coccothraustes coccothraustes*

Description: 16–17 cm (6½ in). Chunky, thickset finch that is considerably larger than its measurements suggest due to its extremely *short tail*. Chestnut-brown above, paler pinkish chestnut below, marked by black wings with single, *broad, white wingbar*, black face, and *enormous, thick and powerful silvery bill*. Short tail tipped white. In flight, huge white wingbar shows especially across underwing. Frequently sits stock still among large trees and easily overlooked.

Voice: A metallic Robin-like *tic*.

Habitat: Mature deciduous woodland, parks with both deciduous and coniferous trees, groves and orchards.

Breeding: Five pale blue-green eggs, lightly spotted black, laid in shallow nest of twigs placed on branch of tree. Incubation 9–14 days, mainly by female.

Range: Widespread and mainly resident over muc of Europe, though only winter visitor to non-wooded areas of western Mediterranean. Extends eastwards throug Russia and Siberia to Kamchatka. Central and eastern Asiatic birds migrate to Japan and northern China.

The huge bill of this species can crack the hardest of seed cases, including those of nuts, cherries and olives, but it is ill-adapted to opening the smaller, softer seed preferred by other finches and may take tw or three times as long to de-husk them.

BUNTINGS (EMBERIZIDAE)

324 species; worldwide fourteen species breed in Europe. Buntings are small, predominantly ground-dwelling birds, wit stout seed-eating bills like the finches. The do, however, take a wider variety of food than those birds and have not developed th specialized bills shown by many species of finch. Most are dependent on grass seeds which are crushed to extract the kernel, bu will also take small invertebrates and fruit available. They inhabit a wide variety of lan forms from deserts to marshes and woodlan to bare mountains, although most are foun in park-like landscapes of groves, orchards and along hedgerows. Though found in bot the Old and New Worlds, the largest varie of both genera and species occupies the latter. These are mainly chubby species wit rounded wings and longish tails. The sexes are the same size, but most species differ in plumage, especially on the head. Males generally have boldly patterned heads whil females, being more uniform, present serio identification problems. Both sexes tend to have white outer-tail feathers. Nests are cup constructed by the female near the ground and she alone performs the incubation, though males join in feeding the young.

p.274 **Lapland Bunting** *Calcarius lapponicus*

Description: 14–16 cm (5½–6½ in). Summer male streaked brown, black and buff above, with *black head and breast broken by bold white supercilium* and backed by *chestnut nape.* Black streaking lines flanks. Female, winter male and juvenile similar, with streaked upperparts and buffy, black-streaked breast and flanks. A clear-cut, *pale central crown-stripe,* dark lateral crown-stripes and pale supercilium create distinctive head pattern. A reduced chestnut nape remains a useful feature, as is black-tipped yellow bill.

Voice: A rolling *tititick,* and a *teeleeoo* of alarm; song a pleasant jingle uttered in flight.

Habitat: Bare mountain slopes and open tundra. In winter along bare coastlines, saltings and among bare inland hills and moors.

Breeding: Five to six greenish, brown-mottled eggs laid in cup placed beneath large rock or among low vegetation. Incubation 11–13 days, by female alone.

Range: Circumpolar summer visitor, from Scandinavian mountains across tundra Siberia to Alaska, northern Canada and Greenland. Winters across central Siberia south of boreal forests and across central North America; in Europe winters along North Sea coasts and from Hungary eastwards.

Known as the Lapland Longspur in North America, this is an Arctic breeder that must be sought by most birders during the winter. It feeds on the ground in flocks and is often difficult to see. The similarity between its winter plumages and the female Reed Bunting may lead to its being overlooked.

p.275 **Snow Bunting** *Plectrophenax nivalis*

Description: 16–17 cm (6½ in). Summer male is unmistakable *white bird marked by black wings and tail.* Female and winter male warm buff above, heavily streaked on back, and white below with warm-buff wash over head, breast and flanks. Some *white always*

shows *in wing* and, in flight, flocks resembl
pieces of paper blowing in the wind.

Voice: A loud *sweep*; song is high-pitched warbl

Habitat: Bare mountain scrub and plateaux, open
tundra; in winter frequents open hills ar
bare shorelines, often of shingle.

Breeding: Four to six pale-blue, reddish-spotted eg
laid in cup beneath rock. Incubation 10-
days, by female alone.

Range: Circumpolar summer visitor, from
Scandinavian mountains across Siberian
tundra, Alaska and northern Canada to
Greenland. Resident in Iceland. Winters
broad swathe south of boreal forests in b
continents; in Europe winters in Scotlan
along North Sea coasts and in a belt
extending eastwards from Sweden,
Denmark and central Europe.

In winter plumage these birds merge we
with scantily vegetated shorelines and ca
be easily overlooked until they fly. Nortl
Sea coasts also hold wintering Lapland
Buntings and Shore Larks, all highly
sought Arctic breeding species.

p.276 **Yellowhammer** *Emberiza citrinella*

Description: 16–17 cm (6½ in). Distinctly more yellow
than any other bunting. Male has *yellow h*
with narrow black markings on crown an
ear coverts. Upperparts *rich chestnut* and
heavily streaked; underparts yellow, with
chestnut streaks along flanks. Female dull
and less yellow, with pronounced dark cro
and ear-covert outline, and clear moustacl
streak, all on pale-yellow background. Bo
sexes show clear *rusty rump*.

Voice: Familiarly rendered 'little-bit-of-bread-
and-no-cheese' with the accent on the
'cheese'.

Habitat: Heaths, scrub, hedgerows, woodland
margins and, in winter, particularly amc
stubble fields and coastal marshes.

Breeding: Three to four purple-blotched, white eg
laid in neat cup placed on or near the
ground among bushes. Incubation 11–1
days, by female alone.

Range: Widespread resident across temperate Europe from France to Scandinavia and Greece, eastwards to central Siberia. Summer visitor to extreme north; winter visitor to northern Iberia and Mediterranean.

This is only a short-distance migrant with birds that winter in the Mediterranean, travelling no more than a few hundred kilometres from the more southerly parts of the species range. Most Yellowhammers are resident, or move only short distances to seek a plentiful food supply.

p.276 **Cirl Bunting** *Emberiza cirlus*

Description: 15.5–16.5 cm (6–6½ in). A well-marked bunting. Male black-streaked chestnut above, marked by bold, and distinctive *black and yellow head pattern*. Underparts yellow, with broad *chestnut streaks* on breast and flanks. Female very similar to female Yellowhammer, but with less yellow on more boldly marked and clear-cut facial pattern. Both sexes lack rusty rump of Yellowhammer.

Voice: Song a quick rattle, like a Lesser Whitethroat, that ends abruptly and lacks terminal flourish. Call a thin *sip* or *sissi-sissi-sip*.

Habitat: Hedgerows, copses, orchards, groves and, in winter, among open fields.

Breeding: Three to four white, black-speckled eggs laid in cup placed on or near the ground in thick bush. Incubation 11–13 days, by female.

Range: Resident endemic of Western Palearctic. In most countries bordering northern shores of Mediterranean, as well as Morocco to Tunisia, extending northwards through France to southwest England and eastwards to Turkey.

The decline of this species in England, paralleled in northern France, has been attributed to climatic change and to changes in agriculture. It is now confined to southern Devon where warm summers and mild winters seem best suited to its lifestyle.

p.278 **Rock Bunting** *Emberiza cia*

Description: 15–16.5 cm (6–6½ in). Adult summer ma
has grey head marked by *white supercilium
and black lateral crown-stripes,* with black
eye-stripe joining black moustachial strip
to enclose ear coverts. Upperparts streaked
black on warm orange-brown; underparts
orange-brown. Female, winter male and
juvenile, all less clear-cut versions of
summer male, with grey head and black-
enclosed ear coverts prominent.

Voice: Song a *zi-zi-zi-zi-zir*; call a thin *zit*.

Habitat: Well-vegetated, rocky upland slopes, wit
trees, olive groves and rock-walled fields.

Breeding: Four to six pale-grey, black-scrawled eggs
laid in neat cup placed among rocks or in
base of bush. Incubation 12–13 days, by
female alone.

Range: Resident, with some local winter
movements, from Iberia across southern
Europe to Turkey, Caucasus and central-
southern Siberia. Also localized summer
visitor to western Germany, Hungary, and
mountains of Romania.

The Rock Bunting colonized both Hunga
and the former Czechoslovakia during the
mid-twentieth century, and since 1967 it
also colonized and spread in Israel. Howev
it has declined in Germany, mainly as a
result of reafforestation schemes. Elsewher
it is no more than a vagrant northwards as
far as Britain, where there are six records.

p.277 **Ortolan Bunting** *Emberiza hortulana*

Description: 15.5–16.5 cm (6–6½ in). In all plumages
upperparts rufous-brown streaked black,
underparts orange. Summer male has *grey-
green head and breast,* brighter green in no
breeding males and virtually brown in
first-year birds, with *yellowish moustachial
streak and bib.* Female similar to first-year
male, both showing streaking on throat a
breast. All plumages have distinctly *pink
bill.* Can be confused with similarly pink
billed Cretzschmar's Bunting.

Voice: A buzzing, melodious song of six to eight notes; call a thin *tsee-ip*.

Habitat: Open, dry countryside from stony hillsides to cultivated lowlands. In winter frequents dry, sparsely vegetated plains and semi-deserts; in autumn, regular on plough.

Breeding: Four to six grey-spotted, pale-blue eggs laid in cup of grasses on or near the ground. Incubation 11–14 days, by female alone.

Range: Summer visitor to much of Continental Europe, from Iberia across southern France to Sweden, Finland and eastwards to central Siberia; also through Italy and Balkans to Turkey and northern Iran. Winters across Sahelian Africa. Regular long-distance migrant across most of Europe in variable numbers, and a regular, if scarce, off-course migrant elsewhere.

Ortolan Bunting is one of a species pair; the other is the similarly pink-billed Cretzschmar's Bunting, which occurs alongside Ortolan in Greece. The obvious head pattern differences (Ortolan with yellow on green, Cretzschmar's with orange on grey) may be far from clear in the field in any plumage other than that of adult breeding males. However, the Ortolan has narrow chestnut fringes, lacking pale tips, to the tertials.

p.277 **Cretzschmar's Bunting** *Emberiza caesia*

Description: 15–16.5 cm (6–6½ in). In all plumages, upperparts chestnut, clearly streaked black, with broad chestnut margins to *pale-tipped tertials*. Adult male has pale-grey head, marked by *pale-orange moustachial streak and bib,* and *rufous-orange underparts*. Adult female has warmer-grey head, with paler-orange markings; non-breeding male has virtually buffy head with even paler markings. Easily confused with similarly pink-billed Ortolan.

Voice: Song, several clear notes with final note on a different pitch, *twee-twee-twee-tee*; call a loud *tyip*.

Habitat: Dry, rocky hillsides with scattered bushes. Regularly sings from telegraph wires.

Breeding: Four to six blue-grey speckled-black egg,
laid in cup on the ground among
vegetation. Incubation 12–14 days, by
female, though male may help.

Range: Western Palearctic endemic; summer
visitor to Greece, Turkey, Cyprus and
eastern Mediterranean coasts. Winters i
Sudan and Ethiopia.

The broad-front migration of this specie
brings large numbers of birds to Cyprus
where it also breeds, in both spring and
autumn. It also accounts for vagrancy
northwards as far as Britain, where it ha
occurred twice in late spring.

p.277 **Cinereous Bunting** *Emberiza cineracea*

Description: 16–17 cm (6½ in). Typical bunting, ma
in summer male by *bright greenish-yellow
wash* over otherwise plain head, most
marked on chin. Upperparts brownish-
with line of *white-margined wing coverts.*
Female with plain face and brown strea
chin and back. Winter male has greenis
yellow chin and olive head. *Plain face, p
eye-ring and silver bill* in all plumages.

Voice: Harsh *zee zee-zee-zee-zaa* similar to Ortol

Habitat: Scrub-covered rocky uplands to tree-lin

Breeding: Three to six brown-blotched blue eggs
in a cup hidden against a rock. Incubati
and roles of sexes unknown.

Range: Breeds western Turkey and offshore Gre
islands of Lesbos and Chios. Also in
southeastern Turkey adjacent to Syrian
border. Winters on coasts of Red Sea.

Decidedly scarce Western Palearctic
endemic that passes through Cyprus on
migration, but is otherwise seldom seen
away from Lesbos, where most birders a
it to their European list.

p.275 **Rustic Bunting** *Emberiza rustica*

Description: 14–15 cm (5½–6 in). A well-marked
bunting with a *distinctive crest.* Summer

male chestnut and black, with *bright-chestnut collar,* distinctive, broadly striped *black and white head* pattern, and raised crest at rear of crown. Underparts white with *chestnut breast-band and flank-streaks.* Winter male, female and juvenile have brown and buff, not black and white, head patterns, but still show *distinct crest and chestnut flank-streaks.* Bill is pale-horn coloured.

Voice: Call a sharp *tic* or *tsip,* repeated.

Habitat: Various wetland habitats among conifer forests; well-vegetated marshy margins, streamside thickets.

Breeding: Four to five pale-blue eggs, speckled grey-brown, laid in cup on or near the ground among dense vegetation. Incubation 12–13 days, by female alone.

Range: Summer visitor to boreal zone from Scandinavia to Bering Straits. Spreading westwards. Winters in Japan and eastern China.

In view of the decidedly eastward migrations of this species, it is a wonder that it is such a regular vagrant westwards as far as Britain, where it averages almost ten records a year. Scandinavian birds move directly eastwards in autumn following their presumed colonization route over the boreal forests before heading southwards to their winter quarters.

---

p.275 **Little Bunting** *Emberiza pusilla*

Description: 13–14 cm (5–5½ in). Smallest European bunting marked by chestnut- and black-streaked upperparts and finely streaked white underparts. Best features are pale *coronal stripe* and black-bordered, rich *maroon-chestnut ear coverts* and supercilium. Facial colouring may be subdued in juveniles, but remains a good feature.

Voice: A Robin-like *tic;* song a musical twitter.

Habitat: Marshy tundra, forest wetlands and marshy birch and alder woods.

Breeding: Four to five black-scrawled, pale-green eggs laid in cup on the ground among vegetation. Incubation 11–12 days, by both sexes.

Range: Summer visitor from extreme north of Norway and Finland across tundra and northern boreal zone of Russia and Siber Bering Straits. Winters in Korea and Ch

The westward colonization by this spec culminated in its appearance as a Europ breeding bird in Finland in 1935. It als spread to the Kola Peninsula about the same time and subsequently reached Norway and finally Sweden. Despite its eastward migration it is a regular vagra westwards to Holland and Britain.

---

p.278　**Reed Bunting** *Emberiza schoeniclus*

Description: 14–16 cm (5½–6½ in). Summer male h *black head and throat marked by prominent white moustachial stripe* and white collar. Upperparts streaked chestnut and blac underparts white, lightly streaked alon flanks. Winter male, female and juveni lack black head and have well-marked supercilium, enclosed ear coverts and prominent *moustachial streak;* underpart streaked on breast and flanks.

Voice: Song, several deliberate notes ending i flourish; call a rasping *tseep.*

Habitat: Reed-beds, marshy margins and, in wir fields and gardens.

Breeding: Four to five olive-grey eggs, streaked ar spotted black, laid in cup among veget near the ground. Incubation 12–14 day by female, though male will sometimes cover the eggs without properly incubating.

Range: Common resident, breeding across temperate and northern Europe, but decidedly local in countries bordering Mediterranean. Extends eastwards acro whole of Siberia to Japan and Kamchat Birds from Scandinavia eastwards are summer visitors, some making lengthy migrations as far as China. Widespread Mediterranean at this season.

The winter male, and particularly femal juvenile, Reed Buntings are easily confu

with the similar-plumaged Lapland, Rustic,
Yellow-breasted and even rarer buntings.

---

p.279 **Yellow-breasted Bunting** *Emberiza aureola*

Description: 13.5–14.5 cm (5½ in). Summer male rich
rufous-brown from crown to back, with
black face, and *yellow and rufous-brown
breast-bands.* Rufous-brown wings show
broad and narrow, white wingbars.
Underparts bright yellow with a few
rufous-brown flank-streaks. All other
plumages lack black face and breast-bands,
but are yellow or yellowish below, with
less prominent wingbars. Head pattern
brown and buff with clear-cut ear-covert
box and prominent supercilium.

Voice: Call a sharp *tic*; song a fast warble.

Habitat: Damp thickets of birch and willow and
overgrown waterside meadows; also found
in dry scrub and grassland.

Breeding: Four to five black-spotted, pale-grey eggs
laid in cup placed low in bush. Incubation
13–14 days, by both sexes.

Range: Summer visitor from central Finland
eastwards through boreal zone to
Kamchatka; regular vagrant westward.
Winters in eastern China and Southeast Asia.

The Yellow-breasted Bunting increased
rapidly in Finland after its first colonization
in the 1920s. Some 300 pairs now breed,
following influxes in the early 1960s and
mid-1970s. It is still a highly sought after
species that even the best spots do not give
up easily.

---

p.279 **Black-headed Bunting**
Emberiza melanocephala

Description: 16–17 cm (6½ in). Male has *bright yellow
below,* extending to chin and nape. *Black cap*
extends below eye to cover ear coverts. Lower
nape, back and rump *warm chestnut,* wings
black with whitish margins. Female has grey
upperparts, with *plain unmarked head,* a row
of dark spots across wing (like a Tawny

Pipit), and unstreaked underparts marked
wash of yellow on breast and undertail.

Voice: Call a hard *zit*; song a fast pleasant warb

Habitat: Open scrub, bushes, hedgerows, groves,
orchards and gardens.

Breeding: Four to five brown-speckled, pale-blue e
laid in cup of grasses placed in bush.
Incubation about 14 days, by female alo

Range: Virtually endemic summer visitor to
Western Palearctic and southeast Europe
from Greece and Black Sea coasts
westwards along coasts of former
Yugoslavia to a few regions of Italy; also
eastwards through Turkey and Middle E
Winters in India and Pakistan.

This is a late arrival in spring, but it is t
widespread and common along roadside
throughout Greece. Vagrants across Eur
must be treated with great care as the
possibility of escape from captivity is hi

---

p.277 **Corn Bunting** *Miliaria calandra*

Description: 17–18.5 cm (6½–7 in). Sexes similar and
resembling undistinguished female
buntings of other species. Upperparts
streaked buff and brown; underparts pal
and *heavily streaked*. Best distinguished b
tubby shape; short, *thick neck hunched int
shoulders,* and trailing legs in flight.

Voice: An accelerating rattle likened to sound
produced by shaking a bunch of keys; ca
harsh *dzip*.

Habitat: Arable fields, grasslands, hedgerows, step

Breeding: Four to six grey-spotted, white eggs laic
cup of grasses hidden on the ground.
Incubation 12–14 days, by female alone

Range: Widespread resident across southern and
temperate Europe and southernmost
Scandinavia, eastwards across southern
Russia to Turkey and Middle East.

The Corn Bunting is decidedly local in
distribution, being absent in some appare
suitable areas. In parts of southern Europe
is locally abundant, with birds singing fro
virtually every telegraph post.

Part III

Appendices

681

LIST OF ACCIDENTAL SPECIES

Accidentals are birds that have strayed from their normal breeding or wintering areas or migration routes and have occurred in Europe at least once, but less than annually during the last 50 years. This list, arranged in taxonomic order, includes birds, such as Pallas's Sandgrouse, which once were more common but are now rare vagrants.

Accidentals reaching Europe come from four main sources: oceanic islands, mainly in the Atlantic (O); North America (NA); Asia (As); and Africa (Af). 'New' birds continue to arrive from North America and Asia, but the combined barriers of the Sahara and the Mediterranean make the influx from Africa rather small.

Pied-billed Grebe *Podilymbus podiceps* (NA)
Wandering Albatross *Diomedea exulans* (O)
Southern Giant Petrel *Macronectes giganteus* (O)
Fea's Petrel *Pterodroma feae* (O)
Black-capped Petrel *Pterodroma hasitata* (O)
Bulwer's Petrel *Bulweria bulwerii* (O)
Madeiran Storm-petrel *Oceanodroma castro* (O)
Swinhoe's Storm-petrel *Oceanodroma monorhis* (O)
Double-crested Cormorant *Phalacrocorax auritus* (NA)
American Bittern *Botaurus lentiginosus* (NA)
Least Bittern *Ixobrychus exilis* (NA)
Green Heron *Butorides virescens* (NA)
Western Reef Heron *Egretta gularis* (Af)
Bald Ibis *Geronticus eremita* (Af/As)
Lesser Flamingo *Phoenicopterus minor* (Af)
Snow Goose *Anser caerulescens* (NA)
American Wigeon *Anas americana* (NA)
Falcated Duck *Anas falcata* (As)
Black Duck *Anas rubripes* (NA)
Blue-winged Teal *Anas discors* (NA)
Lesser Scaup *Aythya affinis* (NA)
Ring-necked Duck *Aythya collaris* (NA)
Spectacled Eider *Somateria fischeri* (As)
Bufflehead *Bucephala albeola* (NA)
Bald Eagle *Haliaeetus leucocephalus* (NA)
American Kestrel *Falco sparverius* (NA)

Sora Rail *Porzana carolina* (NA)
Allen's Gallinule *Porphyrula alleni* (Af)
American Purple Gallinule *Porphyrula*
    martinica (NA)
American Coot *Fulica americana* (NA)
Sandhill Crane *Grus canadensis* (NA)
Houbara Bustard *Chlamydotis undulata* (A
Oriental Pratincole *Glareola maldivarum*
    (As)
Semi-palmated Plover *Charadrius*
    semipalmatus (NA)
Killdeer *Charadrius vociferus* (NA)
Lesser Sand Plover *Charadrius mongolus* (A
Greater Sand Plover *Charadrius leschenau*
    (As)
Caspian Plover *Charadrius asiaticus* (As)
White-tailed Plover *Chettusia leucura* (As
Great Knot *Calidris tenuirostris* (As)
Semi-palmated Sandpiper *Calidris pusill*
    (NA)
Western Sandpiper *Calidris mauri* (NA)
Red-necked Stint *Calidris ruficollis* (As)
Long-toed Stint *Calidris subminuta* (As)
Least Sandpiper *Calidris minutilla* (NA)
White-rumped Sandpiper *Calidris fuscic*
    (NA)
Baird's Sandpiper *Calidris bairdii* (NA)
Sharp-tailed Sandpiper *Calidris acuminat*
    (As/NA)
Stilt Sandpiper *Micropalama himantopus*
    (NA)
Buff-breasted Sandpiper *Tryngites*
    subruficollis (NA)
Short-billed Dowitcher *Limnodromus gris*
    (NA)
Long-billed Dowitcher *Limnodromus*
    scolopaceus (NA)
Hudsonian Godwit *Limosa haemastica* (N
Little Whimbrel *Numenius minutus* (As)
Upland Sandpiper *Bartramia longicauda*
    (NA)
Greater Yellowlegs *Tringa melanoleuca* (N
Lesser Yellowlegs *Tringa flavipes* (NA)
Solitary Sandpiper *Tringa solitaria* (NA)
Spotted Sandpiper *Actitis macularia* (NA
Grey-tailed Tatler *Heteroscelus brevipes* (A
Willet *Catoptrophorus semipalmatus* (NA)
Great Black-headed Gull *Larus ichthyaet*
    (As)

Laughing Gull *Larus atricilla* (NA)
Franklin's Gull *Larus pipixcan* (NA)
Bonaparte's Gull *Larus philadelphia* (NA)
Grey-headed Gull *Larus cirrocephalus* (Af)
Royal Tern *Sterna maxima* (NA/Af)
Elegant Tern *Sterna elegans* (NA)
Aleutian Tern *Sterna aleutica* (NA)
Forster's Tern *Sterna forsteri* (NA)
Bridled Tern *Sterna anaethetus* (O)
Sooty Tern *Sterna fuscata* (O)
Least Tern *Sterna antillarum* (NA)
Brown Noddy *Anous stolidus* (O)
Ancient Murrelet *Synthliboramphus antiquus*
  (NA)
Spotted Sandgrouse *Pterocles senegallus* (Af)
Pallas's Sandgrouse *Syrrhaptes paradoxus* (As)
Rufous Turtle Dove *Streptopelia orientalis*
  (As)
Mourning Dove *Zenaida macroura* (Af)
Black-billed Cuckoo *Coccyzus*
  erythrophthalmus (NA)
Yellow-billed Cuckoo *Coccyzus americanus*
  (NA)
Marsh Owl *Asio capensis* (Af)
Egyptian Nightjar *Caprimulgus aegyptius* (Af)
Common Nighthawk *Chordeiles minor* (NA)
Chimney Swift *Chaetura pelagica* (NA)
White-throated Needletail *Hirundapus*
  caudacutus (As)
Pacific Swift *Apus pacificus* (As)
Little Swift *Apus affinis* (Af)
Pied Kingfisher *Ceryle rudis* (Af/As)
Belted Kingfisher *Ceryle alcyon* (NA)
Blue-cheeked Bee-eater *Merops superciliosus*
  (Af/As)
Northern Flicker *Colaptes auratus* (NA)
Yellow-bellied Sapsucker *Sphyrapicus varius*
  (NA)
Acadian Flycatcher *Empidonax virescens* (NA)
Eastern Phoebe *Sayornis phoebe* (NA)
Tree Swallow *Tachycineta bicolor* (NA)
Cliff Swallow *Hirundo pyrrhonota* (NA)
Bar-tailed Desert Lark *Ammomanes cincturus*
  (Af/As)
Hoopoe Lark *Alaemon alaudipes* (Af/As)
Bimaculated Lark *Melanocorypha bimaculata*
  (As)
White-winged Lark *Melanocorypha leucoptera*
  (As)

Black Lark *Melanocorypha yeltoniensis* (A
Blyth's Pipit *Anthus godlewskii* (As)
Olive-backed Pipit *Anthus hodgsoni* (As)
Pechora Pipit *Anthus gustavi* (As)
Buff-bellied Pipit *Anthus rubescens* (NA)
Northern Mockingbird *Mimus polyglotto*
   (NA)
Brown Thrasher *Toxostoma rufum* (NA)
Grey Catbird *Dumetella carolinensis* (NA
Siberian Accentor *Prunella montanella* (*
Siberian Rubythroat *Luscinia calliope* (A
Siberian Blue Robin *Luscinia cyane* (As)
White-throated Robin *Irania gutturalis*
Moussier's Redstart *Phoenicurus moussier*
   (Af)
Desert Wheatear *Oenanthe deserti* (Af)
White-crowned Black Wheatear *Oenan*
   leucopyga (Af/As)
White's Thrush *Zoothera dauma* (As)
Siberian Thrush *Zoothera sibirica* (As)
Varied Thrush *Zoothera naevia* (NA)
Wood Thrush *Hylocichla mustelina* (NA
Hermit Thrush *Catharus guttatus* (NA)
Swainson's Thrush *Catharus ustulatus* (N
Grey-cheeked Thrush *Catharus minimus*
   (NA)
Veery *Catharus fuscescens* (NA)
Eyebrowed Thrush *Turdus obscurus* (As)
Dusky/Naumann's Thrush *Turdus naum*
   (As)
Black-throated/Red-throated Thrush
   Turdus ruficollis (As)
American Robin *Turdus migratorius* (NA
Pallas's Grasshopper Warbler *Locustella*
   certhiola (As)
Lanceolated Warbler *Locustella lanceolat*
   (As)
Gray's Grasshopper Warbler *Locustella*
   fasciolata (As)
Thick-billed Warbler *Acrocephalus aedon*
   (As)
Booted Warbler *Hippolais caligata* (As)
Desert Warbler *Sylvia nana* (Af/As)
Green Warbler *Phylloscopus nitidus* (As)
Two-barred Greenish Warbler *Phyllosco*
   plumbeitarsus (As)
Hume's Yellow-browed Warbler
   Phylloscopus humei (As)
Radde's Warbler *Phylloscopus schwarzi* (*

Dusky Warbler *Phylloscopus fuscatus* (As)
Ruby-crowned Kinglet *Regulus calendula* (NA)
Brown Flycatcher *Muscicapa dauurica* (As)
Red-breasted Nuthatch *Sitta canadensis* (NA)
Brown Shrike *Lanius cristatus* (As)
Isabelline Shrike *Lanius isabellinus* (As)
House Crow *Corvus splendens* (As)
Daurian Jackdaw *Corvus dauuricus* (As)
Yellow-throated Vireo *Vireo flavifrons* (NA)
Philadelphia Vireo *Vireo philadelphicus* (NA)
Red-eyed Vireo *Vireo olivaceus* (NA)
Red-fronted Serin *Serinus pusillus* (As)
Evening Grosbeak *Hesperiphona vespertina* (NA)
Black-and-white Warbler *Mniotilta varia* (NA)
Golden-winged Warbler *Vermivora chrysoptera* (NA)
Tennessee Warbler *Vermivora peregrina* (NA)
Northern Parula *Parula americana* (NA)
Yellow Warbler *Dendroica petechia* (NA)
Chestnut-sided Warbler *Dendroica pensylvanica* (NA)
Black-throated Green Warbler *Dendroica virens* (NA)
Blackburnian Warbler *Dendroica fusca* (NA)
Cape May Warbler *Dendroica tigrina* (NA)
Magnolia Warbler *Dendroica magnolia* (NA)
Yellow-rumped Warbler *Dendroica coronata* (NA)
Bay-breasted Warbler *Dendroica castanea* (NA)
Blackpoll Warbler *Dendroica striata* (NA)
American Redstart *Setophaga ruticilla* (NA)
Ovenbird *Seiurus aurocapillus* (NA)
Northern Waterthrush *Seiurus noveboracensis* (NA)
Common Yellowthroat *Geothlypis trichas* (NA)
Hooded Warbler *Wilsonia citrina* (NA)
Wilson's Warbler *Wilsonia pusilla* (NA)
Canada Warbler *Wilsonia canadensis* (NA)
Summer Tanager *Piranga rubra* (NA)
Scarlet Tanager *Piranga olivacea* (NA)
Rufous-sided Towhee *Pipilo erythrophthalmus* (NA)
Lark Sparrow *Chondestes grammacus* (NA)

Savannah Sparrow *Passerculus sandwichensis* (NA)

Fox Sparrow *Zonotrichia iliaca* (NA)

Song Sparrow *Zonotrichia melodia* (NA)

White-crowned Sparrow *Zonotrichia leucophrys* (NA)

White-throated Sparrow *Zonotrichia albicollis* (NA)

Dark-eyed Junco *Junco hyemalis* (NA)

Black-faced Bunting *Emberiza spodocephala* (As)

Pine Bunting *Emberiza leucocephalos* (As)

Yellow-browed Bunting *Emberiza chrysophrys* (As)

Chestnut Bunting *Emberiza rutila* (As)

Pallas's Reed Bunting *Emberiza pallasi* (A

Red-headed Bunting *Emberiza bruniceps* (

Rose-breasted Grosbeak *Pheucticus ludovicianus* (NA)

Blue Grosbeak *Guiraca caerulea* (NA)

Indigo Bunting *Passerina cyanea* (NA)

Bobolink *Dolichonyx oryzivorus* (NA)

Brown-headed Cowbird *Molothrus ater* (N

Northern Oriole *Icterus galbula* (NA)

THE ART OF BIRDWATCHING

You can watch birds just about anywhere, including urban areas, and the equipment required is minimal. The only essentials are a field guide and a pair of binoculars; additional equipment is optional though more and more birders carry a telescope and tripod outfit.

While a field guide is intended for use when the bird is in front of you, or at least fresh in the memory, it should also be studied at home. Look at the photographs and study the shapes, postures, and plumage of different types of bird to become familiar with the categories in which they are arranged. Try to memorize the principal field marks; many birds are not identified because an observer fails to notice leg colour, bill shape, or some other key feature. When you see a new bird, make a note of such features as the size and shape of the bill (whether long or short, slender or stout, curved or straight), the tail (long or short, rounded, squared, wedge-shaped, notched, or forked), and the wings (long or short, rounded or pointed). Note any distinctive markings such as a crest, eye-rings, wingbars, or a flashing white patch in the wings, tail or rump. Many species have colour patterns that identify them at a glance; by studying the pictures in this book in advance, you may be able to identify many species at first sight.

The second essential is a pair of binoculars; the range of available makes and models of binoculars is immense. Every pair of prismatic binoculars is marked with a code of two figures, for example 10×40: the first number, 10, is the magnification, 10 times ($10\times$); and the second number, 40, is the diameter of the object lens (the one at the front) in millimetres. Higher magnification brings objects closer, but it also reduces the area that can be seen (the field of view), making it more difficult to locate the object, especially a fast-moving bird. Larger object lenses increase the field of view and the light-gathering power of the

binoculars, but they also make the
binoculars heavier. For birdwatching, the
diameter of the object lens should be five
times the magnification, so, with a
magnification of 8, the diameter should l
(5×8). Magnification should be between
and 10×, and thus the diameter of the ob
lens should be between 30 mm and 50 m
This comparatively narrow range elimina
many instruments not suited to a
birdwatcher's needs.

Birdwatchers soon discover that for
identifying ducks on a large reservoir or
sandpipers on mud flats even a 10× powe
binocular is inadequate. Although it ma
be a nuisance to carry, a telescope is
indispensable for viewing distant birds.
The most useful magnification in a
telescope is 20× to 30× since this is abou
large as can be achieved without loss of
light-gathering power or increased
vibration. The telescope should be moun
on a tripod since it is difficult to keep it
steady by hand.

Many birdwatchers carry a field
notebook. Details of each field trip may I
logged, including date, time, route taker
companions, and weather. Keep a list of
birds observed, with numbers, and make
notes and drawings if possible.

Train yourself to move quietly and
unobtrusively through the countryside; I
alert and observant and avoid chatting w
your companions. Wear dull-brown or
greenish clothing that blends with your
surroundings, and at all times obey the
countryside laws and codes. Remember t
there are other people with an interest in
the countryside besides birdwatchers.

GLOSSARY

accidental A species that has appeared in a given area only a very few times and whose normal range is in another area. Also known as a vagrant.

aquatic Frequenting water.

arboreal Frequenting trees.

axillaries The feathers of the 'armpit', where the underside of the wing joins the body.

arpal patch A patch of feathers at the 'wrist', or bend of the wing.

cere A fleshy, featherless area surrounding the nostrils of hawks, falcons, pigeons, and a few other groups of birds.

ircumpolar Of or inhabiting the Arctic (or Antarctic) regions in both the eastern and western hemispheres.

colonial Nesting in groups or colonies rather than in isolated pairs.

commensal Living near or with another organism.

conspecific Belonging to the same species.

smopolitan Worldwide in distribution, or at least occurring on all continents except Antarctica.

coverts Small feathers that overlie or cover either the bases of the large flight feathers of the wings and tail, or an area or structure (e.g. ear coverts).

crepuscular Active at dawn and dusk.

crest A tuft of elongated feathers on the crown.

crown The top of the head.

cryptic Of form or colouring that serves to conceal.

decurved Curved downward.

dimorphic Of species or sexes having two colour form[s]

diurnal Active during the day.

eclipse plumage A dull-coloured plumage acquired by mo[st] ducks immediately after the breeding season and worn for a few weeks; males then acquire more brightly coloured plumage.

endemic Restricted to a certain area.

eruption An irregular large scale movement from a native range.

eyebrow A conspicuous stripe of colour running above but not through the eye. Also know[n] as the supercilium.

eye-stripe A stripe that runs horizontally from the base of the bill through the eye and beyo[nd] (see Lores).

feral Escaped from captivity and now establishe[d] and self supporting in the wild.

field mark A characteristic of colour, pattern or structure useful in distinguishing a specie[s] in the field.

flight feathers The long, well-developed feathers of the wings and tail, used during flight. The flight feathers of the wings are divided int[o] primaries and secondaries.

frontal shield A fleshy, featherless and often brightly coloured area on the forehead of coots, gallinules, and a few other groups of birds

fulvous Tawny; dull yellowish-red.

gape The mouth opening.

Holarctic Occurring in both Palearctic and Nearctic regions, i.e., in northern and temperate regions of both New and Old Worlds.

immature A young bird in a plumage stage between juvenile and adult.

intergrade An intermediate or transitional form.

irruption An irregular, large-scale migratory movement or increase in numbers into a non-native area.

juvenile A young bird in first post-nestling plumage.

lek A place where males of some bird species, especially gamebirds, gather and perform courtship displays in a group rather than courting females individually and in isolation from one another; females visit a lek to mate, but generally build their nests elsewhere.

lores The area between the eye and the base of the bill, sometimes distinctively coloured.

mandible Each of the two parts of a bird's bill, termed respectively the upper mandible and the lower mandible.

mantle The back of a bird together with the upper surface of the wings; the term is used especially in groups of birds like gulls and terns in which these areas are of one colour.

migrant A bird that regularly passes through an area on its way to or from its normal breeding range.

mirrors White spots or areas in the black wingtips of gulls.

montane Pertaining to mountains.

moult The process of shedding and replacing feathers.

moustachial A streak of colour running from the base of
streak the bill back along the side of the throat.

Nearctic The zoogeographical region of North America and Greenland.

nocturnal Active at night.

ochreous The colour of ochre; yellowish-brown.

omnivorous Eating almost any kind of plant or animal food.

Palearctic The zoogeographical region of Eurasia.

pelagic Frequenting the open ocean.

phase A distinctive plumage-colour variance that occurs in certain groups, such as falcons and skuas, but that is unrelated to race, age, sex or season.

plume A feather larger or longer than the feathers around it, generally used in display.

polygamous Of species that mates with more than one member of the opposite sex.

primaries The outermost and longest flight feathers on a bird's wing, usually numbering 11.

race A geographical population of a species, which is slightly different from other populations of that species; also called a subspecies.

range The geographical area or areas inhabited by a species.

raptor A bird of prey.

resident Remaining in one place all year; non-migratory.

ringing The marking of birds by placing rings of metal or coloured plastic on their legs for future recognition as individuals.

riparian Of, or inhabiting, the banks of a river or stream.

roding The flight of a Woodcock over or around its territory at dusk.

rufous Reddish colour.

scapulars A group of feathers on the shoulder of a bird, along the side of the back.

scrape A shallow depression made on the ground, made by a bird to serve as a nest.

secondaries The large flight feathers along the rear edge of the wing, inward from the primaries.

sedentary Remaining in one place; non-migratory.

shoulder The point where the wing meets the body. The term is also loosely applied to the bend of the wing.

spatulate Spoon-shaped.

speculum A distinctively coloured area on the wing of a bird, especially the metallic-coloured patch on the secondaries of some ducks.

sub-adult An immature bird about to reach full maturity; a term usually used of birds that take more than a year to acquire adult plumage.

subspecies A geographical population of a species that is slightly different from other populations of that species; a race.

supercilium A conspicuous stripe running above, but not through the eye. Also known as the eyebrow.

superspecies A group of closely related species whose ranges do not overlap.

tarsus The lower, usually featherless, part of a bird's leg above the feet.

taxonomy The science of classifying organisms according to their natural relationships.

terrestrial Frequenting the ground.

territory Any defended area.

tertials The innermost flight feathers on a bird's wing, immediately adjacent to the body.

They are often regarded simply as the innermost secondaries. Also called tertiaries.

thermals Currents of warm, rising air used by hawks and other soaring birds to assist flight.

vagrant A species that has appeared in a given area only a few times and whose normal range in another area. Also known as an accidental.

vinaceous Dark red; wine-coloured.

Western Palearctic That part of the Palearctic lying west of the Urals southwards to the central Sahara and including the northwestern Middle East.

CONSERVING BIRD LIFE

The decline in bird populations in Europe
has generally been caused either by the
destruction of a bird's environment, as in
the draining of swamps or the cutting
down of forests, or by more direct
influences such as offshore oil-spills,
pesticides and hunting by man.

Although the destruction of wetlands or
forests is difficult to control, organizations
for the saving of marsh areas, as in Spain's
Coto Doñana, have occasionally been
effective. The use of harmful pesticides can
be curbed by law. To reduce the possibility
of oil-spills, laws controlling safe tanker
construction and operation should be
encouraged in every possible way.
Meanwhile, new techniques for cleaning up
spills and rescuing birds that have been
contaminated are being explored. Every
country in Europe has some legislation that
protects birds from hunters. But the
enforcement ranges from negligible to
adequate. In general, northern European
birds are better protected than those in
southern Europe. The tradition of hunting
over the open countryside is very strong, and
in most areas 'sport' is the primary aim. In a
few countries wild birds are taken for food,
but usually for gourmets rather than as a
source of necessary protein. Because of the
lack of adequate laws and enforcement in
southern Europe, a heavy toll is also taken
of migrants that breed in the north and
pass through the Mediterranean on their
way to Africa. British bird-protection laws
are fairly typical of northern Europe: as a
rule, all birds and their eggs are protected
at all times. The few exceptions include
pest species such as the Wood Pigeon and
the Starling, gamebirds in season, and
some migratory wildfowl. Some birds may
not even be photographed without
permission from the various national
conservation bodies. Although the penalties
for breaking the law are high in certain
cases, they are not nearly as severe as those
in the United States.

The last 20 years have seen a dramatic decline in the number of certain Europea birds. Pesticides and weedkillers are responsible for part of this decrease, but direct persecution has also taken a toll. Ir addition, oil pollution is cutting into the populations of Guillemots, Razorbills, Puffins, and other northern seabirds. Larg spills make the headlines, but the polluti is more or less constant. One wonders which will run out first, the oil or the aul

Among the British ornithological societies of interest to birdwatchers are: 1 British Ornithologists' Union, which hol regular meetings and publishes an outstanding journal, *The Ibis*; the British Trust for Ornithology, an organization of amateur ornithologists that concentrates cooperative field work; and The Royal Society for the Protection of Birds, an eve expanding society of bird conservationist that maintains a string of important reserves and publishes *Birds* magazine.

PICTURE CREDITS

All pictures have been researched and supplied via The Frank Lane Picture Agency Ltd. FLPA would like to thank David and Jean Hosking; Rosemary Foulger; Marcus Webb; the contributing photographers; and the following agencies for all their help with this project: Silvestris Foto Service, Sunset Agence Photographique, Panda Photo, Windrush Photos and Natural Image.

t = top; lt = lower top; m = middle; um = upper middle; lm = lower middle; b = bottom

umbers in **bold** refer to colour plates. The circle preceding
aglish names of birds makes it easy for you to keep a record
the birds you see. Subspecies are not marked in this way.